# Fear, Cultural Anxiety,
# and Transformation

# Fear, Cultural Anxiety, and Transformation

## *Horror, Science Fiction, and Fantasy Films Remade*

EDITED BY SCOTT A. LUKAS AND JOHN MARMYSZ

LEXINGTON BOOKS

A division of
ROWMAN & LITTLEFIELD PUBLISHERS, INC.
*Lanham • Boulder • New York • Toronto • Plymouth, UK*

LEXINGTON BOOKS

A division of Rowman & Littlefield Publishers, Inc.
A wholly owned subsidiary of The Rowman & Littlefield Publishing Group, Inc.
4501 Forbes Boulevard, Suite 200
Lanham, MD 20706

Estover Road
Plymouth PL6 7PY
United Kingdom

British Library Cataloguing in Publication Information Available

**Library of Congress Cataloging-in-Publication Data**

Fear, cultural anxiety, and transformation : horror, science fiction, and fantasy films
remade / edited by Scott  A. Lukas and John Marmysz.
    p. cm.
 Includes bibliographical references and index.
 ISBN-13: 978-0-7391-2488-8 (cloth : alk. paper)
 ISBN-10: 0-7391-2488-9 (cloth : alk. paper)
 ISBN-13: 978-0-7391-3140-4 (electronic)
 ISBN-10: 0-7391-3140-0 (electronic)
 1.  Horror films—History and criticism. 2.  Science fiction films—History and criticism.
3.  Fantasy films—History and criticism. 4.  Film remakes—History and criticism.  I.
Lukas, Scott A., 1968– II. Marmysz, John, 1964–
 PN1995.9.H6F42 2009
 791.43'6164—dc22                                           2008028685

Printed in the United States of America

⊖™ The paper used in this publication meets the minimum requirements of American
National Standard for Information Sciences—Permanence of Paper for Printed Library
Materials, ANSI/NISO Z39.48–1992.

# Contents

# Acknowledgments

We would like to thank our editors, Joseph C. Parry, Patricia Stevenson, and Melissa Wilks, for their assistance throughout the writing of the book.

I would like to the many people who have supported my work during the course of this project, including my parents (Clara Lukas, Frank Lukas), Krista Benjamin, Stuart Henry, and, especially, John Marmysz for his dedication to the book and his patience. Also, thanks to Russell A. Berman for organizing the N.E.H. seminar "Terror and Culture: Revisiting Hannah Arendt's *Origins of Totalitarianism*" that facilitated John and me meeting and discussing the book. Thanks also to director Roger Nygard (*Trekkies*, *Trekkies 2*, *The Nature of Existence*) for his help and to Jerald Harkness for numerous conversations about films. (Scott A. Lukas)

I dedicate this collection to the memory of my mother, Frances Marmysz, who sat through many, many horror movies with me.

I give thanks to Dan Shaw, editor of *Film and Philosophy*, for his permission to reprint "Cultural Change and Nihilism in the *Rollerball* Films" as Chapter 5 of this collection. I also thank the participants at the 38th annual national meeting of the Popular Culture and American Culture Associations, held in March of 2008, for their comments on my paper titled "Plato's Nightmare: Cinema as a Nihilistic Operation." In particular, I am grateful to Tim Madigan for organizing the session on philosophy and popular culture at which that paper was presented. Portions of that paper have been incorporated into the introduction to this collection. Finally, I give thanks to my coeditor, Scott A. Lukas, for all of his hard work and enthusiasm for this project. (John Marmysz)

*Chapter 1*

# Horror, Science Fiction, and Fantasy Films Remade

Scott A. Lukas and John Marmysz

Of all pop cultural phenomena, the film remake may be among the most complex, and among the most controversial. According to some cultural critics, remakes accomplish nothing more than to cheapen filmic discourse. From this perspective, film remakes are seen as mere copies that are derivative, formulaic, and lacking in creativity or artistic inspiration. According to others, including fans and directors, remakes offer the opportunity to revisit classic filmic texts and, whether for pure pleasure or for economic gain, to reimagine them in new ways.[1] In truth, there are many different sorts of film remakes, both of first-rate and inferior quality, that operate in a variety of artistic, cultural, economic, and technological dimensions. It is, thus, impossible to paint the phenomenon of the film remake with too broad a brush. Instead, the most fruitful approach treats each individual film on its own terms, attempting to understand the vision, purpose, and execution of each particular remake within its unique context.

While there have been numerous excellent scholarly works on film remakes—ranging from the study of French-American remakes; the theoretical and cinematographic issues of remakes; specific film genres and remakes (such as film noir); the relationship of remakes to other popular remade forms of film (such as sequels); and the connection of film remakes to major cultural themes (like cultural archetypes)—the essays in this volume focus specifically on the multiple ways in which horror, science fiction, and fantasy films have been remade.[2] The contributors to this collection approach the analysis of these remade films from a variety

1

of perspectives, ranging from the philosophical to the technological. However, what these essays all share in common is a conviction that remakes of horror, science fiction, and fantasy films have the potential to reveal something to us about our recurrent fears, anxieties, and hopes for the future. The inspiration for this collection comes from our hunch that horror, science fiction, and fantasy film remakes offer the opportunity to revisit important issues, stories, themes, and topics in ways that speak to contemporary audiences. Like mythic stories that are told again and again in differing ways, these sorts of remade films offer updated perspectives on timeless ideas. While some may succeed and others may fail aesthetically and politically, they always, nonetheless, say something about the culture in which, and for which, they are produced.[3]

## The Remake as a Nihilistic Category

Leo Braudy wonders whether the remake is even "a useful interpretative or theoretical category?"[4] How to distinguish between an adaptation, a homage, a tribute, a reinterpretation, or any other number of designations that are related to the remake may be a theoretical difficulty that is insurmountable, and thus it may make very little pragmatic difference in the long run. In fact, a discussion concerning how precisely to classify a film as a remake could become so intricate that it might derail our attempt to embark upon an examination of particular films in the first place! Let us start, then, by simply observing that, in the most general sense, film remakes can be thought of as "new versions of old movies."[5] The very term *remake* refers to something that has been made again, and so we can treat any film remake as a film that has, literally, been made again. Note the temporal dimension here. In order to be made again, there must already have been a film that acted as the source material for the remake, and that film must have existed before its own remaking. This may seem an obvious observation, but it highlights an important point that is central to the essays in this collection. While all films engage in re-presentation, the remake is unique insofar as it is a representation of a representation.

Film itself is a medium that operates in the realm of representation. All films are composed, at the very least, of visual images captured and made available for repeated viewing. These images are preserved on film in order, literally, to be re-presented again and again. Usually, cinematic imagery is also accompanied by sounds, such as voices and music, which themselves have been captured, manipulated, and re-presented as an accompaniment to the primary visual imagery appearing on screen. There have even been unusual instances in which various other sensory dimensions, such as smell (Odorama) or touch (Sensurround, Percepto), have been introduced into the cinema experience further to enhance the realism of the representational spectacle.[6] In any case, whether reproducing sights, sounds or smells, film is a medium whose very language is the language of representation.

While all representation involves degrees of borrowing, adaptation, and rewriting (including text), the film remake complicates matters insofar as it is a representation of a representation. For this reason it has been targeted by critics as a form of pure borrowing—as a sort of cultural parasite that infects the high art form known as film.[7] Because the film remake unabashedly re-presents what was already a mere representation, it is often thought to be intrinsically inferior to the work it imitates. This suggests a curious, if not nihilistic, status for the film remake.

The vogue among many contemporary philosophers, cultural critics, and postmodernists has been to utilize the term *nihilism* as an insult to any person or production that denies the existence of truth or value in the world, under the presumption that to deny such things is self-evidently reprehensible. Nihilism, like the category of the film remake, is thus something to be avoided, overcome, or rejected. What could be more awful than to accept the absence of truth and goodness after all?! When understood in a more sophisticated and authentic way, however, nihilism, like the film remake, may be less threatening and more productive than we have been led to believe. Heidegger councils us that "[t]he essence of nihilism contains nothing negative," and it may, in fact, contain one of the most constructive and affirmative of possibilities: the hope for ongoing and never-ending interpretation—something the film remake itself also suggests in its multiple copying and repetition.[8] To characterize the film remake as a nihilistic category, for these reasons, is not necessarily to denigrate or insult it, but to elevate it and to celebrate its potential for encouraging in us an ongoing and never-ending search for truths that, in the end, inevitably slip from our grasp.

As its nihilistic character suggests, the remake questions the nature of meaning itself, and as Mazdon writes, "the decision to remake a film and responses to that remake do have a significance which extends well beyond the movie theatre."[9] In films and their remakes, sight and sound (and sometimes smell or touch) are recreated and intersect in ways that are never actually found in the world as it exists in itself. Yet, nonetheless, in producing their art filmmakers are concerned with conveying something to audiences about the nature of a reality that exists outside of the world of cinema. This is the strange irony of the medium: it attempts to represent and make accessible for repeated viewing worlds that never have existed in order to tell us something about the world that really does exist. By creating illusions, filmmakers strive to create truth. In this, they fail doubly, fabricating something that is neither wholly true nor false. The filmic product, thus, exists in a strange, gray area between the real and the unreal, the authentic and the counterfeit, the meaningful and the meaningless.

Plato tells the story of a prisoner in a cave who faces hardship, torment, and pain in his attempt to ascend out of the darkness of illusion and into the harsh light of reality. When finally gazing upon the sun, the prisoner learns the truth, but when he descends back into the depths of the cave to communicate this truth to his friends, he is at a loss for words.[10] The truth, in Plato's myth, cannot be represented verbally or visually. Yet, in failure, the escaped prisoner nonetheless acts as a guide who points the way to a world beyond representation. Those who are willing and energetic may become curious and engage in their own quest. Those who are not willing or energetic remain comfortable and content in their cave-world. Filmmakers, perhaps, are like the guide in Plato's story, and there is a fitting irony to the fact that they encourage audiences to sit still in cave-like theaters as a prelude to the search for truth. Like the shadows and reflections on the cave wall, the images that flash across a movie screen are representations of another reality, made present in the moment, but also slipping away moment by moment until the conclusion of the performance. In the end, the film itself is more than the sum of its parts, and the intersection of sight and sound merely points the way toward some other absent reality that becomes the subject of debate, discussion, and speculation. What did the filmmaker mean? What was the message conveyed through the film? In what ways was this film successful? In what ways was it unsuccessful? Questions are generated and if these questions are compelling enough, audiences may be drawn again and again to the same movie in order to review and repeat their experience, looking for clues that might help to solve the mystery of the film's ultimate meaning. Repeated viewings of films allow us to linger in the presence of a representation that purports to reflect some truth, and yet the reflection is not the thing itself.

While representations are the basic mechanism and language of film, we find with film remakes that these representations are themselves subject to ongoing representations. This is Plato's nightmare, and it is an amplification of cinema's nihilistic predicament. From the perspective of those, like Plato, who find value only in the Source or the final Truth as it exists beyond all reflections and representations, it may appear decadent that we should experience enjoyment simply by way of multiplying and replaying images and sounds endlessly. The point is not to immerse ourselves in mere entertainment, after all, but to discover the one reality which lies veiled behind the grand diversity of representations, reflections, and shadows. We don't want to remain cave dwellers, but to find our way out of the cave, and so long as we content ourselves with the mere repetition of sights and sounds, according to this view, we remain trapped. For some critics, this collusion of originals and copies—as manifested in the film remake—creates a condition in which film loses its grasp, however fragile, of reality. Akin to the loss of the aura in Walter Benjamin's analysis of the reproduction of art, the film remake represents a lessening of the original, a copying of the original film's symbolism, narratives, character development, and even camera angles, and ultimately, a loss of the original film itself.[11]

The proliferation of images in the world—whether disconnected, as on CNN, or as montages in films—creates an interesting visual scenario in which verisimilitude supplants Truth.[12] As Jean Baudrillard offers in his thesis on the "procession of simulacra," original and copies have become colluded, with the result that we are unable to differentiate between originals and copies.[13] Like the copies referenced in Baudrillard's writings, film remakes are recreations of previous films. It only takes a moment of reflection to realize, however, that no remake is, in fact, an exact replica of the film it has remade, and so there is always some degree of creative originality involved in its production. As Andrew Horton and Stuart Y. McDougal point out, "remakes constitute a particular territory existing somewhere between unabashed larceny and subtle originality."[14] Even Gus Van Sant's controversial remake of *Psycho*, in which virtually all of the camera angles and scenes are mirror images of the original Hitchcock version, demonstrates a certain sly and ironic originality in its manner of mimicry. Van Sant is aware of what he is doing, and he is conscious of the fact that his movie will always operate in the shadow of Hitchcock's previous film. Just as every film involves re-presentation, every remake involves a re-presentation of a previous re-presentation, and as Kierkegaard notes, we should recognize that the urge to repeat and re-present is itself always already a symptom of something creative at work in human consciousness.[15] The desire to remake a film, like *Psycho*, suggests that there is something alluring and attractive about the content depicted in that film and also that there is something to be gained by reworking that content and carrying it into the future.

## The Film Remake as Palimpsest and Technological Intervention

Just as the representational issues of the film remake may be connected to principles of nihilism, the outcome of the film remake—as a media category that folds into society along with other media, informational, and popular culture forms—is to challenge the hegemony of film as well as its reception in society. As Durham remarks, "the remake could be perceived as the epitome of contemporary postmodernist culture."[16] Alongside its nihilistic potential, which challenges the idea of linear interpretation and wholesome truth, the film remake's postmodern potential exists in its challenge to revered categories of the original. While no film is ever original—it is always adapted from some source text—some films can conceal their identity and claim an originality that eludes the remake.

As more films are remade an interesting palimpsest develops. New films allude to or sometimes completely remake past films, and past films—as images—are often interpreted as nostalgic forms, as originary texts that perhaps escaped the fate of the sort of simulacra that concerned Plato. Lucy Mazdon offers that "the remake . . . can be seen as both a feature of an extensive network of cultural reproduction and an echo of the very identity of film itself."[17] As more films converge in forms of remaking, and as more critics and fans debate the merits of such meetings on the Internet and in popular trade publications, a crisis of representation occurs. The study of the filmic remake, like the study of the adaptation of texts into films, is burdened by interpretation. This burden is the result of people being unable to accept the translation of a given form—such as the movement of *Harry Potter* from book to film—or the revision of a given form—such as the updating of a classic Hitchcock film.[18] As the film *Adaptation* suggests, the ability to locate the intent of an (original) author, to translate that new vision into a screenplay, and to negotiate the complex world of filmmaking is problematic.[19] And, as David Wills remarked, "There can never be a faithful remake . . . because there can never have been a simple original."[20]

While some films, such as *Citizen Kane*, become established as iconic examples of great film, of a canon, remakes challenge the hegemony of film itself. As Horton and McDougal argue, "remakes, in fact, problematize the very notion of originality," particularly the metanarrative of film as a form of originality.[21] While some critically received films can escape, if not erase, their original text, such as Stanley Kubrick's film version of Arthur C. Clarke's *2001: A Space Odyssey*, in the case of film remakes no such escape from the original is possible. The remake of *Cape Fear* will always reference the original *Cape Fear*, even to the point of including actors from the original in the new film. Only in rare cases, such as in the remade *Manchurian Candidate*, does the remake suggest the possibility of moving away from the original.[22]

One clear impetus for the remake is technology. As Heidegger, Baudrillard, Benjamin, and others have suggested, technology offers new possibilities for remaking the world. Because film and media technologies have advanced, there exists the new possibility to remake films in new ways—adding more sophisticated special effects (combining live action, CGI, and other effects), using more locations, and bringing in more popular actors (such as in the Soderberg remake of *Solaris*). These alterations do not mean that a film will be received more favorably than the original, but the presence of technology itself allows for further proliferation of film remakes.[23] The advance of technology, in fact, creates a whole new way of thinking about what is really important in filmmaking. Heidegger has suggested that our propensity to think technologically colors the way that we see our world, and not always for the better. When we think technologically, we tend to filter our world through a lens that gives special status to the useful and the instrumental. Because we possess a special technology, we come to believe that we must use it at any cost.[24] Things become useful or "unuseful" according to how they allow us to utilize our latest techniques and devices. Technology often becomes its own end, and rather than serving as a means for the transmission of content, content can become a means to demonstrate the potential of technology. Daryl Frazetti argues, in his chapter on *Star Trek* fan films, in favor of the positive, insurgent possibility of new forms of technology that allows fans to challenge the originary texts of the *Star Trek* genre, but we also see the negative side of this same issue in the technologically advanced, and yet aesthetically problematic, remakes of *Rollerball* and *Van Helsing*. In Frazetti's understanding, the remake becomes a counter-hegemonic form: while remakes typically are produced under the authority and conventions of Hollywood and other film industries, fan remakes allow anyone, given a bit of technological knowledge and a great deal of dedication, to involve him or herself in the remaking of classic texts, in this case *Star Trek*. Frazetti also indicates that this use of technology is more than a fascination with new technological forms. It is in fact is a statement about the possibility of fans remaking (and retaking) the texts that they revere, and often embellishing them with new meanings, contexts, characters, and circumstances that would be too controversial for a major film studio.

Recent technologies have created a circumstance in which revisiting and reviewing films has become easier and more convenient than ever before. In the early years of cinema, the production and projection processes were very specialized affairs, requiring the presence of trained technicians who would operate and maintain the complicated machinery needed to produce and exhibit films.[25] Today, while film technology has become very sophisticated, the actual operation of the equipment needed for the production and exhibition of films requires less specialized knowledge than ever before. In movie theaters, film projectors are now so automatic that they can be operated by the counter staff, and some theaters have even moved to the use of fully computerized projection. At home, we now have videotapes, DVDs, and computer video files (like machinima) that can be played with the press of a button or the click of a mouse. We may even create our own movies using personal video cameras and computers. Additionally, spectators now have the ability to stop, rewind, and freeze the images on their viewing screens, allowing more control and an intensified opportunity to scrutinize, dissect, and manage cinematic representations. While films have always been subject to repeated viewings, the ease with which such repetition may occur is now especially acute. We now take for granted that we may repeat, review, and replay films at will. We build personal libraries of movies just as we build personal libraries of books, and just like our books, the movies in our own collections are available to us at any moment of the day. In this new era of the filmic palimpsest and the technological sublime, as André Bazin once wrote, "we are moving toward a reign of the adaptation in which the notion of the unity of the work, if not the very notion of the author himself, will be destroyed."[26] While some may lament this movement of film (and of reality) further away from the original and the Truth, others will, no doubt, celebrate what is seen as a libratory, democratic, and vital transformation of popular culture.

## The Remake and Repetition

It is not, of course, technology that drives the desire to repeat; it is the other way around. The desire to repeat is what has driven the development of the sort of technology that makes repetition possible. Aristotle, in *Poetics*, observed that human beings have a need to mimic and replay events because in this they gain a sort of control and mastery over the world and themselves.[27] Although Aristotle spoke from a Western perspective, repetition is deeply rooted in all cultures. Films, like religious rituals, have the ability to reflect and reaffirm our commitment to things that we hold to be important. In ritual, certain words are respoken, certain actions are redone, and certain thoughts are reaffirmed, all for the soothing effect of repetition.[28] Aristotle saw special value in the repetition of dramatic performances because each repetition allowed people the leisure to experience a cathartic release of emotion under safe circumstances. A kind of personal knowledge is developed in this process, and the multiplication of dramatic representations has a potentially positive and therapeutic potential. In the contemporary world, with new technology making it possible endlessly to repeat and review films in scrupulous detail, under a wide and varied set of diverse conditions and circumstances, perhaps we have more opportunity than ever to explore ourselves by scrutinizing the different ways that we react as we revisit the same cinematic performances again and again. Perhaps in the endless, nihilistic deferral of final conclusions concerning the Truth of cinema and our relationship to it we also find an endless well of meaningful material with which we may philosophize.

All film, like ritual, plays on the value of repetition, either to make dramatic points or to create suspense in the audience. Film remakes heighten repetition by moving from mere allusion and brief citation, to credited or uncredited remaking of the entire filmic text. This remaking of films allows for not only an affirmation of control and mastery, as Aristotle suggested, but the forging of cultural familiarity within society itself. When people repeatedly experience the same stories, albeit retold in new ways and with new actors and technology, a psychological connection to a shared social world is fostered. Viewers come to realize that the same stories and ideas have been shared and enjoyed by others in their communities, thus connecting the individual and his or her momentary experience to the life and future of the collective. Like the various rituals we engage in, film remakes institutionalize familiarity, contributing to our contemporary way of being. As Mazdon says, "films are made to be reproduced,"[29] and with her we can agree that film provides a form that both clarifies our sense of being and complicates it. As Claude Lévi-Strauss once wrote of culture, like culture itself, the film remake provides a form that is "good to think"—that is, its inherent form creates cognitive dissonance, especially as it challenges people to think in a new way about a classic film that has been remade.[30] In some cases, as Leo Braudy says, remaking is reflected in "cultural nostalgia"—a deep desire to rework things from the past and to recreate historical periods.[31] The need for repetition is foundational, and we constantly find circumstances that allow us to exercise this need. Repetition is important because it gives us the opportunity to mediate between the past and the present, creating a sense of continuity out of otherwise disconnected moments in time, thus facilitating our control over those moments. As we recreate occurrences from the past, we grant them existence in the present, and this allows us the leisure to cherish them, meditate on them, re-experience them, and learn from them again and again. This is particularly evident in Costas Constandinides' chapter detailing the remaking of classic movie monsters. In the case of the film *Van Helsing* a peculiar form of repetition is present. While some film remakes attempt to pay homage to the past—such as in the case of reworking a classic text—*Van Helsing* operates under a different principle. Instead of sticking closely to the classic texts of movie monsters, this film problematizes the idea of the remake as a form of repetition. Not only does *Van Helsing* reference numerous classic film genres—such as *James Bond*, Expressionism, and numerous horror films—but it further complicates the matter of its repetition by developing numerous intertextual references to classic movie monsters. Ultimately, its concern is not the classical archetype of the movie monster but the new visual culture that has given rise to films like *Van Helsing*. In this way, images from our collective past find new, creative life in the present.

Classic myths, including those archetypal ones described by Campbell and Jung, suggest that there is inherent cognitive, political, and existential value involved in retelling, and the authors in this collection agree that remade films have a unique role in the perpetuation of our own modern myths. In some cases, such as in the retellings of *Frankenstein*, the "film has supplanted the novel as a source of myth."[32] As it retells classic stories, the film remake creates a new type of story—one that brings forth new narrative and aesthetic elements. With the remaking of classic horror films like *Psycho*, *The Texas Chainsaw Massacre*, *Night of the Living Dead*, and *Halloween*, classic and archetypal horror texts are recast for new audiences, and "even viewers with no direct experience of [films like] *Psycho* are likely to possess a 'narrative image' of the film."[33] Films and their remakes, in this way, serve fundamental existential, psychological, and cultural needs. The (remade) images flashing on the screens in movie theaters, like those adorning the walls of Paleolithic caves, give us a sense of meaning in a hostile and often confusing world. They also fulfill an important social function, of the sort described by Durkheim, by binding us all together with commonly shared stories that speak to our particular fears, anxieties, and hopes for the future.[34] Zília Papp's chapter deals with this sort of motivation. In her analysis of the *yôkai* (妖怪), she emphasizes the fact that certain cultural forms—in this case, Japanese spirits—provide the realm of film remaking with a rich and salient foundation. While yôkai are present in historical folktales and in forms of popular culture, like the manga, there is an even more telling appearance of them in film. As Papp indicates the yôkai reappear in a variety of Japanese monster films and in each reappearance there is reference to a sense of nostalgia, as well as of patriotism. Whether they are retold in classic or more surreal films, the yôkai illustrate how one of the most powerful inspirations for filmic remaking is the repetition and representation of culturally meaningful mythic tales.

Søren Kierkegaard praises the urge to repeat, seeing in it a means by which humans come to make sense of an otherwise absurd world. In repetition, he claims, we bring continuity to the fleeting moments of life and affirm what is past by attempting to preserve and transport it into the future. He writes, "repetition proper is what has mistakenly been called mediation."[35] What he means by this is that in repeating, there is a transition in our consciousness from what was to what now is. In order to repeat, we must once again bring back into existence something that existed at least once before, at an earlier time. Thus, repetition mediates between the past and the present. There is a difference between repetition and recollection, furthermore, in so much as recollection is a backward movement while repetition is a forward movement. When we recollect something, we think of how that thing was in the past; when we repeat something we bring it to actuality again in the present. Thus while recollection makes us unhappy, repetition makes us happy.[36] Recollection is a symptom of longing for something that is no longer with us. It is tinged with melancholy and sadness for things lost. Repetition, on the other hand, is an expression of our power to recreate something anew, again and again. It is a positive expression of our will toward the future. We find this same observation expressed in the writings of Sigmund Freud when he discusses the "repetition compulsion," which is a tendency in organisms to "restore an earlier state of things which the living entity has been obliged to abandon under the pressure of external disturbing forces."[37] According to Freud, the will to repeat operates at a variety of psychological levels, both conscious and unconscious, but it always attempts to conserve and maintain something from the past, and in this it represents a rebellion against the transitory nature of life as it slips from birth toward death. Moment by moment, time drifts by, each instant unique. In our compulsion to repeat, we grasp on to the moment and attempt to preserve and concretize it; vainly of course, since the instant an event of repetition is carried out, it too slips away to become another moment that has passed. If that event is not to be forgotten, then it must be recollected or repeated yet again and again. Without either recollection or repetition, life is simply a series of transitory moments, and Kierkegaard tells us it thus "dissolves into empty, meaningless noise."[38] Viewed in this way, and contrary to Plato, significance and meaning in life may be found not by forsaking duplication and imitation, but precisely in the ongoing and vain attempt to solidify in the present, through repetition, what will only again fade away the very next moment.

The success of film remakes has been hampered, in part, by the context in which repetition has been defined. As Scott A. Lukas writes in his chapter on the remaking of classic video games as films, the excessive emphasis on the remake as an industrial category, and the subsequent propensity to dismiss the remake as nothing more than a derivative economic strategy, leads to a circumstance in which certain forms of repetition are negated. In his analysis of the relationship of popular video games to their filmic remakes—including *Doom*, *Silent Hill*, and *Resident Evil*—he suggests that it is becoming more difficult to distinguish between forms of adaptation and remakes. While some have argued that remaking occurs within one medium—film—Lukas asks us to consider the idea that remakes may be the products of cross-media dialogue, in this case, between video games and films. Video game releases now often surpass the opening box-office receipts of major motion pictures (such as in the cases of *Halo 3* and *Grand Theft Auto IV*), and combined with this increased popularity of video games is the affinity between producers, writers, engineers, directors, and fans who fluidly move between the virtual worlds of a given video game and its filmic remake. As more video games and films share such affinity, there are more debates about the meaning of such remakes. Some critics argue that the repetition that characterizes the remake produces a loss of meaning, others say it expands the meaning, while others express that it complicates the meaning of the "original" and the "copy."[39] In this context of repetition, playing with the original and the copy, an interesting issue arises. While remakes suggest the value of repetition as an interpretive and representational issue, many fans and critics argue that some forms of repetition are too much—either there are too many remakes of certain types of films or that remaking creates filmic products that are, simply, repetitive.[40] Repetition produces familiarity. In some cases this familiarity, as it references memory, can have a positive effect—such as in the nostalgia that people have for certain films or film styles, like film noir (recast in *Sin City* and other films)—but in others familiarity produces discomfort as viewers come to question the very basis of this medium of representation.[41]

The remaking of films often occurs for economic reasons. Studios that own particular properties may be inclined to remake them multiple times in order to avoid spending money on the rights to other potential properties. Related to this is the fact that there is a ready-made and receptive audience that exists for remakes of successful films. *Invasion of the Body Snatchers*, for instance, has been remade no less than four times, and each of those remakes was ensured an audience since the original film retains a loyal following of fans. There is less of an economic risk involved when remaking a tried-and-true film than there is in springing something completely new on the viewing public. While, as Verevis suggests, "Hollywood studios seek to duplicate past successes and minimize risk by emphasizing the familiar," film remakes also illustrate the powerful impact of brands, media conglomerates, and market synergy characteristic of contemporary popular culture.[42] The synergy of images or narratives across multiple media and audiences comes to fruition in marketing empires like *Harry Potter*. In the case of *Potter*, repetition occurs not as the result of a postmodern tendency but as a market truth: in order better to leverage the product, the company must introduce it in as many markets and within as many demographic niches as possible. The result is a proliferation of remakes and repetitions that span television, print media, film, video games, theme park rides, cartoons, and the Internet. The film *Transformers* (2007) is one recent example of this synergistic trend of remaking that now spans multiple media.

## Remake as Dialogue

An analysis of the contexts in which the English prefix *re* appears indicates a curious and hopeful situation for the film remake. The prefix *re* calls us to consider things that bring us "back from a point reached," "back to the original place." It suggests to us that something will happen "again" and "anew" in the sense of a "restoration to a previous state or condition," or the "undoing of some previous action."[43] All of these connotations reference a condition in which past and present are juxtaposed, something is undone, and then created once again in a new way. This suggests that the film *remake* itself may be rather Janus-faced in its operations. One of its faces is familiar and comforting. When we encounter a remake, we recognize a friend that we have seen before. Yet, the overall appearance of this friend's face has changed, like that of someone we haven't seen in years and years. The general contours remain stable, and yet the details are different. We may both be amused and disturbed by these changes all at once, but we are nevertheless transfixed. With such an encounter, we remember the old appearance of our friend and, both in sadness and in curiosity, we find ourselves comparing the past with the present. We note the toll that time has taken or, equally often, we marvel at how time has improved on a potential that previously was only latent. Nevertheless, we are always comforted by the inherent qualities of our friend as we enter into dialogue with him or her, even if he or she seems unrecognizable and distant at first.

In *The Anxiety of Influence: A Theory of Poetry*, Harold Bloom suggests that poets, as writers who strive to create a new vision of the world, are hampered by the poets who have come before them.[44] The "anxiety of influence" has equal impact on the work of filmmakers who attempt to expound upon a previous text. In film remakes a complex dialogue exists between the various sources of the remake—including the original source text and the remade film or films.[45] As a "textual category" the film remake involves a complex dialogue between multiple authors, various sources, and even multiple media.[46] While some have viewed the film remake as a "one-way process: a movement from authenticity to imitation," following Bakhtin and others' concepts of dialogue, heteroglossia, and pastiche, we might reconceptualize this idea of the one-way nature of the film remake as a two-way process in which originals, copies, and their multiple authors and interpreters engage in a dialogue.[47] As a dialogue among people, and often between different generations and groups of people, film remaking continues a longstanding tradition of storytelling. Even in the cases of so-called bad film remakes, there is value in discussing and debating these new filmic visions in the contemporary agora of film criticism. In the case of film genre, the remake plays an especially significant dialogic role. Shane Borrowman's chapter on the zombie film remake illustrates how the process of remaking introduces dialogue within and between genres. The myth of the zombie, embellished in many films that were inspired by George A. Romero's *Night of the Living Dead* (1968), is cultivated in no small part by the recollection in people's minds of how the image of the zombie has been developed, problematized, and rewritten throughout the numerous films that draw on Romero's original vision. As fans flock to the theaters to see the newest versions of the zombie they, like author Borrowman, await what will appear on the screen: in some cases the new zombies are met with approval, while in others there is disappointment for various reasons, including the rewriting of characters, dialogue, and situations from the earlier films. As Borrowman claims, there are many ways in which the remakes of the classic films rewrite the politics—such as race and gender—of the earlier films, in some cases successfully and in others not. What is significant in Borrowman's reading of the zombie myth is how he highlights the manner in which audiences establish their own kinship with the films, suggesting a significant dialogue between fans and the many film remakes themselves.

The filmmaker who is drawn to retell old stories, or the audience member that is draw to re-view them, is expressing an urge to bring something that has passed into the present once again, and this is a forward-looking, creative act in itself. Horton and McDougal write that remakes are "films that to one degree or another *announce* to us that they embrace one or more previous movies."[48] In this way, the remake calls us actively to mediate the past with the present. As we view remakes of particular fantasy, horror, and science fiction films our minds are drawn back to recall earlier incarnations of those films. This allows us the opportunity to do something above and beyond simply revisiting, recollecting, and reaffirming our previous encounters with heroism, fear, and wonder over technology. In viewing a remake we become more than simply passive viewers of a drama; we also become participants in the active, dialectical construction of a legacy. As we repeat our exposure to the content of a remade film, we, along with the filmmakers, bring the past into the present. We notice similarities and dissimilarities between the remake and the original. We make judgments on how well or how poorly the remake and the original compare with one another. A connection is made between our recollection of an earlier film and our present experience of the current film, and we become the conduits through which that connection becomes manifest. Collectively, our minds bring continuity to the momentary representations and images that flash across the screen, imparting an order and meaning that grants them significance. Thus, films and their remakes potentially promote both internal and cultural dialogue within and between us as viewers. John Marmysz expresses such an idea in his analysis of *Rollerball* and its remake, offering that the ways in which the two films differ—most notably, in how philosophical issues are mediated by the cultural moods of the times in which these films were made—provide an instructive way of thinking about the transition between cultural periods. Marmysz discusses how aspects of the two films, including character and music, are transformed in the remade version. In the first version of *Rollerball* there is an emphasis on the idea of authenticity as a response to the meaninglessness and stress of the futuristic world, while in the remake emphasis is instead placed on the search for trite and superficial values and relationships. Further, the remake emphasizes action and violence, not in the manner of an existentialist critique, which is evident in the first film, but as a stylistic and entertaining distraction.

The issue of the continuity/discontinuity between a film and its remake is further evident in the issue of authorship, which itself is a complex form of dialogue. Constantine Verevis' analysis of Stephen Soderbergh's *Solaris* points to the ways in which film remakes establish a kind of media dialogue. Verevis' use of *Solaris* points to the complexity of both the processes of adaptation and remaking; indeed, it may no longer be possible to distinguish between the two. When a film like *Solaris* is adapted from a book, there are numerous decisions made about the way in which the story, characterization, and action will take place on the screen. Itself a nihilistic, interpretative, and representational process, adaptation works with a story but re-presents it as an incomplete text. When this story is further permuted, additional decisions are made about it. As Verevis explains, in some ways the Soderberg film clarifies unexplained aspects of the Lem story, thus suggesting a more expansive dialogue between the Tarkovsky film, the Soderberg remake, and the original Lem story. Quoting Soderbergh in his chapter, Verevis illustrates how the director saw his relationship with these various sources as dialogic: 20 percent was the Lem book, 20 percent the Tarkovsky film, and the rest the director's own ideas. This understanding of the director's inspiration suggests that remakes may expand the dialogue of culture and film, not diminish it as some have argued.

The director's inspirations—indeed, often his or her status as an auteur—have influenced the cycle of remakes that is now common across the world. In Stan Jones' chapter, much like the case of Verevis' analysis of *Solaris*, we see a director (Peter Jackson) whose work on the Academy Award-winning *Lord of the Rings* trilogy established his global reputation, heightened his auteur status, and thus allowed him to remake the costly *King Kong*. In Jones' study of this cycle of remaking he indicates an interesting and peculiar form of dialogue in film. While certain films like *King Kong* might seem impossible to remake—after all, the Kong myth is filled with racism, stereotyping, the instrumental reason of the machine/city over nature, and the "universalizing interpretations . . . [and] encrustations of meaning attached" to a dominant allegory—Jones illustrates that even a myth as controversial as Kong *can* be remade. *King Kong*, like the forms of drama and theatrical myths identified by Aristotle and Benjamin, *demands* to be retold, and thus like the forms of allegory and literary dialogue that preceded it, it is becoming a universal form.[49] The extent of Jackson's homage to earlier versions of *King Kong* is evident in what Jones calls "illogical" and "absurd" elements that are retained in the remake, precisely for the purpose of engaging in filmic dialogue with the past versions of *King Kong*. At the same time, this reliance of dialogue with the past may, in Jones' view, result in kitsch homage. Perhaps most interesting in Jackson's play on the myth of *King Kong* is that his contribution to this cycle of film remakes suggests an interesting "fate of [remakes] carrying a wide range of meaning" and furthering the multireferentiality of the myth.

Indeed, while many critical accounts of the film remake dismiss the form, without question, as derivative and simplistic, there is another possible interpretation of the remake. In this view, the remake is a site of vitality, a place for the testing of new technology, new authorial and acting visions, and of reworking classic texts for new audiences. For the viewer of films, a remake "demand[s] that the viewer participate in both looking at and reading between multiple texts. . . . and enjoy the *differences* that have been worked, consciously and sometimes unconsciously, between the texts."[50] As Leo Braudy notes, "To remake is to want to reread."[51] Understood in this view the remake problematizes the idea of the original film as a monolithic product and suggests that it, like any other text, is a valid site for a dialectical exchange between the old and the new. In this sense, as Habermas might say of the modern world itself, the film remake interrogates all film as an "incomplete project."[52] While many of the authors in this volume disagree on the success with which filmmakers have remade films, they all agree that the process establishes one of the most significant, enduring, and often critical forms of dialogue between writers, filmmakers, fans, and film critics alike.

## Fear, Cultural Anxiety, Transformation

A major premise of this collection is that the remaking of horror, science fiction, and fantasy films involves an attempt dialectically to work through and linger with our collective experiences of fear, anxiety, and transformation. Fear and anxiety are essential elements in horror films, and it has often been noted that there is something mysterious about the fact that audiences, first of all, derive enjoyment from exposure to fearful and anxiety-inducing performances and, second of all, that they desire reexposure to these stimuli again and again. When zombies appear on the screen or when King Kong beats his chest, why don't audiences run from the theater in terror? Why do they stay seated and continue to subject themselves to the repeated shocks and scares that are sure to come? Furthermore, why do people willingly return to see the same horrors reenacted in sequels and remakes? In the chapters by Juneko Robinson and Ills Huygens, this fascination with fear and anxiety is illustrated through an analysis of the many remakes of the *Invasion of the Body Snatchers*. This particular film has established a cycle that repeats throughout the 1950s, 1970s, 1990s, and 2000s, and what is interesting with each remake is how the trope of fear and anxiety is expressed. Dehumanization, fear of engulfment, fear of others, uncanny doubles, invading forces, hysterical bodies, and castrating and monstrous females are all expressions of the anxious fears that play a role in the many versions of the body snatcher myth. The ways in which these feelings are played out in the films change, but the idea that film is an effective means for conveying these basic emotions has not. In the most recent version of the myth, *The Invasion*, the fear is updated to include references to our contemporary anxieties about Darfur, 9/11, President George W. Bush, and the war in Iraq. There is no indication that this fascination with fear and paranoia will diminish, nor will the filmic remake's use of it.

As suggested earlier, Aristotle and Kierkegaard have taught us that repetition, including the sort engaged in by filmic remaking, can have a positive effect. The desire repeatedly to engage in encounters with fanciful and dreadful characters within the illusory realm of the cinema attests to our need to experiment safely with our own reactions to fear and anxiety. Though we never will know with absolute and conclusive certainty who we are and how we fit into the world, we can gain greater and greater degrees of self knowledge through our repeated attempts to bridge the gap between the past and the present. Remakes of fantasy, horror, and science fiction films provide us with just one type of opportunity to gain practice at this form of creative meditation. As Aristotle claimed, the illusions of drama can be instructive, and though we may never learn everything, we can in the meantime at least learn some things about ourselves and our feelings about the world. Such is the positive potential of the remake.

At the same time, remaking can have a negative effect. While this debate clearly is subjective—particularly as it is impossible to determine what constitutes a successful repetition—there are many who feel that the remake has degraded film and even culture itself. Myoungsook Park's chapter considers the complex relationship of French and Japanese film remakes, particularly the emerging J-Horror genre. While some have celebrated the film remake as an opening up of dialogue between still-distant nations, others have pointed out that the US remake of a foreign film is actually a form of cultural imperialism, cleverly disguised as a multicultural, dialogic, and democratic process. As she emphasizes in her chapter, the film remake, in numerous ways, parallels concerns related to globalization and large-scale shifts in culture, economics, technology, and information beginning in the 1980s. Like the remake, these shifts have been hailed by some and criticized by others. Of great concern is the way in which the film remake functions as one piece of the machine of globalization—in this case expanding the properties of US capitalism. Central to Park's look at the complexity of the remake, globalization, and culture, is the degree to which copyright law and authorship impinge on the efforts to remake films. While many filmmakers and nations would like a piece of the remake, it is clear that a Hollywood remake stands as the authoritative version, and thus it may be impossible to depict the remake as a democratic phenomenon. As she points out with French films remade in the US, the audience is often unaware of the fact that such films are remakes, thus furthering her argument about the remake as a form of cultural imperialism. Also significant in terms of cultural imperialism is the issue of how culture-specific characters, issues, and situations are rewritten in their new filmic versions. As Park observes, because certain cultural traits may not be present in the culture that is remaking a film, these traits may either be deleted or rewritten (often in muted forms) for the new audience. Thus the transformation that results may actually create a watering down of the characteristics hailed by some as virtues of the film remake.

One of the most significant effects of the remake is a cultural one. While some have focused on the remake as a purely textual category—as something that results from a previous "text"—the authors in this volume suggest a shift in how the remake should be interpreted. Many of the contributors to this collection argue that the remake marks significant shifts in how we understand the self, other, society, and numerous cultural and philosophical issues. Thus, the remake becomes a sort of barometer of society, indicating not just technical or stylistic changes in the various genres of film, but also indicating changes within the mythos of society itself.

Daniel Herbert's offering in this collection points in this direction. His analysis of the films *Insomnia, Ju-on* and their remakes suggests that we should look more carefully at the emerging field of transnational film remakes—films made in one cultural context and then remade in another—and what they say about economic, political, and social issues. Herbert argues that one of the predominant issues of the transnational remake is that of space and geography, specifically centering on "a geography of imagination rendered by transnational economic and cultural forces." As more films are remade, Herbert suggests that a global struggle for power occurs, as more and more media and industries compete for the mass consciousness of the planet. At the same time, remakes provide an interesting dialogue between different cultures, even a transnational space of cultural production as he calls it, and this aspect of the transformation of film (and culture) cannot be minimized. Central to Herbert's chapter (and indeed to many in this collection), is his statement that "Film remakes . . . negotiate tensions between repetition and transformation." There is little doubt that film remakes will continue to proliferate, and fans, academics, and film critics will continue to debate the merits of these repetitions and transformations, including the effects they have on us and on the culture of which we are a part.

# Notes

1. As Leo Braudy remarks, "the most apparent reason to remake is economic—the remake as 'presold' property." Leo Braudy, "Afterword: Rethinking Remake," in *Play It Again, Sam: Retakes on Remakes,* ed. Andrew Horton and Stuart Y. McDougal (Berkeley: University of California Press, 1998), 328.

2. These many excellent texts include, Carolyn A. Durham, *Double Takes: Culture and Gender in French Films and Their American Remakes* (Hanover, N.H.: University Press of New England, 1998); Jennifer Forrest and Leonard R. Koos, *Dead Ringers: The Remake in Theory and Practice* (Albany, N.Y.: State University of New York Press, 2002); Ronald Schwartz, *Noir, Now and Then: Film Noir Originals and Remakes, 1944–1999* (Westport, Conn.: Greenwood Press, 2001); Anat Zanger, *Film Remakes as Ritual and Disguise: From Carmen to Ripley* (Amsterdam: Amsterdam University Press, 2007); and, most prescient as to the remake as an emerging cultural form, Constantine Verevis, *Film Remakes* (Edinburgh: Edinburgh University Press, 2006). The bibliography of this collection includes an extensive list of additional readings on film remakes.

3. In terms of aesthetics, academics, fans, and film critics alike have criticized the remake as a formulaic category, and thus one that devalues the aesthetic appeal of film. In terms of politics, a number of authors have written that the remake relegates non-Western films to an inferior status, especially as many non-Western films are remade (such as *The Departed/Infernal Affairs*) even while people are unaware of the originals behind such remakes. The politics of remaking, according to some, are inherently conservative—they favor the repetition of a classic text as opposed to creating new filmic texts.

4. Braudy, "Afterword," 327.

5. Thomas Leitch, "Twice-Told Tales: Disavowal and the Rhetoric of the Remake," in *Dead Ringers: The Remake in Theory and Practice*, ed. Jennifer Forrest and Leonard R. Koos (Albany, N.Y.: State University of New York Press, 2002), 37.

6. When the film *Polyester* (1981), directed by John Waters, was first released, audience members were given scratch-and-sniff cards labeled with numbers that corresponded to numbers flashed on the movie screen at various points in the performance. The smells on the cards corresponded (sometimes in a very disgusting way) with the action in the movie. Sensurround was developed by Universal Studios in the 1970s as a way to enhance the presentation of films like *Earthquake* (1974), *Midway* (1976), and *Rollercoaster* (1977). The process involved the placement of powerful speakers in theaters which would rumble with an intensity that audience members could feel. This was in order to mimic the feel of an earthquake, the explosion of bombs, and the roar of a roller coaster on its tracks. Percepto was a gimmick created by William Castle for his film *The Tingler* (1959). Theater seats were wired to deliver electric shocks at points in the film when the titular monster appeared on screen.

7. Edward Said once offered that "the writer thinks less of writing originally, and more of rewriting." Edward Said, "On Originality," in *The World, The Text, and The Critic* (Cambridge, Mass.: Harvard University Press, 1983), 135. T. S. Eliot, in his influential essay "Tradition and the Individual Talent," wrote, similarly, that "No poet, no artist, of any art, has his complete meaning alone." T. S. Eliot, "Tradition and the Individual Talent," in Frank Kermode, *Selected Prose of T. S. Eliot* (London: Faber, 1984), 38. See also, Walter Benjamin, "The Storyteller: Reflections on the Works of Nikolai Leskov," in *Illuminations* (New York: Schocken, 1969), 83–109; and Julie Sanders, *Adaptation and Appropriation* (New York: Routledge, 2005).

8. Martin Heidegger, *Nietzsche: Volume IV: Nihilism* (San Francisco: Harper, 1982), 221.

9. Lucy Mazdon, "Introduction: Special Issue: Film Remakes," *Journal of Romance Studies* 4, no. 1 (Spring 2004): 3.

10. Plato, *The Republic* (Indianapolis, Ind.: Hackett, 1992), 514–517b.

11. Walter Benjamin, "The Work of Art in the Age of Its Technological Reproducibility: Second Version," in *Walter Benjamin: Selected Writings, Volume 3: 1935–1938* (Cambridge, Mass.: Belknap/Harvard, 2002), 101–33.

12. Susan Sontag, *On Photography* (London: Penguin, 1977).

13. Jean Baudrillard, *Simulations* (New York: Semiotext(e), 1983). Today, the procession of the simulacra may be even more pronounced in visual culture, including film. For more on this idea see, W. J. T. Mitchell, *What Do Pictures Want?: The Lives and Loves of Images* (Chicago: University of Chicago Press, 2005).

14. Andrew Horton and Stuart Y. McDougal, "Introduction," in *Play It Again, Sam: Retakes on Remakes*, ed. Andrew Horton and Stuart Y. McDougal (Berkeley: University of California Press, 1998), 4.

15. Søren Kierkegaard, *Repetition in Fear and Trembling/Repetition* (Princeton: Princeton University Press, 1983).

16. Durham, *Double Takes*, 17.

17. Mazdon, "Introduction," 2.

18. See Deborah Cartmell and Imelda Whelehan, "Harry Potter and the Fidelity Debate," in *Books in Motion: Adaptation, Intertextuality, Authorship*, ed. Mireia Aragay (Amsterdam: Rodopi, 2005), 37–49.

19. Karen Diehl, "Once Upon an Adaptation: Traces of the Authorial on Film," in

*Books in Motion: Adaptation, Intertextuality, Authorship*, ed. Mireia Aragay (Amsterdam: Rodopi, 2005), 89–106.

20. Quoted in Braudy, "Afterword," 329. This point is also verified by Constantine Verevis who writes, "these textual accounts of remaking risk essentialism, in many instances, privileging the 'original' over the remake or measuring the success of the remake according to its ability to realise what are taken to be the essential elements of a source text." Verevis, *Film Remakes*, 2.

21. Horton and McDougal, "Introduction," 4.

22. In this version of *The Manchurian Candidate*, care is taken to remake the film along political and technological lines, most particularly as the new agent of ultimate control is no longer the state but the global corporation known as Manchurian Global. A similar, albeit sloppy, attempt at such updating occurred in the remake of the classic body snatchers films, *The Invasion*.

23. One such example is Ted Turner's goal of colorizing classic films. Gary R. Edgerton, "The Germans Wore Gray, You Wore Blue: Frank Capra, *Casablanca,* and the Colorization Controversy of the 1980s," *Journal of Popular Film and Television* 26 (Winter 2000): 24–32.

24. Martin Heidegger, *The Question Concerning Technology and Other Essays* (New York: Harper, 1977).

25. Jennifer Forrest, "The 'Personal' Touch," in *Dead Ringers: The Remake in Theory and Practice*, ed. Jennifer Forrest and Leonard R. Koos (Albany: State University of New York Press, 2002), 89–123.

26. André Bazin, "Adaptation, or the Cinema as Digest," in *Film Adaptation*, ed. James Naremore (Piscataway, N.J.: Rutgers University Press, 2000), 26.

27. Aristotle, in *Poetics, The Complete Works of Aristotle: Volume II* (Princeton: Princeton University Press, 1995), 2316–2340.

28. Linda Hutcheon writes that "like ritual, this . . . repetition brings comfort." Linda Hutcheon, *A Theory of Adaptation* (New York: Routledge, 2006), 114.

29. Mazdon, "Introduction," 7.

30. Claude Lévi-Strauss, *Totemism* (Boston: Beacon Press, 1963), 89.

31. Braudy, "Afterword," 333.

32. José Ángel Garcia Landa, "Adaptation, Appropriation, Retroaction: Symbolic Interaction with *Henry V*," in *Books in Motion: Adaptation, Intertextuality, Authorship*, ed. Mireia Aragay (Amsterdam: Rodopi, 2005), 226.

33. Verevis, *Film Remakes*, 60. One study of *The Texas Chainsaw Massacre* indicated that 90% of the remake's audience did not see the original but had a vague idea of it. Verevis, *Film Remakes*, 146.

34. Émile Durkheim, *Suicide: A Study in Sociology* (New York: Free Press, 1997).

35. Kierkegaard, *Repetition in Fear and Trembling/Repetition*, 148.

36. Kierkegaard, *Repetition in Fear and Trembling/Repetition*, 131.

37. Sigmund Freud, *Beyond the Pleasure Principle* (New York: W. W. Norton, 1989), 43.

38. Kierkegaard, *Repetition in Fear and Trembling/Repetition*, 149.

39. One such suggestion is found in Derrida's concept of différance and in Hans-Georg Gadamer's hermeneutic circle. Jacques Derrida, *Of Grammatology* (Baltimore, Md.: Johns Hopkins University Press, 1998); Hans-Georg Gadamer, *Truth and Method*, 2nd ed. (New York: Continuum, 1993).

40. Gerard Genette's study of the palimpsestous nature of texts is especially relevant

in this regard. Gerard Genette, *Palimpsests: Literature in the Second Degree* (Lincoln: University of Nebraska Press, 1977).

41. See Hutcheon, *A Theory of Adaptation*, 21; and Schwartz, *Noir, Now and Then.*

42. Verevis, *Film Remakes*, 4.

43. *Oxford English Dictionary*, <http://www.oed.com/> (1 December 2007).

44. Harold Bloom, *The Anxiety of Influence: A Theory of Poetry*, 2nd ed. (New York: Oxford University Press, 1997).

45. Leitch, "Twice-Told Tales."

46. Verevis, *Film Remakes*, 8.

47. Verevis, *Film Remakes*, 58.

48. Horton and McDougal, "Introduction," 3.

49. Walter Benjamin, *The Origin of German Tragic Drama* (London: Verso, 2003).

50. Horton and McDougal, "Introduction," 4, 6.

51. Braudy, "Afterword," 332.

52. Jürgen Habermas, "Modernity: An Incomplete Project," in *Interpretive Social Science: A Second Look*, ed. Paul Rabinow and William M. Sullivan (Berkeley: University of California Press, 1987), 141–156.

# Part I: Fear

*Chapter 2*

# Immanent Attack: An Existential Take on *The Invasion of the Body Snatchers* Films

Juneko J. Robinson

There's something about the horror genre that makes it especially amenable to philosophical examination. In facing threats of death, dismemberment, possession, mind control, or the loss of one's soul, protagonists in horror films typically are confronted with fear, anxiety, and dread concerning human finitude in general and their own personal mortality in particular. Moreover, the characters in horror films generally face crisis situations in which they must assume extraordinary personal responsibility and make exceedingly difficult choices. In seeking freedom from that which menaces them, such characters are often forced into a Homeric-like odyssey as they attempt to escape from whatever evil entities inhabit the "bad place"—the ghosts in the haunted house, the vampires in the foreboding castle, the zombies swarming the mall, the psycho killers, or pernicious people-next-door trolling the neighborhood. Similarly, the protagonists in science fiction films frequently are forced to struggle with maintaining their humanity while doing battle with menacing alien entities in a coldly impersonal and indifferent universe or in a blighted post-apocalyptic landscape. Frequently, such characters wind up unleashing their own worst tendencies, and as a consequence we find powerful and destructive forms of human nature expressed, often through scientific or social experiments gone awry. In complementary fashion, fantasy films often utilize an epic, heroic perspective. Much like the ancient Greek myths, many of these films imagine battles between good and evil that are epic both in their scale and in their ramifications for the lives and souls of the protagonists. In attempting to reverse fate or to save or protect someone or some thing, the characters in fantasy films are often compelled to embark upon what Joseph Campbell referred to as the *hero's journey*, whereby they are forced to confront their own Achilles' heel. The task is to do so without succumbing to evil, without losing one's soul. Inevitably when these characters return home from war, whether real or metaphorical, they are changed: older, wiser, and battle-scarred.

All of these issues—fear, anxiety, dread, passion, death, and human finitude, along with the possibility of individual transcendence, freedom, and personal responsibility—are central concerns not only of horror and many science fiction and fantasy films and literature, but also of much of Western philosophy in general, and existentialism in particular. They are recurring human preoccupations precisely because they form an inextricable part of the human psyche. For this reason, we collectively revisit these themes in film and literature again and again and again. But while all horror, science fiction, and fantasy films share at least some, if not all, of the aforementioned characteristics, some have been remade because they are particularly effective in their ability to illustrate and to articulate these deep-seated preoccupations of ours. Having appeared in no less than four English-language film incarnations, three written versions, numerous translations, and countless spin-offs around the globe, the *Invasion of the Body Snatchers* series is a prime example of a horror/sci-fi/fantasy story that we seem to be drawn to again and again precisely because it speaks to these gnawing, existential concerns.[1]

## *L'enfer C'est les Autres*: Existentialist Themes in *The Body Snatchers* Films[2]

Much has been written about the various versions of *Invasion of the Body Snatchers*. Since the first film debuted over fifty years ago, commentators have typically written of how the film represents the decline of community, modern alienation, the growing distrust of authority, the hypocrisy of provincialism, science and the medical community, the fear of both the communist threat and of McCarthyism run amuck. However, while each of these views has merit and has much to say about the collective fears that were present within the cultural zeitgeist in which each successive film appeared, I share Carl Jung's observation that we tend to revisit the same stories for reasons that are deeply engrained in our human psyche and the human experience. As Stephen King has noted, we make up horrors in order to cope with real ones.[3] My contention is that, at its most fundamental level, the *Invasion of the Body Snatchers* tale has been so enduring precisely because it speaks to our most deep-seated and universal of fears—that of the self-dissolution that comes with death, of which the fear of inundation, of forced transformation, of being absorbed into something larger than ourselves, are merely variations.

The existentialist philosopher Martin Heidegger believed that we humans are alone in our ability to anticipate our deaths. What is significant for Heidegger, however, is not our awareness of death as an event that occurs at the end of our lives, but rather our awareness that, from the very moment of our birth, we are effectively in the process of dying. Because death might come at any moment, our sense of time, with the concomitant awareness of the finiteness of human life, of our personal, individual lives, is paramount and crucial to our sense of self. Precisely because we know that there will be a time when we will no longer "be-there," human beings are the only beings for whom "being" is an issue. It is because we "care" about our being that the confrontation with death is such a frightening experience for us. For Heidegger, in fact, "care" is our basic human state of existence. It is care that conditions how we comport ourselves towards our lives, our deaths, and all other beings and entities in the world. Because of this, we are never simply neutral towards our lives and our world. For Heidegger, care is not merely a mental or emotional attitude, but an ontological state and one which must be present in order for other attitudes even to be possible. Thus, it is only because humans "care" that existence and death are issues for us.

Because this awareness of death is so pervasive, forming such an integral part of the human psyche and affecting how we comport ourselves towards every aspect of our lives, even metaphorical death calls to mind the real thing. This is because metaphorical death, such as tremendous unintended or coerced personal transformation, is experienced as a threat to our physical and mental integrity. But why should this be so? We often speak of personal transformation as a wonderful and even miraculous phenomenon, one that is in fact necessary to achieve great feats such as spiritual enlightenment. However, in order to achieve such a radical transformation we must lose that which we identify with our former selves. Indeed, it appears that in order to achieve such a transformation it may not even be possible to remain what we would normally think of as "human" at all: we must instead become something very different from what we are—something unrecognizable to our present selves. There is, in fact, a long-standing debate within the philosophy of religion—particularly in Eastern religions—as to whether or not it is better to retain some sense of self separate from that which one is about to become or to lose one's self completely in *nirvana*. Given this, it makes sense that the very meaning of nirvana is "extinction," as in a flame being snuffed out. As desirable as such states may be, the reality is that we are also deeply ambivalent about such personal transformations, religious or otherwise. There is a tremendous anxiety that such changes—even if for the better—will result in some sort of fundamental alteration to our sense of self. There is a fear that we will no longer recognize ourselves.

The motifs of engulfment and forced transformation appear in countless movies—particularly horror movies that involve betrayal, such as, *The Thing, The* (original) *Stepford Wives, Alien,* or *Rosemary's Baby.* In these films, the enemy does not wish so much to destroy us physically as it does to appropriate our hearts, minds and bodies for its own use, to transform us from within, so that the enemy might then survive and thrive in our place. In the *Invasion of the Body Snatchers* series, alien pods from outer space inundate Earth, seeking to absorb and extinguish the human race, albeit only incidentally to their own flourishing. Like viruses, which carry no DNA of their own but which utilize the DNA of their hosts, these pods replace their hosts cell by cell until all that remains is an empty shell. In these films, there is an ambivalence portrayed between the attraction of engulfment and the horror of self-annihilation. The attraction of the pods stems from the fact that we have a deep-seated need to escape our fundamental, ontological isolation by merging with others and losing ourselves in something larger than our finite selves. In the *Body Snatchers* films, the extinction of the individual ego is depicted as facilitating an awe-inspiring absorption of human beings into a plant-like organism whose parts are merely manifestations of a unified, functional whole. There is, in certain regards, something both comforting and reassuring about this, and so we see many of the characters in these films welcoming their own loss of self and encouraging their neighbors and loved ones also to give themselves over to the pods.

Yet, being absorbed in a crowd also invokes terror, a fear of being torn asunder or of being engulfed. The *Invasion of the Body Snatchers* series illustrates the duality of this ambivalence. The fact of the matter is that the pods are not *merely* an external threat; they are an external threat that we are forced to *internalize* against our will. "Only true conversion leads men to give up their old associations and form new ones," writes Elias Canetti and the conversion that the pods demand is that we shed not only those social distinctions of rank, status, and property that separate us from the rest of humanity, but also those differences that distinguish us as individuals.[4] In trading our love and loyalty towards particular people, we gain the unconditional devotion that comes upon merging with, and becoming an appendage to, an organism that is greater than ourselves. But this is not all. What makes the first two films so effective is our recognition of the positive consequences that such a transformation would make possible: a placid life without suffering or doubt, fear or anxiety; no more alienation or loneliness, no more war or hatred, no more, in the words of one protagonist, "tears." We are very much aware of such longings. Yet to be one with everything requires the effective destruction of much that stamps us as unique individuals.

## *Invasion of the Body Snatchers* (1956)

The classic, original 1956 version of *Invasion of the Body Snatchers* begins with swirling storm clouds and anxious, threatening orchestral music as the credits appear and inform us that the following presentation is in Superscope. In a scene reminiscent of a noir thriller, the film's opening reveals a police car racing through rain-slicked streets at nighttime and pulling up at an "emergency hospital." A civilian disembarks and as he enters to confer with the on-staff physician, we hear an evidently agitated man ranting, "Will you let me go, while there's still *time*?!" (As we shall see, the element of time is a recurring motif in this series). The new arrival is an on-call psychiatrist, contacted by the emergency ward physician on duty. As he opens the door, a crazed, disheveled man rushes into our view. It is Dr. Miles Bennell, the hero and protagonist of the story. Upon being pacified by the psychiatrist, the crazed man begins his story.

In voice-over, Bennell tells us that the horror began when he was called home from a medical conference the previous Thursday. Upon returning home, Bennell's nurse informs him that there have been a huge number of desperate patients waiting for him—some for the last two weeks—for ailments they are unwilling to disclose either to her or to the on-call doctor. As they head to the office, Bennell and his nurse encounter the first visible sign that all is not quite right in this quiet, picturesque little town: as they drive down the road, they are forced to swerve in order to avoid hitting little Jimmy Grimaldi, who is frantically trying to escape from his mother. Pulling over, Bennell gives chase, but Jimmy eludes him. Jimmy's mother explains to Bennell that the boy doesn't want to go school, and as they are talking Miles notices that the formerly prosperous Grimaldi vegetable stand is closed. "Joe been sick?," he asks. "No," Mrs. Grimaldi says, "we gave the stand up—too much *work.*" This troubles him, because when he last saw the stand a month ago it was "the cleanest, busiest stand on the road."

Later, upon his arrival at the office, Miles and his nurse are greeted with six cancelled appointments and a visit from Bennell's former flame, Becky Driscoll. Fresh from a Reno divorce and several years abroad, Becky says she feels "almost like a stranger in my own country." Their meeting is warm and flirtatious. However, Becky soon reveals that she is worried about her cousin Wilma, who seems to be convinced that her Uncle Ira is not really her uncle. Miles agrees to stop by to check on her and to make a referral to the town psychiatrist. Afterwards, Miles is visited by little Jimmy Grimaldi, literally dragged in by his grandmother, and shrieking that his mother isn't his mother. Administering a sedative, Miles sends Jimmy home to his grandma's. When he finally meets with Cousin Wilma, everything seems fine except for her strange and unsettling conviction that her uncle is an imposter.[5] Wilma tells Miles that "there's something missing" with old Uncle Ira. "There's no emotion, only the pretense of it." That special look in his eyes, which was once reserved only for her, is now gone. Miles tries to comfort her, assuring her that it's more difficult to go crazy than she might think; however, he does tell her that once she thinks about how crazy her accusations are, "then you'll know that the trouble is inside you."

Like the consummate professional, the good doctor temporarily shelves his misgivings about Wilma and at dusk takes Becky to dinner at a new, formerly popular but now empty, supper club. While dancing and awaiting their pre-supper martinis, the two are interrupted by a phone call. His old friend Jack Belicec is in some trouble and in immediate need of a doctor. Pulling up the darkened driveway of the Belicecs, they are met by Jack. As they speak, Belicec's wife Teddy anxiously races out of the house. They are cagey about revealing what the real matter is, instead preferring to let Bennell form his own professional opinion. Entering the rumpus room, they stand by the bar, Belicec indicating a pool table swathed in complete darkness. He tells Bennell to turn the light on over the pool table. Immediately, the music crescendos; brass blaring with the intensity and monotony of a fast approaching car horn. A glistening, wet, white-sheathed, human-like figure is clearly visible on the pool table. The glare from the lamp casts deep shadows on the adjacent wall as Bennell intently examines the body lying on the table. These shadows will become prominent throughout the remainder of the film in marked contrast to the sunny, daylight-inspired optimism of the first twenty minutes of the film. As the wildly swinging lamp cord becomes still, Becky moves in closer and is abruptly startled by the cacophonous chiming of a cuckoo clock, an omen that soon madness will ensue, that time—as measured by human concerns—is winding down.

We witness in the opening scenes of this story, thus, how the familiar, comfortable environs of small-town America have become the setting for an ambiguous threat that cloaks itself in mundane everydayness. In Bennell's own hometown, among the familiar faces of the townspeople, in the rumpus room of his friend's familiar house, the invasion has begun. Superficially, everything looks the same as what it once was, and yet there is something amiss and out of joint. Familiar, friendly faces have become sinister, not due to any external transformation, but due to some sort of internal, unseen change. It is this cloak of familiarity that makes the underlying threat so terrifying and frightening. The alien invaders are taking advantage of everything and everyone that we trust, gaining our confidence even as they destroy our souls. They infiltrate our world covertly, siphoning the individual life force of our loved ones in order to make them into instruments or tools for the occupation of Earth. The rest of the film documents the spread of this invasion as alien pods take over and attempt to destroy the human race, absorbing individuals one by one, and replacing them with shell-like, emotionless imitations of their former selves.

As mentioned earlier, previous interpretations of the original film have typically centered on the threat of oppressive conformity as manifested under communism and McCarthyism.[6] However, such observations don't explain *why* it is that such crushing conformity is so fearful to begin with. Part of what makes the specter of conformity so personally threatening to us in the *Invasion of the Body Snatchers* series is that it is couched in familiar, almost seductive terms that acknowledge our secret yearning for order, simplicity, and contentment, but which also causes us deep suspicion. We yearn for the camaraderie of the crowd and to lose ourselves in something larger than ourselves, but we simultaneously fear such engulfment because the consummation of such a merger would require that we lose our identities and become something very different from who we are now. The loss of personal freedom that is necessarily implicated by such absorption into the crowd would require destruction of that which distinguishes us as individuals. As sociologist William H. Whyte wrote in *The Organization Man*, "It is all very well to say one should belong . . . But how much? Where is the line between co-operation and surrender?"[7]

According to Stephen King, from the perspective of Jack Finney, the story's original author, the worst thing about the pods is that they have absolutely no sense of aesthetics: in the novel, they are neglectful and let the town run down.[8] In the original film version, the Grimaldis close their vegetable stand because it's "too much work." This explanation is subtly disturbing and significant because it is an indication that the pods simply do not care, either in the Heideggerian sense, or in the more commonly recognized sense. These aliens have no ambitions or pretensions; their intentionality is limited to a biological imperative. Simone de Beauvoir has pointed out that the reason why we have historically considered battles and skyscrapers such great feats is because they are taken as evidence of the human ability to transcend nature.[9] But, in the absence of human caring, reflection, and meaning-conferring activity, art, literature, and civilization as we know it would cease to exist. In such a world, war and conflict would come to an end, but the cost would simply be too high. It would be a world without war, not because we had rationally *chosen* to transcend our barbaric nature, but because we had surrendered to the imperatives of our animal (or in this case, plant-like) nature, thereby making war irrelevant insofar as there would no longer be any ideological or other typically human motivations or attitudes that are made possible by care.

It is against the backdrop of such existentialist concerns that the original *Invasion of the Body Snatchers* unfolds. But there are also social and historical issues to take into account. Although one would not know it to look at the television programming of that decade now, the 1950s were a time of tremendous, often threatening, social change. As Roger Eberwein has pointed out, the original version of *Body Snatchers* was released the very year in which Southern schools were being forcibly desegregated on the heels of the Supreme Court decision outlawing "separate but equal" education.[10] If the Red Scare was not enough, school desegregation unleashed a formidable sense of being inundated by an alien threat. According to Eberwein, the language used in the popular press to describe these forces of social change drew on metaphors of disease and contagion, of cure and illness.[11] At a time when public esteem for medical professionals was extraordinarily high, the impotence of the protagonists in the original film is noteworthy in the face of the turmoil associated with desegregation. According to Eberwein, this is not to say that there is some "previously undiscovered allegory about racism" to be discovered in the film "but, rather, to suggest that we ought to remember that the film entered a dialogue . . . of considerable tension."[12] That dialogue was characterized by a fear of engulfment and forced transformation at the hands both of communists and civil rights activists pressing for desegregation. Later, successive versions of *Invasion of the Body Snatchers* would similarly emerge within their own particular cultural and historical contexts, providing interesting insights into the manner in which more elemental, existential fears and hopes become historically manifest.

## *Invasion of the Body Snatchers* (1978)

The first remake to emerge nearly twenty years after the original was undoubtedly the greatest in terms of its philosophical depth and the vividness with which it illustrates these fundamental themes of existentialism, and thus I shall devote the most space in this essay to its analysis. In this version, with a distinguished cast, director Philip Kaufman changes the setting from small-town, mythical Santa Mira (the novel originally takes place in Sausalito, a suburb of San Francisco), to urban San Francisco. Threatening music gives way to shrieking and a soundtrack of pulsing, intrauterine sounds, as the film opens with a view of an alien planet saturated with gelatinous, sperm-like tendrils that become untethered and drift upwards into space. This eerie landscape could be Earth in the distant past or the not-so-distant future. Quickly the picture cuts to satellite photos of Earth in various degrees of resolution. A rainstorm brings the drifting alien organisms to California and, in a nod to the first version, we see a garbage truck, whose import we are not yet clued into, inexplicably "commuting" through the toll plaza that links Marin County to San Francisco.

In marked contrast to the first film, in which the invasion occurs covertly and out of sight, we are immediately made aware of the spread of the viscous spores through rain and groundwater runoff. Ominously, they immediately sprout tendrils, take root, and emit strange blossoms from tiny, cabbage-like pods and it is this novelty that attracts Elizabeth Driscoll, now a professional at the Department of Public Health. Taking a blossom home with her, Elizabeth believes she has discovered a "grex," a new species that emerges when two unrelated species cross-pollinate. "Many of the species are dangerous weeds and should be avoided," she reads. "A characteristic rapid and widespread growth pattern was even observed in many of the large war-torn cities of Europe. Indeed, some of these plants may thrive on devastated ground."

The references to a landscape blighted by war remind us of two of the events most responsible for our twentieth-century existential crisis: the Holocaust and the dropping of the atom bombs at Hiroshima and Nagasaki. First, there were our anxieties about the long-term effects of radiation after the dropping of the atomic bombs, an anxiety revealed through countless horror and science fiction films in the 1950s and 1960s. Secondly, in a manner reminiscent of the mass incineration of people in the Nazi ovens of the Holocaust, as well as in Hiroshima, Dresden, and other cities, the pods' transformations are made possible by the reduction of the human body to blackened ash and fluff. As with the victims of World War II, the protagonists in this version of *Invasion of the Body Snatchers* are rendered disposable; their remains unceremoniously (and sacrilegiously) mixed with those of others, and carted off in garbage trucks to be dumped at mass burial sites.

That humans beings are reduced to blackened fluff is particularly horrifying, because here we are reminded that in death people are most fully transformed back into the unthinking, undifferentiated matter that constitutes what Jean-Paul Sartre terms "being-in-itself." According to Sartre, human beings have two facets. On the one hand, we are the sum of all that we are unable to change: the circumstances of our birth and heritage, the culture and point in history into which we are born, our gender, race, biological needs, and sex drives. All these and more are the brute facts—what Sartre refers to as *facticity*—about the world in which we one day suddenly find our selves and about which we can do little to alter. It is this facticity of our existence that puts us on par with all the other things and entities that comprise the world of *being-in-itself*. Being-in-itself is just all the stuff in the world; the totality that exists independent of human consciousness. Without human consciousness to organize it, create distinctions, and confer meaning upon it, this totality constitutes a single, undifferentiated mass. Uniform, gray, and viscous like cold oatmeal, being-in-itself is superfluous, inundating everything and obliterating all distinctions. Sartre, in his book *Nausea,* has the character Roquentin describe his sudden awareness of being-in-itself while sitting beneath a tree in a park with horrifying detail:

> The root, the park gates, the bench, the sparse grass, all that had vanished: the diversity of things, their individuality, were only an appearance, a veneer. This veneer had melted, leaving soft, monstrous masses, all in disorder—naked, in a frightful, obscene nakedness.[13]

However, we are never *merely* our facticity—the sum of our found heritage and biological dispositions—for humans have the unique ability to confer *meaning* upon such brute facts about ourselves and the world. This is because we are conscious beings and, for Sartre, consciousness is always active and it is always *about* something, that is, it is intentional. In fact, for Sartre, thinking *is* action. However, because of this ability to reflect and confer meaning upon our lives and the world, we have both the blessing and the curse of transcendence. It is transcendence that allows us the ability to choose to overcome the brute facts about our lives. Our lives, then, are the sum total of the actions or projects we have engaged in, but until the point of death, we are always in the process of making and remaking ourselves. It is this freedom of consciousness that characterizes *being-for-itself*. To be human is to be a being-for-itself because we are always conferring meaning onto our existence and making something of our own lives.

This self-awareness is what separates us from the rest of the world's entities, which are seen by Sartre as a seamless, unified whole. Our intentionality allows us to shine the beam of human consciousness on entities and, like a flashlight, make distinctions that are not present in the objective world. Without human consciousness there are no distinctions to be found in the world, and thus there can be no such thing as "destruction" within being-in-itself. According to Sartre, natural disasters such as earthquakes and storms do not destroy—at least not directly. They merely modify the distribution of masses of being. It is only with the introduction of something that is not part of being-in-itself—that is, the negation that is human consciousness, which cares about such events and their implications—that such phenomena can be judged as "destructive." Thus, Sartre described the non-human world of the in-itself as nauseating precisely because its excess lies beyond any human comprehension and it is indifferent to the meaning-conferring activity that human consciousness seeks to impose upon it.

The only thing that keeps humans from being completely reduced to being-in-itself at death is the fact that our deaths, and those of others, hold meaning for us. But as the characters in *Invasion of the Body Snatchers* indifferently watch their own former remains being carted off in garbage trucks, we are made aware of the meaningless of death in a world without people. Without the meaning-conferring feature of human consciousness, there is no destruction in being-in-itself, no extinction of the human race, no murder of individual human beings. There is only the meaningless redistribution of matter, only the matter-of-fact transformation from an anthropocentric world to a pod-infested alien one. Nowhere is this made more apparent than when homeless street musician Harry and his dog—local denizens of the park near Matthew's and Elizabeth's place of work—are merged into one horrific freak: a dog with its owner's human head. Because being-in-itself is undifferentiated and admits of no distinctions, this merging of man with dog is unremarkable in the big scheme of things. For us as meaning-conferring humans, however, it is positively horrifying.

The ingenuity of the 1978 remake lies in its ability to meld the growing alien threat into the familiar background of an urban din. The opening scenes show footage of isolated individuals gazing out of windows, in a manner reminiscent of the stark pictures by the "painter of loneliness" Edward Hopper. Random street shots from overhead reveal the solitary nature of urban life, indicating how even in the midst of the crowd, we are alone in a world long since abandoned by God. It is only upon repeated viewing that one becomes aware that the invasion is already well underway with the rolling of the opening credits. Early on as Bennell (now named Matthew and a Department of Public Health official) is driving through the city, the car radio informs us that there is a multi-county blackout and that utility crews will be working throughout the night to restore power. It is of course the perfect opportunity to secret away pods, but like much of the urban din, we are inclined to dismiss this detail as insignificant. Police sirens blare, a running, wild-eyed businessman runs past an oblivious Elizabeth as she walks to work, a couple seems to notice him and (perhaps, coincidentally?) runs in the same direction.[14] We think we hear an alien shriek in the background, but it is soon drowned out by the noise of traffic. Is this significant or simply the kind of behavior that only appears strange when viewed in isolation? When Elizabeth arrives at work late and blames it on her boyfriend ("I don't know. He was just weird"), a coworker looks at her askance. Is the look one of mere disapproval or something more sinister?

Our sense of paranoia grows when Elizabeth meets Matthew in a hallway. Everywhere, there are people standing around, watching them or staring off into space and waiting (for what?). As the camera circles around, we catch a brief glimpse of a man alarmingly pressed up against the inside of a glass door. Elizabeth bumps into a man who pointedly stares after her. A white lab coat suspiciously ducks back into a doorway just as Matthew's attention is drawn by an approaching public health inspector. In a scene hearkening back to Camus' *The Plague,* the inspector holds aloft a giant, dead black rat. "I got it. I *really* got it!" he says triumphantly. Later, Elizabeth recounts to Matthew how she followed her boyfriend throughout the city. "I keep seeing these people, all recognizing each other. Something's passing between them; some secret," she says in language that calls to mind some sort of "social disease." Later, Dr. Kibner refers to the mass delusion of imposters as "some sort of hallucinogenic flu" and suggests she get a good night's sleep. "Is it contagious?" Matthew asks. Kibner just laughs. The plague has begun and like the protagonists in Camus' novel, these individuals will have to decide how to comport themselves to a hostile world. They will have to take a stand in order to combat the absurdity in which they find themselves.

It is commonly held that the 1978 version of *Invasion of the Body Snatchers* is an indictment of New Age psychoanalysis and this is partly right as it plays on the deep-seated ambivalence and suspicion we have towards psychology and the risks and benefits of personal transformation. Leonard Nimoy's David Kibner is unquestionably more sinister than the benevolent, but ineffective Danny Kaufman from the original film. However, what is objectionable about Kibner is not so much his post-pod personality, but our suspicions about his pre-transformation character. "He's trying to change people to fit the world," Jack says in a tirade directed at Kibner. "I'm trying to change the world to fit people." Again, our ambivalence about the fine line between cooperation and surrender is echoed in this second version of the film. The fact that none of us is surprised when we see Dr. Kibner wielding a hypodermic needle filled with a sedative in order to facilitate Matthew and Elizabeth's transformation is further indication of the fallen status of doctors in our eyes, particularly psychiatrists.

As with the original version, time is a recurrent motif in this film, now made even more prominent. Upon hearing a loud buzzing alarm clock, Elizabeth awakes to find her boyfriend Geoffrey sweeping up the remains of his former self. He is cold and unresponsive. As she follows him to an awaiting garbage truck, which carts off his ashen remains, the incessant ticking of an unseen clock begins. Watching him intently, she is startled by loud chiming, the camera immediately zooming in on the offending clock. The insanity has begun yet again. Later, when Matthew fears for her safety, he sneaks into Elizabeth's house as Geoffrey sits motionless before a television that is inexplicably broadcasting a succession of clock faces. As in the first film, the notion of time is significant insofar as it is a uniquely human construct, one that necessarily emerges for a being that is consciously and uniquely aware of its own impending death.

Driving through the city, Matthew and Elizabeth nearly hit a frantic running man. It is Kevin McCarthy, the actor from the original film who played Miles Bennell, and he is screaming for help. Alarmed, they lock their doors. Banging on the

windows, Miles shouts "You're in danger! Please! Listen to me, something terrible—please, you're next!" We hear shrieking. "They're already here!" He darts
out of view screaming as the crowd runs after him. "He must have done something," says Matthew, and then a sickening thud is heard. When Matthew and Elizabeth drive past the scene of the "accident," a crowd has gathered, but they are
silent and impassive. Sirens sound and a motorcycle cop pulls up, but the officer
is more concerned with directing traffic than with covering Miles' body out of any
show of respect. Later, when Matthew attempts to report the accident, he finds that
there is no record of the gruesome incident.

The first time we see the full-grown pods in this movie, they are swaddled in
cloth like babies, and it is out of the primordial ooze of the Bellicec Mud Baths that
we get our first glimpse of a pod person in transformation. It is a duplicate of Jack
Bellicec, ostensibly the spawn of a houseplant brought as a gift by Mr. Gianni, one
of the bathhouse's customers. Called by the frantic Bellicecs, Matthew examines
the featureless man, still glistening like a newborn, and covered in cobweb-like
material—"like a fetus," as Jack points out. Now concerned and unable to reach
Elizabeth, Matthew races to her home where he finds what at first appears to be her
body in a plant atrium, which of course later vanishes, having been replaced by debris and a broken flower pot in the shape of a face.

In marked contrast to the blackened, dried-out fluff of human remains, the images of the pods and their human duplicates are like mutant overripe fruit from
some nightmarish Bosch painting. With the explosion of giant hairy, veined flowers, mucus-covered adult-sized fetuses emerge gasping, snorting, moaning, shrieking, and shuddering out of grotesquely large okra-like pods. The organic quality is
enhanced by the sickening sounds of moist slithering and the dry, leaf-like crackling of bursting pods set to the backdrop of heartbeats and in-utero pulsations. An
aerial shot views the horror of writhing bodies in the very un-Eden-like garden,
which is inhuman and disgusting. These pod people follow a simple logic: to be
born and procreate. However, according to Beauvoir, neither birth nor suckling
are activities in the existentialist sense because no human project is involved.[15]
"The function of life," according to Kibner, "is survival." For Beauvoir, however,
"life does not carry within itself its reasons for being, reasons that are more important than life itself."[16] Pods "wish" only to survive. Humans, however, desire
to live joyously, deeply, and meaningfully. Accordingly, these pods exhibit neither
the miracle of God's creation, nor the beauty of human birth for what they are carrying out is merely a natural function like mitosis or defecation. It is meaningless
and perfunctory, having nothing to do with humans. They are pure being-in-
itself.

The birthing scenes are especially disgusting because they allow us to regard
the human form and objectify it in a way akin to that of watching the emergence
of maggots. Without the meaning-conferring activity of human consciousness,
birth is no longer a joyous and miraculous beginning of a beautiful newborn child.
Instead, it becomes a monstrous parade of freaks; moaning, shivering, full-grown

adults emerging from plants. Cancer cells replicate by infiltrating an organ and taking on the form, but not the function of its cells. They are cells that somehow lose their ability to differentiate themselves into, say liver cells, or brain cells.[17] They reproduce, but unlike the cells of a liver or a brain they perform no function, have no purpose, other than to replicate.[18] These pods are an abomination because they resemble humans, but only superficially. Like cancer cells, they are mere copies possessing neither originality nor creativity in the fuller, human sense of the term. Their sole purpose is to replicate.

Having been awakened in the midst of his transformation, Matthew attempts to call for help and finds that the operator already knows him by name. As the scope of the conspiracy dawns on all of them, Jack asks, "Matthew? Do you have a gun?" They are now in a Hobbesian state of nature. But before attempting to escape, Matthew cleaves his duplicate's head with a garden hoe and it implodes like an overripe melon. The pods shriek. A sound taken from swine, it is a call to slaughter. Later, in attempting to free the homeless Harry and his beloved dog from their dreamless sleep, Matthew kicks the pod beside them, which promptly hemorrhages like an aborted fetus. Towards the end, upon hearing the haunting siren song of redemption "Amazing Grace" from afar, Matthew, now alone, makes his way towards a ship. Hoping against hope, the audience is caught up in the optimism of the music ("I once was lost, but now I'm found. Was blind, but now I see"), but this hymn is also commonly used at funerals. Arriving at the shipyard, Matthew sees pallets filled with dozens of pods being loaded for shipment abroad. "Oh, God," he cries. But there will be no redemption here.

## *Body Snatchers* (1993)

Of all the film versions of *Invasion of the Body Snatchers*, Abel Ferrara's version least resembles the original. Here, the main protagonist is Marti, an alienated teenaged girl who resents her deceased mother's "replacement" by a stepmother. Her father Steve, a chemist with the Environmental Protection Agency, is charged with inspecting toxic waste sites on military bases, and Marti is forced to spend two months on the road with her dad, stepmother Carol, and their six-year-old son Andy. Using the voice-over technique of the first film, Marti explains that she will "begin with the idea that sometimes things happen that we don't understand. Maybe we shouldn't try to understand those things." As they drive, she reads Ian McEwan's *The Cement Garden*, a tale about a group of orphaned siblings who hide the death of their mother from the outside world by burying her body in concrete in their basement. Marty, it turns out, lost her own mother when she was seven and, like the protagonists in McEwan's novel, cannot let go of the past. Now a sullen teenager, she is resentful of the interloper that has stolen her father's affections away from her.

Arriving at the camp at dusk, soldiers' faces are obscured by darkness. We see them in uniform, blackened silhouettes jogging in unison. The Malones enter what for them is an alien world. In contrast to the reassuring familiarity of small-town living the first film, here the central characters are all at once thrust into an unfamiliar, threateningly homogenized environment. Pulling up to their new digs in their yuppie Volvo station wagon, they are at first unsure which of the identical houses is theirs. Predictably, the interior they discover is bland and undistinguished. Devoid of any personal belongings, the Malones will soon fill it with all their unspoken disappointments, anger, and resentments. This is a house, not a home.

Angry at having to share her room with her stepbrother, Marti leaves and wanders into a restricted area instead of helping her family to unpack. There, she is ominously surrounded by armed soldiers. Warned that she shouldn't be there without security clearance, she is rescued by a convertible driving bad-girl-blond in a leather jacket, who turns out to be Jenn Platt, rebellious teenager, and the commanding officer's daughter. Taking Marti home, Jenn attempts to introduce her to her mother, who is passed out drunk on the sofa with a lit cigarette in her hand. Picking up her mother's glass of vodka, Jenn cavalierly says, "Mom's an alcoholic. According to the experts, that means I'll be one too." As they leave, the camera turns askew and we hear the faint beginnings of crackling and oozing sounds. Nearby, a woman in her nightgown expectantly opens her door to a group of MPs. As they enter, we overhear her husband saying, "I don't know what's wrong with the kids. They don't treat me like I'm their father. They treat me like I'm some stranger." Suddenly awakened in the neighbouring house, little Andy wanders into his parents' room, complaining of nightmares. As they soothe him, they overhear a domestic disturbance with screaming and a struggle. The MPs are wrestling the man into a truck and then they speed off.

Picking up on the family treachery of the original film, *Body Snatchers* clearly focuses on the oppressive nature of family conformity in the face of dysfunction. In a scene reminiscent of *The Stepford Wives*, Marti visits Jenn's house and is greeted by a now meticulously coiffed and highly suspicious Mrs. Platt. Apparently, Mrs. Platt is on the wagon, having replaced her vodka with water. But Jenn is suspicious. There are no delirium tremens, no physical cravings, and, as Mrs. Platt leaves with a group of women to play bridge, Jenn informs Marti that Mrs. Platt doesn't even know how to play bridge.

It is, fittingly, the base's housewives who, being home all the time, make excellent conduits through which to spread the contagion. It is the traditional role of the woman to attend to the processes of birth, and thus to initiate the process that inevitably leads towards death. In this version of the movie we again see a garbage truck making its rounds. At each stop, housewives bring out only small plastic bags filled with loose material no bigger than a melon. Later, we will see that they are bagging up the remains of their former selves. As with other prenatal diseases and injuries, this particular sickness is spread by the mother. Beauvoir provoked much controversy when she wrote that there is something disgusting about motherhood, but in this film we get an illustration of what she was getting at. To be a mother is to be a womb, an instrument for the organic propagation of new life. Traditionally, this function has been held in high esteem by many cultures, but from the existentialist perspective to be a womb is to become a being-in-itself. The natural, organic, and automatic functions of motherhood can be a trap if not freely chosen. Unwanted pregnancies are thought to be tragic precisely because they are cases in which a human being submits to a biological process that is out of her control. She unwillingly loses herself and is transformed into something less than human. In the case of Ferrara's *Body Snatchers*, the military housewife seems to call our attention to this fact. As a housewife, she is not in control of her own life. The very title, "housewife," defines her in relation to the role she plays to her husband and family. She has no identity of her own and has already lost the freedom and uniqueness that is the essence of a being-for-itself. What better place to begin an alien invasion whose ultimate goal is the eradication of individual identity?

This film's focus on, and implicit critique of, traditional family values occurred in tandem with a growing concern in America about health and the role of medicine in family planning issues. The film's release coincided with a time of increased public debate about issues concerning bioethics. The abortion controversy had re-emerged in an even more emphatic form than in 1978. In a nod to the increasingly violent and confrontational anti-abortion movement of that period, the base's transformed general says to a holdout, "You disappoint me, major. You're a man of medicine. You're supposed to preserve life. Not take it." The organic growth of life is a process that must not be interrupted. Human choice must be eliminated and nature allowed to take its course.

In an interesting change from previous versions, the nefarious character of the 1978 film's civic and administrative leaders is now squarely placed upon the American military. As with the civilian population, the military at that time was facing its own medical ethics crisis. Toxic chemical exposure and atropine injections designed to protect soldiers against Iraqi nerve gas were both suspected of causing Gulf War syndrome, a mysterious malady not even recognized by the military until some time later.

At first disturbed by the fact that Tim, a soldier from the base, had killed someone in Kuwait, Marti ends up begging him to shoot her impostor father. By the end of the film, she and Tim are on a mission to save the world by bombing the outgoing convoys of trucks loaded with pods en route to other military bases around the country, and she revels in their destruction. "They destroyed everyone I loved. Our reaction was only human. Revenge, hate, remorse, despair, pity, and most of all, fear. I remember feeling all those things as I watched the bombs explode. How I *hated* them." The expression of emotion is here in dramatic contrast to the emotionlessness of the pods. Marti is rebelling against the lure of motherhood, an oppressive family life, and entanglement in a regimented, military lifestyle where conformity and stoicism are the order of the day. The alien pods offer peace, comfort, and quietude, but they offer these things at the cost of being truly human. Marti, thus, violently rejects the lure of the *in-itself* and, in doing battle with pods, is destined to a state that Heidegger refers to as *homelessness*. This homelessness is more than simply not having a roof to live under. It is a life that is lived without roots and without a connection to a community. In choosing to be an individual, she has chosen to stand apart from the crowd and therefore to renounce the rewards that come from fitting in. With nowhere to go, Marti and Tim eventually land at a military airport. Marti is in tears. "They get you when you sleep," she tells us, "but you can only stay awake so long." As the camera focuses on anonymous ground crewman, we hear a droning, slowed-down, and distorted version of her pod stepmother's warning: "Where you gonna run? Where you gonna hide? Nowhere. Cause there's no one . . . like you . . . left."

## *The Invasion* (2007)

Although the film met with disappointing critical reviews and box-office receipts upon opening in mid-September of 2007, *Invasion* also provides an interesting existential commentary on the times. Released just days before the sixth anniversary of the September 11 terrorist attacks, *Invasion* feels contemporaneous insofar as it is set in the days just before or just after the Halloween of some year either in the recent past or the near future. Taking its cue from the 1993 Ferrara version, the 2007 release focuses more on the idea of contagion and less on the notion of genetic tampering and graphic, freakish, physical transformation.

The film opens with a flash-forward in time: we see a wild-eyed woman frantically racing through an abandoned and looted pharmacy apparently in search of uppers and guzzling pills and caffeinated soda in a desperate attempt to stay awake. We hear voices and pounding from behind a locked door. The next flashback scene reveals that there has been a space shuttle tragedy reminiscent of the Challenger disaster. Upon reentering the atmosphere, the shuttle, appropriately named "The Patriot," burns and disintegrates, cutting a swath and spreading debris from Dallas to Washington, D.C. News footage informs us that NASA has discovered that the shuttle was contaminated with an endo-spore and has taken steps to quarantine the hull of the ship as the president makes his way to the site for a debriefing. As a government official returns to his car after visiting the quarantined site, a young girl—out of civic duty—presents him with a piece of the shuttle that landed on the roof of her house. Reaching for it, he cuts his hand on the debris and a sticky substance adheres to his bleeding hand. Annoyed, he quickly departs, leaving behind the fragment. Upon arriving home, the family dog winces and growls at him when he reaches out to pet the animal with his injured hand. Later that night, deep in sleep, the inspector is wheezing with labored breath, his facial features obliterated by a mucus-like web. A news tidbit informs us that pieces of the shuttle have already appeared for sale on eBay. Conspiracy theories abound as many apparently believe that the shuttle was crashed deliberately. The invasion has begun yet again.

The following scene reveals the woman we met at the beginning of the movie waking to the sounds of her son screaming in a nightmare (an omen that the act of sleeping has the ability to transport us to a frightening world). This is Dr. Bennell, now transformed into a woman psychiatrist and divorced mom. Upon arriving at work, Dr. Bennell is predictably confronted by a patient (this time Veronica Cartright, who played Nancy Bellicec in the first re-make) who claims that her husband is not her husband. It all sounds so familiar.

Although Eberwein is correct to point out that it is impossible fully to situate the meaning of a film within a specific epoch when we are still within that particular historical and cultural moment that has yet to unfold completely, we can offer some preliminary observations. From the outset, the references in *The Invasion* to the post-September 11 American cultural landscape are unmistakable; this is so to such an extent that some audience members have complained of the liberal political subtext of the film.[19] Indeed, even the timing of the release (the last week of August) in the context of twenty-four-hour televised memorials to those events is telling. Like the events of that morning, for Dr. Bennell, the horror begins to unfold at the beginning of a mundane workday. As she walks to work, she notices the unusual silence of the streets. Large groups of people, apparently waiting for the bus, are standing stock-still, vacant-eyed, and silent. One is reminded of the hollow-eyed commuters walking in mass-migration from lower Manhattan the morning of the disaster, apparently, according to observers, in complete silence. Later as the contagion spreads and some come to the realization that resistance is hopeless, in a scene chillingly reminiscent of the mass suicides from the burning Twin Towers, we see a couple atop a building embracing before they leap to their deaths as they are watched by dispassionate, now-alien, observers below. Posters for missing people crop up like those put up all around lower Manhattan that day in September. As on that day, the alien threat comes from above, in this case from an errant space shuttle (there's an interesting cultural reference here: "Patriot" is also a kind of American missile).

Picking up on the thread of contagion that appears in earlier versions of the film, *Invasion* emphasizes the sickness and disease metaphor, but this time rather than merely being powerlessness to stop the spread of disease (such as the first film's Dr. Miles Bennell), physicians are much more clearly responsible for its spread. There is an interesting reversal of the roles of Dr. Miles Bennell and psychiatrists Danny Kaufman and David Kibner in the 1956 and 1978 versions, respectively. From the first two versions to the last, the role of the psychiatrist assumes greater prominence in the plot. But unlike the benevolent but ineffective Danny Kaufman (1956) and the sinister, egoistic David Kibner (1978), *Invasion's* Dr. Carol Bennell is a psychiatrist who early on comes to recognize the ensuing insanity growing all around her and she tries to fight it. This time, it is not the psychiatrist who is doing the pooh-poohing, but the physicians and public health officials. However, Carol is challenged by her ex-husband in a way we wanted to challenge Kibner back in 1978. "You give people pills to make their lives better," he charges. "How is that different?" Similarly, Yorish, a Russian diplomat Carol meets at a dinner party at the Belicecs teasingly (and cynically) asks her, "Can you give me a pill to make me see the world as you Americans?" In a manner hearkening back to the public debates about the safety and efficacy of anthrax vaccines in the wake of anthrax-contaminated letters in the months following September 11, mass vaccinations are touted and demanded by an anxious public. But, in marked contrast to the existential heroism of Miles Bennell, public health officials in *Invasion* organize mass inoculations under the seeming auspices of protecting the public, but which in reality are designed to spread the contagion.

More muted than in the 1956 version, and taking its cue from the maternal spread of disease in the 1993 version, it is clear that this new contagion is spread through acts of "caring" and "kindness." Filmed in Baltimore, Maryland, this is a community characterized by civic duty (the little girl who presents the NASA agent with a broken piece from the shuttle), and loving relationships between mother and son. Indeed, it is under the auspices of love, nurturance, and hospitality that beloved friends and family members are able to help the contagion spread. Carol's patient complains that her formerly abusive husband keeps bringing her things to drink and she doesn't want them. Tucker, Carol's ex-husband, plies their son with hot cocoa. Those mass inoculations are carried out under the pretense of protecting the health of the public and, in a scene that reminds one of a perverse reversal of the heroic flight attendants on September 11's doomed Flight 93, we see uniformed attendants "helping" an elderly train passenger by holding her down and giving her an injection that will presumably lead to her transformation.

The insanity that is spread by the pods is peculiar in that it allows the world a respite from its routine troubles. From the beginning, televised news is ubiquitous in the lives of the protagonists. Now, with the spread of the contagion, long-elusive peace accords are finally reached. There is a cease-fire in Darfur, President Bush is now on good terms with Venezuelan leaders, and the US occupation of Iraq comes to a close. After Carol goes on the run with her son, she hides out in a convenience store and waits for her boyfriend Ben Driscoll. Coming out of the bathroom, she is surprised to find him standing there. Compared to his calm demeanor, it is she who looks feral and insane. "Carol, look at yourself. Is this who you are? Is this who you want to be? Remember when we went to Aspen? You wondered what it would be like if people could live like those trees, in complete harmony . . . In our world, there is no *other*."

The appeal of peace, harmony, and social integration, even if achieved at the expense of individuality and freedom, illustrates the powerful existential attraction of the in-itself. There is a part of us that longs to become being-in-itself, because to be so would mean to escape our fundamental loneliness and anxiety. Yet to do so would not only deny the reality that we are free, conscious, meaning-conferring individuals, but it would catapult us into a state that Sartre refers to as *bad faith*, the state akin to that of the drug addict who so completely identifies with his addiction that he comes to believe that he and his addiction are one and the same. What makes bad faith so egregious is that it is an attempt to deny our fundamental ontological freedom and the tremendous personal responsibility that comes with such freedom. Moreover, even if such a change from being-for-itself to being-in-itself were possible, it would transform us into something inhuman, and hence unrecognizable to ourselves, and deeply at odds with what we hold most dear about our humanity. According to Simone de Beauvoir, as humans, we value transcendence above what she terms *immanence*, for it is our capacity for transcendence that makes us uniquely human. For Beauvoir, immanence is that which is beholden to natural functions, rather than human-directed, freely and consciously chosen projects. By contrast, transcendence is the ability to break free from the world as given; the ability to transcend our animal nature.[20] It is not surprising that we typically react with horror when we see other human beings reduced to meaningless objects, as in the case of the pod people, and treated as if they are not ends in themselves, but rather ends for others to use and dispose of as they please. For humans to be converted into being-in-itself would require that we destroy the very qualities that make us human. For both Sartre and Beauvoir, this would not only be bad faith, but would transform us into something literally disgusting and nauseating (that is, horrifying) to ourselves.

So, though we understand and sympathize with the appeal to harmony, peace, and the promise of belonging and integration, we also reject this appeal when it comes at the cost of our transcendence. As humans, as beings-for-ourselves, we must refuse to become beings-in-ourselves. To do otherwise would be to lose ourselves, to become "things" rather than persons. Perhaps having read Sartre's description of Roquentin's horrific vision of the tree as being-in-itself, Carol's response to Ben's plea to become like "those trees, in complete harmony," is to shoot him in the leg.

After a long and drawn-out detention and chase, at the last possible moment Carol and her son are rescued by a friend in a helicopter, a medical researcher who has found the key to a cure. As it turns out, the alien virus has no real defense. People build up immunity and those cured have no recollection of their temporary insanity. Watching the morning news reports on eighty-three more deaths in Baghdad ("Will it ever end?" her now live-in boyfriend asks aloud), Carol muses that, "for better or worse, we're human again." The film ends with Henryk Belicec's comments from an early dinner party. "In the right situation, we are capable of the most terrible things," we hear him intone as scenes of multiplying blood cells and viruses in a Petri dish fill the screen.

## Existential Projects and *The Invasion of the Body Snatchers* Series

As has been discussed, a number of themes are recurrent across the various incarnations both of existentialism and of the *Invasion of the Body Snatchers*. In addition to a sense of horror regarding the alienation of humans from a hostile world, themes of anxiety and dread in the face of human finitude, of individual choice and personal responsibility, of freedom and a passionate engagement with life are all prominent concerns. Ultimately, however, it is ambivalence regarding engulfment of the self and the relationship between being-in-itself and being-for-itself that form the foundation of the *Invasion of the Body Snatchers* series. Because this existential subject matter cuts to the very core of the human experience, it is no surprise that the public has been drawn to repeat its exposure to no less than four remakes of this of this movie over the course of fifty-one years.

If it weren't for popular films like *Invasion of the Body Snatchers*, which clearly stress these sorts of existentialist ideas, we might be tempted to view existentialism as a purely academic undertaking. That view would be mistaken. As George Cotkin has pointed out, existentialism has had a tremendous trickle-down effect on popular culture beginning with the first English translation of Kierkegaard in the 1930s by theologian Malcolm Lowrie.[21] Public figures ranging from theologian Reinhold Niebuhr, psychologist Rollo May, writers Dorothy L. Sayers, Dashiell Hammett, Norman Mailer, and Richard Wright, playwright Thornton Wilder, and management theorist Peter F. Drucker, were all influenced by proto-existentialist thinkers such as Kierkegaard and Nietzsche. Moreover, the influence went both ways: Camus' *The Stranger* was influenced by James M. Cain's crime classic *The Postman Always Rings Twice* (1934).[22] As we have seen, the relationship between existentialism and popular culture continues today in film.

According to Stephen King, paranoia, as expressed in horror stories, is at bottom a deeply optimistic view; one that allows us the comforting belief that "*Something* rational and understandable is going on here! These things *do not just happen!*"[23] Conspiracies show that there is order in the chaos, a mastermind behind the evil design. Yet the *Invasion of the Body Snatchers* series belies any meaningful sense of comfort. There simply is no "reason" for the invasion other than the mindless biological imperative of virus-like spores that aimlessly drifted across the universe and happened to land on planet Earth. In the final two films, the cause of the invasion is either due to environmental disaster or is the result of an errant space shuttle picking up a contagion on its way back to Earth. In any case, the invasion occurs by happenstance and accident. At the same time, the downbeat or ambiguous endings fail to release us from the feeling of anxiety. In the first version, we gain some small measure of comfort in knowing that Dr. Miles Bennell is finally believed by his skeptical colleagues who were ready to have him committed to an insane asylum. However, there is no indication that humans will ultimately prevail in this war against alien pods. The latest version is similarly far from fully satisfying: the contagion is contained and later cured, but we are forced to return to our normal lives in a deeply troubled and increasingly violent and unpredictable post-September 11 world. The message is tentative: eventually this madness will end and when it does, we won't likely remember it. But regardless, we still have to live with *ourselves* and comport ourselves to this world.

The original unreleased 1956 version, which lacked any voice-over and initially ended with Miles screaming, "They're here! You're next!" was as dismal as the 1978 version; so much so that studio heads nixed it and ordered it to be released with a more comforting opening and closing. To date, the original version has rarely been shown to the public, and then only at film festivals. The 1978 Kaufman version is equally as stark and uncompromising as the original unreleased version. There is no redemption, no solace. All resisters succumb. No one is saved. Even Jack Finney's novel ends with incomplete relief. Although the aliens flee from a hostile planet Earth, thanks to the efforts of a heroic Miles, there is no indication that they have similarly fled other afflicted areas, and we are left wondering why this happened and whether it will occur again.

This notion of tremendous uncertainty and lack of meaning is part and parcel of existentialist philosophy. The senseless slaughter of two world wars, the advent of the nuclear age, and the dehumanization of much of modern life has appeared to us as an alien world; a godless one in which we have found ourselves abandoned (in a state Sartre refers to as *forlornness* and that Heidegger calls *homelessness*). In reality, we have indeed chosen this world. It is in fact the result of a countless number of choices each of us as individuals have made. However, at the moment that those choices become solidified into the past, the past becomes part of our facticity, that aspect of the world which we cannot change. The message of the *Invasion of the Body Snatchers* series, however, is that we are still responsible for choosing our future. We must not merely settle for inauthentic, meaningless lives. We should fight for our humanity, and "not go gentle into that good night."[24]

## Notes

1. As of 2006, according to WorldCat, a catalog of over 25,000 libraries around the world, various versions of the novel have been translated into Danish, Dutch, French, German, Italian, Norwegian, and Swedish. <http://www.worldcat.org/> (5 March 2008).

2. *L'enfer C'est les Autres* translates to "Hell is other people," Jean-Paul Sartre.

3. Stephen King, *Danse Macabre* (New York: Berkeley Books, 1981), 13.

4. Elias Canetti, *Crowds and Power* (New York: Viking Press, 1960), 17.

5. She is played by a young "Mrs. Olson" of 1970s television Folger's Coffee ad fame.

6. See, for example, Stuart Samuels, "The Age of Conspiracy and Conformity: *Invasion of the Body Snatchers* (1956)," in *American History/American Film: Interpreting the Hollywood Image*, ed. John E. O'Connor and Martin A. Jackson (New York: Continuum, 1988).

7. William H. Whyte, *The Organization Man* (New York: Simon and Schuster, 1956), 350.

8. King, *Danse Macabre*, 322.

9. Simone de Beauvoir, *The Second Sex* (New York: Vintage, 1989), 63.

10. Roger Eberwein, "Remakes and Cultural Studies," in *Play it Again Sam: Retakes on Remakes*, ed. Andrew Horton and Stuart Y. McDougal (Berkeley: University of California Press, 1998), 23.

11. Eberwein, "Remakes and Cultural Studies," 23.

12. Eberwein, "Remakes and Cultural Studies," 24.

13. Jean-Paul Sartre, *Nausea* (Norfolk, Va.: New Directions, 1959), 127.

14. "It's always upsetting," director Philip Kaufman remarks in the DVD's commentary, "to see people in suits running in the streets." Particularly, one might add, in this post-September 11 world.

15. Beauvoir, *The Second Sex*, 63.

16. Beauvoir, *The Second Sex*, 64.

17. Sherwin B. Nuland, *How We Die: Reflections on Life's Final Chapter* (New York: Knopf, 1994), 208–209.

18. Nuland, *How We Die,* 208–209.

19. See, for example, selected reviews at <http://www.IMDB.com> (5 March 2008).

20. Beauvoir, *The Second Sex,* 63.

21. George Cotkin, *Existential America* (Baltimore: Johns Hopkins University Press, 2003), 36.

22. Cotkin, *Existential America*, 28–29.

23. King, *Danse Macabre*, 316.

24. Dylan Thomas, "Do Not Go Gentle Into That Good Night" (1956).

*Chapter 3*

# Invasions of Fear: The Body Snatcher Theme

Ils Huygens

The body snatcher theme forms a complex nexus of different and sometimes contradictory fears related to the body—not only the other's body but also the self's body: fear of contact and touch, the contagiousness of paranoia and mass hysteria, fear of dehumanization and alienation, fear of hosting a parasite, sexual fears. The snatching process by which the aliens reproduce relates to questions of the permeability of our skin and the fluidity of identity. By taking a closer look at the bodily themes developed in the different versions of *Invasion of the Body Snatchers,* I will try to untangle the complex constellation of bodily anxieties expressed in the body snatcher narrative and situate them in the context of their times.

*Invasion of the Body Snatchers* has been made into a film three times with a fourth remake released in 2007. The story is based on a sci-fi novel by Jack Finney that originally appeared in three parts in *Collier's Weekly* in 1954, and was first published in its entirety in 1955. The story is about the invasion of a parasitic alien race that lands on earth, first merging with simpler life-forms such as plants, then taking over human bodies by creating exact replicas while they sleep.

The first adaptation was directed by Don Siegel in 1956 and followed the novel quite closely. Rather than adhering to the rather weak resolution of the book, in which the aliens in the end leave earth realizing they cannot beat the humans, Siegel chose a much more open and ambiguous ending, where it remains uncertain whether the invasion will be stopped. An updated remake and sequel to the Siegel film was made in 1978 by Philip Kaufman. Apart from changing the original small-town setting to the city of San Francisco and its free-spirited milieu,

45

this second remake remained quite faithful to the first movie, repeating numerous scenes. The main protagonist, now called Matthew instead of Miles Bennell, is not a family doctor but a national health inspector. His love interest also changes names from Becky to Elizabeth. The ending of the second film was even more bleak as the main character is also turned into a pod person. In 1993 a more loosely adapted version of the story was directed by Abel Ferrara who sets the story on a military base where chemical weapons are stored. The main character is not a doctor but a teenage girl, whose father Steve is doing research on environmental pollution in the military area. The title of the film was shortened to *Body Snatchers*. The fourth remake, *The Invasion*, is the first big studio production of the body snatcher story. Warner Bros. first hired Oliver Hirschbiegel to direct. His original thread of paranoia and claustrophobia gets somewhat lost in favor of the action sequences, explosions, and car chases that were added by a second director (James McTeigue). In this 2007 remake the story is set in Washington DC amidst the post-9/11 climate. The main protagonist is a female psychiatrist, Carol Bennell, who tries to save her son from her alien ex-husband, who works at the White House as a health official. As opposed to the other three films, this last version is like Finney's book in that it has a very happy ending. Thanks to the development of a vaccine, the invasion is stopped and the victims are turned back into their previous human selves. A new version of the body snatcher story has thus appeared almost every decade; each film, reformulating what it means to be human and reimagining the confines of our human bodies.

## Dehumanization

You can drive the same car, you can have the same job, you can eat the same foods, but you are going to be happy because you won't have the anxieties that love causes you to have.

The most general anxiety that emerges in the body snatcher films is the fear of dehumanization, which encompasses all the more specific bodily related fears I will discuss later. When a person is taken over by an alien, his original self is duplicated by an exact replica called a pod person. Apart from his body, the snatcher also steals the victim's identity, knowledge, and even his memories. Once the snatching process is completed, the original human body shrivels to dust and is disposed of. The only difference is that the replica does not have feelings. A line repeated by one of the pod persons in the two first films explains that this loss of emotions is only for the better: "There is no need for love or emotion. Love, desire, ambition, faith—without them, life is so simple." In the body snatcher films, the fight between alien and human comes down to the age-old clash between the ratio of our intellect and the pain and bliss caused by human passions.

The loss of emotion and passion is intrinsically coupled with a loss of personal ambition. The alien bodies only want to serve the greater good of their race. Human emotions merely stand in the way of the perfect conformity and efficiency that will enable their survival. Since the victimized humans do not lust for power, there is no source of conflict anymore and everyone is happy, although a form of sedated contentment is perhaps a better way to express their state of being. As director Don Siegel explained: "To be a pod means that you have no passion, no anger, that you talk automatically, that the spark of life has left you."[1]

In the first three films humanity is defined by its positive characteristics: love, friendship, and loyalty, all of which eventually lose to the aliens. Yet an interesting shift occurs in the fourth film. Here humanity is defined not by its capacity to love but by its tendency towards violence and hatred, showing us the negative effects of emotion and individual freedom. *The Invasion* is almost sympathetic towards the aliens: once they have taken over the world, violent conflicts such as Iraq, Iran, and Darfur suddenly come to an end. Even Bush and Hugo Chavez shake hands. The fourth remake is also the only one in the series in which the aliens are defeated and love conquers all. However, this is not necessarily seen as a good thing. The epilogue shows an idyllic family scene with the newspapers on the breakfast table that are full of violence and atrocities again, leaving main character Carol to wonder if a world without the aliens really is a better place.

## Fear of the Other: Political Metaphors of the Alien Invasion

Both the book and its first film adaptation were released in the fifties. Like most other alien invasion narratives of the time, they were commonly read as metaphors for Cold War paranoia. The aliens' lack of individual goals and secretive groupthink on the one hand, and their lack of feelings and cold behavior on the other, were well-known stereotypes of communists. Secondly, there was a deeply rooted sense of paranoia about communism that parallels the paranoia over the other's body which is part of the body snatcher narrative. There is a sense that anyone could be "one of them." But as stated in *Sight and Sound* after the release of the third remake, Siegel's film offers itself both to left- and right-wing interpretations: it is "alternatively a drama of communist subversion or of suburban conformity unfolding in a hilariously bland atmosphere of hyper-vigilance."[2] A still unresolved debate arose concerning whether the original movie should be read as promoting an anti-communist message or whether it should be taken as a warning against the dangers of McCarthyism. McCarthy inspired America's own paranoid reaction to the Red Menace, which forced everyone to conform and think the same, leading to blacklisting, betrayal, and suspicion amongst relatives, friends, and neighbors.

Philip Kaufman's remake gave rise to similar ambiguous interpretations. Contrary to the first film, the authorities (government and industry) actively take part in the invasion from the beginning. It has been argued that the film was a warning for the counterculture not to conform and turn into the establishment. When female protagonist Elizabeth talks about her suspicions concerning her boyfriend, Matthew asks whether she thinks her invaded lover has changed his political beliefs or perhaps has become a Republican. Yet the film can just as well be read as a critique of how the counterculture laid the path to its own destruction, and of the apathy and nihilism that characterized the late seventies and eighties:

> Joyous, honest rebellion had become garden-variety cynicism; the value of individuality had been supplanted by the enticement of losing one's soul to a group; and the childish dependence upon social institutions to save us all prevented self-preservation. In important social ways, the counterculture became indistinguishable from the establishment and, in doing so, compromised whatever value it had introduced into the culture.[3]

The main protagonists seem to reflect this demise of the counterculture. The central character Matthew is presented as a post-hippie who likes to cook, wears woolen sweaters, and has the remnants of a wild hairdo. Yet he works as a civil servant for the public health department and has become part of the system the hippies once fought against. Matthew's friends, the Bellicecs, who help him fight the alien invasion, are perhaps even more of an example of the ruins of flower power. Jack is a writer of poetry and a cynic, while his wife Nancy runs a downtown mud bath center and believes as much in the powers of natural healing as in the possibility of science fiction. Interestingly enough, this rather naïve character is also the first to realize what is really going on.

Abel Ferrara's *Body Snatchers* takes place on a military base, reflecting the increasing militarization of society in the 1990s. Perhaps one of the most frightening things in Ferrara's film is that there is not really any difference between the pod persons and the soldiers. The film also alludes to the post-Gulf War climate, calling on a fear of terrorist invasions, but moreover of chemical and biological warfare, by explicitly linking the alien invasion to the drug-induced mental syndromes soldiers suffered after the Gulf War. However, the film also deals with the internal subversion of American society and values since it is precisely the American army, our so-called saviors and protectors, that now lie at the heart of the alien invasion. The fourth remake takes this even further by making the source of the infection a White House official who spreads the virus through counterfeit flu inoculations. The post-9/11 fear of media manipulation in America is reflected in the movie's depiction of a government cover-up operation concerning the alien virus, which is consistently reported to the public as a new kind of flu. The body snatcher narrative has proven easily adaptable to the fits of the time, thus interpretations of the story's political meaning may differ. Yet a common feature of each film is the depiction of our paranoia and fear of other bodies.

## The Uncanny Double as Same

The alien invasion in each of the films starts from within the family unit. Wives do not recognize their husbands anymore, children are terrified by their own mothers, and other variations. The familiar bodies of our loved ones are turned into uncanny doubles: strange and sinister, rather than safe and warm. One of the most interesting details in the body snatchers films is that this uncanny and monstrous other is not visually established as either monstrous or as other. Humans that have been invaded look and behave exactly like normal human beings. The snatching process does not result in a contrast of self and other but is, rather, an invisible usurpation of the self by the other, outwardly resulting in a body indistinguishable from the original. This is what causes us to experience the disturbing effect of the uncanny. One of the first scenes in the 1956 film is a perfect example of such an uncanny encounter with the other who is the same. The scene takes place when Miles and Becky are paying a visit to Becky's cousin who is convinced that her uncle has been replaced by an impostor.

> "Have you talked to him? It's him, it's your Uncle Ira."
> "He is not."
> "How's he different?"
> "That's just it, there is no difference you can actually see. He looks, sounds, acts, and remembers like Ira."
> "Then he is your uncle Ira."

Objectively, Uncle Ira looks perfectly normal. The uncanniness of his body, however, is masterfully visualized by means of the camera. In this particular scene, Don Siegel creates a feeling of unease at the sight of uncle Ira's body by inserting it in the frame in unusual ways. First we see him mowing the lawn (an emblem of normal American suburban life) in an extreme long-distance shot. Then the camera captures Becky and Miles talking in a long shot, while suddenly in the foreground the uncle passes by from right to left. Not only is this movement in itself perceived as unnatural, it also captures the uncle in profile, heightening the effect of strangeness. When Becky and Miles are leaving and pass him by, he smiles and says to Miles in a friendly manner: "It's good to have Becky back, isn't it?" The scene ends with a close-up of his face, his eyes staring at the backs of Miles and Becky, his smile deforming into a bizarre grimace.

The pod people may not experience emotions anymore, but they certainly have learned how to fake them. As Becky's cousin puts it: "There is no emotion anymore, just the pretence of it." However, their imitations are not quite perfect, as Ira's bizarre smile shows. Only in small details of behavior and bodily expression can a pod person be recognized. Not only the protagonist, but also the viewer, is forced to scrutinize the image and scan the bodies that we see in search of any word, gesture, or blink of an eye that is just slightly out of the ordinary; or perhaps just simply too ordinary.

# Under the Surface Skin

At first glance everything looked the same. It wasn't. Something evil had taken possession of the town.

The notion of the uncanny infects not only the invaded bodies, but the whole atmosphere of the narrative. The shifting of the familiar into something strange and fearful is emphasized in the Siegel film by initiating the invasion in a small-town setting. The danger arises from within the very heart of the American Dream, as Charles Freund writes:

> Straight out of a Norman Rockwell painting, this community of neighborly Main Street storekeepers and doctors—pushing hand mowers across their spacious lawns and whiling away summer evenings on their big porches—embodied a cherished American self-image: that we are a homogeneous nation whose traditions and values spring from the bosom of these small towns. The loss of Santa Mira to the pod people is more than just an invasion—it's an assault on some basic American fantasies.[4]

Siegel sets up Santa Mira as a perfectly normal-looking town with a grocery store, newspaper stand, a town square, and nice suburban houses. But these small-town scenes are increasingly infused with a growing sense of unease and paranoia. As in the scene with uncle Ira, this is done by oscillating between extreme long shots and abrupt close-ups. Siegel also increasingly uses distorting lenses, *clair-obscur* lighting, and low-angled shots to add a disquieting visual tension to seemingly ordinary scenes.

Kaufman's version transfers the anxiety of modern alienation from American suburbia to the big city. Using spinning cameras, bird's eye views, extreme long shots, and other unconventional viewpoints, the busy city life is gradually turned into an uncanny place, recalling the threatening transformation of Santa Mira. Driving around the city, female protagonist Elizabeth tells Matthew of her worries about the changes, recalling the words spoken by Miles in the beginning of Siegel's film: "Yesterday it all seemed normal. Today everything seemed the same, but it wasn't. It was a nightmare. It became frightening." While she is talking we see flashback images of Elizabeth on a journey through the city with people staring at her from buses and sidewalks. They are just normal city folk yet their insistent staring, combined with wildly spinning and whirling camera movements and a psychedelic soundtrack, infuses the scene with a menacing feeling, as if she was having a bad trip. This scene is almost literally reproduced in the 2007 film where main character Carol Bennell becomes more and more isolated in a city full of people.

In Ferrara's film, set on an isolated, restricted military base, alienation is at once everywhere and at the same time placed firmly into the core of the family circle, with the figure of the alienated teen as the central protagonist. After her stepmother turns into a pod person, Ferrara shows us a family breakfast scene that is disturbed by the mother's cold way of behaving, as she throws knives and plates on the table in a robotic fashion. When her five-year-old son accuses her of being an impostor, she doesn't even react. When Steve looks up at his wife's face, she produces a reassuring yet utterly fake smile, reminiscent of uncle Ira's deformed smile in the first film. This typical family scene becomes highly uncanny due to the contrast between intimacy and breakdown. However, again, nothing is different enough to be perceived as such. The mother might be in a bad mood. Andy may simply be acting difficult. Marti is not paying attention to anything as usual. Objectively, nothing seems really out of the ordinary, but subjectively something feels wrong.

## Included and Excluded Bodies

I keep seeing these people. All recognizing each other.

The pod people are the ultimate bodies of conformity. With a lack of feelings and individual desires, everyone becomes the same. The desire to conform and belong to the pod people community is opposed to the human fight for personal identity and free will. We support the protagonists in their fight for freedom but at the same time witness how they become outcasts in a society where people—despite everything—seem to get along pretty well, content with their 'untroubled' lives. In the body snatcher films the social and public body is the site of this constant clash between wanting to be the same and fitting in, versus the affirmation of one's individuality, of being different. As M. Keith Booker argues:

> The particular form of alienation that was prevalent in America in the 1950s was the fear of not fitting in. Surrounded by a pressure to conform, individuals feared the loss of their distinct individual identities. Yet they also feared their own inability to fit in; they feared being identified as different, as being, in fact, the other. In short, Americans in the 1950s suffered from two principal fears: the fear of being different from everyone else and the fear of being the same as everyone else.[5]

In cinema, inclusion in a community is established through the exchange of looks, the correspondence of the gaze between characters which is conventionalized in the reaction shot. As Richard Bégin writes, the exclusion of the look is a recurring element in each version of the film.[6] The encounter between humans and invaded humans, however, is very often marked by a rupture in the structuring principles of the reaction shot; for instance the scene described earlier with Uncle Ira. The pod people are either staring or diverting their gaze when confronted with humans. As the group of invaded humans grows larger, there is an exchange of looks passing between the pod people from which both viewers and protagonists are excluded. As Elizabeth describes it: "Something is passing between them."

Secondly, each film's cinematography produces a growing sense of isolation and exclusion as the characters become more and more enclosed by the aliens. Claustrophobic framings, extreme darkness, and shadowy lighting refer the human bodies to the edges of the frame. They are almost literally pushed out of view by the growing alien population. In each film the main character ends up totally isolated, and hunted down.

That the 1978 remake takes place in San Francisco is no coincidence. The city is known as a home of nonconformists and free spirits, not only because of its hippie background, but also because it is known as a place where homosexuality and other forms of alternative sexuality found a welcoming refuge. Even within the greatest diversity of bodies, it seems, the dangers of conformity and groupthink remain. Ferrara's film has been criticized for not being as strong as the earlier versions because its military setting did not allow for the creation of contrast between the pods and the soldiers. Even before they are actually taken over by the aliens, the soldiers are already like the pod persons, taking orders, blocking out all emotion, trained to put the greater good of the race over their individual wishes. "It's the race that counts not the individual," one of the army generals explains the alien's philosophy. This lack of contrast makes the film perhaps the most nihilistic of all, suggesting that humanity was lost from the beginning, and that any fight for freedom is in vain. The fourth film plays the role of devil's advocate, focusing mostly on the negative consequences of free will: violence, genocide, war, and starvation. Submission and conformity guarantee survival and peace, even if it is in a world without art, poetry, friendship, or love.

## Clockwork Bodies: The Pod People as Automatons

Both alienation and the dangers of conformity can also be traced to anxieties based in economics. Siegel himself never really admitted to any political references but rather stressed the dangers of conformity that came with the rise of consumerism. In an interview he explains that his inspiration came from the idea that more and more people are becoming like the pods, numbed by our contemporary lifestyles: ". . . the majority of people, unfortunately, are pods, existing without any intellectual aspirations and incapable of love."[7] His statement is echoed twenty years later by Kaufman: "We've taken some of the things that were expressed about the original film—that modern life is turning people into unfeeling, conforming pods who resist getting involved with each other on any level."[8] The fear of dehumanization and disintegration of the self is related to the conformity and uniformity imposed on our bodies by an increasingly technological and industrialized world: standardization, mass production, rationalization, and the growing influence of capitalism and technology on everyday life, coupled with the rise of television, advertising, and franchising.

This connection to the anxieties related to capitalist industrialization is very explicit in all four films. To begin with the parasitic nature of the alien race itself: they imitate, usurp, and ultimately use up all of a planet's resources before simply moving on again in search of a new race to colonize. The invasion is not in the least chaotic but organized in a highly functional and economical manner. Not only do the pod persons set up a logical shipping and distribution system to deliver pods all over the country, they also create an efficient system of waste disposal that is hinted at by the recurring images of garbage trucks that pick up the remains of the original human bodies. In the second film they even set up industrial greenhouses to grow pods on a level of mass production. The humans are transformed into the perfect automatons to put to work in a capitalist society, either to perform mechanized operations in industrial factories or to work as white-collar clones in big corporations. In Ferrara's film these clockwork bodies are ideal soldiers: disciplined, fearless, loyal, but also disposable and easily replaced.

## The Human Body as Hysterical Body

It's some kind of strange neurosis, evidently contagious, an epidemic of mass hysteria.

The pod persons act calmly and talk logically. When they are among humans they smile, wave, and chat as required; in short there is an absolute absence of abnormality. That is why their normal behavior is visually contrasted by human bodies in the grip of fear. The humans are transformed into hysterical bodies—a sign of having too much emotion. Hysterical and paranoid behavior become the only means to distinguish a human body from the perfectly functioning bodies of the pod persons.

The pod people's diplomacy, rationality, and efficiency make them not only the perfect carriers of capitalist expansion and technological progress but, on a biological level, places them on a higher step of the evolutionary chain. From a Darwinist perspective, emotion might be viewed as a burden that works against the survival of the fittest. The irrationality and confusion associated with emotions links humanity to its more primitive and animal side. The Siegel film uses a framing device that places the whole narrative immediately within an atmosphere of insanity and hysteria. The film begins with Miles frantically telling his story to a doctor in a hospital ward, shouting: "I'm not insane." His eyes are wild, he looks like he hasn't slept in days, and his bodily gestures are out of control. In the 1978 film, there is a guest appearance by Don Siegel as a madman running wildly into the street and hitting Matthew's car. With a bewildered face reminiscent of Miles' face in the hospital scene he shouts, "They're coming. You're next. We're in danger." At the beginning of the 1993 film, the main character, Marti, is terrorized by a soldier who lashes out at her in a gas station bathroom, and who rambles incoherently about things that get you while you sleep. Yet these hysterical bodies turn out to be the ones who understand what is going on and are trying to warn us. Once the invasion has really begun, all of the remaining humans are presented in a constant state of hysteria: running, fleeing, screaming, hiding, and desperately trying to stay awake, which pushes their bodies even more to the edge.

A central place in this narrative thread of hysterical behavior is accorded to the psychiatrist, who analyzes behavior in an objective way and tries to normalize it. In Siegel's film the town psychiatrist reassures Miles and Becky that nothing is wrong and that people are caught in some kind of contagious mass hysteria, infecting each other's fantasies with their strange stories. Yet later on, it is the same psychiatrist that tries to manipulate Becky and Miles to give themselves over to the alien lifestyle, saying they will be born again in "an untroubled world." Kaufman portrays the character of the psychiatrist even more as a man of logic and science. Even when it is loud and clear that something is wrong, the psychiatrist keeps convincing Matthew and his friends that it is just their imagination playing tricks on them. In fact both his extremely logical explanations and his hypnotic, mind-soothing talk make us unable to tell whether he was one of the pod people from the beginning. In the Kaufman film psychiatry is treated with condescension, as a form of manipulative brainwashing, perhaps induced by the increasing commercialization of mental health in the seventies. Psychiatry is represented as the new religion of the soul; not a loving, but a mechanical soul that can be repaired or changed for the better. The fact that the psychiatrist in Kaufman's film is played by Leonard Nimoy—who also played Spock, *Star Trek's* most emotionless and logical character—adds to this idea. In the fourth remake this point is made even stronger, with the main protagonist now being a psychiatrist. When one of her patients tells her that "my husband is not my husband anymore," she simply suggests a change of medication. Her actions are perhaps not much different from what the aliens do, and is reflective of the increasing use of psychotropic drugs in society.

## The Castrating Body of the Femme Fatale

Hysteria is traditionally associated with the female body and more specifically with problems of the womb. Anxieties about the female body are expressed in the body snatcher narrative in two ways: first by turning an innocent woman into either an alluring femme fatale or monstrous mother figure, and secondly by linking the female reproductive system to monstrous births and abominable fetuses. The transgressive move of showing male bodies in a state of hysteria can be understood as an expression of fear of the female body and the growing emancipation of women. Michael Hardin interprets the Siegel film from this perspective and claims that the alien invasion expresses a threat that comes from the demise of white patriarchy, with the changing role of wives and mothers, who are becoming more educated and even might prefer a job over housework.[9] This causes anxiety among the male population, which no longer feels it can control and dominate the female body. In Siegel's film, at first glance the gender roles attributed to Becky and Miles are rather traditional. Becky does not seem to have a job and after her marriage ended she simply returned to live with her father. In the narrative she is posited as a passive and scared female that longs to be saved and protected. However, in a crucial scene towards the end of the film, it is Becky and not Miles who gives the final blow to a guy's head, enabling their escape from the pod people who had captured them.

Miles' failure to rescue his loved one—in an equally emblematic and horrifying scene—results in the ultimate empowerment of Becky's body. After he has left Becky alone during their escape from the aliens, he returns to find her sleeping. He takes her in his arms and kisses her. Miles moves away and the camera shows Becky's face in extreme close-up, her eyes opening slowly and looking calm and self-assured, in contrast to the terrified look on Miles' face. If her kiss was cold, her gaze is even colder. Miles' horror is intensified by an extreme close-up of his face. Becky then tries to talk him into joining her. The snatching process has turned Becky from a passive and weak female into a femme fatale, seducing him to cross over to the bad side. As he tries to run away, in a classic act of femme fatale behavior, she betrays her lover by warning her peers.

The alien invasion enables a transgression of the classic active/passive role, with the role of the woman becoming stronger with each new version of the film. Elizabeth, for instance, is presented clearly as a much more emancipated woman than Becky. The psychiatrist in the Kaufman remake even explicitly relates the hysteria that has caught the city to the deterioration of the heterosexual couple, especially blaming women when saying to Elizabeth, "Don't you see, it's people stepping in and out of relationships too fast because they don't want the responsibility. The whole family unit is shot to hell." He goes on to tell her that she only wants to think Geoffrey is changed because she wants an excuse to get out, and orders Matthew to take her home. To protect the natural order, women have to remain loyal to their husbands no matter what.

In the third film, the roles seem to have completely reversed; the true fight is now between Marti and her stepmother. Marti's father, Steve, neglects his daughter and accepts his wife's dominant position. Anything but a hero, he is presented as passive, weak, and unable to take any significant action. Even when it is clear his wife has become a threat to himself and his children, all he can do is fall in her arms and start crying and sobbing. It is Marti who has to pull him from the deadly embrace and luring words of his wife. Soon after that he is taken over by the aliens himself, leaving the care of young Andy in Marti's hands. *The Invasion*'s lead is a single mother with a successful career. She has to save her son from the hands of her evil ex-husband who has fallen prey to the pod people. Ben Driscoll, her colleague and love interest, tries to help her but fails. In a scene reminiscent of Becky's changeover in the first film, he turns on her and becomes one of them.

## The Monstrous Mother

In Siegel's film the first invaded human we encounter is a mother whose young son is running away from her hysterically. When Miles asks her what is going on she answers calmly: "It's just that he doesn't want to go to school anymore." Later on, the boy's grandmother brings him into Miles' medical office, saying that "He's got the crazy idea she isn't his mother." The boy shouts in terror: "She isn't, she isn't. Don't let her get me!" In another scene Miles watches his nurse, Sally, put her baby in his crib while placing one of the pods beside him. She consoles him with the words that tomorrow "there'll be no more tears." In writing about this scene, Michael Hardin observes that by actively and willfully killing her own baby Sally turns around everything our culture has taught us: "that mothers are loving and nurturing, not persons who will take away our 'humanness.'"[10] As mentioned earlier, he relates this to anxieties about the changing roles of women in the fifties. Through the snatching process, the body of the woman is not only changed from passive into active and made dangerously seductive; as a mother she changes from a nurturing and life-giving body to a threatening and death-giving body.

Ferrara's version of the snatcher story is the one most obsessed with this figure of the monstrous mother. Being a stepmother, Carol is already posited as an unwanted intruder from the beginning. After the family moves onto the military base where Steve is doing research on the polluted environment, the stepmother is the first person who is invaded by the aliens. Once her body is taken over, it becomes the center from which the alien threat is spread to the rest of the family. Young Andy (Marti's half-brother) is the only one who is aware of the changes, but nobody takes notice of him. As in Siegel's film, scenes associated traditionally with the comforts of motherhood now become threatening and sinister. In the evening we see Carol telling Andy to go to bed, ordering Marti to take her bath and giving her tired husband a massage in the bedroom. But all these acts of motherly love are nothing more than tricks to make them fall asleep and prepare their bodies for the snatching process. When they finally realize what is going on, they flee from the house as the mother emits a terribly chilling shriek to alert fellow aliens. Her wild curly hair, wide-open mouth, and pointed finger make her look like Medusa, a symbol of the death-giving woman.

## Monstrous Births and Abominable Fetuses

The snatching process itself is presented as a perverted version of human reproduction. In the 1956 film a first hint of how the snatching takes place occurs in a scene where the half-formed double of Jack Belicec (a close friend of Miles) is discovered.[11] Laying in a dead man's position on their pool table, the body is scrutinized by Miles and his friends. Their conclusions conflict. The adult body looks to be in perfect condition, yet there is no sign of life, no lines, no character. "It's like the first impression of a stamp," Jack notices. The body does not breathe and does not have fingerprints. It is a dead corpse and an unfinished fetus, simultaneously. The exact scene is restaged in the 1978 film when Nancy Bellicec discovers a double forming of her husband in a mud bath. The body is much less clean than the first one, covered with the slimy white tendrils. The mutation process is not only shown in more detail but also represented in a much more visceral and abject way than in Siegel's film, where Belicec's double—as well as Becky's double—looked clean and unreal, like dolls. During a later scene we learn even more about the snatching process. When Matthew, Elizabeth, and the Bellicecs are hiding in Matthew's house, they all fall asleep and the snatching process sets in. Small pods attached to plants start emitting tentacles that enwrap the human bodies, sucking them dry and starting the duplication. Doubles start growing inside the seed pods, which become larger and larger and start pulsating, while the original bodies start showing signs of decomposition. When they finally burst open, a mucky fluid oozes out followed by the duplicate bodies that are ambiguous and horrifying due to an uncanny combination of adult size with the face and hands of unborn children. Covered in slime, the yet-unfinished bodies lie wriggling on the ground. Gasping for air they shriek and moan in metallic nonhuman voices.

In Ferrara's film the mutation process is shown with even more detail in an extremely long scene, which shows both Marti and her father being snatched. Marti takes a bath, as instructed by her stepmother. With her Walkman on her head she falls asleep, and a pod placed right above her head in an airshaft slowly sends out its tentacles. They reach Marti's body and enter through her mouth and nose. As the exchange process begins, the red, womblike figure of the pod begins growing and pulsating. As Marti suddenly awakens, her unfinished double falls into the bathtub, accompanied by something that looks like a placenta and other organic waste materials. Her double is equally as revolting as Matthew's, with plucky white hair, a pale and unformed face but of the same weight and size as Marti. She jumps up and wakes her father. Upon this abrupt abortion of the snatching process, Steve's double slides from under the bed and grabs Marti by the legs before turning into dust. As Nicole Brenez notices, his double is oddly old and wrinkled, like "a decomposing corpse" or a "born-dead old person."[12]

As Robert Eberwein has pointed out, these monstrous births may be read in the light of developing research on artificial reproduction, which was more and more reported by the media during the late seventies.[13] In vitro fertilization for instance had its first successful outcome in 1978, but this was preceded by numerous accounts in the media of failed experiments. At a certain point in Kaufman's film, a dog appears with a man's head, clearly the result of a failed or aborted snatching experiment. But the image can also be read as a futuristic look into the age of genetic engineering that allows cross-species DNA hybridity. In the fourth remake anxieties about artificial reproduction are replaced by contemporary fears of genetic engineering and the reality of cloning. Here, the original alien bodies are not presented as plant-like spores but are virus-like entities that interfere with human sweat. This causes a "cellular condensation" that alters the body's genetic expression by integrating the alien DNA. The snatching process as an abomination of human reproduction becomes redundant. Now the aliens interfere directly with our human genes.

## Mutations in the Body Snatcher Theme: From the Surface Skin into the Depths of the Body

In the 1956 film paranoia over the other's body plays on the fact that we never really know what a body can hide. Unlike the other versions of the film, most of the transformations remain invisible from both viewer and characters, making us unable to tell who is "one of them." The skin is treated as an impenetrable surface and as deceptive appearance. In the second, and even more in the third and fourth remakes, skin becomes something that is fundamentally open and permeable, easily entered by viruses and diseases, but just as much by modern technologies or toxic materials.

Whereas the alien bodies in their original form are absent from Siegel's film, Kaufman actually begins his film with images of the aliens: hardly having any form at all they are presented as a whitish, transparent, and floating mass. The original alien bodies are highly ambiguous yet clearly they are some kind of organic life-form, which has the capacity to merge with other organisms. If one thing jumps out in Kaufman's version, it is the ubiquity of seeds, plants, flowers, and greenhouses; yet their artificial locations in the midst of the city make them look oddly out of place, somehow linking the invasion plot to the alienation of our bodies from nature. We live in cities and poison our bodies with elements of the modern lifestyle. As the character Nancy Bellicec at some point wonders, could all the trouble have anything to do with the junk we feed our bodies? The primitive form of the aliens aligns them not only with plants but with other more dangerous, archaic life forms such as microbes, viruses, and parasites that enter the body and cause disease or mutation from within. The 1993 *Body Snatchers* is sometimes read as an AIDS metaphor, but in Ferrara's film the vulnerability of the body to viruses and other unnatural intrusions is also linked to contemporary fears of biological and chemical warfare. When Steve is testing for chemicals in the water, the military doctor comes up to him and asks, "Can they affect the brain patterns? Can they interfere with chemo-neurological processes? Simply can they alter a person's view of reality?" Young Andy is frightened to death in kindergarten when all his fellow pupils hold up the same blood-red drawings of formless viscera, showing how much the alien invasion has infected their young brains. In the fourth film the mind-altering effects of chemicals are not placed in a context of biological warfare but in our everyday lives. An abandoned pharmacy notably becomes Carol's main hideout, a supermarket full of colorful pills to help us make it through the day.

The idea of something entering our bodies through our orifices is a primal bodily fear. This fear is connected in the *Body Snatchers* films to a discourse concerning alien intrusions into our bodies that change our structure from within. But whereas Kaufman links it more to natural biological threats such as viruses and infections, Ferrara and Hirschbiegel equally connect the snatching process to the intrusion of our bodies by modern technology. As Nicole Brenez points out, during the snatching scene in the bathtub a striking visual parallel is drawn between the alien's tentacles and Marti's Walkman.[14] Artificially produced consumer products like Walkmans, BlackBerrys, and iPods are becoming more and more parts or extensions of our bodies. In the third and fourth remakes, this nexus of fears is developed not so much as a notion of alienation anymore, but seems to reflect the loss of the natural body as a valid category. The dehumanizing process at the heart of the body snatcher theme walks hand in hand with the rise of the posthuman body.

# Notes

1. Don Siegel quoted in Vivian Sobchack, *Screening Space: The American Science Fiction Film* (New Rochelle, N.Y.: Arlington House Publishers, 1979), 123.

2. Jim Hoberman, "Paranoia and the Pods," *Sight and Sound* 4, no. 5 (1994): 29.

3. Tracy Knight, "The Rorschach Plot of Invasion II: The Life and Death of Counterculture," in *They're Here: Invaders of the Body Snatchers, a Tribute*, ed. Kevin McCarthy (New York: Berkeley Boulevard, 1999), 123.

4. Charles Freund, "Pods over San Francisco," *Film Comment* 15 (1979), 23.

5. M. Keith Booker, *Alternate Americas: Science Fiction Film and American Culture* (Westport Conn.: Praegar, 2006), 69.

6. Richard Bégin, "C'est ce Regard-là qui a disparu! *Invasion of the Body Snatchers* et l'Altération du Même," in *Les Peurs de Hollywood: Phobes Sociales dans le Cinéma Fantastique Américain*, ed. Laurent Guido (Lausanne, Switzerland: Edition Antipodes, 2006).

7. Don Siegel, quoted in David Zinman, *50 from the 50's: Vintage Films from America's Mid-Century* (New Rochelle, N.Y.: Arlington House Publishers, 1979), 144.

8. Philip Kaufman, quoted in Robert Eberwein, "Remakes and Cultural Studies," in *Play it Again, Sam: Retakes on Remakes*, ed. Andrew Horton and Stuart Y. McDougal (Berkeley: University of California Press, 1998), 19.

9. Michael Hardin, "Mapping Post-War Anxieties onto Space: *Invasion of the Body Snatchers* and *Invaders from Mars*," *Enculturation* 1, no. 1 (1997).

10. Hardin, "Mapping Post-War Anxieties onto Space," 5.

11. While the character's name is spelled as "Belicec" in the 1956 film, it is "Bellicec" in the 1978 version.

12. Nicole Brenez, *Abel Ferrara* (Urbana: University of Illinois Press, 2007), 151.

13. Robert Eberwein, "Remakes and Cultural Studies," 27–28.

14. Nicole Brenez, "Come into my Sleep," *Rouge* 6 (2005), <http://www.rouge.com.au/rougerouge/sleep.html> (10 November 2007).

*Chapter 4*

# Remaking Romero

Shane Borrowman

All earth was but one thought—and that was death / Immediate and inglorious
—Lord Byron, "Darkness"

Early in the 1980s, my veterinarian's good business sense and poor judgment conspired to expose me to zombie films. My family owned a St. Bernard named Gretchen who suffered from arthritis in her hips. We also owned a VCR, and the nearest video rental store was twenty-two miles away. The films there cost $7 each per day—with weekends counting as a single conjoined "day" since the place was closed on Sunday. That price was too high, given that we had the dog's frequent medical expenses to cover, and that rental time was too short. Back then, anything over five or six miles felt like far too much of a commute to waste gas money on, given that gas ran sometimes as high as $1.70 per gallon.

Then the veterinarian solved our non-dog problems: He bought some metal shelving and a wide selection of cheap videotapes—in the early 1980s, "cheap" meant anything under $80 and almost no one actually owned a real video that hadn't been taped off television—and turned the cramped storage closet next to his waiting room into a video rental hotspot. This tiny space reeked of hardcore industrial disinfectant, the wet fur of sick animals, and good-natured greed.

I loved it. I was always there anyway because of Gretchen, and the good doctor charged only $5 per rental tape for seven days. Plus, he allowed anyone, regardless of age, to rent anything—regardless of rating or content. He was also quite forgiving of late fees; I learned this when a copy of *Zombies of Mora Tau* (1957) fell behind my television and went missing for more than a month. His receptionist asked if I could find it, smiled when I returned it, and never charged me an extra dime.

During the years prior to his retirement, while no other video rental place moved into town, this doctor of veterinary medicine introduced me to the breadth and depth of the horror genre, especially zombies. I rented these movies by the armful, cramming such unlikely companions as the classic *White Zombie* (1932) into the same weeklong marathon of watching and re-watching as *Teenage Zombies* (1957) and *Creepshow* (1982). These comparatively tame films were balanced against the video nastiness of *Zombie* (1979) and *Children Shouldn't Play with Dead Things* (1972). These were good times.

Because I rented and repeatedly watched these films in no order other than random, I tended to think of them as part-and-parcel of the same monolithic whole—some older than others, some more wildly bloody than others, but all simply zombie movies. Plus, I was young enough not to make value judgments—which are nearly impossible to avoid when the subject of study is a genre forced to include such cinematic abortions as *Zombie Death House* (1987), *Return of the Living Dead 3* (1993), and *Day of the Dead 2: Contagium* (2005)—no more of a sequel to the Romero classic than was *Zombie* to *Night of the Living Dead*.[1] The quality of such films leaves the genre with serious credibility issues, even among the already often questionable company of other horror films.

The impact on my long-term thinking of this monochromatic and judgment-withholding view of what is often considered to be a crazily swirling genre is significant: I never considered zombie movies to be a progression, a chronological sequencing of films that developed in a linear way. It was a bewildering, amorphous cinematic mix where movies from different film traditions and different decades stumbled along together side-by-side, regardless of director, country of origin, or place in time. In my formative experience, the genre itself was—to deploy an image both accurate and obvious—like a hoard of the walking dead: all members different upon the surface but fundamentally identical beneath.

It was an attitude that fit well both with the early 1980s and the ethos of zombie cinema. In those early Reagan years—some of the hottest of the Cold War—the outside enemy of America was communism. Internally, America had other, possibly more terrifying, enemies. When Randy Shilts' book *And the Band Played On* was published in 1987, there had already been approximately 20,000 AIDS-related deaths in the US alone since 1980.[2] By the time the film version of *And the Band Played On* (1993) won awards, another 140,000 AIDS-sufferers had died—more than double the number of US combat casualties in the Vietnam War. Through 2005, according to reports from the CDC and other agencies that monitor this plague, the cumulative number of US deaths alone from AIDS was greater than half a million.

In this ongoing culture of fear, zombie cinema has enjoyed a renaissance unlike anything seen in its history. It is not my purpose here to write the intertwined histories of US paranoia and the cinematic specter of the walking dead. Such a study would take a book, and the book has already been written—more than once, in fact. Instead, I offer a twofold analysis of the mostly modern history of zombie cinema, with special focus on the remakes of George A. Romero's classics *Night of the Living Dead* (1968 and 1990) and *Dawn of the Dead* (1978 and 2004). Because the remake of *Day of the Dead* has not yet been released in 2008, it bears no part of this discussion. Comparative analysis of these four films says much about the ways in which Americans inscribe their fears upon the cinematic bodies of the undead—particularly their fears of the socio-economic Other and the ever-changing/never-changing place of women in American society.

My analysis of *Night of the Living Dead* (1968) draws upon the "Millennium Edition" released by Elite Entertainment, while the analysis of *Night* (1990) is founded upon Columbia Pictures' home-video release. These are simple enough, obvious enough, selections, given that only single versions exist of each of these films. Multiple versions of *Dawn of the Dead* (1978) exist, however, and the differences among them are many and varied. For the analysis below, I have focused upon the "European Version" from the multi-DVD "Ultimate Edition." While part of this selection—possibly a large part—is personal choice, the personal choice is not a capricious one: Unlike the US release of *Dawn of the Dead*, I find the Continent's narrative arc edited in a more streamlined yet effective manner. More significantly, the "European Version" employs a sober soundtrack that adds to the film's mounting tension and dumps both the campy comic music of the US cut and the majority of the pointless pie fight that drags down the terrifying resolution. Tony Williams argues, in *Knight of the Living Dead*, that these elements of the US release are part of comedic, satiric American culture, possibly even harkening back to the naturalism that characterizes much of American literature.[3] Maybe. But the film still suffers, especially when placed against the remaining sober and somber films in the four-part trilogy. Two versions of the 2004 remake of *Dawn* exist, and I focus herein on the "Unrated Director's Cut"—that is also favored by the film's director, Zack Snyder, because it both presents the gore as he intended audiences to see it and includes further character development that was denied to theater viewers. Also, it is my assumption that readers are more than passing-familiar with the films discussed herein, and I make no attempt to summarize the basic plot events of any film unless such summation is required on a given point of analysis.

Any history of zombie cinema that begins with *White Zombie* (1932) and tapers out with such largely unremarkable 2007 films as *28 Weeks Later* and *Flight of the Living Dead: Outbreak on a Plane* (the former is, of course, a sequel to the wildly popular *28 Days Later*, while the latter is a pirated plot from the cult movie *Snakes on a Plane*) has immediate difficulties. The seventy-five-year chronology, with its easily compiled list of annual entries, implies a linear progression that is, at best, a useful fiction wherein the march of time implies—even if the author of the list does not—a progressive, evolutionary development that leads, directly or indirectly, from one genre entry to the next. It's a nice, simple structure that allows for much analysis.

Among the most useful and intriguing of these chronological histories of zombie cinema is Jamie Russell's *Book of the Dead*—a far more intelligent and exhaustive study than Peter Dendle's *The Zombie Movie Encyclopedia*.[4] Following a largely (though not exclusively) chronological order from *White Zombie* on, Russell divides zombie films into a handful of broad categories, beginning with the Caribbean/African voodoo base of early films through the atomic-age terrors of the twentieth century to the Romero and Italian splatter films from the late 1960s onwards. The history Russell constructs makes good sense, beginning with those mostly forgettable 1930s and 1940s films that were barely encumbered by a budget and progressing through the deliberately low-budget splatter-fests of the 1970s and 1980s to the big-budget zombies of recent decades—*Resident Evil* (2002) and *Land of the Dead* (2005), for example. It's a story of money that has a happy ending, a story of popularity on the rise with only a bright future ahead. It's a good story, as stories go, but a troubled and troubling history.

Unfortunately for Russell and other proponents of this linear brand of history, zombie cinema has developed by accretion and digression, not by logical and natural selection. It's a process of *re*volution rather than evolution, where the line that extends from *White Zombie* to *Land of the Dead* is circular rather than straight. As Stephen King argued in his study of American horror *Danse Macabre*, within a discussion of *Night of the Living Dead* (1968), "It may be that nothing in the world is so hard to comprehend as a terror whose time has come and gone [and] one generation's nightmare becomes the next generation's sociology."[5] His argument is a simple one: horror morphs from one generation to the next, but horror movies remain static. They do not, however, transition from terror to incomprehension. Audiences that viewed *White Zombie* and saw in the walking dead "a nightmare vision of a breadline" are replaced by a new generation of audiences whose members carry their own nightmare baggage—fearing, perhaps, the literal white zombie's sexual slavery to her evil master, or the colonial exploration and exploitation of indigenous people, or the racist appropriation of African and Caribbean bodies by white robber barons.[6]

Fears change year to year, but the films do not. Instead of becoming outdated, the zombie films of the past are reinscribed with the new fears of new viewers. Audiences are especially inclined to write and rewrite their fears on the palimpsest of zombie films, given that such movies, while they may tap various timely terrors, always tap into what R. H. W. Dillard refers to as "a fear of the dead and particularly of the known dead, of dead kindred."[7] Times change, terrors change, but zombie films do not. The years that matter most in this circular, revolutionary model of the history of zombie cinema are those years when the genre both revolves over itself and lurches in a slightly different—but not entirely new or unexpected—direction, the years when Americans write new fears atop old films, especially those all but timeless fears that exist in the tensions between men and women and between social classes. These are the years of the Romero zombie movies and their remakes.

## *Night of the Living Dead* (1968): "I'm Taking the Girl with Me"

By 1968 the peace and love generation had begun to realize, fully, that war and hate were far more likely to change the world, no matter how good anyone's intentions may be. Americans had been dying in Southeast Asia for more than thirty years, with no end in sight, and the US political system itself suddenly seemed to be rotting at the core. John Kennedy had promised that NASA would put a man on the moon, but that hadn't happened yet, either. Worse, perhaps, the USSR had beaten the US into space ten years before, combining Cold War anxiety with fear of the great, dark "out there" of the stars. At home in the US, the civil rights movement had succeeded—or run out of steam, depending on where the individual American stood—and the fight for equal rights for women had been joined.

Had zombie cinema continued to exist—or subsist—on techno-terrors like *The Astro-Zombies* (1968, although occasional references claim, perhaps accurately, a 1967 release), a sad mix of pseudo-Frankenstein mythos and walking dead imagery, then the genre may well have stagnated—spinning its undead wheels in the ever-deepening mud of passing years and worn fears. In Pittsburgh, however, a budget of less than $150,000 in the hands of a fine independent filmmaker lifted the zombie above this sad silliness.

While he retained much of the shambling, vacant-faced, hollow-eyed imagery from zombie films past, George A. Romero introduced perhaps the most significant, viscerally moving element of the modern zombie film: cannibalism. In earlier films of the genre—*White Zombie* or *Revolt of the Zombies* (1936)—the most terrifying aspect of the walking dead was simply that aspect implied by their name: They were dead, and they were still walking. There was an implacable, *Terminator*-ish quality about them, but it was largely mindless. When their master fell to his death in the final reel of *White Zombie*, for example, the dead simply went tumbling after. The zombie could follow orders, but mostly it was scary simply because of what it *was*. What was once a fully functioning human being full of life and potential became an unthinking brute, too stupid to get out of the way of a moving car—as evidenced by the opening scene of *Zombies of Mora-Tau*—but not terrifying enough that the locals needed to barricade their doors (or quit the locale entirely). They couldn't be reasoned with or repaired, but it was possible to coexist beside them, even if it was unnerving and unpleasant.

Romero took this appropriation of the human body in service to dark and unspeakable ends to a new and far more frightening level: He made the zombies flesh-eaters—human flesh-eaters by preference, although bugs and rodents were devoured too. The terror of physical possession remained—as those already dead became zombies and those bitten by zombies also joined the ranks of the undead—

but the root fear of body dismemberment and the taboo of cannibalism were con-
joined to craft a monster that took the zombie's past and remodeled it in the present to create a new and grim future of universal truths overturned, of societal
hierarchies breaking down, of family structures shattered. In the process he also
crafted a familiar spin on the age-old story of female oppression and appropriation
and the tension of class relations in America.

As the film opens, Barbara and Johnny are traveling into the country to visit
the grave of their father; despite the effort and time involved and the remoteness
of the location, and Johnny's general unwillingness to be involved in the venture,
they are making the traditional gestures that honor familial dead. After a close shot
of a shot-up "cemetery entrance" sign, a flapping US flag is featured. This, the
image argues, is America. Johnny fits nicely into the conventions of the horror
genre, with his sarcasm and skepticism identifying him as the sort of individual
from whom crisis will draw heroism.[8] His ugly and nearly immediate end demonstrates that *Night of the Living Dead* isn't about reaffirming conventions; it's about
overturning them.

In Romero's America Barbara is clearly a passive participant. Johnny drives
her to the grave, asking her, like a whiny child, if there's any candy left for him.
He teases his sister, terrifies her, and rushes to her aid when she is attacked. In
short, he does all that an American audience of the time would expect from a
brother. And Barbara—like generations of film scream queens before and after
her—plays her role equally predictably. She begs her brother to stop complaining,
to stop teasing, to stop her assailant from hurting her.

As Johnny and the zombie fight, Barbara watches from a safe distance. When
Johnny is killed, she runs away—screaming, tripping, and falling down. Parallel-
ing her actions in the cemetery, Barbara, once joined by Ben and thus under his protection, refuses to aid in her own defense. As Ben struggles with the dead, Barbara
passively looks on, making no move to help and sinking into a virtually catatonic
and compliant state (breaking silence only long enough to tell her own sad story
after Ben tells his, the telling done in a slow, halting, childlike voice). She can retreat from her reality like this, however, as Ben tells her, early in their meeting, that
"*We've* got to get out of here" (italics mine). Without discussion or the possibility
of dissent, she becomes a part of him. She and he become a we without consideration or comment.

Ben's domination of Barbara is a strangely benign tyranny. As he works to
salvage some safety in their situation and Barbara tells her story, he responds not
with understanding or fellow feeling but with first a largely rhetorical question
followed by a stern admonishment: "Why don't you just keep calm?" and then "I
think you should just calm down!" But of course Barbara does not calm down and,
in fact, offers a plan of her own: She wants to go in search of her brother. Ben rejects this fraught-with-danger plan immediately. "My brother is alone!" screams
Barbara. "Your brother is dead," Ben replies—following this with two slaps, after
which Barbara faints.

This possession of Barbara as an object of male control continues when the two are joined by Harry Cooper and his fellow cellar dwellers. As Ben and Harry argue about where the safest place to be besieged may be—Harry favoring the cellar and Ben favoring the ground floor of the house—Harry ignores Barbara entirely. Suddenly, as he prepares to return to his chosen hideout, he blurts, "I'm taking the girl with me." His motives are unclear and questionable. Put into the most favorable light possible, Harry may be drawing upon a twisted syllogism of manhood: The cellar is safe (as major premise), the girl must be safe (minor premise), therefore the girl will be safe in the cellar (inevitable conclusion). Ben draws upon a similar sort of logic, choosing only to stay out of the basement (though he later leaves open the possibility of fleeing, ultimately, to the cellar). Because he met Barbara first, and she has offered no assertion about where she wishes to be (other than her beat-down plan to search for Johnny), she remains with him.

Barbara belongs to Ben, as does everything else in his vicinity. "You can be the boss down there [in the cellar]," Ben announces to Harry, "I'm boss up here." Both Ben and Harry entirely ignore Tom—a young man also hiding in the cellar— just as Tom has ignored (in fact has not even mentioned, at the time of this pronouncement of Ben's) his girlfriend Judy. And Harry has done no more than mention his wife and daughter. The idea that Tom might have a claim at "bosshood" never enters the mind of either older man, and neither Barbara nor Helen nor Judy is considered for the position.

As Ben dominates Barbara, so Harry dominates his wife—and by extension their mostly unconscious daughter Karen. After his confrontation with Ben and failed bid to take possession of Barbara, Harry returns, alone, to the cellar. Helen argues that they should leave the "dungeon" but is unsuccessful. The two remain basement-bound until Tom calls down with the news that a television has been found.

When Harry and Helen leave the cellar, they join Barbara and Ben and the film's youngest couple, Tom and Judy (who are young and wholesome and look like they've just changed clothing after walking off the set of *Beach Blanket Bingo*). Although they had originally sought refuge with the Cooper family, Tom decided, at Ben's prompting, that he and Judy must leave the comparative safety of the cellar to help barricade and defend the house. Judy's opinion was never solicited. As Ben controls Barbara and Harry holds authority over Helen, so Tom dominates Judy. Later, as she slices swatches of fabric for Molotov cocktails, Tom reminds Judy of the time during "the big flood" when she couldn't decide what to do and had to be convinced that the plans of others were right. Hugging her, Tom adds, "You're sure no use at all, are ya?" They kiss. It's a tender moment filled with gender tension: Judy is helpless without Tom and hopeless as a helper for Tom. Told to remain in the house while Ben and Tom attempt to fuel a pickup truck for a planned escape, Judy rushes to her man's side, and dies there when Ben's plan to obtain fuel falls through and the pickup truck explodes.

Helen's fate is no better than Judy's. As the dead finally force their way into the farmhouse, Helen returns to the cellar—where a now-dead Karen stops eating her father's corpse long enough to stab Helen repeatedly with a trowel. In a terrible inversion of the family dynamic, Helen first watches without noticeable complaint as Ben shoots her husband; she is then devoured by the child to whom she gave life. Like Helen, Barbara's final moments are filled with familial inversion. Although she manages to break out of her near-paralytic state to help free Helen from the clutches of the ghouls, Barbara is confronted with a terror even more awful than the death of her brother: Johnny's murderous return. Last seen as he attempted to save her, Johnny now reaches out to his sister not with love—or even brotherly aggression—but with hunger.

Judy and Tom are killed trying to engineer an escape; Harry is killed by Ben, Helen is killed by Karen, and Barbara is pulled to her death by her brother. Alone and forced to flee from the dead, Ben rushes to what is, as Harry argued, the only safe refuge: the cellar (although he must kill his former comrades in order to be truly safe). The inversion of the natural order comes to completion: The social order has broken down, the family has disintegrated, and even the hero was wrong. Of course, Ben was so certain that he was correct that his certainty led him to shoot Harry—and only slightly less directly cause the deaths of all his companions.

Between Harry and Ben, the gender tension is far more complexly tied to the hierarchical nature of the logic of manhood. Each of these two men acts in what he legitimately believes to be the best interest of those under his protection. Ben refuses to allow Barbara to leave in search of her brother—even going so far as to assault her physically to stop her. Harry never deviates from his stated intention to retreat into the cellar. Possibly cowardly and craven, Harry is barely able to leave his place in the door to the cellar to help Ben rebuild his failing barricade, but he does help Ben nail the door shut. Once they are safe, Ben delivers four unreturned punches to Harry, leaving his face swollen and scraped, and threatens to drag him outside and feed him to the zombies. At a moment when the two men have connected, when Harry has left his chosen place of safety to help Ben in his, the barrier between these men has fallen. The two are not equal: When Ben attacks, Harry makes no attempt to fight back. He has submitted to Ben's authority. "If you stay up here," Ben shouted at Harry earlier, "you take orders from me!" When he does as he's told, however, Ben reacts with violence, ultimately shooting Harry in the chest as the dead crush in.

In one of the strangest tender moments in the film, Harry—shot and dying—stumbles into the cellar and dies reaching for his sick daughter. After he returns to life, Ben shoots Harry another three times, perhaps enjoying the grim pleasure of killing his enemy not once but twice. Whether the killing of Harry is pleasurable or not, "Our hero only manages to survive the *Night of the Living Dead* by cowering in the cellar," just like Harry said the survivors should.[9]

Unlike later films in his four-part trilogy, in *Night* (1968) Romero explains that the living dead have been revived by radiation returned to Earth from a probe to Venus. While this taps nicely into American anxieties of the time concerning enemies beyond the nation's borders, the racial, social, and familial aspects of the movie reach much more powerfully into the psyche of its audiences. Race relations, always strained in the US, had reached critical mass throughout the 1960s. The push for equality extended beyond African Americans to women, especially visible in the push for an Equal Rights Amendment to the Constitution itself. At the same time, the Vietnam War and changing social mores led to a breakdown of traditional family structures once thought to be timeless, possibly even ordained by the Creator. As Jamie Russell argues, "Vietnam lurks in every frame of Romero's film. Hitting cinemas at the height of the war, as race riots, peace demonstrations and angry outbursts of a youthful counterculture raged through America, Romero's debut pulled no punches in its representation of a nation falling apart on every level."[10] The film was so upsetting that critics such as Roger Ebert made special efforts to warn parents of the danger it posed to young minds. The film was so popular that theaters staged special midnight showings.

Night of the Living Dead tapped into all of America's free-floating anxiety and was wildly successful—launching both the career of its director and the future of its genre, no longer mired in tired stories of European colonialism and racist notions of voodoo. However, the women in the story were still objects more than subjects, and the tension between master and slave had simply sidestepped into the tension between social classes and competing visions of social order.

## Night (1990): "You Know I'm Right"

At the opening of his otherwise brilliant analysis of Romero zombie films and their remakes, Gospel of the Living Dead, Kim Paffenroth argues that his analysis will "skip the remake of Night of the Living Dead (1990), which Romero oversaw, as too identical to the original to need further comment."[11] In relation to much of my argument above, Paffenroth is correct. Tom and Judy Rose (an even more "country cracker" name than "Judy" alone) are still background characters dominated by Harry and then Ben. Harry is bossy and belligerent, abrasive and abusive, and convinced that the cellar is the only safe place to hide. Helen, although slightly more helpful in the defense of the farmhouse, is still a victim waiting for her daughter to rise from the dead. And Ben is still a terribly, tragically flawed hero: convinced of his own correct course of action, he brooks no argument about where the best place to be besieged is. All of these points of connectedness make the remake unworthy of further analysis along these lines. But Barbara (1990) demands consideration, given her radical transformation from the character of Barbara (1968).

In the beginning of this Tom Savini-directed remake, Barbara is the same character as she is in the original film. Although her long blonde hair is now short and red, she still carriers herself with the same quiet, wallflower-like quality. If anything, Barbara (1990) has more of the schoolmarm/spinster librarian stereotype about her, an image reinforced when her brother cruelly asks/taunts, "When's the last time you had a date?" Tossing fuel upon this fire, he wonders why visiting their mother's grave is so important to her, given that their mother nearly drove Barbara to become a nun.

While Barbara (1990) does attempt to help Johnny as he wrestles with the zombie that attacks her, the effort is more harmful than helpful: Using a cross-shaped floral arrangement as a weapon, Barbara stabs the zombie in the shoulder—stabbing her brother's hand in the process. After Johnny is killed, Barbara (1990)—like Barbara (1968)—flees, falls, wrecks the car that could provide safety and possible escape, and screams quite a bit. Confronted by more of the undead, the new Barbara retreats into the same sort of whimpering helplessness as did the original, leaving her savior Ben to keep her safe.

But the vacation Barbara (1990) takes from the reality of her situation is a short one. As Ben fights to force a ghoul out of the kitchen, Barbara seizes a fireplace poker and bludgeons the animated remains of the house's former owner to a second death. Ben gives her some comfort—and Barbara seems to let him take the lead in deciding how the farmhouse must be fortified against attack—but she takes active part in her unfolding fate. She is no background figure over whom the men argue possession; instead, Barbara (1990) is an agent of change, a force in the construction of the story around her. Instead of arguing possession of Barbara, in fact, Ben and Harry argue possession of the home itself—an argument cut short when Judy Rose angrily asks, in her only assertive moment, what would happen to them if Tom threw them out of his uncle's home.

As tension develops over the most likely means of escape and Ben and Harry take their opposing positions, Barbara offers an alternative: escape on foot, no gasoline required. While Ben, Judy, and Tom nail boards across doors and windows, Barbara states calmly of the undead, "They're so slow. We could just walk right past them." Ben vetoes this idea out of hand but becomes wildly excited when Tom remembers where more wood can be found to reinforce the windows and doors. Later, as other survivors search the body of Barbara's first kill, looking for the keys to the gas pump, Barbara advances her argument again. Carefully aiming and firing, Barbara shoots down the zombie that killed her brother. "We can get away," she tells Ben, who responds that her idea to walk out is simply "too dangerous." Ben, like Harry, has committed to a plan and will harbor no deviation, and Barbara can see this clearly. "You know I'm right," she tells him, and they all retreat into the house.

Rather than seeing Barbara's choice to remain with Ben and the others as a sign of her acquiescence to male authority, it is more consistent with her remade character to see this as a choice to remain where she is most needed. In 1968 Barbara tuned out when confronted by shock trauma, only coming back long enough to be snatched away by her now dead brother. In 1990 Barbara only broke down briefly and incompletely; when she put herself together, she was greater than the sum of her parts.

Barbara (1990) is not a simplistic reversal of Barbara (1968), not simply a scream queen transformed into a warrior woman. Barbara (1990), although she becomes a surprisingly good shot with a rifle in a shockingly short amount of time, is something new in the Romero mythos: a strong woman with ideas of her own, ideas better than those of the men around her. Harry and Ben choose static defense against the walking dead, while Barbara sees them for the shambling scarecrows that they are: keep moving and keep safe. But Ben rejects Barbara's plan, and Barbara remains with him. Ben relies upon Barbara's strength to make his own plans reach completion. He refuses to leave the farmhouse with Tom and Judy Rose until he knows that Barbara (and her rifle) will be watching his back. After the disaster at the gas pump, Barbara gives covering fire as Ben makes his run back toward the house.

As the siege comes to its inevitable end, and the dead stream into the house, Ben and Harry repeat their final moments from 1968, with both of them being injured this time, Ben mortally. Harry flees to the attic—a far superior hiding place, actually—and Ben retreats to the basement, where he shoots Helen and finds the gas pump key that would have made escape possible for everyone. As in 1968, salvation did, in fact, exist in the cellar. Barbara, armed with a zombie policeman's revolver and unable to carry the injured Ben, puts her own plan into action. While zombies force Harry upstairs and Ben down, Barbara walks away. When zombies come close, she aims her revolver at their heads, but it isn't necessary to shoot—until she is confronted by the horrible sight of a zombie woman carrying a doll. Breaking into tears, Barbara shoots the zombie in the head and completes her escape from the farmhouse and its environs.

Throughout *Night* (1990), a subtle subtext of class status runs. Johnny drives a nice car and wears leather driving gloves, both upper-class paraphernalia. The Cooper family are also dressed quite nicely, Harry in a tuxedo and Helen in a dress and pearls—the attire of wedding guests. Even Sara, the dying daughter, wears a party dress and black shoes. Ben's attire is that of middle management—jacket, tie, and dress shoes. Barbara seems to carry the same class markers, wearing a long skirt and light blouse. Tom and Judy are pure country, from their jeans to Tom's baseball cap. As socioeconomic markers go, these are all largely benign, with the exception of the couple's clear dismissal by their social betters.

The real depths of class consciousness in Savini's remake appear in the last few minutes, as Barbara makes good on her escape. Standing beside a seemingly abandoned pickup truck, Barbara is startled when a shot suddenly rings out. She hurls herself into the bed of the truck, shouting at the shooter. In the truck she finds the twice-dead remains of her brother Johnny; recoiling from them, she is grabbed across the shoulders and chest by a man dressed like a stereotypical country hunter. His two laughing and smirking companions bear the same attire—jean jackets, boots, flannel, hunting orange. It's an uncomfortable moment filled with a strange and creepy sexual tension, exaggerated when the man holding her smiles and waggles his eyebrows before releasing her.

The strange nature of this post-nightmare scene continues when Barbara awakens sitting upright in a jeep, surrounded by other vehicles and dozens of people involved in the cleanup of the living dead. The scene has a carnivalesque atmosphere, and Barbara stumbles in slow wonder through this surreal landscape. A pig barbecues in the background, while bikers taunt and wrestle with zombies staggering about in a tiny corral. More disturbing, lynched zombies hang from a huge tree while their attackers repeatedly shoot their jerking bodies. All of the people involved in this odd reversal of victim/victimizer from the *Night* before seem to be either working class, rural, or, most simply, "white trash." They serve as a scathing indictment of the survivors and as a continuing reversal of conventional truths begun in *Night* (1968). "They're us, and we're them," pronounces a bemused Barbara.

In the final scene of *Night* (1968), Ben is shot down by whites who are there to rescue him. In *Night* (1990) Ben is also put down—by one of the men who "rescued" Barbara, in fact—but only after he has succumbed to his gunshot wounds and become a zombie. Harry, on the other hand, has survived, and he is amazed that Barbara actually returned. If the death of Ben in 1968 is a statement on race relations in America, then Harry's sudden and immediate death at Barbara's hands is an even more powerful statement on gender in America in the last decade of the twentieth century. Ben's death, however tragic and perhaps laden with symbolic meaning, was an accident—a hunting accident, as it were. When Barbara (1990) shoots Harry in the head it is a deliberate act of murder—justified or not. Given the opportunity to destroy the man who made the previous night even more terrible, the man whose decisions caused the death of at least Ben, Helen, and Sara, Barbara doesn't hesitate to kill and then cover her crime: "There's another one for the fire," she tells the men who rush up behind her at the sound of the gunshot.

When I first saw *Night* (1968), everyone groaned—moaned, really—when Ben was shot down like a zombie. It seemed fundamentally terrible and unfair for him to suffer so much only to die. When I first saw *Night* (1990), everyone in the theater cheered wildly when Barbara shot Harry in the forehead without a moment's hesitation. It seemed fundamentally right and just for her to take such vigilante justice into her hands, even though Harry himself, jerk or not, had suffered as much as Barbara and lost even more.

## *Dawn of the Dead* (1978): "We Can Deal With It"

The racial tensions raised in *Night* (1968) continue in *Dawn's* opening reel. The mostly white police force storm a tenement filled with Puerto Rican immigrants and African Americans—"niggers" and "dumb little bastards," in the words of one officer—unwilling to turn over their dead to the proper authorities. This is unsurprising in an America still struggling with the same racial divides of the 1960s. The on-screen bigotry continues as the film's central quartet—Peter, Roger, Fran, and Steven—fly over the Pennsylvania countryside and, quite literally, look down on orange-clad hunters, uniformed civil servants, and National Guardsmen. The scene of these zombie killers drinking coffee and beer and laughing with their women bears more than a passing resemblance to the final scenes of *Night* (1990).

The scene is one of revelry and mirth, with zombies as an awkward impediment to the fun. The fleeing quartet—all professional people, two police officers (SWAT, more accurately), and two television journalists—sneer at the fools beneath them as they steal a network's helicopter and fly blindly north toward Canada (a vague and nearly formless plan referenced in edits of *Dawn* other than the European Version). Take away a sense of class pride and privilege, and there's little or no reason for these four to feel superior to the armed, semi-organized, and (presumably) official resistance beneath their feet.

When they reach and claim their consumer paradise—a shopping mall where everything's free, even the cash in the bank tellers' drawers—the quartet sets itself up in luxury, after perhaps one night of sleeping on the floor and eating SPAM: stereo equipment, fine furniture, gourmet food, stylish clothes. In the storage room of an unused civil defense post, Fran, Steven, Roger, and Peter become masters of all they survey. However, in this paradise gendered tensions exist.

Among the men, Roger and Peter are clear equals. When the survivors find the mall, it is the two policemen who make plans to raid the place for such necessary supplies as lighter fluid. Steven is not invited and is not included in the informal planning that leads to the decision to claim the mall rather than to abandon it. As Steven joins the pair, nearly getting killed by a lone zombie on the way despite the fact that he carries both a rifle and a pistol, he is given provisional acceptance after finding a safe passage back to Fran and the helicopter. Later, he is allowed to fly above Peter and Roger and watch while they hotwire trucks and use them to block the doors to the mall. While Steven presumably gave the two a ride out to the first truck, the purpose for his continuing presence afterwards is unclear.

Despite his provisional status as a man, both Roger and Peter repeatedly refer to him as "Fly*boy*" (italics mine). He's a terrible shot with a rifle and a worse wrestler, and the implications of the name are clear: In a world of men—two men, anyway—he is a boy. But as a boy in a world of men, he is, at least, a step in the hierarchy above Fran.

From the opening scenes of the film, Frannie is an object to be handled rather than an agent in her own narrative. Steven must harass and nearly threaten Fran in order to get her to agree to meet him to flee—and even then, she seems to agree only after a camera operator assures her that her "responsibility is finished." Steven has engineered an escape—even if he doesn't seem to have thought through the destination very thoroughly—and Fran is both his fiancé and his hostage to fortune. The fact that Steven clearly understands their relationship in this way is revealed when Fran demands that she be kept informed of the group's plans and that she be left with a weapon. Steven sulks and scowls and thumps around like a tantrum-throwing child. Fran is his and, it seems, has no business making decisions of her own—including her demand to be taught to fly the helicopter, a demand supported by the two officers and grudgingly allowed by Flyboy.

Like Barbara (1968) and Barbara (1990) (early in the remake), Fran is of limited value in her tiny, well-stocked world. When Steven wrestles, awkwardly and badly, with the undead during a stop for fuel, Fran offers no help. As the two cops plan and execute their initial raid into the mall, they leave Fran with a gun, which Steven takes away from her without a fight. Caught without a weapon, Fran is nearly overpowered by a single bespectacled zombie in Hare Krishna robes. Later, while Roger and Peter park trucks around the mall's doors, Fran delivers questionable covering fire—occasionally scoring hits, even fatal ones, but creating more tension by her poor marksmanship than her skill. "I'm not going to be den mother," Fran declares early on, but that's virtually all she becomes. She does not, or cannot, fight the dead in the mall, so she remains behind while the men do the killing. She nurses the zombie-bitten Roger while Steven and Peter illogically pile the decomposing dead in a walk-in cooler, among various food supplies. She cuts Steven's hair during the "settling-in" montage. She is even shown cooking, despite her earlier joke about not having her "pots and pans."

Most significant in regards to Fran's position in this tiny society is her physical condition. While she sits in the dark, smoking a cigarette and eavesdropping, the men discuss their future, deciding to stay in the mall rather than to blindly flee further. When Peter asks if Fran is all right or ill, Steven spills the metaphorical beans: "She's pregnant." Following this revelation, a brief and tense discussion ensues, driven mostly by Peter. "We can deal with it," he asserts, asking only one question of Steven: "Do you want to abort it?" Steven hangs his head and shrugs a vague and halfhearted negative. Peter's approach to the situation's sudden complication seems, at a glance, to be both strong and calm, harsh, even, but no more than is perhaps necessary in this dark and violent postapocalyptic world of the dead.

The problem with Peter's statement and question is in that vague pronoun reference. Peter doesn't tell the other two men, "We can deal with this problem," and he doesn't assert, "We can help Fran," or some other such positive sentiment. The complexity of the situation is reduced to an "it" that can be aborted. Steven, as the man of the couple, has the say, and Fran listens to the discussion but never joins it. There is no clear reason for her to be excluded, and it would be inconsistent to think that suddenly she had been forcefully ejected from the palaver. Yet she sits, smokes, and broods. When Steven comes to bed, she snaps at him: "All your decisions made. 'Do *you* want to abort it?'" The men have spoken, and Fran doesn't put up a fight—aside from some verbal sniping at Steven.

As Fran's pregnancy moves toward term, the trio of survivors is attacked by what Peter calls "a professional army"—a *Road Warrior*-like mixture of hippies and bikers and assorted "white trash," along with a sombrero-wearing mustached man who may be Hispanic: *Easy Riders* in Romero's hell on Earth. Aside from their predilection toward random destruction, the priorities of the looters seem strikingly similar to those of the original quartet: They take money, jewelry, weapons, clothes, and various luxury items. The European cut of *Dawn* avoids the absurd and pointless pie fight that mars the American theatrical cut.

Steven, unable to suffer the looters silently, picks a fight he cannot win. He is wounded by the bikers and, ultimately, killed by multiple zombies. Becoming a zombie himself, he goes in search of Fran—a typically Romeroesque inversion of the traditional couple dynamic. With the bikers gone and the zombies once more in control of the mall, Fran prepares to flee. Showing weakness for perhaps the first time, Peter tells her quietly, "I don't want to go. I really don't." While there's a certain sad logic to Peter's self-destructive decision—where, after all, will he and Fran flee to in their helicopter with its nearly empty gas tank?—it is hardly in keeping with the macho character of the previous acts. Without a word of explanation, he chooses to abandon both Fran and her unborn child.

Although Peter rejects suicide in favor of flying away with Fran, the film's ending is, if anything, as bleak as that of *Night* (1968). Perhaps even more. In *Night* (1968) there was reason to hope that order had been restored; the authorities were, after all, working their way through the countryside, killing the dead along the way. No one from the besieged farmhouse survived, but Ben's death was bad luck more than anything else. *Dawn of the Dead* deploys perhaps the most bleak happy ending in film history: Peter, Fran, and the unborn child fly away into the dawn sky, escaping the shopping mall where they nearly lost their lives. But they have almost no fuel for the helicopter, and they have nowhere to go. The odds of their story ending well are cruelly small.

I first saw *Dawn of the Dead* on a Halloween night, just after a Helloween concert ended on MTV. Having watched the concert to its end, I came into the film late—after the mall had been claimed, cleaned, and remade by the already reduced band of survivor types. Days before, my girlfriend and I had attended a double feature at the drive-in, its end-of-the-season hurrah: *Rocky IV* and *Red Dawn*. In retrospect, this seems a poor choice of films for a drive-in date, but it was the Cold War, after all. Both of these movies have happy and sappy endings, soft-boiled political commentary delivered with appropriate pathos. It just didn't ring true, not when President Reagan was always talking about the dangers posed by the Soviet's Evil Empire. Then I caught the last act of *Dawn of the Dead*. That was an ending that rang true in a world that seemed to be on the brink of nuclear holocaust. As Peter and Fran flew off into the sunrise, I slowly shook my head in wonder. They *might* live, but it sure won't be happily ever after.

## *Dawn* (2004): "You Wanna Kill My Family?"

While *Night of the Living Dead* (1990) ended with Barbara's survival and the possibility of order being restored, Zack Snyder's 2004 remake of *Dawn of the Dead* made no such significant change to the tale's outcome. What it did manage, however, was to bulk up the number of survivors and incorporate virtually every character type from both the Romero films *Night* (1968) and *Dawn* (1978), as well as the remade Barbara from *Night* (1990).

Ana, the primary character of the remade tale, is a skilled nurse—with a sharp and sarcastic wit and healthily developed instinct for self-preservation. She's strong enough, both physically and mentally, to survive the shock trauma of both her husband's death and his rising from the dead to attack her, to survive the first wave of the zombie plague, to survive in the closed environs of the Crossroads Mall, to survive the panic-filled escape to waterborne semi-safety. She is cut from the same character-cloth as Barbara (1990), with some of the nurturing mother-figure qualities of Fran thrown into the mix. She is, however, not a completely independent agent: When Ana declares of the mall, "I don't want to die here," she immediately turns to Michael for an escape plan, which he provides.

Set in complement and contrast to Ana are several other (lesser) female characters. Luda—a pregnant Russian immigrant—serves primarily as the vehicle by which Snyder incorporates perhaps the most disturbing reversal of accepted truth into his film: Ana, the nurse, kills Luda's zombie child. Norma, a late middle-aged truck driver, shows some of the same strength and resourcefulness as does Ana, surviving the initial outbreak and managing to save others—and even showing the strength to shoot both the undead Luda and Andre, father of the zombie child. Nicole and Monica serve as opposite sides of the same coin—like Mary Ann and Ginger from *Gilligan's Island*, the Madonna and the Whore. Nicole—physically quite similar to Barbara (1990)—is the wholesome girl-next-door type, a tragic figure because we witness the death of her father (or hear the shotgun blast that kills him once he rises from the dead, specifically). She develops an almost immediate relationship with Terry, the youngest of the three mall security guards, and the two play out the role of young lovers for nearly the entire film, perhaps most memorably as they giggle and cuddle while stargazing. She is Judy (1968), Judy Rose (1990)—a good girl through and through. Monica's place in the film's narrative arc is a different one. Introduced as she struts through the mall, glad to be out of "that fucking truck," Monica is soon shown not only having sex with Steve, the only white-collar survivor, but both allowing him to videotape it and demanding, "Fuck me harder, Steve."

Among the female characters in *Dawn* (2004), Monica is the most original—although her character type is certainly an old one in Western culture, one that stretches at least as far back as Homer's *Iliad* and *Odyssey*. In the Romero films and their remakes, she is nearly unique, a foul-mouthed, sexually liberated woman. The closest representation appears in the European edit of *Dawn* (1978), where Fran is shown both in bed with Steven and dolled up like a saloon girl, complete with revolver.

The men in *Dawn* (2004) provide a much more eclectic mix than do the female characters. While both CJ and Bart are familiar crackers—especially Bart—CJ is a competent and capable survivalist, although he is capable of making bad decisions; he is Ben, both in *Night* (1968) and its remake. Terry, the third member of the security guard trio, is different from his partners; he is the generally whole-some young man who is not without some flaws—including a strange penchant for televisual voyeurism and a liking for soy mocha lattes with foam. There's a bit of Tom in him, especially Tom from *Night* (1990), and some of Johnny, especially from *Night* (1968). Together with Nicole, he becomes part of the pair of lovers present in both films. Andy, Glen, and Tucker are facets of the same character type, specifically the figure of Roger in *Dawn* (1978). They are skilled, have some well-developed instincts for both self- and other-preservation, and are ultimately doomed. Like Roger, Andy ends his life as one of the undead, while neither Glen nor Tucker suffer this fate.

In Snyder's remake of *Dawn of the Dead*, the character of Harry Cooper makes an appearance, divided among two characters: the criminal-turned-family-man Andre and the white-collar alcoholic Steve. Like Harry, Andre is driven by a desire to save his family; like Harry, Andre is also unable, or unwilling, to do what must be done once a member of his family becomes a zombie. When Norma shoots the zombie Luda, in fact, Andre immediately draws his own weapon and re-turns fire. While Harry's class status may be the same as that of Steve—certainly the suggestion of upper-class status is there in both films, if only in clothing style—the personalities of the two men overlap in a number of behavioral patterns. Like Harry in both *Night* (1968) and *Night* (1990), Steve is both cowardly and unreli-able. Worse, he is willing to put his own survival over that of other members of the group.

Michael, Ana's love interest, displays the same sort of survivor instincts as does Roger, the sarcastic policeman/SWAT team member with knowledge of hotwiring cars. Despite the fact that he is a television salesman at Best Buy, Michael is able to fight and kill a zombie using only a broken croquet mallet, fire a pistol with startling accuracy, and engineer the group's ultimate escape from the mall. Not bad for a guy who used to work at a stationery store and, later, repaired photocopiers. Like Roger, Michael is bitten by the undead, although Michael chooses suicide over post-mortem zombification.

The most significant male character in the film *Dawn* (2004) is, of course, Kenneth—known as "Officer" throughout most of the film. He is a former military man turned cop, a man able to lead a raid through the zombie-infested parking garage and another across the zombie-filled parking lot. Initially concerned more with his own survival than that of the others around him (not counting his brother at Fort Pastor), Kenneth eventually develops a bond with Andy, and it is Kenneth who first proposes leaving the mall, despite its relative safety. Kenneth is this *Dawn's* Peter, from the shared color of their skin to their shared knowledge of re-ligion—Peter of voodoo and Kenneth of "church" (revealed in his bathroom-based discussion of the "end of days" with Andre). And like Peter, he is one of the few survivors to reach the marina after the flight from the shopping mall.

Although Snyder's incorporation of these character types into a single (mostly) coherent narrative—he never really explains why, exactly, the survivors choose to go to the shopping mall—is impressive, it is the familial dynamic, and its inversion in the land of the dead, that provides much of the internal tension of the film. Family is this movie's focus from the beginning, as Ana returns to her suburban home to "date night" with her husband—who becomes a zombie and attempts to kill her the next morning. Childless herself, Ana is shown discussing backwards skating with her young neighbor; once the little girl becomes a zombie, however, Ana does not hesitate to heave her down the hallway.

This focus upon familial inversion spreads across the other survivors. Shortly after Norma's truck-bound band of refugees reach the mall, Kenneth shoots Frank while Frank's daughter Nicole is forced—by proximity, if nothing else—to listen. Nicole lost her mother and siblings to the undead, Frank tells everyone; now she loses Frank to both the undead and the survivors themselves. In a strange twist, Nicole recreates a sort of familial bond with Chips, the dog found during the raid into the parking garage, and is then forced to release him into the zombie hoard surrounding the mall. When Chips is trapped in Andy's Gun World, Nicole risks her life—and ultimately causes both Tucker's death and the sudden collapse of the mall-bound society—to save him; later, in the film's final scene, she loses Chips again as he charges, barking, onto a zombie infested island.

The ultimate inversion of family values, however, comes when zombie Luda gives birth to her zombie baby girl. Andre allows his love for Luda and the child to blind him to the danger she poses to the group after being bitten by a ghoul; he ties her to the bed but does not reveal her condition to the others, knowing what their response would be. He births the zombie child and swaddles it, holding it with love even as he shoots down Norma and is himself shot to death. When the other survivors come upon this scene, they do not hesitate to destroy the zombie child in what, arguably, may be one of the most disturbing scenes ever released in a theater since the demon-possessed child in *The Exorcist* masturbated with a crucifix.

It is this terrible act of value-inversion that finally pushes the survivors to make their run for freedom, although it's the attempt to send food to Andy and Nicole's subsequent decision to rescue Chips that actually sets the plan in motion five days early. The trip to the marina is a terrible one fraught with danger, and only a handful of survivors make it onto Steve's yacht: Ana, Kenneth, Terry, Nicole, and Chips. It's a perfect family structure for the first time since Ana's husband Louis was killed—mom, dad, and two kids. There's even a dog.

Of course, in this postapocalyptic world of the dead, this family has no more chance of lasting than does any other human institution. Audience members who rushed the exit—or turned off the film at home—when the credits began to run may have been left with the same sort of grim hope as were audiences of Romero's *Dawn* (1978): The survivors got away, but they might not really have any place to go. They might find something, maybe, if their luck holds. Audience members who stuck around through the credits are left with far less optimism: the boat runs out of gas and suffers some sort of fire in the engine compartment, while the survivors themselves seem to run out of both food and water. When they do find an island, they don't even make it off the dock before the living dead swarm them.

Snyder never makes it clear if Ana, Kenneth, Terry, and Nicole manage to flee back to their yacht (although Chips seems to have run off entirely, judging by how far away his bark sounds). But like Peter and Fran in the helicopter, the odds of these folks reaching safety seem virtually nonexistent. Like *Dawn* (1978) and *Night* (1968), *Dawn* (2004) takes it as a truth that once the zombies appear, there's little hope for a happy ending for anyone, whether they survive the zombies or not.

When this remade *Dawn* came out in 2004, I was ready. I had planned for weeks, rearranging appointments and orchestrating my teaching so that I wouldn't have any student papers to read. On opening day I was there—appropriately enough, I attended the film at a theater in a mall—and I didn't move from my seat until the final credits ran. As I walked to my car and drove home, I couldn't stop smiling. I'd been worried that Zack Snyder wouldn't have the nerve to make a film as violent and grim as had Romero, and my fears were groundless. If anything, this movie was less optimistic than *Dawn* (1978).

Too young when I saw the original to really make much of the subtext, I was considerably older in 2004. The opening scene of Muslims at prayer preyed on me, as did the final image, sandwiched amongst the credits: zombies charging the dock where the survivors of the mall have finally fetched up. These are the images of power in the post-September 11 world. It didn't take much to splice these images together, leaving me with an image of Islamic extremist hoards storming the last infidels. I couldn't stop smiling over my enjoyment of *Dawn* (2004), but it was a smile founded on a grimace and deployed in place of tears.

## Zombie Films and/as Remakes

Zombies really started off on the wrong foot, for they had no great literary or mythological foundation upon which to build. Vampires and revived pseudo-scientific sorts of monsters had *Dracula* and *Frankenstein*, respectively, to lend them some credibility. The werewolf, in one form or another, had a long folklore tradition in virtually every country of Europe, Africa, and among Native Americans. Even the mummy—that shambling zombie wrapped in bandages—gained acceptance because of the always-present public fascination with Egyptian funerary practices. Other creatures gained acceptance in other ways: *King Kong* had its at-the-time revolutionary special effects to give the big monkey a boost of sincerity (or authenticity, anyway), while even such a lame monster as the Phantom of the Opera had both a literary parentage and an upper-class ethos to give it some respectability.

The zombie had none of this. Its mythological roots reached back, in the West, only to the religious practices of the Afro-Caribbean diaspora. This alone presented a problem, given that at the time of *White Zombie*'s 1932 release, America was sixty-seven years away from the end of slavery and more than thirty years away from the end of legalized segregation.

Compounding the zombie's credibility issue, its literary roots were of the most spurious and questionable kind: William Seabrook's *The Magic Island* (1929). Seabrook was an adventurer, and his books reflected this, sensationalizing his travels and going to great lengths to define the indigenous people he encountered as radically inferior and often disturbing Others. The only book of his that deviates from this outsider looking in and not liking what he sees approach is *Asylum*, his tale of his "adventures" in a mental institution where he was committed to cure himself of alcoholism. Not exactly a canonized text.

Worse, zombies were monsters on a budget. While creating a vampire or other creature required some style and a certain special effects budget, zombie-hood could be achieved with some torn clothing and a shambling walk. Anything else was—and often still is, to some extent—gravy. For a filmmaker looking to spend as little as possible, a more perfect budget-conscious creature couldn't have been devised (unless the monster were invisible, perhaps). So once *White Zombie* set this shambling corpse of a genre in motion, others quickly joined the fray. And nothing could have lowered the zombie's status more completely than a slew of bad movies. Already in disrepute, the zombie immediately sank to the bottom rung on the ladder of horror.

Then in 1968 George A. Romero gave the zombie everything it needed. It was decades too late for the zombie to have a literary heritage, but Romero provided what a literary heritage would have: common plot lines and character types. Doctor Frankenstein and Van Helsing are the archetypes in their respective tales, for example. More significantly, he gave the zombie a purpose. While previous films' zombies had relied on some evil mastermind to set them in motion and to give their second lives purpose, Romero gave them their own agenda: flesh eating.

*Night of the Living Dead* gave the zombie tale its "literature"—its basic monster qualities and plot outline, in the same way that *Dracula* defined the basic characteristics of the vampire and *Frankenstein* set out the general agenda of its story-type. In post-*Night* (1968) zombie tales, there's an outbreak wherein zombies are created—by radiation, disease, voodoo magic, scientific experimentation gone awry, or causes unknown—which may be part of the story's plot or may simply be either assumed or alluded to later. The main characters encounter the zombies and flee in search of refuge. Once found, the refuge is barricaded, and the zombies lay siege. In the end one of two basic plot lines unfolds: The zombies break in or the surviving humans break out. Sometimes there are no survivors of the break in/out, and, if anyone does survive, that survivor is irreparably changed by the experience—and may not have much longer to live, anyway. As Kim Newman argues of the grim finale of *Night* (1968), "Fifteen years after Ben got shot in the head, the unhappy ending was a commonplace," not only within the horror genre—*Easy Rider*, for example.[12]

This was the pattern Romero established in 1968 and reinforced in his later films, *Dawn* (1978), *Day of the Dead* (1985), and *Land of the Dead* (2005). More importantly, this became the general narrative pattern for the vast majority of true zombie films that followed, from Italian films such as *Zombie* (1979) and *Zombi 3* (1988, both directed by Luciano Fulci), to the Japanese movie *Living Dead in Tokyo Bay* (1992), to the Australian action/zombie crossover *Undead* (2003). In American cinema, the use and abuse of Romero-style zombies and plot lines continues unabated in movies such as *Return of the Living Dead 5: Rave to the Grave* (2005) and *28 Weeks Later* (2007). Additionally, modern technology has allowed for an explosion of amateur zombie films—with most enjoying budgets considerably smaller than Romero's for *Night* (1968)—from *Zombie Night* (2004) to *Zombie Killers* (a 2000 high school production that, without the Internet, never would have reached an audience beyond its own classroom of creation).

While a remake of Romero's *Day of the Dead* is said to be in production (and presumably there will, some day, be a remake of *Land of the Dead*), the plot lines and character archetypes established by Romero in 1968 ring across the genre, from amateur films released online and major Hollywood studio productions to video games such as *Dead Rising* and the ongoing *Resident Evil* series. Some of these films and games have more of a claim to quality or originality than do others. All of them, ultimately, are remakes of Romero.

# Notes

1. The film *Night of the Living Dead 3D* (2007) may be among the most egregiously exploitative remakes in film history and deserves mention here only because it exists. The 3D angle is no more skillfully done herein than it was in either *Jaws 3D* (1983) or *Friday the 13th 3D* (1982). In this unauthorized and ill-conceived film, Ben is white, Judy spends virtually all of her limited on-screen time nude, and Cooper is a marijuana farmer. Cooper's suicide and Barbara's sudden surrender to the undead are both underwhelming events in a narrative arc nonsensical even by the most generous of standards. Worst of all, Sid Haig—a regular player in other zombie films, such as the surprisingly decent *House of the Dead 2* (2005)—plays a mortician with bad judgment and an accent that seems to come and go at random. He swings a shovel like the gravedigger in *Dead Meat* (2004) and has all the mannerisms of the hitchhiker in Tobe Hooper's *Texas Chain Saw Massacre* (1974). All of them. Aside from a visually clever opening scene and one witty line of dialogue, this film represents the worst that the horror genre has to offer: "When the dead walk, you gotta call the cops."

2. Randy Shilts, *And the Band Played On: Politics, People, and the AIDS Epidemic* (New York: Stonewall Inn Editions, 2000).

3. Tony Williams, *The Cinema of George A. Romero: Knight of the Living Dead* (New York: Wallflower, 2003).

4. Jamie Russell, *Book of the Dead: The Complete History of Zombie Cinema* (Surrey, England: FAB, 2005). Peter Dendle, *The Zombie Movie Encyclopedia* (Jefferson, N.C.: McFarland, 2001).

5. Stephen King, *Danse Macabre* (New York: Berkley, 1983).

6. David J. Skal, *The Monster Show: A Cultural History of Horror* (New York: Norton, 1993), 169.

7. R. H. W. Dillard, "Night of the Living Dead: It's Not Like Just a Wind That's Passing Through," in *American Horrors: Essays on Modern American Horror Film*, ed. Gregory A. Waller (Champaign: University of Illinois Press, 1988), 14–30.

8. Kim Newman, *Nightmare Movies: A Critical Guide to Contemporary Horror Films* (New York: Harmount, 1988).

9. Newman, *Nightmare Movies*, 3.

10. Russell, *Book of the Dead*, 69.

11. Kim Paffenroth, *Gospel of the Living Dead: George A. Romero's Visions of Hell on Earth* (Waco, Tex.: Baylor University Press, 2006).

12. Newman, *Nightmare Movies*, 4.

# Part II: Cultural Anxiety

*Chapter 5*

# Cultural Change and Nihilism in the *Rollerball* Films

## John Marmysz

In 2002, a remake of the 1975 film *Rollerball* was released in theaters. It flopped at the box office, disappearing quickly from movie screens and reappearing shortly thereafter on home video. Although popular success is not the best indicator of a film's aesthetic worth, in the case of this 2002 atrocity, box-office failure and bad filmmaking did indeed go hand in hand. This was especially disappointing, as I had been looking forward to this remake for quite some time. I consider the original version of *Rollerball* to be something of a classic; prescient in its vision of a world dominated by corporate monopolies, and philosophically perceptive in its depiction of nihilism. The remake, though faintly echoing some of the same themes as the original, fails to treat these issues in anything but the most superficial manner. Rather, it distracts the audience with unexciting action sequences, insipid dialogue, and characters that are just plain uninspiring. Whereas the original version of *Rollerball* artfully contrasts the flash and violence of a warlike future sport with the inner existential crisis of that sport's superstar, the remake fails even to convey the excitement of the titular game.

While aesthetically horrendous, the remake of *Rollerball* is instructive, as it provides a point of contrast to the original film, highlighting a change in our culture's manner of engagement with the difficult philosophical problem of nihilism. Both films share a roughly similar plot, yet in the differing manners that they explore and develop that plot, we can glimpse two separate ways in which nihilism may be discovered, confronted, and dealt with. The differences are quite striking.

In the original 1975 film, nihilistic melancholy is depicted as a situation stemming from individual strength and the aspiration toward excellence. The forces of culture, and of nature itself, are portrayed as conspiring against any individual who strives for absolute spiritual fulfillment, with the ultimate message that personal honor, nobility, and success can be had only at the cost of forsaking public adoration and the economic rewards offered by corporate culture. In the 2002 remake, on the other hand, the encounter with nihilism is depicted as a result of personal inadequacy and individual weakness. This version portrays the entanglements of mass culture more sympathetically, in the sense that they offer the failing individual a way out of personal hopelessness. Whereas the original 1975 film ends with the main protagonist resolutely and fatalistically braving his destiny alone, the 2002 remake ends with the main character taking part in a mass movement against the powers that be.

The different sensibilities of these two films are best summed up in this last contrast, which also points to a characteristic difference between the ways that modern and postmodern cultures tend to view the philosophical issue of nihilism. Whereas modernists view nihilism as arising out of the individual's confrontation with a world naturally hostile to the innate strivings of authentic and self-reflective human beings, the postmodernist perspective sees nihilism as merely a transitional stage in the evolution of mass culture; one that might be overcome with the abandonment of older, more individualistic ways of thinking. Thus, in the relatively brief interval between the releases of the two versions of *Rollerball*, we can detect a shift from a modernist to a postmodernist rendering of the predicament of nihilism.

## The Existential and Ontological Axes of Nihilism

Friedrich Nietzsche puts matters quite correctly when he observes that the term nihilism is "ambiguous."[1] Though the general phenomenon is familiar to most of us, the philosophical meaning of the term remains quite unclear and often misunderstood. Too often, nihilism is thought to refer to situations or states of affairs that are absolutely negative, and which have no redeeming qualities whatsoever. However, this loose usage of the term does not do justice to its subtleties as a philosophical concept.

Understood in its richer, philosophical sense, nihilism describes a distinctively human state of separation from the highest objects of aspiration. As human beings, we have the capacity to formulate notions of absolute Being, Truth, Justice, and Goodness, yet so long as we live we must constantly fall short in our pursuit of these perfections. According to the nihilist, human finitude necessarily separates us from the full realization of any form of absolute perfection, and so we must forever remain frustrated in our attempts to achieve those goals that are the most important to us. Human life is, as Albert Camus puts it in "The Myth of Sisyphus," "absurd," being characterized by an ongoing battle between the individual, human demand for meaning and fulfillment, and the resistance of the world around us to deliver on that demand:

> The world itself, whose single meaning I do not understand, is a vast irrational. If one could only say just once: "This is clear," all would be saved. But men vie with one another in proclaiming that nothing is clear, all is chaos, that all man has is his lucidity and his definite knowledge of the walls surrounding him.[2]

In this sense, nihilism is not simply a synonym for despair or negativity, but is, rather, a philosophical doctrine that attempts to characterize the human condition.

Though nihilists claim that all humans are necessarily alienated from the absolute, most of us are not fully aware of, or even interested in, this predicament. Humans commonly ignore their nihilistic separation from Being, Truth, Justice, and Goodness, focusing their attention on more humble, and more attainable, worldly goals. While the pursuit of these sorts of modest objectives may produce feelings of potency and happiness in the short run, such pursuits also have the effect of distracting us from our actual state of alienation from the ultimate. This underlying alienation, claims the nihilist, can never fully be covered over. Though it may become obscured in the course of pursuing our everyday activities, it nevertheless reasserts itself and makes itself known in a number of different ways.

An existential feeling of alienation frequently offers us our first access to the phenomenon of nihilism. For an individual whose fundamental aspiration is for the absolute, the modest, attainable goals ordinarily pursued in the course of living life must at some point lose their sustaining power. It is then that life, as commonly lived, becomes shallow, flat, and unsatisfying. Lived existence becomes "a desert-like emptiness, a malaise, an illness of the spirit and the stomach."[3] These feelings of distress may provoke individuals to embark on an inquiry into the causes of life's deficiencies, and in the course of such an inquiry, they may be forced to recognize the pervasive scope of the phenomenon of nihilism.

From an existential encounter with personal meaninglessness, the nihilist discovers that all is not right with the world. As Camus asserts, "We must despair of ever reconstructing the familiar, calm surface which would give us peace of heart."[4] The source of this existential discontent is the perception of an incongruity between the aspiration toward infinite perfection, on the one hand, and the finitude of human being, on the other. This incongruity is, in its very essence, irresolvable. Humans are finite, and so their very being is at odds with the state of being that they wish to achieve. The existential struggle with this state of affairs opens the way for an encounter with ontological nihilism. Ontologically we have "fallen away" from Being. We are separated from the absolute and there is no hope of ever mending this rift. Our relationship to reality is naturally defective, and like puzzle pieces that fit nowhere, we are doomed to remain out of place and estranged from Being itself.

Ontological alienation and the existential sense of anxiety that accompanies it have often been pointed to as self-evidently negative aspects of nihilism. In modernist accounts of nihilism, these negative aspects are often viewed as grounds for a kind of despair that, while incapable of fully being overcome, may nevertheless be faced with heroic or superhuman resolve. We find such accounts in the writings of Nietzsche and Camus. For Nietzsche, because humans are fated to struggle against the chaos of reality, and in the process eternally to suffer, they should develop the psychological capacity to endure this struggle and suffering, and even to take pleasure in it. Thus we find Nietzsche advocating the goal of the "Superman." The Superman understands "every kind of 'imperfection' and the suffering to which it gives rise [as] part of the highest desirability."[5] Such an individual can endure recurrent feelings of alienation and despondency, utilizing those feelings as a motivation actively and creatively to affirm life. For Nietzsche, existential and ontological nihilism are realities that, once faced, may serve the positive end of cultivating individual strength and nobility of character. Likewise, Camus suggests that while the recurrent struggles and sufferings of life never end, a heroic and strong individual can resolve to rebel against the ontological injustice of the world and, like Sisyphus, take pride and joy in affirming that "the struggle itself toward the heights is enough to fill a man's heart."[6]

On the contrary, the postmodern approach to existential and ontological nihilism sees them as something to be overcome and left behind, like bad dreams are forgotten upon waking from an unsettled sleep. Jean-François Lyotard provides perhaps the clearest and most straightforward articulation of this viewpoint when he characterizes postmodernism as a sort of "war on totality."[7] Being, Truth, Justice, and Goodness are viewed by Lyotard as outdated ideals and totalizing "metanarratives" that vainly attempt to sum up the absolute. In focusing our attention on these ideas and aspiring toward them, humans doom themselves to despondency and despair in the pursuit of the unattainable. It would be better, then, to turn our backs on these traditional values and immerse ourselves in creative and ongoing play aimed at no final, totalizing goal. According to the postmodernist, existential and ontological nihilism are conditions of modernism that may be overcome and left behind if we can just give up on our antiquated aspirations. Nihilistic thinking is a sort of nostalgic longing for a bygone era, according to this point of view, and it is about time that we move on into the future. Once we abandon the desire for the absolute, we can get on with life, untroubled by the worries that accompany nihilistic alienation. The freedom to pursue diverse ways of thinking about the world will be more frequently exercised, and we will no longer be concerned with dogmatic assertions concerning the "reality," "truth," "justice," or "goodness" of human creations. All of these creations will be understood as equally legitimate and not in the least bit substandard, since we will no longer judge them according to totalizing and absolute ideals.

Whereas the modernist is an idealist, the postmodernist is a pragmatist. This, in a nutshell, is what defines their difference. The modernist is constantly struggling to attain the unattainable; the postmodernist finds satisfaction in what is attainable. While the modernist aspires to the ideal, and thus remains unsatisfied with the real, the postmodernist considers what has been made real, in all of its diverse forms, as good enough. There is, then, an inherent conflict between modernist and postmodernist approaches to the phenomenon of nihilism. According to modernists, nihilism (in both its existential and ontological guises) cannot truly be overcome, but must merely be endured and resisted. In this view, existential nihilism results from the awareness of an ontological reality that can never authentically be denied. For postmodernists, however, nihilism is simply a way of thinking, not a final description of reality, and so it may be overcome if we can become adept at creating new ways of thinking that are not reliant on absolutes. For modernists, it takes strength to endure the ontological truth of nihilism. For postmodernists, languishing in nihilism is a sign of weakness, as it indicates one's inability to break free from a nostalgic longing for the past. While both consider the struggle against existential nihilism to be a potential source of vital activity, they disagree on its ontological origins, and as a result, modern and postmodern perspectives tend to characterize the struggle with nihilism differently. From the modernist perspective, nihilistic struggle has a hint of fatalism and tragedy to it as the nihilistic superhero vainly battles reality alone and isolated from those who have chosen to ignore the Truth. From the postmodern perspective, on the other hand, the confrontation with nihilism is seen as a transitionary stage after which an individual might successfully break free from the outdated mode of thinking that had previously constrained his or her manner of being. In this liberating struggle, the postmodern nihilist tends to develop sympathy for the viewpoints and aspirations of others, accepting that there are many different and divergent ways of conceptualizing the "truth."

In the old and new versions of *Rollerball*, we see these differences illustrated and played out to their logical conclusions. The 1975 version represents the modernist perspective, portraying the main protagonist, Jonathan E. (James Caan), as a professionally successful, yet tragic, individual who has no choice but to engage in a vain battle against the world around him. The 2002 remake, on the other hand, takes up a postmodernist perspective, depicting its hero, Jonathan Cross (Chris Klein), as a professionally unsuccessful, but opportunistic revolutionary who ultimately leads an insurrection against his oppressors. Contrasting and comparing these films will produce several concrete illustrations of the internal vicissitudes of nihilism that are not only philosophically instructive, but which also offer insights into the shifting landscape of American culture over the last twenty-seven years.

## *Rollerball* (1975): A Modern Nihilist Superman

The original version of *Rollerball*, starring James Caan as the hero Jonathan E., begins and ends ominously with Bach's *Toccata and Fugue in D Minor* playing on the soundtrack. This is a significant detail that sets a tone quite different from that of the 2002 remake. *Toccata and Fugue in D Minor* is popularly associated with tales of terror, and so the feeling produced in the audience is one of foreboding and danger. At the very start of the film, as track lights and instrumentation are tested, as the audience for the game streams in, and as the corporate executives take their places, deeply menacing organ music dominates the soundtrack and creates a mood that will remain a major undercurrent throughout the course of the movie. We are not encouraged to feel excitement or enthusiasm by this mood-setting music, but rather anxiety about some sort of looming threat. Furthermore, the danger that represents the threat we are encouraged to be anxious about is not easily identifiable. It could be the violence of the game to come, it could be the crowd of spectators, or it could be the corporate executives dressed in suits and ties who seem somehow in control of all that is going on. In fact, it will turn out that the danger faced by the film's hero is composed of all these things. The very being of Jonathan E's lifeworld is made up of the culture that surrounds the ultraviolent sport of rollerball, and as the plot develops, we watch him become increasingly alienated from this world. His fall occurs not as the result of his choices, but rather is due to forces beyond Jonathan E's control and understanding. Ultimately there is nothing that he can do to change his fate, and though he is the captain of a championship sports team, he will end up alone as he rebels against his world and the forces that control it.

This opening scene of the 1975 version economically and artfully blends together many of the major elements that will be important to the rest of film. From the outset we know all is not well, and we quickly suspect that Jonathan E. is a sort of tragic hero on a collision course with destiny. According to Nietzsche, the tragic hero is a figure who "prepares himself pre-sentiently by his destruction, not by his victories," and as we watch him we, the members of the audience, experience the "joy to which the path through destruction and negation leads."[8] Jonathan E. embodies the tragic reality that there is always, even for the most successful individuals, an abyss that separates humans from Being itself. The longing for heavenly tranquility is doomed to failure, and even champions like Jonathan E. are destined to fall, no matter how heroically they assert their individual strength. We sense this as the first players assemble in formation on the rollerball track at the start of the film. As our hero stands with his team and impatiently endures the playing of the "corporate anthem"—his impatience illustrated by the fact that he nervously beats his fist against his leg for the duration of the anthem—we get a feeling for what he is up against and of how hopeless his struggles will be. Corporations rule the world now, and the game of rollerball is a rationalized, formalized, and highly controlled substitute for the old-fashioned forms of warfare engaged in when political states dominated the Earth. The corporate anthem is an organ piece, heard by the characters within the film, that reminds us, the audience, of the foreboding organ music we heard during the opening sequence. The multinational corporations, like God or Big Brother, are everywhere and control everything. Each time that the corporate anthem is played, we are reminded of the ever-present threat that Jonathan E's world poses to him. His destruction seems certain, yet we anticipate that he will exhibit the sort of personal authenticity and strength of character that we expect from a tragic hero.

The first rollerball game between Madrid and Houston (Jonathan's team) introduces us to the breathtaking action, violence, and frenzy that are integral facets of this "sport." While the game is certainly vicious, it has strict rules of conduct that must be observed. Penalties are called for illegal moves and time limits for play are set. Players who violate the rules are pulled from the game, and in particular we see Jonathan's friend, Moonpie (John Beck), penalized for unnecessary roughness. The staging of the match is masterfully executed, giving us the sense of a highly stylized and organized gladiatorial competition. The choreography of the players' moves, the color of the costumes, and the design of the rollerball rink (which is actually the Olympic bicycle stadium in Munich, Germany), all contribute to a sense of realism and energy that helps us to understand why Jonathan is led to exclaim toward the end of the match, "I love this game!" It is in the midst of the action and the excitement of play that Jonathan feels most at home. He feels as one with this world that has predictable rules, a predictable duration, and clear-cut goals. Uniforms differentiate those who are with him from those against him, and he feels comfortable counting on the people around him to carry out their duties. Yet, as he leaves the arena, surrounded by chanting crowds of fans, the organ theme from the opening sequence booms out again. The camera pans upward and zooms in to reveal the looming presence of the office building of the Energy Corporation, the company that owns Jonathan's rollerball team. We are thus reminded that, despite his victory in the roller rink, all is not well. Though Jonathan may be a great team captain, his world is far more complicated than he can understand, and it is about to fall apart.

We soon see how uncomfortable and out of place Jonathan feels when taken out of the rollerball arena. A meeting with Mr. Bartholomew (John Houseman), the head of the Energy Corporation, reveals that the game is only part of a much larger reality, and that this larger reality has "rhythms" and "rules" that override those within the world of rollerball itself. While Jonathan may be the consummate athlete, he is completely out of his element when it comes to understanding the world beyond his sport. As a symbol of this awkwardness, in the corporate office he stumbles, cuts his finger on a decoration, and generally feels ill at ease as Bartholomew proclaims rollerball to be a "stupid game" from which Jonathan should be happy to retire. When Jonathan expresses his surprise at being asked to retire, Mr. Bartholomew explains that the game was never supposed to be a tool for individual glory, but rather was designed by the corporations in order to demonstrate to the masses that team effort is what makes for greatness. Though not made explicit during this conversation, it later becomes clear that Jonathan has undermined this purpose by rising to superstar status. He has become too much of an individual figure, a sort of Superman in the sport. For this reason he must leave the game and eventually fade from the public consciousness. Jonathan is merely an instrument used by the corporations, and since he has ceased to serve his assigned purpose, the corporations want him out. It is interesting that even Bartholomew admits he alone is not fully in control of this decision concerning Jonathan's fate. Rather, there are a variety of corporate forces pressuring Jonathan to accept a generous retirement package that will include a television program celebrating his life and career. What is important is not *why* Jonathan must retire, but *that* he must retire, for whatever reason.

After this first meeting with Bartholomew, an abyss opens up in Jonathan's world and he begins to fall away from all that previously brought him comfort and security. His entire identity and sense of self-worth stems from his rollerball-playing acumen, and now all of that is going to be taken away. As it turns out, Jonathan had a sense that something was wrong long before this crisis. His wife, Ella (Maud Adams), was taken from him because a corporate executive desired her for his own. Presumably, Jonathan did not make a big deal over this at the time, since the corporations were otherwise being so generous to him. But now that he is threatened with retirement, Jonathan starts to reexamine his feelings and he realizes that these two episodes in his life—the loss of his wife and now of his career—result from some common cause. He repeatedly expresses a sense of bewilderment over just what this cause is, claiming that he doesn't understand why things seem to be falling apart in his life. He tells his friend Moonpie that "someone is pushing" him and that "something is going on," but that he doesn't know what it is. A sense of existential anxiety and emotional discomfort attunes Jonathan to the fact that he is not in control of his own world, that something is out of joint, and that his spiritual health is deteriorating as a result. Jonathan's growing uneasiness, and his consequent reflection and meditation on his situation, are encouraged by the fact that now, like never before, the smooth functioning of his life's routines has been interrupted. These routines, in a Heideggerian sense, have now become "unhandy," and so, like a carpenter clutching a broken hammer, Jonathan must stop and thoughtfully consider what to do next.

Moonpie laughs all of this off. Unlike Jonathan, Moonpie has no concerns other than the acquisition of more wealth and luxury. He tells Jonathan, "We're living good! You know we are!" yet Jonathan is too far along the path of nihilism to take Moonpie's comments seriously. Moonpie is so distracted by all of the luxuries that his career brings him that he doesn't even care to question why he is of value to the corporation and the crowds that adore his team. Jonathan does wonder about this very issue, if only because now his personal strength and charisma have become more of a threat than an asset to the powers that be. As his relationships with those around him disintegrate, Jonathan is led to the realization that although he is physically surrounded by people, he is also spiritually alone. His fans still adore him and cheer his victories, and his friends still profess their loyalty to him, but Jonathan nevertheless develops a progressively contemptuous attitude toward them and their placid manner of existence. He views them as participating in a way of life that makes them into tools of the system rather than fully developed and autonomous agents. While people like Moonpie cannot even conceive of leaving such a world behind, Jonathan is in the process of becoming ever more alienated from it. The further that this alienation progresses, the more isolated Jonathan becomes and the more suspicious and hostile he is toward the crowd and its complicity with corporate culture.

In the world that Jonathan and Moonpie inhabit, the masses and the corporations are mutually dependent on one another. The corporations require a large consumer base, which the masses provide, and the masses require easy access to goods and services, which the corporations supply. So long as products and luxuries are readily available, the crowd will continue enthusiastically to support corporate control and domination, regardless of how much freedom must be surrendered by particular individuals. In the event that someone did come forth to threaten the authority of the corporations, and consequently to endanger the economic comfort of the people, the "herd" would instinctively defend the status quo, siding with their corporate benefactors in order to resist and subdue any threat to predictability and tranquility. Jonathan foresees this, realizing that he will continue to be adored by the masses only so long as he submits to his role as an instrument of the corporation. At one point in the film we even overhear debauched partygoers at an Energy Corporation gathering who speculate that rollerball players are simply robots programmed for the purpose of playing the game. If Jonathan's rebelliousness were to result in any sort of decline in the efficiency with which the necessities and luxuries of life were delivered to these people, they would be certain to do away with him the way that they would do away with a malfunctioning machine. He himself would have become "unhandy" to those around him. As Nietzsche repeatedly observes, the herd's love of the Superman is never unconditional. When working toward purposes and goals that promote their group interests, the herd loves the Superman. However, since his strength cannot invariably be controlled, the herd also fears the possibility that the Superman may go his own way, becoming an impediment, rather than an asset to the group's way of life. Under such circumstances, it would be usual for the masses to turn against such an individual in an effort to protect their familiar and comfortable routines. Jonathan has now reached the point at which he is being forced to make a choice between retirement to the junk heap or resistance to the corporate machine. Furthermore, since the purposes of the corporate machine have the unwavering support of the herd, Jonathan, if he chooses resistance, is taking on the entire world, and this is a battle that he is bound, tragically, to lose.

The characters of Jonathan and Moonpie represent two aspects of the human attitude toward nihilism. In Moonpie, we see a character that does not care to reflect on the value or worth of his life. Since, unlike Jonathan, he has never been put in a position where he has to worry about his place in the world, he has never had the motivation to question the meaning of life. He remains content and happy with the things that he has earned, and which have been granted to him by the corporation. Moonpie is mystified as to why Jonathan would even be curious about the be-hind-the-scenes workings of corporate culture, since he himself has never had the occasion to experience discomfort or anxiety as a result of the outcomes of these workings. He represents that aspect of the human personality that doesn't want to make waves, but would rather take what the world has to offer without question. Moonpie desires stasis, predictability, and the absence of anxiety, and he rejects anything that threatens to destabilize this contented state of being. Yet his state is one of ignorance and, in the terminology of Heidegger, it consequently "covers over" the true nature of Being itself. In his contentedness, Moonpie refuses to raise the question of Being in the first place, and by refusing to raise such a question, he remains alienated from Being, and thus in a state of unreflective, though non-anxious, ontological nihilism. Thus, Moonpie exhibits the characteristics of an "in-authentic" individual, or one who has become "tranquilized" by the distractions of his world. As Heidegger writes, "The supposition . . . that one is leading a full and genuine 'life' brings a tranquilization to Da-sein, for which everything is in 'the best order' and for whom all doors are open. . . . This tranquilization is inauthen-tic being."[9]

Jonathan, on the other hand, experiences a chronic state of anxiety through-out the film. At one point he too was like Moonpie, but now a sense of existential nihilism has become overwhelming for him. Though he may wish that he could turn back and become more tranquil like his friend, Jonathan is unable to do so. His existential angst has opened the doors of reality to him, revealing that there is more to life than just his own comfort. To remain passive and content is no longer an op-tion now that he has caught a glimpse of the world beyond his rollerball career. What would he do once he retired? Certainly he would have luxuries, women, and money. But Jonathan has come to realize that these sorts of things are not ends in themselves. For him, material goods are worthwhile only as measures of his indi-vidual struggles. As he says to his ex-wife at one point in the film, "It's like peo-ple had a choice a long time ago between all them nice things or freedom. Of course they chose comfort." For Jonathan, happiness and material goods are not equivalent. For him, happiness is to be found in struggle, contest, and the freedom to push himself to new heights.

Despite their opposing reactions to the threat of nihilism, Jonathan neverthe-less cares for his teammate. We see this when, in a game against Tokyo, Moonpie is injured and falls into a persistent vegetative state. Since Moonpie apparently has no other family to see to his affairs, it is up to Jonathan to sign the papers that would authorize ending life support for his friend. Jonathan refuses to do so. Ear-lier, Moonpie had tried to convince Jonathan that his life was perfect, and now Jonathan sees in Moonpie's brain-dead state the sort of stasis, predictability, and lack of anxiety that Moonpie sought all along. There are beautiful nurses to take care of him, fresh cut flowers to add color to his quiet room, nutrition provided in-travenously, and perhaps even dreams to keep him entertained. When Jonathan tells the doctor to "Just leave him as he is," he is, in fact, recognizing that Moonpie's life is not substantially different now from how it always was. The corporation always did (and now always will) supply him with the comforts of life. Now, at least, he doesn't have to play rollerball to get them.

When Moonpie's doctor tells Jonathan that there are hospital rules that must be followed, Jonathan reacts in a controlled, yet angry manner by responding "No there aren't! There are no rules!" It is in this statement that Jonathan finally articulates an important insight that he has been grasping at throughout the course of the film. As he has fallen farther and farther away from his old, comfortable, and predictable way of life, he has come to see that, as Nietzsche warned, "the total character of the world is in all eternity chaos."[10] Rules are human-created illusions useful only for fending off the chaos of reality. Though we often fool ourselves, taking comfort in the thought that there are objectively valid guidelines and standards of judgment existing "out there" in the world around us, the truth is that we, as individuals, are ultimately responsible for making our own way and carving our own path through life. There are no rules, no universal values, and no absolutely certain set of "facts" about reality that can serve as the cornerstones of an authentic life. Instead, human beings are radically alienated from the totality of Being, and in our vain struggles to understand Being itself, the human mind always falls short of its goal. Anytime that we try to bring an end to our struggle with reality by claiming that one set of rules or facts is indisputable, we lapse into laziness, inauthenticity, and self-deceit.

This point is driven home to Jonathan when, earlier in the film, he seeks out information about corporate decision making and corporate history. Since all of the world's books have been summarized and digitized as computer files, he must travel to the world's storehouse of information: a supercomputer named Zero. Upon his arrival, Jonathan is informed by the head computer scientist (Ralph Richardson) that Zero has misplaced the entire thirteenth century. "Not much in the thirteenth century," he is told. "Just Dante and a few corrupt popes." The sheer volume of facts that Zero has been entrusted with is overwhelming, even for a machine. There are just too many details about the world to store or to recall, and Jonathan is told that Zero is continually confused as a result. Not even a supercomputer can recollect everything that has ever happened, and if there is no brain big enough to recall the "truths" of history, what good are those "truths"? Jonathan is told, in fact, that it is as if Zero "knows nothing at all." When Jonathan asks Zero about corporate decision making, the computer answers in a series of tautologies: "Corporate decisions are made by corporate executives. Corporate executives make corporate decisions." All of the bits of information, all of the "facts" that Zero has stored, amount to nothing in the final evaluation. Absolute certainties are, when it comes right down to it, useless tautologies. As David Hume observed, propositions that offer us certainty tell us nothing new or useful about the world, and those statements that do tell us something new or useful are always uncertain. But whereas Hume recommended a form of "mitigated skepticism" in response to this state of affairs, suggesting that we go along with convention rather than struggling against it, Jonathan follows another path. He concludes that no authority, no so-called expert can tell you what is real. In the end, it is up to you as an individual to aspire to your own vision of the Truth, to struggle toward it, and to ignore the distractions that always threaten to pull you away from it. It is up to each individual human mind to impart meaning, coherence, and significance to the information that it collects. When our hero turns to Zero for an answer to his nagging questions about life, he is rewarded with nothing—zero. Here lies Jonathan's most profound lesson: No one, not even those who are the smartest, strongest, and most erudite, are in touch with absolute Truth or Being.

At the end of the film, Jonathan will play one last game of rollerball, during which all rules have been suspended. This final match is intended as a fight to the death, and the corporation heads anticipate that Jonathan will be killed during its course; thus reducing him to "zero." Jonathan, however, has learned his lessons very well, and as his awareness of ontological nihilism grows, so too does his resolve to fight even harder against it. In the final scene of the film, the ominous sounds of *Toccata and Fugue in D Minor* once again resonate. As the crowd of spectators chants his name, and the corporate executives angrily look on, Jonathan E. remains the last man standing in the rollerball arena. Alone, he skates around the track until the movie ends in freeze-frame, and we, the audience, are once again, as at the beginning of the film, left with the feeling that no good will come of this. Though Jonathan may have triumphed in the roller rink, he is still a stranger to the vast, hostile world "out there." When he steps off of the track, the qualities that allowed him to excel as a sports star—individualism, nonconformity, iconoclasm, and a thirst for victory—will be the very qualities that are sure to bring him, yet again, into conflict with the herd and corporate culture. Nothing has been resolved at the end of the film, in other words, and our suspicion is that as one man against the entire world, Jonathan E. is certainly fated for eventual destruction. His struggles have led nowhere and accomplished nothing, and yet we are left with a feeling of admiration for Jonathan's integrity and strength of character. Herein lies his nature as a tragic hero.

## *Rollerball* (2002): A Postmodern Nihilist Opportunist

The tone set at the beginning of the 2002 remake of *Rollerball* is more frenetic, more action-packed, and ultimately, far more superficial than that of the original. We are introduced to the main character, Jonathan Cross, as he rockets down the winding streets of San Francisco. Now transformed into a twenty-something airhead, in this opening scene Jonathan skillfully avoids collision with cars and eludes the police while taking part in an illegal street luge contest. His competitor ends up losing control, smashing through a storefront window while Jonathan is rescued from arrest by his friend Marcus Ridley (LL Cool J), who pulls him off of his street-luge board and into a speeding car. Instead of the ominous and unsettling tone of Bach's *Toccata and Fugue in D Minor*, all of this is played out against a rock-and-roll soundtrack that reinforces a feeling of speed, action, and excitement.

It is in Ridley's car that we learn Jonathan is a failed hockey star. He has been unable to make it into the major leagues, and instead has had to pursue his quest for fame in the world of illegal extreme sports. Unlike his precursor in the original film, Jonathan Cross is introduced to us as an outsider who lacks the talent required to excel in his first choice of career. His friend suggests that he abandon hockey and instead sign up to play on a rollerball team. In this film it turns out that rollerball is no longer a product of corporate powers that rule the world, but is, rather, a moneymaking spectacle created by Eastern-European gangsters who are riding the wave of chaos that resulted after the breakup of the Soviet Union. This is quite an interesting reversal. Recall that in the original film, rollerball was a means of social control, utilized by ruling corporate entities to demonstrate the futility of individual effort. It was depicted as a product of the artificial, yet strict order that corporate forces had imposed upon the world. In the 2002 version of the film, on the other hand, rollerball is a sport arising out of chaos and the breakdown of order. The climate of corporate control has been replaced by the climate of anarchy. Whereas Jonathan E. struggled against a powerful, unified, and omnipresent corporate threat, Jonathan Cross struggles against the threats of fragmentation and lawlessness.

Jonathan Cross, like his precursor Jonathan E., is caught in the grip of existential nihilism. However the root cause of his malaise, and thus his response to it, is quite different from Jonathan E's. For Cross, his feeling of existential alienation derives not from being torn away from success, but from personal failure in his professional career. Cross, unlike E., never was a success. His desire to become a rollerball player is a second choice, pursued only after he fails at everything else that he really wanted to do. When he departs for Zhambal, Kazakhstan, and joins the "Horsemen," Jonathan discovers a sense of place and at-homeness that is new to him. He is transformed from an outsider and a criminal into an integral part of a bigger sports machine. Here we get to see a different, postmodern perspective on the problem of existential nihilism. The problem, it seems, is not that Jonathan has fallen away from his world, but rather that he never was part of any particular world in the first place. His feelings of unease might, hence, be alleviated by pursuing, and integrating himself into, any environment whatsoever. The particular sport that he plays and the particular set of rules or ideals that he follows are not so important. All that is important is to become a success, and in this remake, success is defined by all of the trappings that Jonathan E. rejected in the first film: money, possessions, sexy women, and screaming fans. So it is that we see Jonathan Cross racing around in expensive sports cars, going to trendy night clubs, sleeping with models, and so forth. He is happy here, and for a while, at least, his sense of existential angst dissipates.

As has already been noted, one of the characteristics of the postmodern response to nihilism is to reject old ideals and goals that, from the postmodernist's viewpoint, appear simply to be pipe dreams, incapable of fulfillment. Why torture yourself by working toward objectives that will never be reached? Why continue struggling to hit a target that is infinitely far away? As Lyotard has observed, such a life can only end in despair, and the experience of nihilism results from the failure to realize this fact. Instead, Lyotard has advised that we wage "war on totality." The postmodern hero, in this regard, is one who recognizes the absurdity of struggling toward absolute ideals, and who rejects despair and frustration by "lowering the bar," so to speak, setting new, attainable goals in place of the old, unattainable ones. Like Jonathan Cross, the postmodernist is a sort of opportunist and a pragmatist who is not committed to any particular vision of perfection, but is willing to bend in order to fit whatever world will accept him or her into its domain. Prewritten "metanarratives" are to be rejected and instead we are encouraged to make up the rules as we go along. Success and happiness may be discovered in compromise, accommodation, and flexibility rather than in single-minded commitment and determination. Thus, for Jonathan Cross, hockey is no more desirable than rollerball. What matters is to find a niche, a home, and a place to fit in. This is the only escape from existential nihilism according to the postmodernist. Because nihilistic feelings derive from a silly attachment to outdated ideals and old-fashioned goals, all that is needed in order to overcome these feelings is to reject the traditional pursuits that have led to frustration, and so Jonathan Cross leaves the US and finds his contentment in the chaos and anarchy of Eastern Europe. Though in his home country he is an outsider and a criminal, in another, more unstable culture, he can be a hero and a role model.

However, as he quickly distinguishes himself overseas as the star of the Horsemen, Jonathan begins to sense that his triumph is had at the expense of other people. The irony of Jonathan's newfound success is that the very conditions that allow him to prosper are also the conditions that are repressing those around him. His teammates are treated as expendable parts by the team's owner. Not only are their player numbers tattooed on their faces, marking them as property, but when the viewing audience enjoys seeing players killed in action, the owner organizes the deaths of various members of the team. Furthermore, it turns out that the main audience for rollerball is composed of economically disadvantaged mine workers who toil like slaves for the very individual who owns Jonathan's team. It is here that we get a faint echo of one of the themes that was first sounded in the original film. There is some sort of nefarious force that is orchestrating rollerball in order to keep the proletarian masses placid and content. The difference in the remake, however, is that the force behind rollerball is a greedy individual who is out to exploit the current social disorder. In the original film, on the other hand, the force behind rollerball, though represented by Mr. Bartholomew, is more shadowy and corporate. It was not out of greed that the corporations created the game, but out of a desire to maintain comfort, safety, and security for the entire world. In the original film, the enemies are a corporate suit, a culture of conformity, and a world in which the individual is subsumed by the masses. In the remake, the enemies are the leather-clad, unshaven Eastern-European gangster Alexi Petrovich (Jean Reno), a culture of disorder, and a world in which the masses are exploited by greedy individuals.

Though the new version of *Rollerball* was obviously intended as an action-packed adventure film, the action sequences are so ill-conceived and executed that they are ridiculous rather than exciting. The rollerball matches take place on a roller rink that is tiny and too filled with gadgets and contraptions to give us a clear view of the contest as it takes place. Because there is no letup in the violence even outside of the roller rink, the games do not shock us or even hold our attention for very long. Instead of the somber and foreboding organ music of the corporate anthem, the matches are accompanied by rock bands playing on the sidelines. Instead of Bach, it is Pink, Slipknot, and Rob Zombie that provide the soundtrack for the film. The mood that is thus conjured up is not contemplative, but frenzied and distracted. We are not encouraged to care about the feelings of the main character but to anticipate his next violent and audacious maneuver. Action instead of reflection seems to be the keynote here. Whereas in the original version the three pivotal game sequences were masterfully executed, providing important anchor points around which the rest of the story unfolded, in the new version, the game sequences seem almost incidental to everything else that is occurring in the movie. During the rollerball matches, the actors are filmed in close-up, so the audience misses out on the overall scope and sweep of the games. Each character is given an "outrageous" name, costume, and personality, transforming them into cartoon characters that resemble contemporary professional wrestlers. There are even sequences where a trading card of each of the players is superimposed over (and thus allowed to obscure) the rollerball action scenes. All of this contributes to a very particular vision of individuality that distinguishes the message of this remake from that of the original.

In the postmodern world, individuality is expressed through superficial diversity. To be a postmodern individual is to be unique in appearance, thought, and orientation, though at the same time to be tolerant of the differences that others exhibit. As Richard Rorty puts it, the aim is to pursue "an expanding repertoire of alternative descriptions rather than The One Right Description."[11] For the postmodernist, one's individuality derives from the willingness to take action and to resolutely construct a unique vision of reality. Such visions have no grounding in absolute Truth, but are simply interesting expressions of particular perspectives and viewpoints. The personal narrative, rather than the overarching "metanarrative," is the model. The only real "sin" for the postmodernist is to impose one's personal narrative too vigorously on others. Toleration, liberality, and openness to the "other" are defining characteristics of postmodern ethics, and in the new version of *Rollerball* we see an expression of this view. While Jonathan Cross searches for his place in the world, he is depicted as someone who is not content to occupy that place to the detriment of others. Though intent on fulfilling his individual desires, he does so with the presupposition that everyone else is free to do so as well.

When he discovers that there is a domineering force behind the game of rollerball that is keeping others from their own desires, he revolts and vows to lead the oppressed in a war against this force. Thus Jonathan becomes a revolutionary leader precisely because he desires to be an individual among other individuals. The players and spectators that he rallies are of all different colors, nationalities, appearances, sexes, and dispositions. This sort of diversity is good in itself, according to the postmodernist hero. On the other hand, the sort of individualism that the team owner embodies is of a different kind. It is the individuality of the tyrant, and this is a type of individual that the postmodernist detests. Such an individual disregards the diverse views of others, believing that his or her view is the "One Right Description" of reality. But this is intolerable for the postmodern hero for whom there is no one right description, no overarching Truth concerning the nature of reality. The freedom to pursue diverse forms of happiness is what is important, and anything that gets in the way of this, including artificial standards of Truth, is rejected as oppressive.

The 2002 version of *Rollerball* ends, unlike the 1975 version, on an optimistic, and distinctively non-tragic, note. During the climax of the film, Petrovich trades Jonathan's teammate/love interest, Aurora (Rebecca Romijn-Stamos), to a rival rollerball team. As the final game commences, both teams turn their violence not against each other, but rather toward the owners and organizers of the match, leading the audience in a mass rebellion against the corrupt gangsters who have exploited them. Whereas the original version of the film ends with Jonathan E. alone and in freeze-frame as that ominous organ music plays, this film ends with Jonathan Cross and Aurora in the midst of a mob of rioting mine workers. Aurora says to Jonathan (as they make their way through the crowd and into the back of a truck), "You have started yourself a revolution." She then tells him that she wants to take him home "to her bed," kissing him as a rock song by Rob Zombie fills the soundtrack. The revolution is thus ushered in, not as a frightening and ominous prospect, but as a sexy, exciting, and hopeful adventure.

## The Ethical, Political, and Cultural Implications of Nihilism in the *Rollerball* Films

Traditionally, nihilism has been viewed as an unequivocally negative and life-denying phenomenon that should be avoided, left behind, or overcome at all costs. Philosophers tend to emphasize the anguish, despair, and torment that is associated with nihilistic struggle, suggesting that the experience of nihilism has nothing at all positive about it. If our examination of the old and new versions of *Rollerball* has taught us anything, however, it has taught us that this traditional viewpoint is simplistic. In truth, "[t]he essence of nihilism contains nothing negative."[12] While the separation of human beings from their highest objects of aspiration certainly is a situation that promotes frustration, torment, and anxiety, at the same time it creates the potential for activity, struggle, and the progressive pursuit of greater and greater levels of achievement. As finite creatures, absolute perfection always remains beyond our grasp, and yet the unending aspiration toward perfection may be the very thing that bestows dignity and worth upon us as human beings. Though this aspiration may often be accompanied by feelings of negativity, it would be a mistake, for that reason, to blind ourselves to the potentially positive power of nihilistic struggle. Both Jonathan E. and Jonathan Cross are examples of characters that use their experience of nihilism, not as an excuse to give up on life, but as a motivation for continued aspiration and activity. While the particular targets they pursue may differ, neither character simply gives up and rolls over in order passively to accept the injustices of the world. Rather, these characters remain alive, vigorous, and vital in the face of a hostile environment.

While it is clear that both versions of *Rollerball* confront the threat of nihilism, neither film advocates the variety of nihilism that Nietzsche has labeled "passive nihilism." Passive nihilism is a symptom of "decline and recession of the power of the spirit."[13] It occurs at the point when the individual is no longer motivated to pursue humanly created goals. Because all worthwhile goals seem out of reach to the passive nihilist, this individual comes to think that all actions in the world are inconsequential and therefore meaningless. For this reason, the passive nihilist withdraws, submissively giving in and renouncing any concern or care for the struggles of life, or for Being itself. This is, of course, quite unlike the attitude of either Jonathan E. or Jonathan Cross. Both of these characters are supremely active in their nihilism, finding in it an opportunity for the expression of strength, energy, and concern for the world.

However, the mere expression of "will to power" is not an unequivocally commendable thing, and so active nihilism is not, in and of itself, necessarily to be lauded. One of the dangers faced by the active nihilist is that this individual can all too easily fall into a distracted state of busyness, squandering his or her energies on pursuits and goals that lead farther and farther away from, rather than closer to, an attuned awareness of Being itself. This, I think, is the main distinction to be made between the activities of Jonathan E. and Jonathan Cross. Whereas Jonathan E. embodies the active nihilism of a modern Superman who retains an authentic, individual attunement to Being itself, Jonathan Cross embodies the active nihilism of a postmodern pragmatist who has become distracted by the world of the crowd. In his eagerness to overcome nihilism, the character of Jonathan Cross, ironically, becomes ever more entangled in it by losing himself and willfully becoming an instrument for social revolution. As Heidegger writes, "The will to overcome nihilism mistakes itself because it bars itself from the revelation of the essence of nihilism as the history of the default of Being, bars itself without being able to recognize its own deed."[14] Like Jonathan Cross, those who are too concerned with overcoming nihilism tend to forget that nihilism is itself an aspect of Being. As such, nihilism is not something to be avoided, or left behind as quickly as possible. Rather, it is a phenomenon that should be lingered over and taken as an opportunity to develop a greater, more authentic, understanding of ourselves, our world, and the relationships that hold between the two.

By scrutinizing the plots of both versions of *Rollerball*, I have revealed a number of common issues that are explored in these two films. In both movies we are introduced to a character that is caught in the grip of existential anxiety. This anxiety in both cases derives from the main character's inability to harmonize with the world around him, and this disharmony, in each case, provokes a search for solutions. In both films, furthermore, the main characters undergo a sort of philosophical transformation in the course of their search. By actively choosing to reflect on the underlying ontological circumstances that have contributed to their anxiety, these characters confront the issue of nihilism. But this is where similarities end, for the original version of *Rollerball* depicts the confrontation with nihilism from a modernist perspective, while the remake depicts it from a postmodernist perspective. In the former case, Jonathan E. is compelled by his conscience tragically to face his destiny alone, rejecting all of the social distractions that threaten to pull him away from the one thing that remains valuable to him: an authentic and conscious awareness of himself and his relationship to Being. Conversely, in the latter case, Jonathan Cross optimistically embraces the "crowd," discovering an escape from the anxiety of nihilism through his entanglement with others in their common rebellion against tyranny and domination. Who he is is nothing more than who he appears to be to those around him. Whereas Jonathan E. attempts to reconnect with his own Being in the course of a struggle against the herd, Jonathan Cross attempts to find a place and function within the herd. In these differing approaches to the problem of nihilism, we see the initial development of a number of themes that never gain full voice in the text of the films, but which deserve more extensive articulation nonetheless. One concerns the ethical implications of nihilism, and the other concerns nihilism's political ramifications. Before closing, I would like briefly to discuss these issues and to suggest that what we find here casts an interesting light on contemporary American attitudes concerning Goodness, Justice, and the meaning of life itself.

Implicit in the plot of the original version of *Rollerball* is an ethical message. That message states that the best way to live one's life is not in the pursuit of pleasure, prestige, and fortune, but rather in the pursuit of personal authenticity. Jonathan E. is a tortured and profoundly unhappy man, an individual who, as his friend Moonpie tells him, "has it all!" yet who finds no comfort in this fact. There is more to life than shallow pleasures, Jonathan seems to think, and insofar as we, the audience, are led to sympathize with this character, we agree with him. What makes him so sympathetic to us is his desire to understand himself and his purpose in life, even if this leads to professional and personal ruin. Public adoration, money, and prestige are, for Jonathan E., all distractions that have pulled him away from an awareness of his authentic self. The powers of the corporation have transformed Jonathan into a "thing," a marketable product, a veritable instrument that, in the end, has outlived its usefulness. It is only when discarded and cast aside by the

Energy Corporation that Jonathan rediscovers his true life's ambition. It never was his purpose to acquire goods, fame, and wealth. Rather, all along these were only ways to understand his place in, and his connection with, the world around him. By becoming too focused on things at the expense of an awareness of himself, Jonathan became distracted and forgot what is really important in life. His message to us, the audience, is that the best life is one in which the individual refuses to forget that the adoration of the crowd is incidental, and even detrimental, to understanding who you are. In the short story that inspired the film, Jonathan E. ineloquently sums up these feelings in a conversation with Mr. Bartholomew:

> [Bartholomew] "You don't want out of the game?" he asks wryly.
> [Jonathan] "No, not at all. It's just that I want—god, Mr. Bartholomew, I don't know how to say it: I want more."
> He offers a blank look.
> [Jonathan] "But not things in the world," I add. "More for me."[15]

This point is lost, and an entirely different ethical message is conveyed, in the remake of the film twenty-seven years later. Instead of pulling away from particular "things in the world," Jonathan Cross actively pursues those things, finding happiness and purpose in his worldly entanglements. The crowd becomes a means of escape from his personal dissatisfaction. In solidarity with the group, Jonathan finds himself not only loved, but endowed with a purpose and meaning to his life. Whereas the open-endedness of the original film (and short story) suggests that the threat of nihilism has not been, and never will be, overcome, in the new version Jonathan's transformation into a revolutionary leader suggests that he has not only found his place, but that he will, in fact, change the world and make it a better place for everyone. Though the audience may find it hard to sympathize with this poorly-drawn character, the message that he delivers is clear: we should not withdraw into ourselves and reclusively contemplate who we are. In fact, we are nothing until we make ourselves into something, and we make ourselves into something by doing things, making connections with others, and bending the world to suit our will. The best way to live life, in sum, is to find a place in "the crowd" and to make a contribution. In this, we hear the voices of Lyotard and Rorty drowning out the pleas of Nietzsche, Camus, and Heidegger, and we also get the hint of a political message.

The original version of *Rollerball* takes place after the "Corporate Wars," which presumably were times of chaos and disorder. After these wars, the world has become safe, comfortable, and predictable. The inner, existential crisis that Jonathan E. faces is largely a reaction against the life of comfort and conformity that he otherwise enjoys. Jonathan E., in rejecting his success as a part of the "establishment," is the type of individualistic rebel who wants nothing to do with corporate culture. We get the sense that he, like Socrates and Plato before him, holds a very dim view of the masses and their group choices. Most people would "choose things over freedom," as Jonathan tells Ella, and so most people are not equipped to know what a good life really consists of. In this we sense a sort of antidemocratic sentiment. The masses are stupid followers. They chant slogans taught to them by those who give them what they want, and to put political power in their hands would be to produce a world where, instead of Justice, things, goods, and consumer products are the targets of collective decision making.

On the other hand, the remake of *Rollerball* takes place in the midst of political and social disorder. Jonathan Cross initially finds his place in this milieu, but he soon reacts against it, the way that Jonathan E. reacts against the stability of corporate culture, forming alliances with others in order to pursue effective revolutionary activity. Furthermore, it is with the working classes, the "people," that Jonathan finds his allegiance, not with the exploitative gang bosses. The political message delivered here seems to be that it is only because of oppression that the people appear to be stupid followers. If given the opportunity, the means, and the proper leadership, the masses will pursue the best course of action. This will draw them into a public realm where they will be less concerned with selfish desires, and more concerned with collective justice. Collective justice, furthermore, is understood as the freedom of each individual to be happy, and so, in the final analysis, political activity must be focused on the utilitarian ideal that the best government is one that brings the largest number of people the most amount of happiness.

One suspects that Jonathan E. and Jonathan Cross would not like one another very much. The change in how this main character has been depicted is quite interesting, not only from the perspective of a film critic, but also from the perspective of an American citizen. While it is difficult to fault the democratic sentiments of the remake, it is also hard to sympathize with the shallowness of its characters and the disregard that they seem to have for personal authenticity. American culture changed between the times that these two films were made, and not necessarily for the better. While we may be increasingly confident about our group causes, and more aggressive about asserting our collective will, we have also become less philosophical and, perhaps, concerned with "things" and with manipulating the details of the world more than ever before. The two versions of *Rollerball* are not just movies. They are, in fact, symptoms of the way that Americans think about themselves and their relationship to Being itself. Made shortly after America's defeat in the Vietnam War, the original film was the expression of a people seeking a deep, personal, and reflective understanding of who they are as individuals separate from the crowd. The remake, on the other hand, was made during a period of time when America was gearing up to fight terrorism and foreign enemies. In it we find the expression of a people more concerned with directing their attentions outwards, away from the self, and with banding together in order to alter reality in accordance with collective desires. Whereas the original film is structured around settings of meditative quiet and reflection that are punctuated by action and violence, the remake consists of an uninterrupted barrage of violence, rock music, and unreflective action. Things certainly have changed quite a bit in twenty-seven years, and, it is worth repeating, not necessarily for the better.

# Notes

A previous version of this essay appeared in *Film and Philosophy* 8 (2004): 91–111. The author wishes to thank the editors of the journal for permission to reprint it.

1. Friedrich Nietzsche, *The Will to Power* (New York: Vintage Books, 1967), 9.

2. Albert Camus, "An Absurd Reasoning," in *The Myth of Sisyphus and Other Essays* (New York: Vintage Books, 1955), 20–21.

3. Michael Novak, *The Experience of Nothingness* (New York: Harper Torchbooks, 1970), 11.

4. Camus, "An Absurd Reasoning," 14.

5. Nietzsche, *The Will to Power*, 520.

6. Camus, *The Myth of Sisyphus and Other Essays*, 91.

7. Jean-François Lyotard, *The Postmodern Condition: A Report on Knowledge* (Minneapolis: University of Minnesota Press, 1997), 82.

8. Friedrich Nietzsche, *The Birth of Tragedy* (New York: Dover Publications, 1995), 77.

9. Martin Heidegger, *Being and Time* (Albany: State University of New York Press, 1996), 166.

10. Friedrich Nietzsche, *The Gay Science* (New York: Vintage Books, 1974), 168.

11. Richard Rorty, *Contingency, Irony and Solidarity* (Cambridge: Cambridge University Press, 1989), 39–40.

12. Martin Heidegger, *Nietzsche, Volume Four: Nihilism* (San Francisco: Harper Collins, 1991), 221.

13. Nietzsche, *The Will to Power*, 17.

14. Heidegger, *Nietzsche, Volume Four: Nihilism*, 240.

15. William Harrison, *Rollerball Murder* (New York: Warner Books, 1975), 81–82.

*Chapter 6*

# Hollywood's Remake Practices under the Copyright Regime: French Films and Japanese Horror Films

## Myoungsook Park

Trade is much more than goods and services. It's an exchange of ideas. Ideas go where armies cannot venture. The result of idea exchange as well as trade is always the collapse of barriers between nations.—Jack Valenti (2000)[1]

For contemporary filmmakers outside the United States, it often seems that festival prizes, worldwide box-office revenue, and unanimous critical applause are mere stepping-stones to the ultimate achievement of having their film consigned and co-opted by an American studio. As Hollywood runs increasingly dry of original ideas, it is little surprise that foreign remakes are becoming more profitable and, thus, more prevalent in the industry. It is a (moderately) greater surprise that the preferred format for critical response to these Hollywood remakes of foreign originals remains as uninventive as the films they purport to assess. Most critical reception surrounding a remake continues to focus primarily on textual analysis. The twin texts, Original and Remake, are critically contained and compared to one another, so that the qualities of each are seen only as reversals of the other's failures. The comparison often ends with a value judgment determining that the Hollywood remake ultimately fails to maintain the authenticity established by the text and aesthetics of the original.[2] This dominant trend of textual analysis is based on the binary poles of the original/copy dichotomy. The original vs. copy dichotomy harkens back to traditional art criticism, and makes assumptions that are almost certainly misleading in regards to the film industry. This critical response is based on the idea of the artist as an originator. Since fidelity to the artist's 'original' vision is considered good, the prioritization of original/originality is embedded in the dichotomy. The copy is immediately assigned a negative value. Thus, it is not surprising that debates usually view remake practices negatively, and Hollywood products are concluded as being aesthetic failures.

This tendency of previous academic research to favor textual analysis, and the relative paucity of legal and economic perspectives in regards to remakes, is certainly problematic. I feel it is of greater importance not to determine how Hollywood remakes inevitably fail, either aesthetically or artistically, but to show how the studios themselves ultimately prevail by exploiting current copyright laws and guidelines. I want to shift interest from the original/copy dichotomy to the issue of property ownership, as related to intellectual property rights, more commonly known as copyrights.

These rights establish ninety-five years of exclusive, protective ownership of intangible properties, variously called content, knowledge, information, or entertainment. Copyright is a legal protection for exporters/producers, not for importers/consumers. Hollywood has no interest in limiting its role in the distribution of foreign originals. The copyright regime motivates Hollywood to fill its libraries with domestic remakes of foreign films, in order to claim total control over its property. Thus, remake practices are fundamentally economic practices, which work to minimize foreign imports into the US domestic market, and to maximize Hollywood exports into the worldwide market. Remake practices are an integral part of Hollywood's strategy to maintain the global dominance of its products, while concurrently suppressing the products of its competition, that is, other national cinemas. The current remake practice further serves a political function; it is an example of cultural imperialism. Not only do Hollywood films generate extensive global revenue, as unique products which can be sold and resold an unlimited number of times, but they also act as commercials promoting other popular American products through their content. Of course, the product they most clearly promote is the illusory idealism of the American Dream itself, the capitalistic pride in style and material success that Hollywood itself has come to represent. In an era when 85% of the world's audiences are paying to see American films, one way in which the cultural Goliath of Hollywood perpetuates the current monopoly of content flow is by purchasing and remaking foreign hits.[3]

Hollywood studios are keenly aware of these accusations of cultural imperialism and, thus, they have developed various rhetorical strategies and rationales to justify their practices. I will try to explore and expose some of their strategic responses, including the discourse of the superiority of original texts, and the rhetoric in regards to exchange of culture. Hollywood has purposefully taken a humble stance, claiming that a remake is a way of showing respect to another story and another culture. In fact, Hollywood utilizes the remake trend as counterevidence of their continued global dominance. The first cycle of remakes I will focus on includes Hollywood remakes of French original films, produced from the mid-1980s until the early 1990s. During this cycle, the Hollywood argument defending remakes as exchange of culture and homage was more pronounced in order to ameliorate antagonistic French responses. My second area of focus occurs two decades later, when Hollywood entered another remake cycle, this time centered on Japanese horror films. The traditional defense claim of the remake as cultural exchange was augmented by the rhetoric of auteurism. By inviting Japanese directors to remake their own originals, Hollywood completed the rhetoric of homage/respect and utilized the notion of auteurism to claim that the director's vision remained intact, and that the remakes preserved the integrity of the originals. In the Japanese cases, this strategic auteurism smoothed the transfer of texts, and served to generate the warm, even celebratory, reaction by the Asian film industry of the remake trend, generating such responses as: "Takashi Shimizu, director of *The Grudge*, has become the second proud Japanese directing in Hollywood filmmaking 13 years after Akira Kurosawa."[4] "It is great that [the remakes are] happening. It's also giving [Asian] filmmakers a chance to work in the United States."[5] It seems evident from these comments that the Hollywood remake system benefits both parties, and this has proven to be true for certain individuals, in certain cases. However, the benefits for the foreign filmmaker are usually defined by a onetime payment, and the possibility of joining the same industrial power whose cultural dominance made their success so remarkable in the first place. Thus, by joining with the conquering force, these filmmakers may actually help to lessen the likelihood that one of their peers might repeat their own success.

In any case, in order to better analyze Hollywood's objectives and strategies in regard to remakes, as well as the ensuing repercussions of the remake trend, we must pay special attention to the grand scheme. In this paper, I will offer possible reasons why French and Japanese films were specifically chosen to be remade at certain points in time. This should help demonstrate how Hollywood's restructuring of global markets is intrinsically intertwined with the prevailing intellectual property paradigm. In the French case, I will focus on the broader political and historical context of the rise of copyright, and how Hollywood has worked to make these laws suitable to their various purposes over time. It is significant to mention the dramatic reversal of the US's approach to copyright. Until the mid-1980s, the US, now an avid patron of copyright, refused to join in the fight for copyright protection. Briefly, the context of copyright law can be used to connect the Hollywood remake craze for French films in the 1980s and the subsequent demise of this trend after the World Trade Organization (WTO) replaced the General Agreement on Tariffs and Trade (GATT), and began regulating legal issues of cultural trade.

I will then examine how the current remake practice, as exemplified by Japanese horror films, serves the globalization of Hollywood by offering both protection in the US market and intervention in the foreign market, all in the name of cultural translation. As mentioned, auteurism is highly promoted in order to conceal the remake as a cinematic takeover and shift focus from the studios, which are the real producers/beneficiaries of the film. I am also interested in determining the motivations behind the American tendency to overlook culturally specific semantics in Japanese horror films. The horror genre is inevitably labeled as one of the most universal genres whenever American film critics discuss Japanese horror remakes. Borrowing the methodology of previous textual research, I will show specific cultural elements of the original films that Hollywood has chosen to exclude in the remakes. However, as opposed to many previous critical analyses, my purpose is not to elevate the status of the originals by demonstrating the locality and cultural specificity of the Japanese horror genre. Rather, I argue that the original vs. copy reading actually conceals the arbitrariness of choices made in the remake. Textual choice is a mere disguise for financial choice. In the end, by securing ownership of the original under copyright protection, Hollywood benefits financially from both the critical elevation of the original and the favorable evaluation of the remake. In fact, whether positive or negative, any discussion at all surrounding the original/copy dichotomy is beneficial, as audiences are motivated to pay for both films, which often means double the profit for the studio.

## The First Remake Cycle: France

Since copyright protection has been successfully naturalized, it is difficult to envision the concept of copyright as an artificial invention of the nineteenth century. Its creation followed the new emphasis on authorship, a notion which allowed for artwork to be reduced to being the vision of a sole creator, the individual artist. Copyright laws were intended to provide security that authorship would ensure ownership.[6] The first notable international attempt to regulate the author's protective rights to prevent infringement occurred in 1878 at the *Congres Literaire International* in Paris. In his famous opening speech, Victor Hugo, one of the most successful writers of international readership, proposed a then-new idea that immaterial art work could be just as much a property as much as material goods.[7] Authorship was not yet tied to ownership, and popular opinion favored prioritizing fair use and public access to intellectual/intangible work. Thus, Hugo underplayed the theory of copyright as a property right and instead promoted the artist's noble cause by claiming that his/her works exist for the public's cultural good. He flamboyantly elaborated that copyright should be an incentive to create.

His speech greatly appealed to those people who had previously sided with producers and exporters, such as the French and British writers whose languages and cultures enjoyed elite status worldwide.[8] However, culturally developing countries which relied on imports in cultural trade did not fail to detect the imperialist implications of copyright. There was considerable anxiety that the new regulations of public use would contribute to reinforcing the supremacy of the few dominant national cultures. The US, then still a fledgling country, with a history marked by British colonialist rule, was especially hesitant about entering the domain of copyright law. The US held to the contentions of the developing countries, which ad-

vocated piracy and unauthorized use in order to help recover and construct a social and cultural infrastructure separate from the colonial past. It is fascinating to
revisit how the US justified various copyright infringements by claiming English
literature as a cultural heritage that could not be materialized as property:

> All the riches of English literature are ours. English authorship comes free as the
> vital air, untaxed, unhindered, even by the necessity of translation, into our coun-
> try; and the question is, Shall we tax it, and thus interpose a barrier to the circu-
> lation of intellectual and moral light? Shall we build up a dam, to obstruct the
> flow of the rivers of knowledge? . . . Shall we refuse to gather the share of this
> harvest, which Providence, and our own position, makes our own?[9]

The argument concerning copyright and cultural imperialism remains almost
identical today, but after a century of prosperity and growth, the US has dramatically reversed its argument. There is nothing mysterious about the reversal; it is
merely a condition based on the US position of power. Since World War II, the US
has shifted its identity to the side of exporter/producer in cultural trade, an area of
industry that has been radically accelerated by technology. Another contributing
factor in the momentous shift by the US in terms of copyright stance has been the
global trend of restructuring towards knowledge-based societies, in which the most
valued property is knowledge/information/content.[10] Once the US officially
switched its position, it moved at full throttle. In 1986, the US, once a bystander
in regards to copyright, finally joined the Berne Convention for the Protection of
Liberty and Artistic Works, the international convention first adopted in 1886 at
Hugo's instigation. The Uruguay Round of GATT also began in 1986 and, for the
first time, conflict over intellectual property was the main agenda. The US began
to take an active role in the arguments, which concluded in 1994 with the abandonment of GATT and the establishment of the WTO instead. GATT had regu-
lated trade during postwar years without significantly addressing copyright issues.
The replacement of GATT by the US-supported WTO, which deals with entertainment and intellectual property as its main commodities, marked a sea change
in the arena of international commerce. Ideas, rather than resources or materials,
were recognized as the most sacred commodities and those most in need of protection and regulation. Not coincidentally, this time span (between 1986 and 1994)
also marked the approximate boundaries of Hollywood's avid cycle of producing
remakes of French (and other European) films. The end of the French remake trend
overlapped with the inclusion of the entertainment sector in the WTO, and Hollywood's international dominance has been intricately interwoven with the WTO
regime ever since.
    It is well known that Hollywood has always kept a keen eye on the interna-
tional market.[11] However, beginning in the affluent 1980s and continuing to the
present time, the level of intensity with which Hollywood exports were pushed
steadily increased. From 1950–1980, overseas receipts had accounted for approximately one-third of Hollywood's annual revenue. It is important to note that these

figures did not change for three decades. By 1998, however, overseas box-office sales finally reached the same level as domestic income.[12] During the 1980s and 1990s, several nearly bankrupt major film studios completed lengthy restructuring programs and achieved economic resuscitation through the development of the blockbuster format. The Age of the Blockbuster marked the culmination of a full-fledged post-classical Hollywood. Finance capital created a pattern of movies with huge budgets, saturation advertising and release, and short-run cycles ("For a limited time only at a theater near you!"). The promotion of films as major cultural events has made the opening weekend gross the determining factor of a film's success or failure, and also made the courtship of a predominantly young audience absolutely imperative.[13] This filmmaking practice required a cost of (post) production unattainable by any other developed country.[14] By their very nature, the new Hollywood blockbusters were aimed at the widest audience possible in order to guarantee the biggest return on investment. The huge cost of production, marketing, and distribution went beyond the level that the US domestic market could support alone; it could not exist without securing the foreign market. Hollywood's global audience represents a quantity of capital essential to the industry's growth and success, and that capital requires that Hollywood entertainment be included in free trade pacts.[15]

Western Europe has always been the most lucrative foreign market for Hollywood.[16] The European and Hollywood film industries have influenced each other since the birth of the medium, although the relationship has often been oversimplified as a dichotomy between "film as art" vs. "film as entertainment/commodity."[17] An exodus of European talent took place between the two World Wars, and Hollywood had the opportunity to incorporate many art-cinema directors into its system, including Hitchcock, Lang, Renoir, and Murnau, to name just a few.[18] This influx of talent and capital helped Hollywood to establish and reinforce its unrivaled dominance of worldwide cinema. However, from the end of World War II until the 1980s, although Europe remained its top foreign market, Hollywood's share of European ticket sales did not noticeably increase. In the 1980s, the European audiences were increasingly drawn to their own domestic films.[19] Most notably, French cinema emerged as the most competitive, especially in art film venues. 'Cannes' and 'French cineastes' became the credentials of art movies, and French film succeeded in preserving a contrasting image to Hollywood's 'disposable' pop culture. Like Hollywood, the French film industry was one of the very few national film industries that cited foreign ticket sales as a significant portion of its national gross product. This threat of competition caused Hollywood to begin to localize French film and reassert itself as the predominant exporter in global cultural trade. The initial steps in this process were to identify French films that were box-office successes, acquire their rights, and remake them. Examples are numerous: *Trois Hommes et Un Couffin* (Coline Serreau, 1985)/*Three Men and a Baby* (Leonard Nimoy, 1987), *La Femme Nikita* (Luc Besson, 1990)/*Point of No Return* (John Badham, 1993), *Mon Père, ce Héros* (Gérard Lauzier, 1991)/*My Fa-*

*ther the Hero* (Steve Miner, 1994), *La Totale* (Claude Zidi, 1991)/*True Lies* (James Cameron, 1994), and many others.[20] The huge financial success of *Three Men and a Baby* convinced studios that the remake was profitable, and precipitated the later remake boom—the same function later served by *The Ring* in the Japanese case.

The French, having once been the world's most important cultural exporter, and being wary of practices of cultural imperialism, reacted against the Hollywood remakes. In order to disparage remakes, the popular rhetoric was judgmental of the quality of these cinematic texts. The remakes were viewed as easy copies plagiarized through Hollywood commercialism. However, there was also speculation about how remakes worked in terms of transferring ownership from the original to the remake. There were significant cultural and financial repercussions surrounding the reach these 'mere copies' could achieve outside of the French domestic market, where audiences are routinely bombarded with Hollywood product through the aid of its peerless distribution and marketing arm. The French called the remake a cultural form of theft, which worked by subverting the hierarchy between the original and its translation/copies. These remake practices established Hollywood's text as the universal version, capable of the international reach needed to invoke copyright protection.

This subversion of the hierarchy between the original and its copies/translation is paralleled by similar instances in literature. Specifically, when a non-English original is translated into English, the global ubiquity of the English language inevitably grants the translation a greater readership than the original. An English translation from another language, say, Danish, becomes the standard, and, consequently, any further translations come from the English text. In other words, eventually more people refer to the English translation than to the Danish original. For example, as Eva Hemmungs Wirten points out in regard to the international bestseller *Frøken Smillas fornemmelse for sne* (*Smilla's Sense of Snow*), the English translation has become the standard text from which non-English translation occurs due to English supremacy.[21] Nonetheless, literary authorship/ownership is still attributed to the Danish author, Peter Høeg. On the contrary, in the case of the remake, the original author—whether it be the director, the production company, or whomever—is easily replaced by Hollywood media conglomerates. For instance, *True Lies* is definitively a Twentieth Century Fox commodity with no obligation to reference *La Totale*. *True Lies* has access to countless places where *La Totale* cannot go.

With its remake practices, Hollywood has creatively manipulated the rhetoric of homage by claiming that its remakes remain as true to the originals as possible. One way to address this claim might be to state that extensive fidelity to a French original eventually serves to discourage an international audience from seeing the original, an argument which points towards the inherent contradiction of remakes. That is, if the original is such a masterpiece, and if Hollywood is willing to express such aesthetic respect for it, why not distribute *the original* worldwide with Hollywood's matchless distribution capacity? Why bother to spend millions more to remake a film that has already proven its drawing power?

First of all, the films Hollywood chooses to remake are rarely cinematic masterpieces. More often they are uncomplicated commercial films which have demonstrated box-office success by outperforming Hollywood in their domestic/regional markets. More importantly, as Luc Besson points out, when Hollywood studios acquire distribution and remake rights of French originals, they work actively to withhold, rather than to distribute, them.[22] In most cases, if the originals receive any theatrical distribution, it comes after the remake has completed its run in the theaters. Thus, by purchasing distribution rights, Hollywood keeps those works from competing with their remakes. In some cases, originals are not even distributed in the video market, which proves that importing and distributing them is never the main purpose of acquiring their rights. This is how the remake became the main tool used to marginalize imports and protect the domestic market.

The US domestic market has always been the biggest interest for Hollywood, even since 1998 when overseas box-office totals finally equaled domestic gross. As statistics show, the worldwide theatrical admission gross in 2003 was $21,680,000,000 ($21 billion, 680 million), and the US gross was 43.8% of that total, around $9,500,000,000 ($9.5 billion). From 1999–2003, people in the US went to theaters an average of 5.4 times in a year—which is the highest figure in the world. In other words, the US audience is 21.5% of the worldwide audience, and they go to the movies most frequently. Americans are the most loyal audience to their domestic film product with one exception—the Indian audience. 95% of film tickets bought in India are for domestic fare, and in the US that figure is 94.96%.[23] The loyalty of the American audience to Hollywood fare has been observed in terms of their strong resistance to subtitles and their cultural isolation, along with their indifference to world history and geography. But this stereotype of American audiences is partially due to the fact that Hollywood never allows foreign style and aesthetics to infiltrate theaters, even (or especially) when they remake foreign films. Hollywood remakes of foreign films typically go to great lengths to remove specific cultural and historical references and demystify the filmic narrative in order to universalize the text for global reception. The films are usually redone according to the blockbuster formula, which calls for the elimination of any element superfluous to the narrative, and the addition of big-budget attractions, such as stars and special effects. The remake trend reflects an unspoken cooperation between the American audience's resistance to non-Hollywood fare and a Hollywood that frames its American audience in a particular way and wants them to stay loyal.

In sum, the remake serves two distinct purposes: to provincialize non-US films and to protect the US domestic market from foreign films. Thus, from Hollywood's perspective, the remake is one of the most efficient tools for expanding their properties. Hollywood's remake process is fundamentally motivated by copyright ownership. The desire to capitalize on a film's proven popularity (i.e., profitability) is merely a secondary concern. As the contribution of copyright industries to the eco-

nomic gross continues to grow, the attention to copyright as property right necessarily prevails in terms of international business.[24] This business model is perhaps
best represented by the late Jack Valenti, who was one of the most influential pro-
copyright lobbyists during his thirty-eight years of tenure in MPAA (1966–2004).
As he proudly said:

> The facts are these: The Copyright industries . . . are America's greatest trade ex-
> port prize. They are responsible for some five percent of the GDP of the nation.
> They gather in more international revenues than automobiles and auto parts, more
> than aircraft, more than agriculture. They are creating NEW jobs at three times the
> rate of the rest of the national economy. The movie industry alone has a SUR-
> PLUS balance of trade with every single country in the world. No other Ameri-
> can enterprise can make that statement.[25]

As intellectual property law scholars point out, the copyright industry is marked
by a history of expansion, accumulation, and extension.[26] In an exporter/importer
matrix, an exporter of intellectual property has an inherent propensity towards ac-
cumulating more properties under its protection. The remake is an efficient, transformative instrument with which the importer becomes the exporter. In business
terms, a potential expense becomes revenue, and a competitor becomes a partner.
A Hollywood remake represents the cinematic version of the corporate buyout,
wherein a large conglomerate financially absorbs a successful smaller operation
with a niche market. It is no coincidence that Hollywood's worldwide exports increased twofold in value during the remake era (1987–1991), particularly thanks
to a conspicuous rise in the European markets. The remake practice can only be
contextualized in regards to this big picture.[27]

## The Second Remake Cycle: Japan

What happened in France then provides insights into what is happening in Asia in
the new millennium. The French remakes were surrounded by the rhetoric of the
remake as homage, cultural exchange, or Hollywood's search for creativity in foreign films. What is more remarkable now is the strangely celebratory reaction in
Asia to the current situation.[28] Many Asian filmmakers and critics have remarked,
with a strong tone of pride, that Hollywood is finally showing due respect to the
long-neglected Asian culture. Certainly, both sides have benefited financially from
remake fever. Hollywood obtains new ideas and commercially competitive narratives while paying what is, by its standards, a small portion of money. However,
these acquisition sums are much more financially significant for Asian filmmakers.[29] Furthermore, the Asian film industry gains a new market (albeit mainly DVD,
rather than theatrical), which had been formerly nonexistent. Thus, the Asian film
industry has tended to interpret the current trend favorably. However, the long-
term ramifications of the remakes, as forms of cinematic takeovers, have hardly

been mentioned. The immediate approval of the remake trend overlooks the fact that there is a decreased likelihood of the Asian originals being commercially distributed. The impact that the Hollywood Asian remake craze will have on Japanese and other Asian films is ambiguous. It is surely significant that the Japanese remake cycle accompanies the recent rapid economic rise of Asia, which will become Hollywood's largest foreign market within a decade. Another area for future attention should be possible reasons as to why, at the turn of the century, Japanese horror suddenly became worthy of remaking. Hollywood's strategies for foreign remakes have continued to develop since the success of the French case. First, the rhetoric of respect and fidelity to originals has evolved to fully embrace the concept of auteurism, which has led to invitations for certain Asian directors to accompany their films to Hollywood. By assigning the directorial job of the remake to the original directors, Hollywood claims that the remake stays true to the original and pays ultimate respect to the 'authors.' Another strategy involves the more thorough removal of cultural specificity from the films. These two points are absolutely interrelated.

When DreamWorks' *The Ring* (Gore Verbinski, 2002) grossed an estimated $129 million domestically and $249 million worldwide, it proved the marketability of the remake of Asian movies in the US.[30] Soon afterwards, Hideo Nakata, the director of *Ringu* and *Ringu 2*, was invited by Hollywood to direct *The Ring 2* (DreamWorks, 2005), based on his original *Ringu 2*.[31] Prior to Nakata, Takashi Shimizu, the director of the Japanese film *Ju-On*/呪怨, was invited to direct *The Grudge* (Sony Pictures Entertainment, 2004), based on his original. As verification of the lucrative economic possibilities of these remakes of Japanese horror movies, *The Grudge* and *The Ring 2* became, at the time, the biggest and the second biggest opening horror films in the United States.[32] The success also secured each director the ultimate Hollywood stamp of approval—the sequel. Shimizu directed *The Grudge 2* (Sony Pictures Entertainment) in 2006, and Hideo Nakata signed on to direct *The Ring 3* (Dreamworks, 2009 scheduled release). In today's Hollywood, a successful film spawning a sequel is far from noteworthy, but these two cases were exceptional for two reasons. First, despite a long history of remakes based on foreign originals, Hollywood has rarely assigned directorial jobs to non-European directors, or even to European directors, with the notable exception of the émigré directors of the interwar period. There is a distinct national boundary surrounding directorial jobs in Hollywood. So, for instance, *The Ring* was directed by an American director, Gore Verbinski, as was typical of foreign remakes up to that time. Also, as opposed to the long pre-Hollywood careers of John Woo or Akira Kurosawa, it is not an exaggeration to say that these Japanese directors boasted no international reputation before receiving Hollywood invitations.

To a great extent, the employment of Asian filmmakers in Hollywood proved to be a panacea. When the director of the original is allowed to direct the remake, the remake practice is predominantly considered a cinematic form of respect, even by fans dedicated to the superiority of the original. It virtually eliminates hostile responses, such as the following, which is common from 'fans' of Asian films. David Leong, online news editor of Kung Fu Cult Cinema (www.kfccinema.com), commented:

> Unfortunately, the studios don't think American audiences are intelligent enough to follow a movie plot that's not American. There's a lack of respect by Holly-wood studios that, in the end, irritates people. They change the flow of a movie, the intent of a scene; you change the original director's vision, and you end up with trash.[33]

Certainly there have been cautionary responses, although they are a distinct minority. For example, Chris Doyle, the cinematographer most well known for his collaborations with Wong Kar-Wai, said that "I don't care about the remakes . . . Let's put the money in our pockets. Asian society is moving ahead at full throttle, so you just go ahead and try to catch up. But this is also like a hostile takeover. I think it prefigures a talent grab."[34] Here, Doyle is referring to the fact that Holly-wood's attempted assimilation of Hong Kong noir films led to an exodus of talent. However, although it has been recognized that a director is not an equally signif-icant legal subject as a literary author, popularity of the traditional idea of author-ship prevails in the discussion. Moreover, Hollywood conglomerates want to keep it that way so that the talent grab becomes a respectful act.

In this context, the Japanese *Ju-on* (2000) and Hollywood *The Grudge* (2004) are important texts, because of the remake's claim of minimal difference from the original, thanks to Takashi Shimizu's presence as director. *The Grudge* was par-ticularly fanatical in regards to the rhetoric of faithfulness to the original. Takashi Shimizu directed the same story, in the same location, and even used the exact same house from the original. Given the fact that the film depicts a series of peo-ple trapped in a house haunted by a ghost child and his mother, the decision to use the same house is a clear attempt to 'copy' the original.[35] The 'minor' difference here, as the production company claims, is *people and language.*[36] As Sam Raimi, the producer of *The Grudge*, said:

> There's a large American audience that won't go see a film made in Japan, star-ring Japanese actors, in Japanese . . . I felt this was such a great story that the rest of the world should see it . . . That's what led to the decision to remake it *with American actors, in English, so that the American audience could appreciate it.*[37]

Notably, according to Raimi, the presence of a Japanese director posed no obsta-cle for the discriminating tastes of American audiences. More significantly the "great story" was cross-cultural, an idea that has been critically proclaimed in re-gards to the Japanese horror remake cycle. The following quote demonstrates a popular reception to the current remake practice, privileging the genre of the films in terms of their reception by the American audience:

Asian action and horror films are ripe for Hollywood remakes because *the genres travel well across borders*. In contrast, comedies and dramas tend to be culturally based . . . Horror films in general, *they're not dependent upon cast or dialogue* but on mood and storytelling . . . What any great director can do is convey a story to people who may not understand what's happening at the moment.[38]

This leads us to the second point: Hollywood's strategic overlooking of cultural specificity and its concurrent promotion of universality in the Japanese remake cycle. As discussed earlier, the cultural supremacy of the English language makes all other languages 'minor' languages, which are marked, while English is the standard, and thus unmarked. Works of minor languages must be translated into English if they hope to gain exposure to international attention. Analogous to English, a Hollywood remake makes Hollywood the primary site of global versions. Sam Raimi's claim that differences in language and actors/actresses are minor reveals the arbitrariness of typical Hollywood judgment. The two quotes illustrate how the case of *Ju-on/The Grudge* reveals that language is the supreme issue in terms of American spectatorship. The American audiences' inability to identify with foreign bodies speaking foreign languages is rendered, ironically, through the claim that language is merely a minor difference.[39] Even if we could dismiss the changes in cast and language as minor elements, *The Grudge* demonstrates that the remake is an inherently independent text from its original, even with the same director and 'all the efforts of minimizing changes.' This is primarily due to issues of cultural specificity, especially, in the case of *The Grudge*, the *kaidan* (怪談) tradition. Substantial changes/deletions of kaidan elements are deliberately silenced under the regime of Hollywood as universal/standard translator.

*Kaidan*—in literal translation, scary/frightening story—recalls elements of Japanese folklore, and at the same time serves as a contemporary urban myth to deal with the uncanny, the supernatural, and the incomprehensible. The essential sentiment of kaidan is *on(怨)*, a term referring to an emotion that is an integral part of the genre. *On* is a sentiment of the minority, and is best expressed as a feeling accumulated due to long-lasting oppression or injustice, particularly when one does not have a voice or means of resisting that oppression. The defining quality of *on* is its very inability to be expressed. It is an acceptance of unfairness that must be constantly absorbed and contained internally and thus, *on* is inherently a fatalistic sentiment.[40] This explains why *Ringu*, *Ju-on* and other Japanese horror genre products are obsessed with *onryou/怨靈*, avenging ghost, instead of living figures. Kaidan usually involves a deceased minority figure who was unfairly mistreated, oppressed, and abused. As a result of this abuse, the spirit is compelled to return to interrupt the living world. Significantly, the focus of the kaidan genre is not necessarily bloody vengeance. Rather, a great portion of a narrative is spent on the details of the oppression the figure had to endure, which often leads to an ending in the form of a cleansing ritual. The minority figure was abused and ignored when she was alive, but with the supernatural powers of an avenging ghost, she is heard and understood. The avenging ghost seeks recognition for her mistreatment, for an apology to be issued. While the male psychopath killer from many slasher films seems to enjoy the act of killing itself, often without contextualization, the avenging ghost from the kaidan genre remains communicative and sometimes humane due to the sentiment *on*.

If a genre refers to the social circumstances and participates in ongoing negotiations, then we must consider which society is being addressed and who participates in those negotiations.[41] Although horror as a psychological and physical sensation might be universal, every culture has different semantics of horror, tied to different taboos and myths. Some of the Japanese horror semantics that are weakened or lost entirely in remakes include the virus structure, the female avenger, and the culturally specific signification of the female high school student, who is indelibly interconnected with the *on* sentiment. These three genre semantics pose a distinct threat to Hollywood's claim of universality.

The virus structure in Japanese horror refers to the sense that Japanese society as a whole is haunted by an avenging spirit. Set in a typical, old Japanese house, *Ju-on* placed extreme emphasis on the actual space itself. The house itself emerges as the most essential character in the film. The unfortunate people who step into the house are never individually important. Their existence is secondary compared to the autonomous presence of space. The characters happen to be there, but there is no inherent reason why they are chosen as victims. They are mere fodder, whose deaths serve to demonstrate the displeasure of the spirits. The characters are primarily connected by their passage through the house. The loose relationship among victims suggests the inevitability of tragedy, and the myth of safe, individual anonymity is attacked. By undermining the centrality of a main character through the depiction of a group of loosely related victims—and by closing the narrative with juxtapositions of ghostly, empty Tokyo streets littered with washed-out posters of the missing—*Ju-on* conveys the atmosphere of the virus structure encroaching upon Japanese society

In *The Grudge*, rather than the house being the central narrative element connecting the characters, the story is neatly reorganized around the main female character, Karen. The random victimization and the format of separate stories with loose connections are abandoned in favor of a central protagonist. Although *The Grudge* leaves open whether Karen will be the last victim or not, she is the sole investigator of the serial murders. The audience is strongly encouraged to see through her eyes and to identify themselves with her. Karen's counterpart in *Ju-on*, Rika, is simply one more victim of the haunted house. She may get a bit more screen time than other characters, but she never emerges as a hero who is the focus of narrative, like Sarah Michelle Gellar's Karen. By restructuring the original story so that the actions and desires of Gellar's character become the most important motivation of the story, Hollywood removed the culturally specific implications of the text in favor of a universal star protagonist who would better encourage global audience identification.

   *Ju-on* also served as a prime example of the Japanese horror trope of the female avenger figure. In *Ju-on*, the ill-spirited kaidan figure is a murdered housewife, and the most important victim is also female. More significantly, Rika, the
victim, sees herself becoming the avenging housewife. The attacker and the victim are inseparable and female, and the cycle of oppression continues. This idea
also plays a role in *Ringu,* in which a girl trapped in a deep well has held her rage
for thirty years. Her tragedy began with her doomed psychic mother. In *Ringu,* the
first recipient of the lethal videotape is a single mother who acts as a sympathizer
with the potential to understand the girl's curse. The fact that female suffering is
so privileged, and that the female avenger is the evocative figure in Japanese horror as opposed to a male psychopathic serial killer in mainstream Western horror
films, seems to demonstrate the specific presence of gender-related anxiety in
Japan. Discussing the female avenger in Takashi Miike's *Audition* (1999), Steffen
Hantke argues that the figure invites misinterpretation by the Western audience:

> The fact that Miike can draw from a Japanese tradition of the female "avenger"
> that precedes American horror films suggests that the meaning of the trope will
> differ depending on the audience. For those capable of perceiving Asami as a
> reincarnation of a specifically Japanese "premodern archetype," the source of
> horror in *Audition* may be located in cultural anxieties about the success or fail-
> ure of modernization. For those less susceptible to this reading, she may appear
> specifically *as a backlash phenomenon against late 1960s feminism*. It would be
> reasonable to assume that western audiences, given their cultural predispositions,
> may lean more towards the latter interpretation.[42]

   Whether we agree that Asami in *Audition* is a Japanese "premodern archetype" or not, the point here is the predominant trope of a troubled woman returning as an avenger in Japanese horror, as well as in the kaidan tradition. It occurs
over and over in kaidan, such as in the kaidan classic, *Yotsuya Kaidan (四谷怪談).*
Written in 1825 by Tsuruya Nanboku IV as a kabuki play originally titled *Tôkaidô
Yotsuya Kaidan (東海道四谷怪談),* the tale involves a wife who is not only abandoned by her husband for another lady, but also physically deformed by poison he
has administered to her in small doses. Maimed and mistreated, she dies with *on,*
and comes back as an avenging ghost.[43] This female victim-avenger figure encompasses any female adversity in Japanese society: a widow whose chastity is insistently sustained due to her family, a single mother who suffers abandonment, a
daughter who lives with an abusive stepmother, a married woman who suffers a demanding mother-in-law, and other variations. All of these figures represent the collective female suffering and sacrifice upon which Japanese society is based. Since
male-centered society perpetuates its status quo only by demanding incessant female sacrifice, it is the return of the oppressed that is the deepest source of the collective anxiety. As Hantke argues, if the Japanese premodern female archetype is
still a powerful trope to communicate social anxiety, it reveals that individual sub-

jectivity in the era of globalization is still a problem in Japan. This type of character is directly opposed to the psychopathic male who typifies the most popular Hollywood horror cycles (*Halloween, Friday the 13th, Nightmare on Elm Street, Saw*). In Hollywood, horror is known to be a male-dominated genre because the customers who buy tickets for horror films are primarily male. While the female-dominated horror genre is not the exclusive domain of the Japanese (Western Gothic tradition has a history of depicting women in peril), it is significant to note that *The Ring, The Grudge*, and *Dark Water* are the most prominent examples of recent Hollywood horror films featuring both female protagonists and aggressors. Even within these films, however, the intensive focus on female avengers is dissipated in the Hollywood versions. This is due to the fact that the United States simply does not have a tradition of supernatural female anger to match that of Japan.

Lastly, schoolgirls, who are often the main characters and the majority of the audience of contemporary Japanese horror films, represent one of the most culturally charged figures in Japan and are thereby more difficult to translate. For instance, *Ringu* begins in a domestic setting, with two girls talking about the deadly videotape that kills whomever watches it after one week, and also depicts interviews of girls from an all-girl high school. *The Ring* eliminates these references, and does not utilize horror involving the specific culture of high school girls. *Ju-on* also devotes a significant portion of screen time to high school girls. The fourth episode of *Ju-on* is named for Izumi, a high school girl. As in previous episodes wherein Rika (a young female nurse), Katsuya (an ordinary middle-class office worker), Hitomi (a single female office worker), Toyama (a man more related to blue collar work), and Mariko (a single female teacher), served as representative figures of social groups, Izumi stands for the female high school student. For the Japanese audience, as well as other national audiences from South Korea, Taiwan, and Hong Kong (where there have been similar kaidan traditions), these schoolgirl figures often represent contemporary versions of the female victim/avengers in kaidan. However, for the American audience, the horror genre often deals with teenagers in terms of anxiety from peer pressure, which is not distinctively female.

In Japanese cinema, high school girls, especially from an all-girl high school, represent the inherent contradiction of school as both a modern, socially approved developmental institution and also, to a great extent, an oppressive site to naturalize and educate female subjugations. In many countries, including the United States, high school often represents the last carefree days of youth before familial independence and individual responsibility accelerate the maturation process. In Japan and some other Asian countries, all-girl high schools are often a space where the femininity of patriarchal/Confucian ideology—which requires woman's secondary status within its own system—is propagated. Various educational tools, such as textbooks, define girls only in relation to men, rather than as women themselves, in a celebratory tone. Systemically glorified female figures, such as the good wife or good daughter, serve to prevent student girls from envisioning themselves outside the context of men. Of course, the subtle maneuver of patriarchy is found in elementary and middle schools. However, the high school girl's maturity, both physically and mentally, creates a problematic environment of lingering oppression. The Asian high school girl is most often represented as a sexual object, a Japanese Lolita, with highly fetishized visual codes, such as the school uniform with an extremely short skirt. In terms of gender politics, the all-girl high school often serves as the location of the Asian society's unease. This unease often results in the cinematic persona of the Asian high school girl as horror icon. While an all-girl high school has been associated with a place of horror in the Japanese context, there has been no similar association of horror with an all-boy high school. High school boys are encouraged to anticipate more access to resources and networks and to embark on lives of social control. They have no viable reason to seek vengeance.

The importance of the high school girl figure is again lost in the translation of Hideo Nakata's *Dark Water* (2002), which was remade in Hollywood three years later. Yoshimi, a young mother, sacrifices herself to an avenging ghost girl in order to save her daughter, Ikuko. Yoshimi, like Rika in *Ju-on* and Reiko in *Ringu*, is the main victim. Because Yoshimi herself was abandoned as a child, she sympathizes with this avenging figure. The film depicts Yoshimi being spirited away, before switching to the future, where Ikuko is a high school girl. The film concludes with a shot of Ikuko looking at a girl waiting for her mother. The past and the present are conflated, and fear of abandonment by the mother does not seem to be resolved. It is important to see that this symbol of the high school girl, Ikuko, has no counterpart in the Hollywood remake *Dark Water*. Outside of Asia, the figure of a high school girl loses its evocative power to trigger horror, causing Hollywood to delete or replace the figures.

## Hollywood Remakes as Cinematic Takeover

Japanese (and other Asian) films which have recently been remade are hardly film classics. Unlike some remakes, such as Werner Herzog's *Nosferatu* (1979), a remake of F. W. Murnau's original *Nosferatu* (1922), the Asian remakes make little effort to revisit and adapt an original as a contemporary attempt to communicate with film history. On the contrary, all they have in common is the fact that they are current commercial films which have demonstrated box-office success by outgrossing Hollywood in their domestic markets. They are not categorized as art movies, which are shown only to a small number of people, and which thereby might gain wider status through popular versions made for a wider audience; a practice which is considered Hollywood's specialty. By downplaying cultural specificity and emphasizing universality through budget and genre, Hollywood remakes provide the lure of agency to a global audience. The films are scaled and sanitized for general approval by replacing cultural context and reference with stars and spectacle. To Asian filmmakers, remakes open up the possibility of a wider audience, which provides them with the misguided belief that the traffic between Hollywood and Asia is two-way. By setting itself up as the center of event supply, Hollywood has succeeded in catalyzing a certain excitement over the sudden remake trend. Curiosity regarding which movie is sold to which studio, how much it will pay, which movie tops the record for the highest price, which stars will appear—all these are reasons why remakes are interesting to the Japanese and other Asians.[44] All of this discussion further benefits Hollywood through free publicity and more exposure in the Asian market, which will be the biggest foreign market within a decade. Given that the consumer's attention is a huge commodity in commercial film marketing, there is no reason for Hollywood to refuse the remake practices. The practice of remaking popular foreign films benefits Hollywood both economically, as they concurrently acquire viable texts for themselves while suppressing their competition, and politically, by serving as a convenient way of intervention in the foreign market without being accused of cultural imperialism/expansionism. If a remake such as *The Ring* or *The Grudge* happens to become a hit, the box-office gross serves as an added bonus, and effectively conceals Hollywood's primary objective in acquiring the rights to popular foreign films. Each remake represents a corporate cinematic takeover on a global scale as Hollywood homogenizes its market and universalizes its product, one text at a time.

# Notes

I thank Phil Maher, my *yeobo*, for his support and crucial interventions.

1. Quoted in Toby Miller, Richard Maxwell, Nitin Govil, and John McMurria, *Global Hollywood* (London: BFI Publishing, 2001), 100.

2. Research has been conducted on Hollywood's remakes of French cinema, including Lucy Mazdon, *Encore Hollywood* (London: BFI Publishing, 2000), David I. Grossvogel, *Didn't You Used To Be Depardieu?: Film as Cultural Marker in France and Hollywood* (New York: Peter Lang Publishing, 2002), and Carolyn A. Durham, *Double Takes: Culture and Gender in French Films and Their American Remakes* (Hanover, N.H.: University Press of New England, 1998). As for the overall European-American filmic relationship and the remake as a cultural practice, see James Morrison, *Passport to Hollywood: Hollywood Films, European Directors* (Albany: State University of New York Press, 1998) and Jennifer Forrest and Leonard R. Koos, eds., *Dead Ringers: The Remake in Theory and Practice* (Albany: State University of New York Press, 2002). For examination of the remake as a formative genre in filmmaking, see Michael B. Druxman, *Make It Again, Sam: A Survey of Movie Remakes* (New York: A. S. Barnes, 1975).

3. See David Walsh, "Artistic and Cultural Problems in the Current Situation," World Socialist Web Site, <http://www.wsws.org/articles/2006/mar2006/dwa1-m21.shtml> and also refer to MPAA, <http://www.mpaa.org/researchStatistics.asp> (20 January 2008).

4. My translation is from Sujin Sim, "Japan Encroaches on Hollywood's Idea Bank," Empas, 10 March 2005, <http://movie.empas.com/focus/read.asp?menu=4&type=24&type2=1&id=9330> (10

January 2008).

    5. M. J. Peckos, president of Tartan U.S.A. It launched Tartan Asia Extreme in January 2004.

    6. See Jane Gaines, *Contested Culture: The Image, the Voice, and the Law* (Chapel Hill: University of North Carolina Press, 1991), James Boyle, *Shamans, Software, and Spleens: Law and the Construction of the Information Society* (Cambridge, Mass.: Harvard University Press, 1996), Rosemary J. Coombe, *The Cultural Life of Intellectual Properties: Authorship, Appropriation, and the Law* (Durham, N.C.: Duke University Press, 1998), and Eva Hemmungs Wirten, *No Trespassing: Authorship, Intellectual Property Rights and the Boundaries of Globalization* (Toronto: University of Toronto Press, 2004). Siva Vaidhyanathan in *The Anarchist in the Library* (New York: Basic Books, 2004), 93–94, revisits copyright as the idea of democratic safeguard. He argues that the original idea of copyright was not "primarily meant to grant control and benefits to authors and artists. Historically it's a publisher's law more than an author's, and the ultimate beneficiary is supposed to be the public. . . . Authors and publishers would get a limited monopoly for a short period of time, and the public would get access to those protected works and free use of the facts, data, and ideas within them."

    7. See especially, Wirten, *No Trespassing*, chapter 1, "Wearing the Parisian Hat: Constructing the International Author." This book vividly depicts Hugo's opening speech (1878) at *The Congres Litteraire International* in Paris as the nascence of internationalization, which eventually led to the formation of the Berne Convention for the Protection of Literary and Artistic Works in 1886. In response to the *Congres* in 1878, a Portuguese person being asked to participate said, "How would you have me take part in the work of the *Congres*? At the end of the day, doesn't *l'Association Litteraire Internationale* work exclusively for the profit of French authors and playwrights, whose productions dominate the world market to the great detriment of other literatures?" Wirten, *No Trespassing*, 39.

    8. Regarding differences between Anglo-Saxon copyright and French right of the author (*droit d'auteur*), see Coombe, *The Cultural Life of Intellectual Properties* and Wirten, *No Trespassing*, 56. She argues, despite differences, "both rely on colonial prowess to organize the world according to an economic, political, and cultural infrastructure that serves its interests."

    9. Quoted in Wirten, *No Trespassing*, 95.

    10. Arjun Appadurai, "Disjuncture and Difference in the Global Cultural Economy," *Public Culture* 2, no. 2 (Spring 1990). According to Appadurai, the global trend of restructuring towards knowledge-based societies is not an equal process. The practices of media imperialism produce and distribute the fantasy images of Hollywood on a global scale, and they lead to a certain view which he called *the imaginary*. I am especially interested in the concept of the imaginary by which individuals in the global era maintain the lure of agency.

    11. See Victoria de Grazia, "Americanism for Export," *Wedge* 7–8 (Winter–Spring 1985) and Ruth Vasey, "The Open Door: Hollywood's Public Relations at Home and Abroad, 1922–1928," in *The Silent Cinema Reader*, ed. Lee Grieveson (New York: Routledge, 2004). In the 1920s, when Hollywood incorporated synchronized dialogue in order to guarantee continued universality in the foreign market, studios eliminated politically or culturally controversial issues and strategically edited movies to maximize a specific country's friendly reception.

    12. Miller, Maxwell, Govil, and McMurria, *Global Hollywood*, 6.

    13. A great deal of scholarly research exists on post-Classical Hollywood. Refer to Graeme Turner, ed., *The Film Cultures Reader* (New York: Routledge, 2002), Jon Lewis,

ed., *The End of Cinema As You Know It* (New York: New York University Press, 2001), and Jon Lewis, ed., *The New American Cinema* (Durham, N.C.: Duke University Press, 1998).

14. For example, in 1997 *Titanic* cost $200 million, and it was not rare for American blockbusters from major studios to have budgets over $100 million. The average production costs of feature films in the US in 1997 was $53 million, while it was $6 million in France. Miller, Maxwell, Govil, and McMurria, *Global Hollywood*, 7.

15. Capital as auteur has been theorized by several film scholars. Joshua Clover, in his book *The Matrix* (London: BFI Publishing, 2004), quotes Louis Schwartz as saying, "in the context of Hollywood films, it's actually rather hard to conceive of the director's artistic vision as such, and that we would do better to assume that any given movie is 'directed by money.'" Also see Jonathan Rosenbaum, *Dead Man* (London: BFI Publishing, 2001). Rosenbaum uses the example of *Dead Man* to demonstrate that, because of their control over distribution and marketing, studios can dictate a film's possible audience, even with a supposedly financially independent director like Jim Jarmusch.

16. According to Miller, "Measured in box-office receipts, Europe is Hollywood's most valuable territory. Overall revenue there in 1997 was half the size of the US, but twice that of Asia and four times larger than Latin America. The majors collected over 60 percent of their box-office revenues from outside the US in the top five European markets." Miller, Maxwell, Govil, and McMurria, *Global Hollywood*, 8.

17. See Miriam Hansen, "The Mass Production of the Senses: Classical Cinema as Vernacular Modernism," *Modernism/Modernity* 6, no. 2 (April 1999). In this article, she points out how the binary opposition of Hollywood vs. avant-garde art film is false. Russian avant-garde films and French Nouvelle Vague, for example, are interrelated with Hollywood, and vice versa. The dichotomy satisfies a political need to maintain filmic hegemony within the first world. The European film venues challenge Hollywood supremacy via international film festivals, which have traditionally been a window for third-world cinema to be introduced. Films in the third world have been picked up by major film festivals, such as Cannes, Venice, and Berlin, and have thus gained international attention that they could not have otherwise achieved. In many third-world countries, international acclaim and domestic success are closely related. That dependence is the source of the hegemony with which waning European countries sustain themselves as a counterpole of Hollywood.

18. As for what those directors did in Hollywood, and how their ideas of "foreignness" were conceptualized, see Morrison, *Passport to Hollywood*.

19. Miller, Maxwell, Govil, and McMurria, *Global Hollywood*, 4.

20. Refer to Mazdon, *Encore Hollywood*, 52. She illustrates how much French originals and American remakes earned in theatrical admission gross in the US *Trois Hommes et Un Couffin* (1985) earned $2,150,000, while *Three Men and a Baby* (1987) earned $168,000,000.

21. See Wirten, *No Trespassing*, chapter 2, "Inventing F. David: Author(ing) Translation." She says, "According to UNESCO, almost 50 percent of all translations are made from English into various languages. But only 6 percent of all translations are into English. A mere 2.96 percent of the books published in the US in 1990 were translations; in Britain the number was 2.4 percent that same year. In 1994, 1,418 of the 51,863 books published in the US, or 2.74 percent, were translations. . . . As it is, English is the vernacular of the world because power is assigned in the interstices between linguistic supremacy *and* control of the industries that capitalize on content, information, knowledge, or other assets of intellectual property *in that language*." Wirten, *No Trespassing*, 52–54.

22. Mazdon, *Encore Hollywood*, 4.

23. Statistics come from research in 2004 by KOFIC (Korean Film Council). The third highest number for domestic fare is South Korea (45.34%), followed by France (34.56%), Japan (32.76%), and Italy (21%). These figures are the average from 1999–2003, and the statistics only considered the world's ten largest national markets.

24. Bruce A. Lehman, "The United States and the Global Intellectual Property System: Leadership and Responsibilities," <http://www.iipi.org/Views/Leadership0601.pdf> (12 January 2008).

25. Jack Valenti, "If You Cannot Protect What You Own, You Don't Own Anything!" presented to the Senate Committee on Commerce, Science, and Transportation on 28 February 2002, <http://commerce.senate.gov/hearings/022802valenti.pdf> (12 January 2008).

26. Wirten, *No Trespassing*, 10.

27. Wirten, *No Trespassing*, 90.

28. Certainly the South Korean film industry believes the recent attention to their products from Hollywood is an exciting event. It seems the lure of agency is irresistible. Another benefit to the Korean film industry is that "the massive sale of remake rights is the only way that Korean production companies—which are quite unable to prevent widespread piracy, it seems—can actually keep their heads above water." Richard Clarke, "Why Hollywood Is Brimful of Asia," *The Independent*, 20 February 2004, <http://enjoyment.independent.co.uk/film/features/story.jsp?story=493102> (12 January 2008). While Hollywood continues its trend of rushing to acquire remake rights from the Japanese film market, South Korean films have also been garnering feverish attention from the studios in the past two or three years. Although the Japanese market remains dear to Hollywood—Japan is the biggest international market as a country, providing 10–20 percent grosses of Hollywood blockbusters—and Japan and Japanese have been often represented in Hollywood films, Hollywood's recognition of Korean films and its market is certainly unprecedented. Roy Lee, a partner in the independent production company Vertigo Entertainment who carved out a niche market for Asian films in the US said, "[Remake sales of Korean films] is like zero-to-60 in one year." A few examples among many are *Il Mare*/시월애 (Warner Bros.) *My Wife is a Gangster*/조폭마누라 (Miramax), *Hi! Dharma!*/달마야, 놀자! (MGM), *Tell Me Something*/텔미 섬딩 (Fox), *My Sassy Girl*/엽기적인 그녀 (DreamWorks), and *Old Boy*/올드보이 (Universal). These are films which outperformed Hollywood blockbusters at the Korean box office. In addition to the outstanding figures of Korean remake rights, there are also Hong Kong remake sales such as *Infernal Affairs*/無間道 and *The Eye*/見鬼. *Infernal Affairs* is considered a step towards the resuscitation of the long-waning Hong Kong film industry and Warner Bros. purchased the remake rights to it. Martin Scorsese directed the Academy Award winning best picture remake, *The Departed* in 2006. *The Eye* was released in 2008.

29. For example, the average production cost in South Korea was $4,300,000 in 2004.

30. See Box Office Mojo, "Horror Remake: 1982–Present," <http://www.boxofficemojo.com/genres/chart/?id=horrorremake.htm> (12 January 2008).

31. When *Ringu* was the highest grossing horror film in Japanese film history in 1998, and the success was followed in other Asian countries, the phenomenon became known as *the Ringu syndrome*. The widespread subculture of horror in Asia at the end of the century might be contextualized by the Asian financial crisis and the return of Hong Kong in 1997.

32. Brian Fuson, "*Ring Two* Tops Weekend with $35.1 Million," *The Hollywood Reporter*, 21 March 2005, <http://www.hollywoodreporter.com/thr/film/brief_display.jsp?vnu_content_id=1000846752> (12 January 2008).

33. Renie Graham, "Hollywood Warms to Asian Movies, American-style," *azcentral*, 15 February 2005, <http://www.azcentral.com/ent/movies/articles/0215asianinfluence15.html> (12 January 2008).

34. Richard Clarke, "Why Hollywood Is Brimful of Asia," *The Independent*, 20 February 2004, <http://enjoyment.independent.co.uk/film/features/story.jsp?story=493102> (12 January 2008).

35. Regarding *Shall We Dance?*, the remake of the Japanese original with the same title, it is said that the director and the screenwriter "remain entirely true to the original. Like lounge singers working up a decent cover version of a hit tune, they faithfully track the Japanese film shot-by-shot and line-by-line, with only minor variations." Peter Powell, "Japanese Classic Is Worth an Encore," *The Star*, 15 October 2004, <www.thestar.com> (12 January 2008).

36. The 2001 film *Just Visiting*, produced by Hollywood Pictures and Buena Vista Pictures, is a slightly different example. The director, Jean-Marie Poire, remade his French original, *Les Visiteurs* (1993) with the same French actors, including Jean Reno and Christian Clavier, and set the story in New York instead of France.

37. Quote taken from a documentary featured on the DVD, *The Grudge*, my italics.

38. Pat Nason, "Feature: Japanese Horror-Film Wave?," 29 July 2004 <http://www.upi.com/view.cfm?StoryID=20040729-055142-2377r>, (12 January 2008), my italics.

39. Since there are only a few countries with commercially viable film industries, for most global audiences watching a film usually means watching foreign bodies speaking foreign languages. Thus, the making of meaning depends upon temporal and psychological delays and translations. Most audiences have learned to adjust to such delays and imperfect translations. They eventually develop comfortable tolerances and approximations. In the US, the major studios have constantly rejected the disembodied voice by dubbing and subtitling imported films, "for the sake of" the audience, though "their balanced books depended . . . exactly on the widest possible spread of that practice abroad." Natasa Durovicova, "Local Ghosts: Dubbing Bodies in Early Sound Cinema," in *Film and Its Mulitiples,* ed. Anna Antonini (Udine, Italy: Forum, 2002) and Ginette Vincendeau, "Hollywood Babel," *Screen* 29, no. 3 (Spring 1988).

40. James McRoy, "Case Study: Cinematic Hybridity in Shimizu Takashi's *Ju-on: The Grudge*," in *Japanese Horror Cinema*, ed. Jay McRoy (Edinburgh: Edinburgh University Press, 2005). Also, So-young Kim and Chris Berry, "'Suri suri masuri': The Magic of the Korean Horror Film: Conversations," *Postcolonial Studies* 3, no. 1 (2000).

41. Rick Altman points out that various social agencies, with their specific needs, are involved in the process of genrification. As for the process of negotiations of genrification, see *Film/Genre*, "Where Are Genres Located?" (London: BFI Publishing, 1999).

42. Steffen Hantke, "Japanese Horror Under Western Eyes: Social Class and Global Culture in Miike Takashi's *Audition*," in *Japanese Horror Cinema*, ed. Jay McRoy (Edinburgh: Edinburgh University Press, 2005), 61, my italics.

43. See Popurasha Collection, *Tokaido Yotsuya Kaidan* (Tokyo: Popurasha, 2002), and James De Benneville, *The Yotsuya Kwaidan, or, O'Iwa Inari* (Philadelphia: J. B. Lippincott, 1917).

44. I think it makes sense to try to incorporate other Asian film industries and markets when discussing a Japanese case, given the increasing interrelation among Asian countries. This interrelation creates a unique cultural terrain in which Japanese film and animation

are influential on Taiwanese film, Hong Kong film on Korean film, and Korean film on Chinese film, intermingle. This factor, along with the high market share of domestic films in the Asian market, is recognized as a challenge that Hollywood must address. See David Desser, "Global Noir: Genre Film in the Age of Transnationalism," in *Film Genre Reader III*, ed. Barry Keith Grant (Austin: University of Texas Press, 2003) and Koichi Iwabuchi, *Recentering Globalization* (Durham, N.C.: Duke University Press, 2002). Iwabuchi reassesses Japan as a subcenter of production of consumer culture. His research focuses on manga, anime, and television entertainment which is pervasive in Asian regions.

*Chapter 7*

# Monsters Reappearing in *Great Yôkai Wars*, 1968–2005

Zília Papp

Takashi Miike, the Japanese director infamous for films such as *Koroshiya Ichi* (*Ichi the Killer*) or *Zebraman*, surprised his audiences by taking up the task of directing the 2005 remake of the 1968 horror/fantasy film, *Yôkai Daisensô* (*Great Yôkai Wars*). It is the first time that Miike, who is known for his infatuation with excessive violence, gangster stories, and on-screen blood spilling (Miike is frequently mentioned as the Japanese Quentin Tarantino), produced a children friendly movie, with cute folklore monsters as its main characters. Not surprisingly, Miike delivered something that was unexpected with his remake of the 1968 classic. Compared to the 2005 film, its predecessor is a rather simple and straightforward horror/fantasy story aiming at family entertainment. This chapter aims to focus on and point out the changes between these two films which are separated by nearly forty years. I shall show how the seemingly apolitical, ancient folklore entities, *yôkai*, are positioned in the two films to communicate two distinctively different messages to the audience.

Yôkai (妖怪) is a compound word where both Chinese characters mean "uncanny" or "eerie." The term *yôkai* can refer to eerie phenomena, feelings, sounds as well as animals or humans. As Foster points out the term itself is relatively new and was commonly used since established in the Meiji period in Inoue Enryo's *yôkai-gaku* (*yôkaiology*) to describe all supernatural phenomena recorded in Japan.[1] Other words to describe these phenomena are *bakemono* or *henge* in the Edo period or *mononoke* in the Heian period. Bakemono and henge refer to and emphasize the shape-shifting attribute of these creatures whereas

129

mononoke is a more complex term expressing the untamed energy associated with the monsters. However, by the Meiji period, the supernatural entities of Japanese folklore would be referred to under the collective term of yôkai. These entities include monsters of the mountains and forests, of waterbeds, and human dwellings.

Japanese mountains contain the most ancient and basic forms of yôkai in folk belief, among which the most characteristic ones are the *Oni* (demon), *Tengu* (crow demon), *Yamabiko* (echo), or *Kodama* (tree spirit). Yôkai associated with water usually take the form of transformed water animals, such as giant toads (*Gama*), water buffalo (*Ushi Oni*), snakes (*Nureonna*), or ghost-like creatures which attack fisherman on rough seas (*Umi Bozu*).[2]

Some yôkai enter the village, such as the shape-shifting fox (*Kitsune*) or badger (*Tanuki*), while others reside with humans and are part of daily life, including the cat (*Bakeneko*), the rat (*Bakenezumi*), or the spider (*Tsuchigumo*). Not only animal yôkai are associated with village or domestic life. The Floor Child (*Zashiki Warashi*), which takes the form of a little child, resides in the uninhabited corners of the house and can bring good luck to the family. Other entities include the Ceiling Licker (*Tenjo Name*) or the Slime Licker (*Aka Name*) which lick off the mold and dirt of the ceiling and the bath areas respectively. Objects and utensils can also turn into yôkai upon reaching one hundred years of age. In short, yôkai is a Japanese term for supernatural beings and phenomena, the central idea behind which is the transmutability of all beings, including humans.

Visual renderings of these creatures are specific to Japanese visual culture. Yôkai paintings originating from the Muromachi period take up a considerable part of Edo and Meiji period art. Toei created the first postwar yôkai boom in sixties cinema by producing the *Yôkai Hyaku Monogatari* (*One Hundred Scary Monster Stories*, Kimiyoshi Yasuda, 1968), *Tôkaidô Obake Dôchû* (*Journey with Monsters Along the East Sea Road*, Yoshiyuki Kuroda, Kimiyoshi Yasuda, 1969), and *Yôkai Daisensô* (*Great Yôkai Wars*, Yoshiyuki Kuroda, 1968). As the visual imagery of yôkai was first introduced to the big screen on these occasions, care was taken to depict yôkai authentically and thereby to educate the viewers (mainly children and families) about these traditional folklore characters. In this respect, Miike's film follows the original closely. The yôkai depicted are well researched by eminent yôkai experts such as screenplay writer Hiroshi Aramata, Natsuhiko Kyogoku, and consultant Shigeru Mizuki, who himself remade the 1968 film in an animated version (*Gegegeno Kitaro Yôkai Daisensô*, 1986)

However, while the 1968 Toei version—made in the year Japan's GNP became the second largest in the world, a turning point in Japan's unprecedented postwar economic growth—tells the story of a war fought between traditional Japanese yôkai and foreign (Babylonian) monsters in an Edo period Japanese setting, the 2005 Miike film is situated in a futuristic Tokyo, where yôkai fight the embodiment of pollution and alienation (namely robots created from discarded rubbish and yôkai souls). The 2005 film, shot during the war against Iraq, does not display monsters from Babylonia, but rather emphasizes a strong anti-war message, delivered by Second World War veteran yôkai-manga artist Shigeru Mizuki. By analyzing and comparing the character design, plot, and story line of the original film and the 2005 remake, this chapter aims to shed light on the characteristics of yôkai representation in the two eras, with a special emphasis on the differing political roles these originally apolitical creatures are assigned in both films.

## The Changing Role of Yôkai

Seemingly innocent yôkai have always served an agenda for artists. Monsters in Japanese visual media first appear in the medieval *Rokudo-e* or Paintings of the Six Realms, which grew out of Buddhist iconography representing the realms of the underworld and suffering. Although not many remain, hell paintings are reported to appear in Buddhist illustrations in Japan from approximately the tenth to the twelfth centuries. It was in the twelfth century, corresponding with the decline of the prosperous Heike clan, that scrolls depicting the six worlds (hell, hungry ghosts, evil spirits, humans, and demigods), as opposed to the Pure Land or Paradise, were increasingly produced. The sudden and increasing appearance of such scrolls at the critical time of social confusion supports cultural anthropologist Kazuhiko Komatsu's theory, which postulates that monsters tend to appear at times of social crisis.[3]

These scrolls are important in laying the foundation for a tradition of visual representation of the deteriorated, the gruesome and the filthy, of which monster art and later yôkai manga, animation, and film is part. As Buddhism is based on the fundamental teaching that life is rooted in the Four Sufferings (birth, old age, sickness, death), it is one task of Buddhist art to confront viewers with such realities. No topic, no matter how gruesome, is excluded from artistic depiction. Horror and humor both serve to awaken audiences to the Four Sufferings in life, and the scrolls thereby serve the Buddhist worldview and philosophy that produced them. As art historian Ienaga points out, these scrolls were born as a natural result out of the spiritual atmosphere of the time in which they were produced.[4] It was a time when the Buddhist practice of the "Contemplation on Filthiness," of gazing at decomposing corpses at cemeteries, was actively practiced in an attempt to confront the tragic reality which arose after the relatively luxurious period of the Heike rule.

The Hell scrolls do not depict folk monsters in the guise of yôkai as their iconography is strictly based on Buddhist ideas. On the other hand, the style in which these scrolls are drawn, which is uniquely grotesque, morbid, and humorous at the same time, sets the tone for yôkai art starting from the Muromachi period. The Muromachi period (1338–1573) marks the beginning of yôkai, or monster art, in Japan with the appearance of the *Hyakki Yagyô*, or *Parade of One Hundred Demons Picture Scroll*, as well as the *Tsukumogami Emaki*, or *Utensil God Picture Scroll*. The early Muromachi period witnessed increasing prosperity and stability in which the once-dreaded spirits of the disease gods and yôkai could be expressed visually with levity and humor. This new era is celebrated even by the yôkai with euphoric *matsuri* (festival). The *Parade of One Hundred Demons* picture scroll later becomes the basis for future monster parade representations including film and animation.

The medium of the Muromachi period picture scrolls is color and ink on paper, which produces the distinct color palette associated with yôkai—ambivalence, levity, colorfulness, melancholy, and antiquity—which will resurface in the costume and mask design of the yôkai films. As censorship of the media emerged by the late Edo era, yôkai became a powerful symbol substituting for and ridiculing political figures and dignitaries. The triptych *Minamoto Yorimitsu Yakata Tsuchigumo Yôkai wo Nasu Zu* (*Minamoto Yorimitsu in Bed, Haunted by the Earth Spider and his Demons*, 1843) is an often-cited example of *ukiyo-e* artist Kuniyoshi Utagawa's (1797–1861) satire, where yôkai are used as a comic allegory for political figures.[5]

The militaristic buildup starting from the late Meiji period found a new role for yôkai and local spirits. Foretelling their fate in the Meiji period, artist Kyosai Kawanabe's *Bake Bake Gakko* (*School for Spooks*, 1874), depicts yôkai being forcefully reformed and combed for a new era at a monster reformatory school. Yôkai became sterilized enough by the end of the Meiji period to take on the new roles assigned to them by state-controlled media. The first instance of equating yôkai with foreign enemies of war appears in Yoshiiku Utagawa's (1833–1904) print *Kokkei Wanishiki* (*Comical Notes on Japanese History*, 1895), a comical imitation of the traditional demon parade scrolls. The composition of this print follows closely that of the original *Parade of One Hundred Demons* scroll. Each yôkai in this painting is depicted as ridiculing soldiers from the Chinese army who have been conquered in the Sino-Japanese War (1894–95), Meiji Japan's first important military victory.[6] The rising sun at the end of scroll is none other than the *hino maru* sun disc of the Japanese navy flag.

By the time of the Pacific war, yôkai, mainly demons (oni), were routinely used in wartime cartoons to represent the Allied Forces.[7] Along with caricatures and manga, animated film was also used as a means of war propaganda. The most relevant examples are the Momotaro short films, *Momotaro of the Sky* (*Sorano Momotaro*, Yasuji Murata, 1931), *Momotaro of the Sea* (*Umino Momotaro*, Yasuji Murata, 1932), *Momotaro and the Sea Eagles* (*Momotarono Umiwashi*, Mitsuyo Seo, 1943), and *Momotaro, Divine Troops of the Ocean* (*Momotaro Umino Shinpei*, Mitsuyo Seo, 1945). The final version, *Divine Troops of the Ocean*, is an intriguing animated work, produced in collaboration between the Ministry of Navy and Shochiku Studios. While the seventy-four-minute-long animated film used up resources considerably, its April 1945 release proved to be too late to generate significant social response. Nonetheless, the symbolism used in Momotaro animation—what John Dower calls the *Momotaro paradigm*—gives significant insight into war propaganda tactics and the extent of flexibility of the archetypal symbolism of folklore monsters.[8] While strong Chinese Taoist symbolism can be detected in the original Momotaro story, it was reworked under the guidance of the Ministry of Education to feature an indigenous Japanese folk hero.[9] The story became simplified to accommodate parallels with the war effort, such as Momotaro being the pure Japanese hero, his grandparents the spirits of ancestors, his companions the "liberated" Asian nations and the monsters, residing on a remote island, the Allied Forces. The 1945 animation depicts this parable in its fullest version, rendering the monsters as the British "demons with human face" who surrender to the pure-hearted hero.[10]

The Momotaro animations were banned and copies destroyed by the US troops in the early years of the occupation. However, as Dower points out, the archetypal outsider remained to be used in postwar symbolism, and the old clichés were quickly reassigned in the new world order. Political cartoonists would start to draw horns on the heads of communists by the end of the 1940s.[11] In the postwar years, state censorship of manga and film was gradually lifted. Artists emerging with new vitality after the war, such as Osamu Tedzuka, revolutionized comics and animation. The postwar years would also see the resurrection of the yôkai in the works of manga artist Shigeru Mizuki.

## *The Great Yôkai Wars* (1968)

Shigeru Mizuki, the creator of the *Gegegeno Kitaro* yôkai manga series, is one of the most important manga artists of postwar Japan. The *Great Yôkai Wars* was originally a Gegegeno Kitaro manga episode, published in April 1966 in *Weekly Shonen Magazine*.[12] In order to understand Mizuki's approach to depicting a monster war in the mid-sixties, it is important to outline shortly Mizuki's war experiences in the Japanese Imperial Army during the Second World War.

Enlisted in 1942 at the age of 20, according to his autobiographical manga Mizuki was one of the least-disciplined cadets in the army.[13] He neither completely mastered the correct military behavior towards his seniors, nor was he enthusiastic about the war effort. Mizuki, the bespectacled manga character, is a sort of Japanese version of Czech satirical writer Jaroslav Hašek's *The Good Soldier Švejk* (1921–1922) as depicted in the world-famous illustration by Josef Lada.[14] Mizuki's calamities in the Divine Emperor's Army readily match Svejk's idiocy, which undermined the First World War effort and brought down the Austro-Hungarian Monarchy. It would be an exaggeration to say that manga-Mizuki himself caused the doom of Japanese militaristic expansion; however he contributed to this outcome in his personal way. Characteristic of his surreal adventures in the military, Mizuki was first cast as an army trumpeter, but he couldn't get any proper sounds out of the trumpet. After complaining to his annoyed seniors, he was asked the question, "Do you prefer North or South?" As Mizuki didn't like the cold very much, he answered "South." This is how he was soon embarked on a battleship to the South Pacific front line. He reached New Britain Island (Rabaul) in 1943 while the battleships sailing before and after Mizuki's both perished at sea.[15]

At Rabaul his troops perished in combat and Mizuki spent days in the jungle alone trying to return to his main camp. After catching malaria and barely escaping hostile native tribes, he managed to return, only to be scolded and beaten up for "not dying properly" for the Emperor together with his comrades.[16] In the same year (1944) Mizuki lost his left arm during an air raid, battled malaria, and he was treated in the Rabaul army hospital until the end of the war. By his own recount, he was the only Japanese soldier who befriended the local Tolai tribe and who requested to be left behind on the island after the war. However, he was taken back to Japan where he became a prolific manga artist, the first and most successful one to use yôkai as manga characters, channeling pacifist messages through his monsters.

## The Origin of the *Great Yôkai Wars*

Shigeru Mizuki's manga, *Yôkai Daisensô* or *Great Yôkai Wars* was published in the *Gegegeno Kitaro* series in April 1966.[17] This is the first work with this title and theme. It was followed by an animated version that aired on Fuji TV on March 6 and 13, 1968, produced by Toei Animation. In 1968, a film with the same title, also partly based on Mizuki's original, debuted as the second part of a yôkai film trilogy directed by Yoshiyuki Kuroda and produced by Daiei Motion Pictures.

The main heroes of the manga story, as is the case in any Kitaro episode, are Gegegeno Kitaro, a yôkai boy, his father, who is a mere eyeball, the rascal Nezumi Otoko (Ratman), and peripheral characters derived from folkloristic yôkai. While each episode of this long-running series narrates a fight between Kitaro, his friends and a malevolent yôkai entity, this episode centers on the theme of warfare between monsters. While this theme might partially derive from the *Tsukumogami Emaki* tradition, in which animated utensils go to war with humans, this is the first instance in yôkai narrative where the monsters fight each other in a war. The yôkai soldiers become metaphors in Mizuki's hands.

The story begins with an exotically dressed boy on the streets of Tokyo asking for people's help because his island has become occupied by monsters. The boy addresses the crowd "dear Japanese people," establishing his foreignness during the opening sequence.[18] Kitaro approaches the desperate boy and offers his help. "Do you believe me?" asks the boy, to which Kitaro answers, "Yes, your body emits monster vibes. This is not Japanese vibe. It comes from there (the West)."[19] The "foreign" boy states that he comes from an Okinawan island, Kikaiga-jima, meaning Monsterworld Island. However, the boy wears a conical Vietnamese leaf hat (*nón lá*). Kitaro's father warns the boy, "Western monsters are cruel."[20] Nonetheless, Kitaro gathers pure-blooded Japanese yôkai to go to war with the cruel Westerners on an Okinawan island, thus answering the call of a helpless Vietnamese-looking child, who has asked the Japanese for assistance. Nezumi Otoko is rejected from the Japanese monster squad because he is impure. As he puts it,

"Kitaro, are you insinuating that I am not a pure-blooded monster?" It is Kitaro who refers to Nezumi Otoko as half monster and half human.[21]

The Western monsters include a generic witch and a werewolf as well as a Dracula-like figure derived from Béla Lugosi's character in the 1931 film *Dracula* (Tod Browning). There is also a monster based on Boris Karloff's character from the 1931 film *Frankenstein* (James Whale). They claim that "the monsters of the world gathered on this island to create a country for monsters."[22] Kitaro and the Japanese monsters have to take a stand. Is it "the world" against the Japanese, or monsters against humans? The Japanese monsters do not hesitate with their answer: their identity as Japanese far outweighs their identity as monsters and they are ready to defend the island with their lives.

The central concept of the battle comes with Kitaro's magical vest, Chanchanko, which is taken hostage by the Western forces. Mizuki ascribes different roles to the Chanchanko in different episodes without coherence. In this instance, Kitaro's father claims, that the Chanchanko is woven from the hair of the deceased ancestors of the Hakabano Kitaro lineage.[23] "Our kind, when we die, we leave one thread of spirit hair that keeps on living. Your vest is woven from those hairs. Your superpowers . . . are all thanks to the power of the spirit hair of your ancestors. . . . If we cannot get back your vest, it will be a great insult to your ancestors."[24] When the situation of the Japanese forces gets desperate, however, "the vest started to emit tremendous power to help its descendants. Now, the final member of the Japanese ghost lineage is about to die. At that moment, the Chanchanko turned stark red! That is the colour of anger it felt against the Western monsters!" and the vest starts to kill Western monsters, which saves the Japanese monster forces.[25]

While Kitaro and his monsters fight their patriotic war, the villagers passively hide in a cave waiting for death. The visual rendering of the cave is a close copy of the *kamekobaka*, or turtle-back tombs, which are ancient Okinawan tombs built on cave openings that Japanese defensive forces and local Okinawans used for cave warfare during the Second World War. Tombs and caves were also put to similar use during the Vietnam War, which is explicitly mentioned within the narrative.[26] The Western monsters, trying to trick Kitaro into creating a demilitarized zone, claim, "Hey Kitaro, we don't want to fight a meaningless war, like Vietnam."[27] Mizuki later published a six-volume manga, in which Kitaro fights in the Vietnam War. Titled *War Notes from Vietnam* (*Betonamu Senki*, 1969), Kitaro's yôkai army goes to Vietnam to help the local people there, joining the national liberation front against the American forces.[28] In one instance, Old Crybaby monster fights a Scorpion submarine.[29] The story, which appeared in mainstream children's comic magazines, also narrates the history of Vietnam. The war ends when Kitaro starts a fire on the island that evokes images of nuclear test sites as seen from a distance.[30] The Western monsters disappear in a fireball. The story comes full circle as the Vietnamese-looking boy with a teardrop in his eye keeps waving to the departing Japanese liberators who he begged to come to his island in the opening sequence.[31]

## *The Great Yôkai Wars* in Animation

The animated version, which aired two years later on Fuji TV, in the same year as the *Yôkai Daisensô* film was produced, tones down some of the notions from the manga original, while leaving others intact. References to the Vietnam War are cautiously avoided, and the little boy asking for help is clearly represented as Okinawan. On the other hand, the notions that Western monsters smell different, and are cruel, aggressive, and dangerous are restated several times. The reference to pure-blooded yôkai-ness also stays in the animated version while the fight scenes are considerably diluted. Monsters die in this version as well; however the cave fights do not resemble historical images as readily as in the manga version. Still, the Western monsters pull out a Japan map and plot their landing on the southern main island of Japan, Kyushu, with the help of "biological warfare," that is, using a local monster to spread diseases among the Japanese.

Kitaro's character does not become naked, bald, unconscious, and weak without his vest, but is able to fight despite losing it. The central message of the story is, however, unaltered. The Chanchanko is the symbol of one's ancestral lineage, and without the help of the ancestors, the Japanese fight cannot be won. In the end, Kitaro sadly comments, "All our troops died. Even if we won, I am not happy." "That is war," answers his father.

## *Yôkai Daisensô* Film (1968)

The film *Yôkai Daisensô*, directed by Yoshiyuki Kuroda, is the second in the yôkai film trilogy produced by Daiei Motion Pictures in 1968–1969. The two other pieces, *Yôkai Hyaku Monogatari* (*One Hundred Scary Monster Stories,* 1968) and *Tôkaidô Obake Dôchû* (*Journey with Monsters Along the East Sea Road,* 1969) follow story lines borrowed from period dramas (*jidai geki*) with narratives filled with overtones romanticizing Edo period samurai virtue. The monsters in these two films only appear as a supporting cast with minimal dialogue and act as metaphors for human weakness.

In *Yôkai Daisensô* (1968) monsters take central stage. Loosely based on Mizuki's original narrative, in this film Japanese monsters fight a war with an invading monster from the West. While international monsters appear in the manga and English ones in the animation, in the film version it is an ancient Babylonian monster Daimon, who invades Japan and threatens the habitat of local monsters. The film takes place in Edo period Japan; therefore neither the invader, nor the occupied land draws parallels with contemporary events. The film, as it was more accessible internationally than manga or Japanese animation were in the late sixties, toned down visual and verbal references to the Second World War and the Vietnam War and distilled the theme of the monster war as a metaphor of Japanese patriotism to its most politically correct and nonconfrontational form.

The character design and iconography of Daimon is partly based on the Bur-ney relief, a Babylonian terra-cotta wall carving (circa 2000 BC) from Southern Iraq, often associated with Lilitu, the Babylonian female blood-sucking demon de-picted with bird wings and claws.[32] Lilitu, as mentioned in the *Epic of Gilgamesh* (circa 2000–2150 BC), is a vampire-like night demon that, similar to Daimon, lives on the blood of children and women. On the other hand, Daimon's characteristic of entering the bodies of its victims can be related to another Babylonian mythi-cal being, Ekimmu, a vampire-like spirit that lives off the life force of its human victims. Daimon's body structure is based on the late Assyrian (circa 1800 BC) monumental sculptures and reliefs found in today's Iraq at the current geographic area of Babylonia and Assyria, depicting anthropomorphic demon beings with human heads wearing pointed caps with horns and upright winged torsos and the hindquarters of birds of prey.[33]

In the film, Daimon is a giant, dormant in statue form since around 2000 BC in the ancient Mesopotamian city of Ur, who is awakened by treasure hunters. When disturbed, he flies to Edo period Japan, where he enters the body of a local feudal lord. He lives off the blood and life energy of children and women, takes over the bodies of victims, and multiplies into an army of demons, also growing to giant size and emulating the giant reptile Godzilla, which has been popular in *kaijû* monster films since the mid-fifties.[34] Daimon's first act against the Japanese spirit beings is to tear down the Shinto shrine and the Buddhist altar at the feudal lord's home. His atrocities soon awaken the Kappa water monster, which is first defeated by Daimon. Following that, local monsters gather to protect their home-land and, after several comical encounters, they finally defeat the monster by stab-bing it in the eye, its weak point. The monster is not killed, but flies away from Japan. Despite the film's painstaking attempt to stay inoffensive to postwar and Cold War sensibilities, the film's structure partially follows the Momotaro para-digm established in the animated films produced during the Second World War.

The Western monster is a tall, thin figure with sharp bodily features and a long face and nose. It is a lonesome figure. It is dark, scary, and monochromic, a generic monster without many features, and its cold temperament more closely matches the kaijû reptile entities of the Godzilla and Gamera films. The group of Japanese monsters, on the other hand, lacks an adult, male leader figure. It consists of a fe-male, a utensil, and animal monsters: all comical creatures with childlike features like big round heads, small bodies, and weak voices. Daimon acts as a simple prop, a background to accentuate the colorfulness of the Japanese yôkai. Daimon only enters the bodies of male authority figures. He is a serious male adult character throughout the story, similar to the oni devil characters in the wartime animation *Momotaro Divine Troops of the Ocean* (1945). Stabbed in the eye, he is defeated in the same way as the chief deity of Japanese folklore, the *yamano kami* (moun-tain god) as described in the *Kojiki* (*Records of Ancient Matters*, 680 AD) and *Ni-hongi* (*Chronicles of Japan*, 720 AD). Following the Momotaro paradigm, the monster is not killed but "sent off" the islands.

In summary, the three versions of the *Great Yôkai Wars* produced in the late sixties—the manga, animation, and film—all center on the idea of a Western invasion of Asian regions: Vietnam and Okinawa in the animation and manga, and Edo Japan in the film version. In all cases, the adult-like foreign forces are defeated by the collaboration of childlike local monsters. In the manga and animated versions, the importance of ancestor reverence is also accentuated. The important deviation from the Momotaro paradigm lies in the way that the yôkai now represent "Japaneseness," while until the end of the Second World War, yôkai were used as metaphors for foreigners and outsiders in popular media. This important change can be attributed to the artwork of Shigeru Mizuki, who contributed to the mascotization of the monsters, changing their roles from outsiders to representatives of imagined, shared nostalgic Japanese past.[35]

In an era when Japanese postwar economic recovery was at its turning point, the reappearance of Japanese monsters in media, in the disguise of innocence, nonetheless reinforced the myth of justified vigilance against, and the propagation of, a demarcation line and constant rivalry between "Western" interests and Japan, as well as portraying Japan as the protector of Asian cultures against Western occupation. This testifies to the ambivalent relationship of Japan towards the United States during the Cold War.

## *The Great Yôkai Wars* (2005)

Thirty-seven years later, the remake of the *Great Yôkai Wars* mirrors a different worldview through the characters of the monsters and their opponents. Shigeru Mizuki was production consultant on the 2005 Kadokawa Pictures film directed by Takashi Miike and published the story in manga form one day after the film's release.[36] The film's main antagonist is based on the novel *Teito Monogatari* (*Tale of the Capitol*, 1971) written by yôkai researcher Hiroshi Aramata.[37] The fantasy film, following a story line that heavily borrows from the *The Never Ending Story* (*Die Unendliche Geschichte*, Wolfgang Petersen, 1984), narrates a war between the Japanese monsters and Kato Yasunori, the evil master of *Onmyô-dô* wizardry.

The yôkai become less and less powerful with each remake. While the monsters bravely fought off the enemy on the Okinawan island in the manga and animation versions, they were more timid and vulnerable in the first film version. In the case of the 2005 remake, the yôkai are rendered useless, childish, senile, and cowardly. It is their utmost incompetence, however, which leads them to victory. While not readily clear from the film, audiences familiar with Japanese popular culture are expected to know that Kato Yasunori, the main character of Hiroshi Aramata's popular novel, *Teito Monogatari* and its consequent manga and film versions, is the descendant of the native non-Japanese tribes that lived on the Japanese islands and who were annihilated by the Yamato court and the ancestors of today's Japanese. Kato's parents are killed by the Onmyô-dô wizard Abeno Seimei, and Kato is born from a dying mother. He is in fact the human manifestation of the wrath of the annihilated tribes.[38] Also raised in the Onmyô-dô wizardry tradition, Kato returns to Japan throughout history to cause mayhem, including the Great Kanto Earthquake that shook Tokyo in 1923 and claimed 140,000 lives.[39]

This time Kato combines the supernatural powers of yôkai with the wrath of used tools that were thrown away by people to create *kikai*, a play on words meaning "machine monsters."[40] The wrath of thrown away utensils is already the main theme of the *Tsukumogami Emaki Muromachi* period picture scroll, in which the angered utensils come to life and swear vengeance on people. However, the utensils in that narrative are comical and weak characters, which finally transform into Buddhist saints and attain enlightenment. The monsters in the 2005 film, on the other hand, manifest full-blown anger and hatred towards the Japanese people. Mizuki since the early seventies often used yôkai characters as metaphors for environmental pollution in his manga and animation series *Gegegeno Kitaro*. This is the first instance, however, in which yôkai and *mecha* are combined and that the machines lack any degree of nuanced characteristics.

While yôkai until the Meiji period were equated with the outsiders and were feared for their dangerous powers over humans, in the contemporary narrative they are treated as a fragile and vulnerable endangered species, the symbols of a nostalgic, rural Japanese communal life.[41] They do not fight but simply gather for a festival in the capital. Eighty-three-year-old war veteran Shigeru Mizuki appears in the final scenes of the film as the Great Yôkai Elder, who keeps the balance between monsters and people.[42] His final message resonates with his 1968 manga, "War is meaningless. You only get hungry." According to Takashi Miike's instructions, the actress playing the Sand Throwing Witch was instructed to throw sand towards the imagined direction of Iraq, as the war against Iraq was taking place during filming. While Kato is the wrath of the native tribes that once occupied Japan, there is no mention of foreigners in the story. The scope of the narrative changed, the fight takes place in the psyche of the opponents, as the main fuel of the evil side is wrath, while on the part of the yôkai and the little boy, love for the Other. However, given the intricate story line and characters, Miike's cynical genius as director is well utilized in creating a surreal setting and downplaying the melodramatic overtones that fantasy films often risk.

## Monsters March On

The role of yôkai can be manipulated in media because of their inherent ambiguous nature. Yôkai appear on the borderline between the worlds of gods and humans, when night turns into day or day turns into night. Yôkai are mutational forms of humans, animals, plants, or utensils. This aspect is also mirrored in the function the yôkai undertake in their activities. Yôkai are known to do the following: surprise, trick, possess, harm or help people. Many of them are also known for doing nothing at all. In this respect yôkai also stand on the borderline between beneficial and harmful supernatural entities, with the liberty of turning either way depending on their temporary status.

Yôkai symbolize the moment of change when turning from one way of life to another. They represent the anxiety and fear associated with the uneasiness of change from known to unknown, from certainty to uncertainty. Yôkai also symbolize the moment of change from male to female, from winter to summer, from the wet season to dry season. They symbolize the ultimate nature of things, which is constant transformation and change. They give shape to the anxieties associated with historical and social change as well; not surprisingly yôkai mostly proliferated at the dusk of late-Edo to the dawn of early-Meiji periods. Yôkai also give shape to the fear associated with losing the support of one's group within the strict social structure of the village. For this reason, yôkai are often associated with outsiders: the Kappa with foreigners from the Korean peninsula and China, the Oni and the Tsuchigumo Earth Spider with rebels and bandits living in the deep forests, outside of legal authority.

Following the Second World War, yôkai were transformed in the media to represent a nostalgic Japanese past, as they are portrayed in all versions of the *Great Yôkai Wars*. Whether be it Miike's surreal contemporary vision or the narrative of a West versus Japan power struggle from the sixties, yôkai in the twenty-first century serve the narrative as patriotic and righteous entities that guard Japan from outside forces. Yôkai live on in contemporary media such as manga, film, animation, and video games. Their role will undoubtedly change with each new war to protect the Japanese homeland from invaders. Nonetheless, their core feature remains unaltered: they live in a liminal land between good and evil, right and wrong, which readily lends them to new interpretations in their constant visual evolution within Japanese popular culture.

# Notes

1. Michael Dylan Foster, "Morphologies of Mystery: Yôkai and Discourses of the Supernatural in Japan, 1666–1999" (PhD diss., Stanford University, 2003), 7.

2. Iwai Hiromi, *Nihonno Yokai Hyakka–E to Shashinde Mononokeno Sekaiwo Saguru 2* (Tokyo: Kawade Shobo Shinsha, 2000), 45.

3. Gerald A. Figal, *Civilization and Monsters: Spirits of Modernity in Meiji Japan* (Durham, N.C.: Duke University Press, 1999), 22.

4. Kadogawa Shoten, ed., *Jigoku Zoshi, Gaki Zoshi, Yamai Zoshi* (Tokyo: Kadokawa, 1960), 3.

5. Robert Schaap, *Heroes and Ghosts: Japanese Prints by Kuniyoshi, 1797–1861* (Leiden, Holland: Hotei, 1998), 18.

6. Stephen Addiss, ed., *Japanese Ghosts and Demons: Art of the Supernatural* (New

York: Spencer Museum of Art, 1985), 18.

7. Noriko T. Reider, "Transformation of the Oni from the Frightening and Diabolical to the Cute and Sexy," *Asian Folklore Studies* 62, no. 2 (2003): 133–157.

8. John W. Dower, *War without Mercy: Race and Power in the Pacific War* (New York: Pantheon Books, 1986), 255.

9. Dower, *War without Mercy*, 252.

10. Dower, *War without Mercy*, 255.

11. Dower, *War without Mercy*, 310.

12. Mizuki Shigeru, *Gegegeno Kitaro Dai Ichi Maki* (Tokyo: Chuo Koronsha, 1988), 918.

13. Mizuki Shigeru, *Manga Mizuki Shigeru Den* (Tokyo: Kodansha, 2004).

14. Jaroslav Hašek, *The Good Soldier Švejk and His Good Fortunes in the World War* (New York: Everyman's Library, 1993).

15. Mizuki Shigeru, *Manga Mizuki Shigeru Den* (Tokyo: Kodansha, 2004), 481.

16. Mizuki, *Manga Mizuki Shigeru Den*, 140.

17. Mizuki Shigeru, *Gegegeno Kitaro Dai Ichi Maki* (Tokyo: Chuo Koronsha, 1988), 918.

18. Mizuki, *Gegegeno Kitaro Dai Ichi Maki*, 152.

19. Mizuki, *Gegegeno Kitaro Dai Ichi Maki*, 153.

20. Mizuki, *Gegegeno Kitaro Dai Ichi Maki*, 154.

21. Mizuki, *Gegegeno Kitaro Dai Ichi Maki*, 157.

22. Mizuki, *Gegegeno Kitaro Dai Ichi Maki*, 167.

23. Mizuki, *Gegegeno Kitaro Dai Ichi Maki*, 173.

24. Mizuki, *Gegegeno Kitaro Dai Ichi Maki*, 174.

25. Mizuki, *Gegegeno Kitaro Dai Ichi Maki*, 188.

26. Mizuki, *Gegegeno Kitaro Dai Ichi Maki*, 175, 179.

27. Mizuki, *Gegegeno Kitaro Dai Ichi Maki*, 187.

28. Mizuki Shigeru, *Kitarono Betonamu Senki. Tokusen Kaii Tan 2* (Tokyo: Bungen Shunju, 2000), 12.

29. Mizuki, *Kitarono Betonamu Senki*, 40.

30. Mizuki Shigeru, *Gegegeno Kitaro Dai Ichi Maki* (Tokyo: Chuo Koronsha, 1988), 198.

31. Mizuki, *Gegegeno Kitaro Dai Ichi Maki*, 203.

32. Thorkild Jacobsen, "Pictures and Pictorial Language (the Burney Relief)," in *Figurative Language in the Ancient Near East*, ed. M. Mindlin, M. J. Geller, J. E. Wansbrough (London: University of London School of Oriental and African Studies, 1987), 1–11.

33. Anthony Green, "A Note on the "Scorpion Man" and Papazu," *Iraq* XLVII (1985): 75–83.

34. Ion, ed., *Gamera Gahô: Daiei Hizô Eiga Gojyûgô Nenno Ayumi. The Gamera Chronicles: The History of Daiei Fantastic Movies 1942–1996* (Tokyo: Take Shobo, 1996), 101.

35. Michael Dylan Foster, "The Otherworlds of Mizuki Shigeru," in *Limits of the Human*, Mechademia vol. 3 (Minneapolis: University of Minnesota Press, 2009), 13.

36. Mizuki Shigeru and Aramata Hiroshi, *Mizuki Han Yôkai Daisensô* (Tokyo: Kadokawa, 2005).

37. Aramata Hiroshi, *Teito Monogatari 1* (Tokyo: Kadokawa, 1985).

38. Yôichi Iwasa, ed., *Yomigaere! Yokai Eiga Daishûgô!!* (Tokyo: Take Shobo, 2005), 28.

39. Satoshi Gunji, ed., *Kwai* vol. 19 (Tokyo: Kadokawa Shoten, 2005), 7.

40. Nashimoto Takanori, ed., *Yôkai Eiga Natsuno Jin. Kyogoku Natsuhiko [Ubumeno Natsu] vs [Yôkai Daisenso]* (Tokyo: Yosensha, 2005), 53.

41. Michael Dylan Foster, "The Metamorphosis of the Kappa: Transformation of Folklore to Folklorism in Japan," *Asian Folklore Studies* 57, no. 1 (1998): 1–24.

42. Zennihon Yôkai Suishin Iinkai, ed., *Shashinde Miru Nihon Yôkai Daizukan. Great Japanese Yôkai Illustrated Reference Book Seen in Photographs* (Tokyo: Kadokawa, 2005), 84.

*Chapter 8*

# Trading Spaces: Transnational Dislocations in *Insomnia/Insomnia* and *Ju-on/The Grudge*

## Daniel Herbert

The film remake is as old as cinema itself. Consider the multiple, extremely similar versions of a train pulling into a station as photographed by the Lumière brothers, including *L'Arivée d'un train à la Ciotat* (1895, "Lumière no. 653") and *L'Arivée d'un train* (1895).[1] Despite resemblances, these films can be distinguished from one another, as they were shot at different times and in different locations. Likewise, *transnational* film remakes—films made in one national or regional context and then remade in another—are just as historically established.[2] Transnational remakes were vital, for instance, in the development of cinematic narrative technique, perhaps the clearest example being Pathé Frère's *The Physician of the Castle* (1908, a.k.a. *A Narrow Escape*) and D. W. Griffith's remake, *A Lonely Villa* (1909).[3] These films developed cinematic time-space relations through the sophisticated use of parallel editing, creating the sense of simultaneous action in distant locations.

Early examples of transnational remakes reveal a number of issues characteristic of modernity: the shocks and anxieties around new technologies of transport and communication, tensions about new forms of mobility and interconnection. That these issues arise in cases of cinematic production and reproduction, and that they are caught up in a system of transnational exchange, only affirms that the cinema is a component of larger changes in the social arrangements of time and space and in new constructions of history and geography. Just as these films depict new modes of spatial extension, so too are they the means of a spatial extension in their own right, providing multiplied views of previous moments and distant locations— a mobilized and virtual gaze.[4] As films made in one geo-cultural context and then remade in another, these early examples demonstrate the transnational mobility and cultural flexibility of the cinema. They become their own allegories.[5]

Thus, the transnational film remake is nothing new. Although intense and historically significant, the flurry of Hollywood remakes of French films during the 1980s and early 1990s, such as *Breathless* (1983), *Three Men and a Baby* (1987), and *Point of No Return* (1993), was just one stage in a larger process of transnational remaking between Hollywood and European cultural producers. More recently, this flow appears displaced by the cycle of Hollywood remakes of films from East Asia, most notably seen in *The Ring* (2002), *The Grudge* (2004), and *The Departed* (2006), but evidenced also in such films as *Shall We Dance?* (2004), *Eight Below* (2006), and *Pulse* (2006).[6] Although these remakes of East Asian films also have historical precedents, they represent a significant rearrangement of the flow of existing economic and cultural resources at the macro-regional level.

This essay reflects upon these themes, issues, crises, and tensions, and identifies some of the relations among them. All are connected by the rearrangement of *space* as a category of human experience and *geography* as a category of social practice. As this essay participates in the continuing theorization about space within cultural analysis, I begin by situating contemporary critical geography within the historical context of discourses about postmodernity. In this respect, I chart the contemporary analysis of space and cultural geography within shifting discussions about time and history.

Conforming to the recent shift in the cultural geography of transnational remakes, this essay then examines two recent films from different foreign cinemas and the Hollywood remakes that followed: the Norwegian film *Insomnia* (1997) and its remake by Warner Bros. (2002) as well as the Japanese film *Ju-on* (2003) and its remake *The Grudge* (2004) by Sony Pictures. These films indicate transnational cultural flow in their objective material conditions, each forging a transnational identity by migrating to different national contexts in the remake process. Film remakes always negotiate tensions between repetition and transformation occurring along several different registers.[7] As transnational remakes, the films reveal tensions between national and transnational forces, between the local and the global, and between cultural specificity and abstraction. These tensions manifest themselves in financing, production locations, distribution channels, and reception contexts. These cases not only reveal internal points of contradiction, but they moreover differ from one another in ways that reflect continuing disparities between Euro-American cultural exchanges and those between the US and the Pacific Rim.

In the same way that a nation comes about through cultural imaginings, so does the space of the transnational gain resolution through cultural representations. These films give allegorical expression to the problems of transnational spaces and identities. Specifically, these films dramatize spatial dislocations of identity. The Norwegian film *Insomnia* depicts psychic confusions of spatial dislocation from the perspective of a Swedish detective that is unable to adapt to the twenty-four-hour sunlight of northern Norway, leading to his psychological breakdown. Similarly, in the Hollywood remake, a Los Angeles detective is overwhelmed by the Alaskan midnight sun. In both films, the protagonists *internalize* an aberrant and alienating condition from their rural surroundings. Conversely, *Ju-on* depicts the *externalization* of subjectivity into space. This ghost story details the haunting of a house by the spirits of a murdered family. In this case, the film depicts an interpenetration of the human psyche and domestic spaces of habitation. However, the Hollywood remake *The Grudge* takes on transnational connotations, as all of the protagonists are American while the haunted location remains a Japanese home. In this respect, the domestic space becomes the medium through which a Japanese subjectivity invades American psyches. Seen in combination, these films map ordinary places transformed into liminal spaces of metaphysical trauma, charting a geography of imagination rendered by transnational economic and cultural forces.

## A Spatial Turn: From the Postmodern to Globalization

If *postmodern* was a dominant buzzword in critical discourse during the 1980s, both extending and splitting from conceptions of *modernity*, then since the 1990s it has been replaced by the equally problematic and contested term *globalization*.[8] In this shift, *space* has played an instrumental role, gaining new vitality as a category of critical analysis over the last few decades. Largely drawing from Marxist critical geography, issues of space and place have moved to the fore in many analyses of society and culture. Much of this work draws upon Henri Lefebvre and his assertion that space is entirely interconnected with the production of social relations.[9] Within discussions of postmodernity, this forged new connections between geography and culture, both fields concerned with issues of alterity under a new phase of capitalist accumulation. Edward Soja, for instance, notes the trend toward spatialized thinking in social theory and critical geography, prompting him to argue for spatial conceptions of the postmodern.[10] In the areas of culture and aesthetics, Fredric Jameson characterizes postmodernism as marked by a decrease in historical awareness and an increasing dominance of a spatial logic.[11] In these respects, the postmodern became highly associated with space even as spaces were increasingly described as postmodern.

David Harvey's work in critical geography facilitates the turn from postmodernity toward globalization and transnationalism. Harvey argues that the shift in material and social relations from modernity to postmodernity, from Fordism to post-Fordist "flexible accumulation," rendered drastic transformations in the production of space.[12] He asserts that the world has undergone an intense phase of

"time-space compression," by which he means a speeding up of time and a reduction in the relevance of physical distance.[13] Mapping a different spatial
metaphor, Arjun Appadurai theorizes globalization as a matrix of overlapping
"landscapes" comprised of "global cultural flows."[14] The work of Doreen Massey,
Saskia Sassen, and many others demonstrates that globalization demands new,
often competing considerations of social and cultural spaces.[15] This suggests that,
in a general way, the development of contemporary spatial analysis went hand in
hand with discussions of globalization, even as these discussions were as contested
as the spaces produced under globalization. To a great extent, the problem of space
in general has been a problem of global space in particular.

The complex geography of globalization is profoundly intertwined with the
media. Appadurai situates the media as one of the five transnational "scapes," comprised of the images that flow around the world as well as the networks by which
they travel.[16] Likewise, David Morley and Kevin Robins situate the media centrally within contemporary transnationalism.[17] Similar to the way that economic
forces have altered the landscape of the media industries, producing global communications networks as well as local production centers, so too do the media reshape space by creating more direct relationships between the local and the global.

Within these characterizations, issues of representation as well as of individual and collective cultural identities remain highly contested. As Harvey argues,
"time-space compression is challenging, exciting, stressful, and sometimes deeply
troubling," forcing changes in "how we represent the world to ourselves."[18] Indeed, how are people to inhabit or represent a global space, a "space of flows, an
electronic space, a decentered space, a space in which frontiers and boundaries
have become permeable"?[19] Thus in many accounts, globalized mediascapes en-
gender a disorienting virtualization of identity characterized by fluidity and mobility. However, as globalization places the global and the local into proximity, it
also reconfigures the relationship between locality and identity. Whereas some
warn of the increasing formation of regressive, nostalgic, or idealized place-based
cultural identities in reaction to globalization, Doreen Massey argues for a more
progressive view, asserting that "the local" specific place is as heterogeneous as
any other kind of space.[20] Thus she calls for a more interconnected understanding
of the global, the local, and identity: "a global sense of the local, a global sense of
place."[21]

Conceived as a transformed and transformative landscape, globalization profoundly alters the relations among space, the media, and identity. First, although
it might be an overstatement to claim that the "spatial turn" was a direct discursive
response to globalization, the two discourses do appear mutually constitutive in the
recent period, as spatial analysis found one of its major topics in this keyword. As
such, the ongoing analysis of globalization demands continued development of
spatial models and theories. Second, this highlights the centrality of media within
the geography of globalization. Yet the relations among media networks, representations, and geography are highly dynamic and also require continued analysis.

Finally, this discursive trajectory equally indicates the strong interrelations between space and identity, which under globalization fluctuate between the local and the global, between fixity and mobility.

## *Insomnia* as Transnational Mediascape

The Norwegian film *Insomnia* and its Hollywood remake of the same title illustrate some of the reconfigurations of space under globalization. In their industrial and intertextual relations, as well as within their aesthetic and narrative strategies, these films navigate and thereby chart a complex transnational mediascape. In so doing, they demonstrate a struggle for cultural power within a dynamic transnational geography, and further, highlight the particular role of the transnational remake within this struggle among the global cultural industries. These films reveal various strategies to reconcile the local and the global, and just as importantly, they demonstrate the interrelation and mobility of these terms.

*Insomnia* may seem like an odd example, since Norwegian cinema operates in a very "local" manner. Typically comprised of modest dramas that draw upon local cultural traditions, Norwegian films have rarely attained popularity outside Norway's borders. Only one Norwegian film has ever won an Academy Award, the film *Kon-Tiki* in 1950, and almost none gain theatrical distribution in the United States. Within the greater Nordic region, Norwegian films have traditionally been overshadowed by the Swedish and Danish film industries, which have not only dominated the Nordic scene but produced various successes throughout Europe and beyond. In the areas of production, distribution, and marketing, Norway has historically operated according to a "national cinema" paradigm, a mode of production that continues to this day.[22] As with many national cinema systems, the Norwegian government uses public funds to help the production of feature films, with the caveat that a government board will judge the artistic merit and cultural value of scripts in advance of their production. This process creates a strong relationship between the state and cultural production, conflating artistic values with those of national culture.

Norway's film exhibition system is even more distinctive, however, and much more pointedly local. Rather than private or federal ownership, *municipalities*, similar to counties, own and run the majority of film theaters in Norway.[23] In this respect, an entire segment of the industry is controlled by powers within a small geographic space, a system that creates a number of potential "flaws." Gunnar Iversen notes that very little revenue from film exhibition travels back into film production, but rather municipalities use "the profit from film screenings to build hospitals and schools, to subsidize the theater proper, and to build art institutions."[24] In his estimation, this severely hampers the production of Norwegian films. Moreover, this system may reinforce the popularity of foreign films in Norwegian theaters, particularly those from Hollywood. Local exhibitors are interested in high-grossing films, and due to existing imbalances in film production, this could easily benefit Hollywood films with their vastly higher production and marketing budgets. Indeed, the domestic market share of Norwegian films was under 10% throughout the 1990s, and reached a low of 5% in 1997, the year *Insomnia* was released.[25] In this regard, the localization of exhibition perpetuates the marginalization of Norwegian films within the national cultural market.

Nevertheless, the apparent locality of Norwegian cinema operates in a transnational field. Norway has held partnerships with other Nordic nations in cultural production for many years, contributing however minimally to a regional cinema. Despite Norway's resistance to joining the European Union, the nation participates in pan-European cooperative film programs, including the MEDIA Program and Eurimages.[26] These programs augment the efforts of the International Division of the Norwegian Film Institute to publicize and distribute Norwegian films throughout the world, primarily at international film markets and festivals.[27] Iversen also notes that, economically and stylistically, Norwegian cinema began moving in a distinctly international direction in the mid-1980s.[28] Films like *Orion's Belt* (1985) and *Pathfinder* (1987) indicate a shift toward more thrillers, adventure films, and other "action-driven movies, often intended for an international audience."[29] The relative success of these films prompted new financing partnerships between Hollywood and Norwegian film producers.[30] In these respects, Norwegian cinema has been increasingly situated within a greater global space of media, economic, and cultural flows.

In its overtly spatial narrative, *Insomnia* manifests the tension between locality and transnationalism, between fixity and mobility. The film tells the story of a Swedish detective, played by Stellan Skarsgård, who travels with his partner to a small town in northern Norway to investigate the murder of a teenage girl. However, the detective is assailed by the pervasive twenty-four-hour summer sunlight. During an attempt to capture a murder suspect, the detective's disorientation in a cloud of fog causes him to shoot his partner and allows the criminal to escape. As the film continues, the detective grows wearier and more disoriented by the midnight sun. He covers up his crime and even colludes with the murderer to hide both their misdeeds. After defeating the murderer in a violent confrontation, the detective returns to Sweden with no one knowing of his guilt.

This narrative dramatizes external space interacting dynamically with the subjectivity of the protagonist. Just as the midnight sun disorients the detective, so too does the sunlight reflect his interior sense of guilt. In one scene, he struggles to block out the light from his windows with tape, but he still cannot sleep. In this regard, his subjectivity is dislocated out of his body into the material world, as simultaneously the world impinges upon his psyche. Further, *Insomnia* designates "the local" through its specific representation of material space. Yet by conflating the representation of material space with a psychological space, the film situates "the local" as alien and psychologically dangerous. As the detective encounters this space as a traveling outsider, the dislocation of his psyche resonates not only with his guilt about killing his partner, but more importantly, with his physical dis-location in a "foreign" space, with his ineffectualness as a transnationally mobile figure. The dislocation of subjectivity seen in *Insomnia* thus corresponds with an irreconcilable tension between fixity and mobility, between the local and the transnational. The film constructs global space as a traumatic psychic space.

This polarity between the local and the global takes on greater cultural sig-nificance when viewed in relation to the film's intertextual connections. *Insomnia* draws upon and transforms conventions of film noir in ways that correspond to a tension between locality and transnationalism. As a genre, film noir evokes a his-tory of transnational cinematic and cultural exchange between Europe and Holly-wood. Many directors working in this genre of Hollywood crime films, detective films, and melodramas were European émigrés, such as Fritz Lang and Billy Wilder, who inflected their films with dark themes and expressionist approaches to mise-en-scène.[31] Further, noir was first recognized and discursively organized by French critics.[32] Although produced by Hollywood and, in most accounts, re-flecting American social and psychological preoccupations following World War II, film noir came about through a complex European-American exchange of peo-ple, cultural works, and reception discourses.

*Insomnia* maintains many tropes of film noir, including a morally ambivalent protagonist and a crime-centered mystery narrative, thus drawing upon this transnational cultural history. Yet it radically alters the traditional mise-en-scène of film noir in a critical reconfiguration of the genre. Director Erik Skjoldbjærg stated that he was "struck by the idea of a reversed 'Film Noir' with light, not darkness as its dramatic force."[33] Indeed, *Insomnia* exchanges the interior, urban, shadowy spaces typical of classic film noir for rural, outdoor spaces flooded with sunlight. As Iversen notes, the dramatic and distinctive use of the local landscape is a long-standing, constitutive convention of Norwegian cinema.[34] In this respect, the pic-tographic foregrounding of the landscape seen throughout *Insomnia* localizes film noir in a Norwegian geo-cultural context.

The film's exhibition at film festivals and commercial theaters, as well as its critical reception, reveals a complex navigation of diverse cultural spaces. Selected as part of the prestigious International Critics Week at the 1997 Cannes Film Fes-tival, *Insomnia* quickly garnered acclaim as a major new European film. It made its US premier at the Nantucket Film Festival in June 1997, but more importantly, it screened that September at the Toronto Film Festival, which historically has served as a vital film market for foreign and independent features seeking distri-bution deals for North American theaters.[35] And indeed, its Norwegian owners, Norsk Film A/S, sold *Insomnia* to First Run Features, who put the film into lim-ited release throughout the United States where it earned a modest return.[36] Amer-ican reviewers of the film situated it within divergent spatial-cultural associations. Although many praised the film, they regularly characterized it as an "art-house hit," as a "foreign" film that would appeal to a limited group of upscale, educated, and eclectic filmgoers.[37] These reviews consistently discussed the film's arctic set-

ting as a noteworthy and exotic draw. Yet other reviewers noted the film's inter-
nationalism and generic appeal, as when one wrote that "*Insomnia* seems more interested in smartening up and dressing down Hollywood conventions than locating
its own aesthetic or voice."[38] In these respects, *Insomnia*'s North American reception was marked by its marginalization as an exotic cultural import *and* as an imitation of Hollywood.

If *Insomnia* imitated certain cinematic conventions associated with Hollywood, then Hollywood imitated *Insomnia* overtly by remaking the film, creating
yet another transnational cultural bridge. After reading one of *Insomnia*'s positive
reviews, Hollywood producer Paul Junger Witt asked Norsk Film to send him a
print to view.[39] After this viewing, Witt-Thomas joined forces with Warner Bros.
and secured an option to remake the film.[40] Warner Bros. and several associated
production companies, including Steven Soderbergh's Section Eight, developed
the project, attaching actors Al Pacino and Robin Williams as well as British director Christopher Nolan, whose prestige in Hollywood would increase substantially following the success of his film *Memento* (2000). In this way the Norwegian
*Insomnia* became integrated within Hollywood, a geo-cultural migration that took
the precise form of a cinematic remake.

The narrative, aesthetic strategies, and themes of the Hollywood *Insomnia*
closely resemble those of the Norwegian film, but the remake alters geographic and
psychological details. The film relocates its narrative from Norway to a remote
town in northern Alaska, while maintaining the exoticism of its locale. The film establishes Alaska as a rugged wilderness in the opening sequence, depicting a small
plane flying over glaciers, mountains, and forests in spectacular vistas; stunning de-
pictions of the northern wilderness recur throughout the film. The opening also
establishes the detective, played by Pacino, as an outsider to the space, who arrives
from Los Angeles with his partner. Like the Norwegian film, the remake depicts
an expressionistic relationship between its protagonist's psyche and the rural,
ceaselessly sunlit external space. The Alaskan sunlight invades his consciousness,
keeping him from sleep and also reflecting his interior state of guilt and confusion. As in the earlier film, the detective kills his partner, covers this up, and struggles to outwit the teenage girl's murderer while hiding his own crime. By the end
of the film, however, a younger local female detective realizes the detective's crime
and tries to bring him to justice. In a tidy narrative conclusion that elides the moral
ambiguity of the Norwegian film, the protagonist defeats the murderer in a confrontation but is mortally wounded himself. The film ends with the younger detective absolving him as he dies.

These differences impact the film's portrayal of a transnational space. Although it depicts a dynamic exchange between material and psychic space, the remake forgoes any direct reference to international travel, as the detective and his
partner come to Alaska from Los Angeles, rather than another country. In this regard, the expressionistic relation between psyche and landscape resonates with
confusions about divisions between urban and rural spaces, nature and civiliza-

tion. In dramatizing such polarities, the Hollywood *Insomnia* evokes the western genre and an imperialist frontier mythology. Indeed, the film draws upon well-established tropes of the outsider lawman arriving at a remote frontier town to bring law and order, thereby establishing civilization and continuing the spatial-temporal thrust of progress through manifest destiny. Whereas the prominent use of the natural landscape in the Norwegian *Insomnia* connected that film to a tradition of Norwegian filmmaking, the similarly grand depiction of the landscape in the Hollywood remake connects it to pictorial traditions of the western genre.[41] In this respect, the Hollywood remake of *Insomnia* appears to re-nationalize the transnational implications of the narrative, thematics, and pictorial strategies of the earlier film. Rather than serving as an allegory for the psychic confusions of international mobility, the Hollywood *Insomnia* relocates these confusions within a complex history of the United States' geographic expansion across North America.[42]

This imperialistic depiction of space resonates with greater ideological forces, at once national and transnational, political and cultural. At the same moment that *Insomnia* represented Alaska as a sublime landscape, both beautiful and daunting, Alaska stood centrally within wider political debates about how the state would treat nature; most specifically, the Bush administration's vigorous attempt to open the Alaskan Arctic National Wildlife Refuge to oil drilling while numerous other groups argued to maintain a conservationist approach to the area. Alaska was torn between serving as an economic and a natural resource. Whereas one side sought to further the commercialization of the natural world, the other maintained an ideology of preservation. This polarity, in fact, reveals a general tension in American ideology at this cultural moment. On the one hand, the United States advocates the limitless expansion of capital as part of its promise of social progress and individual self-improvement; on the other hand, there remains a sense of the unbounded freedom endowed by the vast American landscape, the frontier. As even in the western genre the American west had long ago been settled, Alaska now served as a site that evoked the frontier and captured the imperialist imagination of the United States—both within political debates as well as the remake of *Insomnia*. In this respect, the confusion of the film's protagonist resonates with a contemporary cultural confusion about the role of nature and frontiers in the contemporary world.

The political economy of this remake raises transnational issues even more directly, revealing an asymmetry of power as Hollywood strategically exceeds and exploits geographic and cultural boundaries. Although *Insomnia* appears to re-nationalize an expressionistic, imperialistic representation of space, the actual spaces of the film's production were international, as the film was a "runaway production." This phrase refers to films that present narratives set in the United States and that are produced by companies housed in the USA, most typically in Los Angeles, yet which are shot outside the United States. This phenomenon represents one element of the post-Fordist restructuring of the Hollywood studios, and has increased notably since the 1980s.[43] Attracted by favorable currency exchange rates, foreign nations' tax incentive programs for media production, as well as well-trained, non-union film and television labor, Hollywood has increasingly made film and television programming outside the USA while maintaining its managerial, decision-making, and financial apparatus in sunny southern California. The writers of *Global Hollywood* consider this a fundamental part of Hollywood's strategic place within the "New International Division of Cultural Labor," or NICL, whereby the transnational mobility of capital exploits site-specific economic conditions.[44] The Hollywood studios outsource media production to reduce costs and increase revenue.

This represents an important spatial contradiction between the textuality and material conditions of the remake of *Insomnia*. Aside from some B-unit location photography, the majority of *Insomnia* was filmed not in Alaska but rather in British Columbia. Although Australia, New Zealand, and several other nations have recently become regular hosts to Hollywood runaways, Canada has been the most consistent site of Hollywood productions made outside the USA.[45] In addition to economic factors, Canada has held this place due in part to shared language and geographic proximity. Thus, the spaces of *Insomnia* comprise a transnational field, where geography and representation simultaneously overlap and diverge. Whereas the Norwegian *Insomnia* dramatized confusions about international mobility, the Hollywood remake effaced this issue. However, although the interaction between space and subjectivity dramatized in the narrative do not correspond with an international diegetic world, the Hollywood *Insomnia* allegorically represents the transnationalism of its actual production. This also recontextualizes the film's construction of an imperial diegetic space. The expansionist logic of capital in Hollywood propelled the international production of the film, implicitly aligning with the imperial representation of space within the film. Most notably, this marks a severe discrepancy between the two *Insomnia* films, implicating the asymmetrical arrangement of power driving the production of Hollywood transnational remakes.

## *Ju-on/The Grudge* as Transnational Mediascape

If the two *Insomnia* films articulate different transnational spaces, the confusions they induce, and asymmetrical arrangements of power within them, then the films *Ju-on* and *The Grudge* help present a fuller, more complex map of contemporary cultural globalization. As an intertext comprised of a Japanese film and its Hollywood remake, *Ju-on* and *The Grudge* rearrange and "reorient" the asymmetries of power endemic to transnational remakes. Moreover, these films invert many of the narrative and pictorial devices found in the *Insomnia* films, yet they analogously construct transnational space as a confusing and dangerous interaction between the psyche and the material world.

Without discounting the long, rich history of filmmaking throughout East Asia, it is safe to say that in the last several decades Asian cinema has become increasingly important within its regional contexts and throughout the world. The cinema of Hong Kong, from the action spectaculars of Tsui Hark to the cosmopolitan art films of Wong Kar-wai, has had a particularly strong impact on world cinema. More recently, the popular cinema of South Korea has found unprecedented domestic and international success with numerous melodramas and action thrillers. Japanese cinema, however, has been somewhat different. Following the severe decline in the domestic industry during the 1970s, Japanese cinema has gained only marginal success abroad, mainly through a continued presence at international film festivals, with such films as *The Eel* (1997) and *Fireworks* (1997). More prolific and significant, however, has been the Japanese animation industry, which Susan Napier observes held "an inverse relationship with the decline of the Japanese film industry."[46] Yet beyond animated films, Japanese cinema has not gained the same transnational impact as other East Asian cinemas.

Nevertheless, Japanese cinema recently became culturally dialogized in particular ways with Hollywood as part of an overall response by Hollywood to the increasing global popularity of East Asian cinema. Indeed, numerous directors and actors moved from Hong Kong to work in Hollywood during the 1990s, including John Woo, Chow Yun-Fat, and Jackie Chan. Likewise, Hollywood has incorporated certain aesthetic conventions of Hong Kong action cinema, notably exemplified by the combination of wire-work acrobatics and martial arts seen in *The Matrix* (1999). However, the most remarkable contemporary interaction between Hollywood and Japanese cinema has been through film remakes, an exchange that has facilitated a broader series of remakes between Hollywood and other East Asian cinemas; *The Departed*, a remake of the Hong Kong film *Infernal Affairs* (*Mou gaan dou*, 2002), and *The Lake House* (2006), a remake of the South Korean film *Il Mare* (2000), present two examples of this larger trend.

Considered geo-culturally, this represents a dramatic change in Hollywood's transnational remakes, which have predominantly taken European films as their sources. During the 1950s and 1960s, of course, Hollywood remade a number of samurai films directed by Akira Kurosawa, including *The Magnificent Seven* (1960), a remake of *Seven Samurai* (1954), and *The Outrage* (1964), a remake of *Rashomon* (1950). Through a process of generic, geographic, and historical transformation, these films were made into western genre films set in the North American frontier of the late 1800s.[47] However, this cycle of transnational remakes came to a close along with the decline in the western genre through the late 1960s and 1970s. It was precisely out of this moment, from the late 1970s through the 1990s, that Hollywood ravenously remade films from Europe. Although French films provided the majority of source-films, Hollywood remade films from numerous European nations, including the West German film *Wings of Desire* (1987), the Dutch film *The Vanishing* (1988), and the Spanish film *Abre los Ojos* (1997).[48]

The shift toward remaking films from East Asia thus coincides with a larger cycle of activity and transnational significance of those cinemas. In this respect, Hollywood's remakes of Japanese and other East Asian films should be seen as part of a larger reaction to the competition posed by them. This represents a strategic respatialization of Hollywood toward Asia, a redirection of the economic and cultural flow through which Hollywood operates and seeks to command. Moreover, this "Asian turn" in Hollywood resonates with the growth in importance of many East Asian nations within the world economy, or more accurately, the increased economic interdependence of European and North American powers with East Asian powers. In this respect, the contemporary cultural dialogue between Hollywood and East Asian cinema is one cultural manifestation of new social and economic relations. Like any cultural process, this dialogue does not simply reflect social or economic realities, but rather operates with "relative autonomy" and indeed exerts real force upon the construction of these realities. Just as these remakes delineate a transnational space of flows between "East" and "West," between Hollywood and select East Asian cultural industries, so too do these remakes redirect these flows, reshape the space of them, remake them.

*Ju-on* distinguishes Japan's particular role within this process and articulates a number of themes and tensions that pervade it. *Ju-on* was initially produced in 2002 by Oz Productions, a company owned and run by Takashige Ichise. Directed by Takashi Shimizu, the feature film *Ju-on* follows two shorter productions of the same title made for the Japanese straight-to-home-video-market. Within Japan, such straight-to-video fare is referred to as V-Cinema, or OV for "original video," a phrase that was initially coined by the Toei company but soon became associated with the Japanese straight-to-video market in general.[49] As Mark Schilling notes, V-Cinema functioned quite differently than the straight-to-video market in the United States.[50] Rather than merely being a wastebasket of bad films, the Japanese V-Cinema market allowed a number of filmmakers to make sometimes outrageous, at other times innovative films with relative artistic freedom, due in part to their inexpensive budgets and the support of the then-booming home-video market. This was the proving ground for a generation of filmmakers who have since gained worldwide recognition, including Shimizu, Kiyoshi Kurosawa, and Takashi Miike.[51] Within the Japanese national media market of the 1990s, V-Cinema facilitated the production of live-action films aimed at the domestic home video market, making V-Cinema "domestic" in a literal way (that is, in the home), but also nationally domestic in subverting the dominance of Hollywood films in Japanese theaters.

Alongside the financial crisis of the 1990s and the decline of the home-video market within Japan, most likely due to a wave of multiplex theater construction, the V-Cinema market dwindled in the late 1990s. Nevertheless, Ichise and Shimizu found a hit with the original *Ju-on* video in 2000, prompting the company to quickly produce a sequel.[52] This also led to the production of a feature-length version of the film, known (somewhat confusingly) as *Ju-on: The Grudge* (referred to in this essay simply as *Ju-on*). Produced quickly with a modest budget, this film also became a popular hit in Japan and screened at several international film festivals throughout 2003.[53] Capitalizing on the success of a wave of Japanese horror films, exemplified by such films as Kiyoshi Kurosawa's *Cure* (1997), Hideo Nakata's *Ringu* (1998), and Takashi Miike's *Audition* (1999), *Ju-on* sought audiences in Japan and abroad.

The film begins with a printed text explaining its central premise: the spirit of anyone who dies in the grip of a terrible rage will haunt the place of their death and will curse all who enter. This "grudge" can also follow its victims to new locations. The narrative begins as Rika, a social worker, visits a nice but messy Japanese home in Tokyo to find an old woman left there unattended. Rika wanders through the home, curiously and anxiously exploring the empty hallways and the dark corners of every room. Soon enough, she encounters the spirit of a young boy, Toshio, who startles her, and then the spirit of the boy's mother, Kayako, who assails the social worker. The film then progresses in a non-linear chronology, documenting the various victims of these spirits, who succumb merely by entering the unassuming domestic space. Before Rika, a young married couple lived in the home and is killed there by the ghost Kayako. Following this episode, the married man's sister brings the curse with her to her high-rise apartment, where the ghost stalks her through the hallways, into her apartment, and kills her in her bed. After this series of vignettes of spectral encounters, the film concludes by insinuating that the ghosts of the boy and his mother were the victims of the patron of the household.

Similar in some respects to the *Insomnia* films, then, *Ju-on* depicts a dislocation of subjectivity into the world, a dynamic interaction between psychic and material space. *Ju-on* depicts a space infused with the will of dead human subjects; that is, material space becomes the home to the soul after the demise of its bodily existence. Not only do the spirits of those who died in the house remain there, but the house becomes a space of traumatic metaphysical interaction for those who enter. In these respects, *Ju-on* resembles any number of haunted-house films. Yet the film compounds its conflation of psychic and material space by obeying a spatial logic in its narrative. As the film's sequences appear out of a linear chronology, with numerous flashbacks and flash-forwards, and as the house becomes the locus around which all the film's narrative events occur, the house in fact organizes the film's narrative. Thus the traumatic interaction between space and subjectivity is reflected by the construction of the film itself, which fragments time but maintains a consistent location; indeed, the film presents a severe localization of narrative. In these ways, *Ju-on* allegorically represents the horrors of local space, a domestic space of domestic violence.

This depiction has a complex relationship with Japan's larger social and artistic contexts. The construction of space in Japanese cinema has a contentious discursive history, particularly in relation to European cinema and Hollywood. In his classic study, Donald Richie describes Japanese films as having an atmosphere or mood [that] is always the result of a sense of place . . . to a degree uncommon in other countries. It is based upon that attitude toward one's surroundings—which sees them as an extension of self. In the West the tradition has been man against nature . . . It is difficult, therefore, for us to comprehend a culture that does not see man as powerful and immortal, at the center of the universe. The Japanese see him, rather, as part of the world he inhabits.[54]

Richie thus asserts a national characteristic manifested through the cinematic representation of space, establishing divergent national/cultural divisions between Japan and the West specifically in relation to man's psychic relation to external space. Analogously, Noël Burch also differentiates Japanese from Western cinematic spaces. Burch draws upon Heinrich Engel, a scholar of Japanese architecture, and claims that representations of interior, domestic spaces in Japanese films are distinctively static.[55] In cinema, he argues, domestic spaces become "*cellular subdivisions of the screen-surface,*" rather than elements within a deep space.[56] However, Burch claims that the standardization of Japanese interiors limits their use as expressions of characters' psychological states.[57] Whereas for Richie Japanese cinema places individuals in strong relation to external space, for Burch this same cinema places them at a psychic distance from their surroundings.

Thus, despite the emphasis on locality seen in *Ju-on*, it is difficult to align the film with a specifically "Japanese" spatial aesthetic, as there are already discrepancies in the discursive constructions of this category. Alternatively, in his analysis of the film, Jay McRoy characterizes the *Ju-on* as a hybrid of "classic" Japanese horror films, such as *Onibaba* (1964) and *Kwaidan* (1965), and Hollywood "slasher" and "splatter" films, such as *A Nightmare on Elm Street* (1984).[58] In McRoy's assessment, the film's incorporation of different styles demonstrates an ambivalent interrelation between cinematic and cultural spaces. McRoy argues that the film's focus on extreme trauma experienced within the home correlates with the "rapidly transforming social landscape" of post-1990s Japan, and that the film "exposes many of the socio-cultural anxieties that permeate Japan's increasingly hybrid, transitional culture."[59] This reading thus aligns the domestic space of the home with that of the nation, but situates both as complex places of heterogeneous forces and tensions. Further, although Shimizu has indeed stated that he was influenced by Hollywood "splatter" films, and that he appreciates the deliberate pacing of the films of Yasujiro Ozu and Kenji Mizoguchi, he cites an altogether different inspiration for the spatial logic of *Ju-on*: Krzysztof Kieslowski's *Dekalog* series of films (1989), which feature coincidentally affiliated stories that occur in the same apartment building and are thus connected by several characters' shared space of habitation.[60] Here, we find a cinematic articulation of "the local" migrating from one director to another and from one geo-cultural context to another, getting substantially transformed in the process. Yet, more than resolving the "ultimate" source for *Ju-on*, this reveals the myriad, complex intertextual connections of the film.

McRoy's discussion of the cinematic hybridity of *Ju-on* intersects with a larger discourse concerning a Japanese tendency for, according to Koichi Iwabuchi, "cultural borrowing and appropriation," wherein hybridization "is strategically represented as a key feature of Japanese national identity itself."[61] As Iwabuchi observes, such a discourse can lead to "fluid essentialism," whereby "identity is represented as a sponge that is constantly absorbing foreign cultures without changing its essence and wholeness."[62] And indeed, McRoy punctuates his essay with declarations of *Ju-on*'s cultural specificity, in spite of, or perhaps as a result of, its hybridity, such as when he asserts "Shimizu's films is [*sic*] very much a product of contemporary Japanese culture."[63] Yet he also situates the film in strong contradistinction to "Western" cinema and culture, specifically with warnings about the artistic and cultural pitfalls that the film's remake may encounter. (McRoy wrote his essay before *The Grudge* had been released). In a rather complex formulation, McRoy warns that the upcoming remake must, on the one hand, not change too much of the original film else it become a trite Hollywood product, and on the other hand, that it must translate its Japanese cultural specificities for those of the United States.[64] McRoy contrasts the stylistic hybridity of *Ju-on* with the kinds of hybridity seen in a number of Hollywood remakes of "foreign" films, valorizing this type of transculturation over the other and, more problematically, potentially reinforcing a rift between "Japan" and "the West" through differing modes of hybridity.

In fact, the Hollywood remake of *Ju-on* demonstrates an incredibly complex cultural geography. Not only does *The Grudge* construct an overtly transnational space, but in doing so it alters the apparent localism of *Ju-on*. Following the production of *Ringu*, which was enormously successful in Japan and spawned several sequels and a prequel, Takashige Ichise became associated with Hollywood producer Roy Lee, and the two worked on the remake, *The Ring*. At the time, Lee was making his entry into producing Hollywood remakes of East Asian films, which have since become the trademark of his company, Vertigo Entertainment.[65] Lee was given copies of the V-Cinema versions of *Ju-on 1* and *2*, and a day later he met with Stephen Susco and began developing a feature-length remake of the videos, with Susco acting as writer and director.[66] Studios were initially hesitant to produce the film, but after the phenomenal success of *The Ring* in US theaters, and just as the Japanese feature *Ju-on* was completed, there was much interest in doing a Hollywood remake of these films. Remarkably, the original Japanese feature-length version of *Ju-on* was produced with the Hollywood remake fully in mind, indeed, with the notion that a Hollywood feature could be produced simultaneously, a plan that nevertheless did not come to fruition.[67] Further, as Ichise and Lee worked together on producing *The Grudge*, and additionally made co-financing arrangements for a number of films to be produced in the United States *and* Japan, *Ju-on* was enmeshed from the start within an emergent transnational flow among cultural producers on both sides of the Pacific.

The making of *The Grudge* reveals even more profound transnational interconnections. As momentum behind the production of the remake grew, Ichise and

Lee shopped the project to different companies. Sam Raimi's company Ghost House was the first, and they agreed quickly to make the film.[68] It was at this point that Shimizu was brought on to direct the remake, with Stephen Susco retained as writer.[69] Although the remake had yet to secure a distributor, Ghost House worked with a German finance company to secure a production budget by pre-selling the film's territorial rights at the 2003 Cannes Film Festival.[70] Although numerous studios offered distribution deals following this, Columbia Pictures, owned by Sony Pictures Entertainment, became the film's theatrical distributor, likely due to the close relationship between Sam Raimi and Sony Pictures following the success of his film *Spiderman* (2002). With Shimizu directing, this internationally financed, Hollywood-owned and distributed film was shot in Japan, connecting capital and labor from around the world; not exactly a runaway production, but not dissimilar either. The fact that Sony is a Japanese-owned yet transnational corporation complicates this portrait even further. Moreover, the remake differed from the Japanese production in another fundamental way: although a few actors from *Ju-on* reprised their roles in *The Grudge*, American actors and actresses, including Sarah Michelle Gellar and Bill Pullman, played all the lead roles in the remake. In these respects, the remake occurred as an industrial hybrid that mapped out a vast transnational space of cultural production.

The Grudge resonates with this transnational hybridity through its representation of psycho-spatial dislocation, which transforms that seen in *Ju-on*. Much of the remake replicates the narrative of the original. As various people enter a house in Tokyo they become cursed and die at the hands of a vengeful spirit, who had been previously murdered in an act of domestic violence. Although the remake slightly rearranges the temporality of the narrative, the sequences largely maintain a non-linear, episodic structure similar to that found in *Ju-on*. In this respect, *The Grudge* retains a strong sense of localization, as the house remains the focal point of the narrative. Notably, whereas *Ju-on* was shot in a real house in the Saitama prefecture of Tokyo, the house in *The Grudge* was constructed on a Tokyo soundstage.[71] Yet, with only a few, very minor differences, the houses in the two films appear nearly identical.

Rather than transforming the space directly, then, the remake alters the house by placing American characters within it. Sarah Michelle Gellar plays an American exchange student who lives in Japan and does social work for extra credit. In another sequence, an American family resides in the cursed home while the husband works for a Japanese company. In one of the few narrative additions that *The Grudge* makes to *Ju-on*, we find through a series of flashbacks that an American professor working in Japan stands at the center of the entire curse: the woman Kayako became obsessed with the instructor without his knowledge, and when her husband found this out, he murdered her and their son. In this respect, *The Grudge* becomes a story of transnationally mobile people, all white Americans, coming into horrific and deadly contact with "the local," specifically in Japan. Indeed, the film goes to lengths to correlate the house with Japan. For example, it features an extended sequence of Sarah Michelle Gellar's character roaming the streets of Tokyo as she first searches for the house. Similarly, when a Japanese police detective explains the nature of the house's deadly curse to Gellar's character, the two stand atop a building with the expanse of Tokyo pictured behind them, implicating all of Japan as a haunted and murderous place. As the house becomes transnationalized by the encounters with the Americans, the film represents these Americans as ineffective in their transnational mobility. The film portrays failed attempts to reconcile the global and the local.

Nevertheless, this depiction of transnational terror did outstanding business upon its release in US theaters in October 2004, earning over forty million dollars during its opening weekend alone.[72] Although the box-office success of *The Ring* in 2002 precipitated the exceptional, even unexpected success of *The Grudge*, this film confirmed the commercial viability of Hollywood remakes of Japanese horror films and, in many respects, of Hollywood remakes of East Asian films in general.[73] In some ways *The Grudge* had much more of an impact on this cycle than *The Ring*, which could have been viewed as a fluke before the success of *The Grudge*. Propelled by a commercial/cultural logic of repetition and variation, of product differentiation analogous to that of genre cycles and blockbuster franchises, Hollywood studios have concertedly fostered this transnational cinematic exchange.

This should not suggest, however, that the players within this exchange hold equal power or that there are not cultural consequences to these asymmetries. Some reviews of *The Grudge* in US papers succumbed to simplistic cultural binaries typically found in reviews of Hollywood remakes of foreign films, while others lamented the film as a failed cultural hybrid.[74] More strikingly, *The Grudge* followed *Ju-on*'s release in US theaters earlier that summer, where it earned a mere $300,000 over thirteen weeks.[75] Such meager returns are typical of foreign-language films in US theaters, of course, with only the rarest exception. Yet compare that "cultural discount" with the success of *The Grudge* in Japan, where it earned nearly three million dollars.[76] Although box-office figures do not adequately indicate a film's cultural importance, the discrepancy between the success of *Ju-on* and *The Grudge* does demonstrate how the transnational film remake functions as an exercise in power and control, a strategic form of commercial domination through cultural accommodation.

## The Mobile Spaces of Film Remakes

*Ju-on* and *The Grudge* thus join with the two *Insomnia* films in demonstrating struggles for cultural power in the form of transnational film remakes. They articulate this contest in their economic conditions, in the forms of their circulation, as well as in their narratives and aesthetic strategies. They articulate it in their production of conflicting spaces. Although transnational remakes, like the cinema in general, have a long history of dealing with issues of mobility and interconnection, these recent examples provide pointed insights into the tensions that pervade contemporary cultural globalization and the confusions of postmodern, transnational geographies. While the *Insomnia* films, *Ju-on*, and *The Grudge* cannot represent the abstract space of transnational flows directly, they reveal symptoms of the transformation of space by such flows. They map multiple connections between the local and the global through the interpenetration of economics, culture, geography, representation, and imagination. And although these films appear to demonstrate Hollywood's continued dominance among the global cultural industries, they also reveal Hollywood's increased need for financial and geographic flexibility, demanded by the genuine competition posed to its hegemony throughout the world. Like the precarious identities and fluctuating spaces seen within these films, they equally reveal the shifting and mobile conditions—the dislocations—of the contemporary global cultural industries.

# Notes

1. *L'Arivée d'un train à la Ciotat* can be found on the *Landmarks of Early Film* laser disc distributed by Image Entertainment. *L'Arivée d'un train* can be found on the video "The Movies Begin: A Treasury of Early Cinema, Vol. 2" distributed by Kino Video.

2. Thomas Edison made a version of *L'Arivée d'un train* as *Black Diamond Express* (1896), this film depicting the eponymous train speeding through a rural landscape toward and past the camera; although *Black Diamond Express* visibly differs from *L'Arivée d'un train*, its primary conceit and attraction remains the same. As Charles Musser notes, *Black Diamond Express* "was [itself] remade several times over the next six years," creating multiple versions. Charles Musser, *Before the Nickelodeon: Edwin S. Porter and the Edison Manufacturing Company* (Berkeley: University of California Press, 1991), 96.

3. *A Narrow Escape* and *A Lonely Villa* have been extensively described and compared by Richard Abel and Tom Gunning, respectively. Richard Abel, *The Ciné Goes to Town: French Cinema 1896–1914* (Berkeley: University of California Press, 1994), 193–95; Tom Gunning, *D. W. Griffith and the Origins of American Narrative Film: The Early Years at Biograph* (Urbana: University of Illinois Press, 1991), 195–204.

4. Anne Friedberg, *Window Shopping: Cinema and the Postmodern* (Berkeley: University of California Press, 1994), 2–3.

5. David James argues, "as every film . . . internalizes the conditions of its production, it makes itself an allegory of them." David James, *Allegories of Cinema: American Film in the Sixties* (Berkeley: University of California Press, 1989), 12.

6. For an analysis of the various incarnations of *The Ring*, particularly as they delineate a larger technological, economic, and cultural formation across the Pacific Rim, see my essay, "Circulations: Technology and Discourse in *The Ring* Intertext," in *Second Takes: Critical Approaches to the Film Sequel*, edited by Carolyn Jess-Cooke and Constantine Verevis (Albany: State University of New York Press, 2009), forthcoming.

7. Drawing upon Rick Altman's theorization of film genres, Constantine Verevis provides an astute taxonomy of film remakes' intertextual relations. *Film Remakes* (New York:

Palgrave Macmillan, 2005), 84–85.

8. Caren Kaplan engages in an extended analysis of the complex relations between modernity and postmodernity, specifically in relation to space, movement, and travel, in *Questions of Travel: Postmodern Discourses of Displacement* (Durham, N.C.: Duke University Press, 1996). Rosalind Galt also notes that "space" has played a vital role in the critical analysis of modernity and postmodernity, and somewhat similarly to my account here, that contemporary spatial analysis is specifically responding to "the renewed importance of space as a defining feature of postmodernity." Rosalind Galt, *The New European Cinema: Redrawing the Map* (New York: Columbia University Press, 2006), 93.

9. Henri Lefebvre, *The Production of Space* (Malden, Mass.: Blackwell, 1991).

10. Edward W. Soja, *Postmodern Geographies: The Reassertion of Space in Critical Social Theory* (London: Verso, 1989), 6.

11. Fredric Jameson, *Postmodernism, or, The Cultural Logic of Late Capitalism* (Durham, N.C.: Duke University Press, 1991), 6, 25, 44.

12. David Harvey, *The Condition of Postmodernity* (Malden, Mass.: Blackwell, 1990), 147.

13. Harvey, *The Condition of Postmodernity*, 240, 284.

14. Arjun Appadurai, *Modernity at Large: Cultural Dimensions of Globalization* (Minneapolis: University of Minnesota Press, 1996), 33.

15. Doreen Massey, *Space, Place, and Gender* (Minneapolis: University of Minnesota Press, 1994); Saskia Sassen, *Globalization and Its Discontents* (New York: New Press, 1998).

16. Appadurai, *Modernity at Large*, 35.

17. David Morley and Kevin Robins, *Spaces of Identity: Global Media, Electronic Landscapes and Cultural Boundaries* (London: Routledge, 1995), 1–2.

18. Harvey, *The Condition of Postmodernity*, 240.

19. Morley and Robins, *Spaces of Identity*, 75.

20. Massey, *Space, Place, and Gender*, 137, 155.

21. Massey, *Space, Place, and Gender*, 156.

22. "About NFI: Mission and Primary Objective," *Norwegian Film Institute*, <http://www.nfi.no/english> (17 September 2006).

23. Gunnar Iversen, "Norway," in *Nordic National Cinemas* (London: Routledge, 1998), 106–107, 139; "Overview of the Norwegian Audiovisual Market," *Kulturdepartementet of the Ministry of Cultural Affairs*, <http://www.odin.dep.no/kkd/engelsk/publ/veiledninger/018001-990016/index-dok000-b-n-a.html#fotnote_ref_5> (17 September 2006).

24. Iversen, "Norway," 107.

25. "Overview of the Norwegian Audiovisual Market."

26. "Eurimages: Member States," *Council of Europe*, <http://www.coe.int/T/E/Cultural_Co-operation/Eurimages/About_Eurimages/Members/index.asp#TopOfPage> (18 September 2006).

27. "About NFI."

28. Iversen, "Norway," 136.

29. Iversen, "Norway," 136–137.

30. Iversen, "Norway," 136.

31. Paul Schrader, "Notes on *Film Noir*," in *Film Noir Reader*, ed. Alain Silver and James Ursini (New York: Limelight Editions, 1996), 55–57.

32. Schrader, "Notes on *Film Noir*," 53; detailed by Vivian Sobchack, "Lounge Time:

Postwar Crises and the Chronotope of Film Noir," in *Reconfiguring American Film Genres: Theory and History*, ed. Nick Brown (Berkeley: University of California Press, 1998), 167n2.

33. "*Insomnia*," press release from First Run Features, viewed at the Margaret Herrick Library of the Academy of Motion Picture Arts and Sciences.

34. Iversen, "Norway," 102.

35. Monica Roman, "Nantucket Sets Sked," *Variety*, 29 May 1997.

36. "Film Shorts," *Hollywood Reporter*, 17 November 1997; "Toronto Deals," *Screen International*, 19 September 1997.

37. Frank Scheck, "*Insomnia*," *Hollywood Reporter*, 29 May 1997; Joanna Connors, "Shining Endless Summer on a Crackerjack Murder Thriller," *The Plain Dealer*, 24 October 1998.

38. Michael Atkinson, "Guilt Trip," *Village Voice*, 2 June 1998.

39. John Hazelton, "Case Study: *Insomnia*," *Screen International*, 17 May 2002.

40. Hazelton, "Case Study: *Insomnia*."

41. Many have noted that the epic depiction of landscape is constitutive of the western. Scott Simmon, for instance, traces this to photographic conventions of the nineteenth century, particularly in the work of Timothy O'Sullivan. Scott Simmon, *The Invention of the Western Film: A Cultural History of the Genre's First Half-Century* (Cambridge: Cambridge University Press, 2003), 41–42.

42. Quite remarkably, this dynamic occurs again in the Hollywood remake (2007) of the Norwegian film *Pathfinder*. Whereas the earlier film depicts eleventh-century Sami people fending off attacks by roving bandits, the Hollywood remake resituates the narrative in North America in a plot that recalls James Fennimore Cooper's *The Last of the Mohicans*. Turning a "first peoples" story into one of "first contact," the remake has a Viking child raised by Native Americans defend this tribe against a subsequent wave of Viking marauders.

43. Audrey Droesch, "Hollywood North: The Impact and Costs of Demarcation Rules on the Runaway Film Industry" (master's thesis, Stanford University, 2002), 4, 46.

44. Toby Miller, et. al., *Global Hollywood* (London: BFI Publishing, 2001), 56–64.

45. Miller, et. al., 58, 61.

46. Susan Napier, *Anime: From Akira to Princess Mononoke* (New York: Palgrave, 2000), 16.

47. Conversely, David Desser's classic study of Akira Kurosawa's samurai films details how "Kurosawa utilizes Western motifs and makes them his own." David Desser, *The Samurai Films of Akira Kurosawa* (Ann Arbor, Mich.: UMI Research Press, 1981), 4.

48. These films were remade as *City of Angels* (1998), *The Vanishing* (1993), and *Vanilla Sky* (2001), respectively. For a discussion of *Abre los Ojos* and its Hollywood remake *Vanilla Sky*, particularly as they raise issues about transnational identities, see my article, "*Sky*'s the Limit: Transnationality and Identity in *Abre los Ojos* and *Vanilla Sky*," *Film Quarterly* 60, no. 1 (Fall 2006): 28–39.

49. Mark Schilling, *Contemporary Japanese Film* (New York: Weatherhill, 1999), 29.

50. Schilling, *Contemporary Japanese Film*, 29.

51. Tom Mes devotes a chapter of his study of Miike to the director's work for the V-Cinema market. Tom Mes, *Agitator: The Cinema of Takashi Miike* (Surrey, UK: FAB Press, 2003), 35–61; David Cook, *A History of Narrative Film*, 3rd ed. (New York: W. W. Norton and Company, 2004), 761, 766.

52. Takashige Ichise, interview with author, translated by Chiho Asada, 4 October

2006.

53. "*Ju-on: The Grudge*," *New Cinema from Japan*, Toronto 2003 Issue (Tokyo: Uni-Japan Film, 2003), 10.

54. Donald Richie, *Japanese Cinema: Film Style and National Character* (New York: Anchor Books, 1971), 14.

55. Burch thereby counters notions that traditional Japanese domestic architecture creates a space of "free flow." At one point he states, "the filmic image becomes, *predominantly*, the planar projection of the three-dimensional cells, static in each of their successive arrangements." Noël Burch, *To The Distant Observer: Form and Meaning in Japanese Cinema* (Berkeley: University of California Press, 1979), 199–200.

56. Burch, *To The Distant Observer*, 200.

57. Burch, *To The Distant Observer*, 201.

58. Jay McRoy, "Case Study: Cinematic Hybridity in Shimizu Takashi's *Ju-on: The Grudge*," in *Japanese Horror Cinema*, ed. Jay McRoy (Honolulu: University of Hawaii Press, 2005), 175–176, 181.

59. McRoy, "Case Study," 179, 180

60. Takashi Shimizu, quoted in Wheeler Winston Dixon, "An Interview with Takashi Shimizu," translated by Shoichi Gregory Kamei, *Quarterly Review of Film and Video* 22, no. 1 (January–March 2005): 2, 4–5, 7, 12. Alternatively, in my judgment, the combination of styles and themes found in *Ju-on* resembles the neo-gothic Hollywood horror films of the 1970s, such as *The Exorcist* (1973), *The Omen* (1976), or *The Amityville Horror* (1979), more closely than the slasher movies mentioned by McRoy and Shimizu.

61. Koichi Iwabuchi, *Recentering Globalization: Popular Culture and Japanese Transnationalism* (Durham, N.C.: Duke University Press, 2002), 53.

62. Iwabuchi, *Recentering Globalization*, 54.

63. McRoy, "Case Study," 181.

64. McRoy, "Case Study," 182.

65. For more information about Roy Lee, see my interview, "Remaking Transnational Hollywood: An Interview with Roy Lee," *Spectator: The University of Southern California Journal of Film and Television Criticism* 27, no. 2 (Fall 2007): 94–100. For a sensationalized but informative account of Lee and his business practices, see Tad Friend, "Remake Man: Roy Lee Brings Asia to Hollywood, and Finds Some Enemies Along the Way," *The New Yorker*, 2 June 2003, <http://www.newyorker.com/archive/2003/06/02/030602fa_fact> (19 September 2006).

66. Stephen Susco, interview with author, 1 June 2007. According to Susco, his initial idea was to make more of a sequel than a remake. In this unproduced version of the story, an American architect brings the grudge to the United States from Japan after visiting there and building a house that resembles the cursed Japanese home in an American suburb.

67. Susco, interview with author.

68. Tad Friend recounts the situation of this deal in his article.

69. Susco, interview with author.

70. Susco, interview with author.

71. Takashi Shimizu, quoted in Patrick Macias, "The Scarist [*sic*] Horror Ever? 'Juon' Director, Takashi Shimizu Interview," *Japanattack*, 26 July 2003. <http://www.japattack.com/main/?q=node/72. (11 June 2007)> In fact, this same soundstage was used in the production of *Seven Samurai*. Stephen Susco, e-mail to author, 12 July 2007. More details regarding the construction about this set can be found in "Designing *The Grudge* House," a video produced and directed by Michael Gillis and one of the extra features on Sony's

DVD release of the film. In this segment, the film's production designer, Iwao Saito, explains that certain aspects of the house differed from traditional Japanese homes and were designed to accommodate American cultural notions; specifically, it was larger than a traditional Japanese house and had a long hallway that is uncharacteristic of Japanese houses.

72. Gabriel Snyder, "'Grudge' Match: Sony Pic Scares Up Big Aud for $40 mil," *Variety.com*, 24 October 2004, <http://www.variety.com/article/VR1117912389.html> (5 July 2007).

73. Snyder, "'Grudge' Match."

74. Owen Gleiberman, "The Grudge," *Entertainment Weekly*, 29 Oct. 2004, 47–48. Manohla Dargis, "A House Even Ghostbusters Can't Help," *New York Times*, 22 October 2004, E1: 20.

75. Snyder, "'Grudge' Match."

76. "Foreign Box Office: *The Grudge*," *Box Office Mojo*, <http://www.boxofficemojo.com/movies/?page=intl&id=grudge.htm> (5 July 2007).

# Part III: Transformation

*Chapter 9*

# Second Chance: Remaking *Solaris*

## Constantine Verevis

In *The Solaris Effect*, Steven Dillon sets out to explore a fundamental aspect of the cinematic image—the "paradoxical experience of cinematic presence" or what he calls "the *Solaris* effect"—with reference to a select group of contemporary (mostly independent) American films.[1] As the title suggests, the paradigmatic example for Dillon's book is Andrei Tarkovsky's third feature, *Solaris* (1972), a film that "provides a detailed and complex model for cinematic illusion [and self-reflexivity]."[2] Based on the 1961 science fiction novel by Polish author Stanislaw Lem, Tarkovsky's *Solaris* tells the story of psychologist Kris Kelvin who is sent to a space station orbiting Solaris, a distant planet whose surface consists of a vast sentient ocean.[3] The planet reacts to the scientists probing its surface by sending "visitors"—living beings created from their deepest memories and desires—to the station. Kris's visitor is his wife Hari (Rheya in the novel) whom he has mourned since her tragic suicide many years before.[4] According to Dillon, the science fiction world of Solaris not only provides Tarkovsky with an opportunity to pursue his interest in poetic cinema, but "the relationship between Kris and his dead, perfectly real wife [is also] the archetypal relationship of audience and screen at the cinema. There is photographic reality, sensual and emotional immersion, but also a concurrent knowledge that the reality is all along an artifice, a constructed hallucination."[5]

Throughout his book, Dillon argues that the Solaris effect is the essence of self-conscious filmmaking, and that recent American feature films such as *Mulholland Drive* (David Lynch, 2001) and *A. I.: Artificial Intelligence* (Steven Spiel-

167

berg, 2001) "turn out to be contemporary versions of Tarkovsky's [*Solaris*] masterpiece."[6] For Dillon, the Solaris effect is evident, too, in the commercial-inde-
pendent career of director Steven Soderbergh, one that begins with a "landmark of
cinematic self-reflexivity" in *sex, lies, and videotape* (1989), and from its outset
"has been aimed towards a remake of Tarkovsky's *Solaris*."[7] Budgeted at $47 mil-
lion, Soderbergh's *Solaris* (2002) figuratively sits midway between the director's
commercial blockbusters—*Out of Sight* (1998), *Erin Brockovich* (2000), *Ocean's
Eleven* (2001)—and those more "idiosyncratic personal films"—*sex, lies, and
videotape, Schizopolis* (1996), *Full Frontal* (2002)—"that are synced [just like the
narrative of *Solaris*] to his [Soderbergh's and Kelvin's] own bio-rhythms, immediate perceptions and imaginative processes."[8] *Solaris* is a work, then, that directly
invokes earlier properties—Lem's book, Tarkovsky's film and, in terms of its "second chance" scenario, Alfred Hitchcock's *Vertigo* (1958)—but also reveals itself
in relation to Soderbergh's oeuvre and to strategies of "authorial remaking."[9]

## As It Is When It Was

Review articles and commentaries dealing with Soderbergh's *Solaris* remake typically exploit a familiar strategy whereby the ins and outs of the remake—and remake practice in general—are evaded by calling up the new version not as a
"remake" of Tarkovsky's film, but as a fresh "adaptation" of the original literary
source.[10] Tarkovsky's filmed version follows the outline of Lem's novel (retaining
the basic structure and some of the dialogue) but, as Vida Johnson and Graham
Petrie point out, Tarkovsky's film is ultimately less interested in the novel's scientific speculation and psychological insights than in developing questions of family and morality.[11] Indeed, Lem is said to have reacted with hostility to Tarkovsky's
adaptation, in particular its Earth story line (and earthbound prologue) which
served to "shift the film radically away from Lem's primarily philosophical and
technological approach . . . [towards] an exploration of family relationships, themes
of guilt and betrayal, and a celebration of the natural beauty of Earth and humanity's inescapable links with it."[12] By contrast, early production reports indicated that
Soderbergh's new adaptation would steer closer to the themes of the novel, but
upon its release reviewers noted that the remake had transformed the source material (even more than Tarkovsky's version), abandoning its broad philosophical
questions to focus primarily on the love story: the relationship between Kris (Chris
in the remake) and his wife Rheya, and—in a reprise of Hitchcock's *Vertigo*—
their opportunity for a "second chance."[13]

The "making of" extras on the Twentieth Century Fox DVD release of *Solaris* reinforce this type of interpretation. For instance, in an episode entitled "Inside *Solaris*," producer James Cameron states: "this [picture] isn't really a remake
of the Tarkovsky film. It's a *different* adaptation of the underlying novel by Stanislaw Lem." In another segment, "*Solaris*: Behind the Planet," Soderbergh similarly

intones: "my interest in *Solaris* was really driven by the ideas at the center of the book." Curiously enough, the screenplay that is reproduced in the extras package admits its debt to the earlier film version, stating that the remake is "based on the novel by Stanislaw Lem *and* the screenplay by Friedrich Gorentstein and Andrei Tarkovsky." But throughout the documentary extras Soderbergh consistently pushes away from the Tarkovsky version towards the earlier source, underlining his interest in a "great love story" and his own unique (auteur) vision: "it [the novel] just seemed to be about everything I [was] interested in personally."[14] Along with a review comment (in the US trade journal *Variety*) that Soderbergh takes *Solaris* in a "more personal direction to make it something close to 'Scenes From a Marriage in Outer Space,'" the *Solaris* DVD commentaries indicate the ways in which Soderbergh's remake not only overwrites Tarkovsky (and others) but provides evidence of the filmmaker's own traceable signature.[15]

The suggestion that *Solaris* can be understood as a kind of authorial *re*-vision—a property transformed, according to auteur predilections, into "an intimate two-hander between a man and a woman"—is further supported by various review articles that draw attention to the thematic similarities between *Solaris* and Soderbergh's other film work.[16] For instance, Andrew O'Hehir argues that Soderbergh's previous feature, *Ocean's Eleven*, and *Solaris* are in some ways *the same film*: "both are meditations on lost love, in which George Clooney (who is Soderbergh's muse, mirror, and canvas) recovers a dark-eyed beauty from his past."[17] Similarly, Philip Strick states that *Solaris* provides Soderbergh not only with an opportunity to exploit his favorite color schemes—especially blues and purples—but also to comfortably transplant its protagonist, Chris Kelvin (George Clooney), into the "remarkably familiar territory" of Soderbergh's own earlier authorial (and cinematic) remakings:

> [Soderbergh's] *Solaris* is almost if not quite a rerun [a remake] of *Ocean's Eleven* (out-of-towner invades hi-tech labyrinth in order to win back wife), *The Underneath* (out-of-towner pursues former wife for second chance), *Traffic* (stranger-in-town searches for lost daughter to reunite family), or *The Limey* (troubleshooter from another continent arrives in town to avenge lost daughter).[18]

The list of features provided by Strick is instructive, too, for the fact that—like *Solaris*—each one of these films is, in some sense, a cinematic remake: *Ocean's Eleven* is a loose revision of Lewis Milestone's 1960 Rat Pack feature of the same name; *The Underneath* (1995) is an update of classic noir *Criss Cross* (Robert Siodmak, 1949); *Traffic* (2000) follows the six-part UK mini-series *Traffik* (Alastair Reid, 1989); and *The Limey* (1999) is an uncredited remake of *Point Blank* (John Boorman, 1967). Dillon extends this approach to argue that Soderbergh "doubles" the repetition already inherent in these remakes by focusing—in films such as *The Underneath*, *Schizopolis*, *Ocean's Eleven*, and *Solaris*—on a remarriage plot, "one that brings with it the Solaris effect, the present desire [to recapture the past] and broken love of the cinephile."[19] Dillon's description of

Soderbergh's impulse to remake not only suggests a director who is continually resurrecting the ghost of *Solaris*, but also one who is simultaneously revising his own earlier auteur themes. In a further example, one that underlines the way in which remaking can be understood in terms of a filmmaker's desire to repeatedly express and modify a particular aesthetic sensibility and worldview, Amy Taubin identifies *Solaris* as "the most personal, interiorized narrative of [Soderbergh's] career, [a film that] could be his *Pierrot le fou* [Jean-Luc Godard, 1965] or *Vertigo*."[20] Soderbergh himself concurs, stating that:

> [*Solaris* is] about 20 percent the [Lem] book, 20 percent the [Tarkovsky] movie, and the rest my own preoccupations. The conceit of the film is Lem's, and, based on that, *I'm building everything I'm interested in*. It's a relationship. It's a love story . . . [Ultimately] I understood [that *Solaris* is] about acceptance, if I had to use one word.[21]

As these comments suggest, *Solaris* reveals itself to be thematically consistent in relation to Soderbergh's oeuvre, with which it shares (at least) two characteristics. First, Soderbergh returns, in the character of Chris Kelvin, to his favored theme (or portrait) of solitude, of a loner-protagonist: "alienated, isolated, estranged, [an] outsider, underdog."[22] This recalls not only the persona of "the sullen voyeur in *sex, lies, [and videotape]*, the disenfranchised gambler of *The Underneath*, [and] *The Limey* in Los Angeles," but also describes the pensive Chris Kelvin, burdened with the guilt of a specific emotional trauma from the past: the suicide of his wife Rheya.[23] As Soderbergh describes it, "protagonists in my films tend to be at odds with their surroundings and/or the people around them."[24] Not unrelated to this, the second connecting thread across Soderbergh's work is his interest in fractured narratives: "[a] fascination with the manipulation of time, and breaking [away from] the conventions of . . . linear storytelling."[25] In the case of *Solaris*, Soderbergh assembles an elliptical and fragmented tale, one that "systematically and stealthily blurs the dividing lines between past and present, rationality and irrationality, 'flesh and blood' reality, and psychic fantasy."[26] Dave Kehr describes the cumulative effect of Soderbergh's "overlapping narratives and shifting time frames" as one that creates "a haze of passing time, ambiguous memories, partial perceptions, and false assumptions."[27] And in a description of the (subjective) manipulation of time in the editing patterns of *The Limey*—a description that seems to also communicate the form (and content) of *Solaris*—Soderbergh observes: "I was trying to get a sense of how your mind sifts through things."[28] In *Solaris*, Soderbergh's career interest in two recurring features—an isolated protagonist and non-linear narrative—comes together in Chris Kelvin's "desperate need to connect."[29]

## Dreams Never End

Soderbergh's *Solaris* begins (without titles) with a poetic shot of drops of water running down a windowpane. It is an opening which cannot help but recall the first, lingering shots of water weeds which, in the Tarkovsky version, give way to the tracing of Kris's last day in the countryside around his father's house (dacha) before leaving Earth for Solaris. Kris is seen absorbing the sights and sounds of his home planet: strolling through the spacious garden, dipping his hands in the lake, and later allowing himself to be caught in a sudden sun shower. In a significant departure from anything in Lem's novel, which is set entirely on the space station, the first quarter of Tarkovsky's film is devoted to the careful documentation of the natural beauty of Earth, and to establishing Kris's close family and other personal relationships. The extended Earth prologue provides background information to Kris's mission—for instance, astronaut Berton's video recording gives details of an earlier, ill-fated expedition to Solaris, and a television program introduces the crew (Sartorius, Snaut, and Gibarian) presently operating the space station—but the emphasis is to "establish for the film a terrain of memory, a human landscape of loved things to be looked back on with longing and desire."[30] In the scene immediately before his departure, Kris stands outside the dacha at dusk, burning papers and photographs at a bonfire. Among the material Kris sorts through is a photograph of a young woman wearing a shawl: she is later identified as Kris's dead wife, Hari. Together with the initial shots of gentle water weeds (which are later linked to the hair of the sleeping Hari, spread out on Kris's pillow), the photograph connects the appearance of Kris's visitor to his subjective perception and memories of home. As Tarkovsky describes it: "[*Solaris*] is an adventure that happens to one man, within his conscience."[31]

Dillon describes the opening of Soderbergh's *Solaris* as a "hyperdeliberate" quotation of Tarkovsky, but at the same time the Soderbergh version—a film which runs a mere ninety-five minutes—signals its departure from Tarkovsky's two and three-quarter hour long meditative exercise, establishing (in the narrative economy of its opening six minutes set on Earth) the film's future setting, the nature of Chris' mission to Solaris, the sullen protagonist's interior mood, and (most importantly) the film's broad theme of romantic love.[32] Specifically, the first shot of Soderbergh's film is followed by a three-shot sequence of Chris sitting pensively on the edge of his unmade bed. Each of the three shots (#2–4) is accompanied by the sound of rain and a woman's (Rheya's) voice-over: "Chris, what is it?", "I love you so much," and "Don't you love me anymore?" The melancholic mood is broken by a tracking shot (#5) of Chris purposively striding through a crowded and rainy, urban landscape of the near future (this is not only rain from Tarkovsky, but a future Earth washed by the same interminable drizzle of *Blade Runner's* 2019) and then another sequence of three shots (#6–8) which at once documents Chris' profession as psychotherapist and grief counselor and underlines his own isolation. The next five shots (#9–13)—Chris seated on a subway train, Chris moving toward the exterior staircase of an apartment building, and a sequence of three shots which has Chris accidentally cut his finger while slicing vegetables (each one of these shots is repeated, with difference, towards the end of the film)—lead to Chris receiving a mysterious transmission from his friend Gibarian (Ulrich Tukur) who implores him to leave for Solaris to help resolve problems unspecified. "I hope you will come to Solaris, Chris," he says. "I think you need to." The opening sequence (twenty-three shots, including the final shot of the screen displaying Gibarian's message dissolving to a shot of Chris' craft approaching the space station Prometheus in orbit around Solaris) insistently follows the character of Chris Kelvin, striving to put the viewer inside the mind and experience—the memory and desire—of the protagonist.

The narrative economy of the opening of Soderbergh's *Solaris* marks it out from its esteemed predecessor, but even though radically shortened, the remake at once clarifies and refines many elements of the earlier film.[33] Chris arrives on the Prometheus to find the floor and ceilings of the labyrinth space station stained with blood. Gibarian has killed himself, other members of the crew are dead or missing, and Chris catches a glimpse of a young boy, later (though inexplicably) revealed to be Gibarian's son, Michael. Chris also meets (individually) the two surviving members of the crew—Snow (Jeremy Davies) and Gordon (Viola Davis)—who are unwilling (or unable) to communicate what they are experiencing in their encounter with Solaris. As Snow puts it: "I could tell you what's happening, but I don't know if that would really tell you what's happening." Chris subsequently requests a formal interview with Snow and Gordon during which the latter describes the privatization of the Solaris project and how her assignment to assess the economic potential of the planet was interrupted when "this shit started happening." Much is revealed in the extended sequence (around the twenty-minute mark of the film) that documents Chris' "first sleep" on the Prometheus. It is at this point that the viewer begins to understand "that the space station [and oceanic planet below] is a metaphor for Kelvin's mind, not [only] because of the metaphysical arguments that are spelled out in the [film's] dialogue, but [most tellingly] through the mise-en-scène."[34]

The "first sleep" sequence begins (shots #1–3) with Chris locking (as Snow has advised him to do) his cabin door and getting into bed. As Cliff Martinez's shimmering electronic score displaces the ambient sound of the space station, a series of six alternating shots (#4–9)—close-ups of Chris sleeping intercut with ever closer shots of the blue orb of Solaris—motivate a point-of-view shot (#10) of hands holding in a lap what appears to be a doorknob with a central keyhole (the overtly sexual imagery—which recalls the clutch purse of Hitchcock's *Marnie* [1964]—seems a Freudian "joke" about the unconscious). This sets up a pattern of alternation with shots of Chris sleeping (#11–14) before a view of the doorknob (shot #14) tilts up to reveal that it is Rheya (Natascha McElhone) who holds it. A reverse-shot (#15) and eye-line match shows Chris seated opposite her on a subway train (similar to the one seen at the film's opening). At this point the film returns to a shot of Chris sleeping (#16) and, as Rheya gets up to leave the train (shots #17 and 19), the view is at once a dream-image, generated by the sleeping Chris (shots #18 and 20), and a recollection-image, (implicitly) from the point-of-view of the waking Chris seated on the train.

The sleeping Chris frowns (shot #20) and there follows next a shot of the shimmering blue of Solaris (#21), a shot of Chris in an elevator (#22), and then another shot of Chris sleeping (#23). The series of shots (#24–28) that follows depicts Chris and Rheya's first (spoken) encounter at a party, apparently held to mark Gibarian's imminent departure for Solaris. If the shots up to this point have been coded principally as Chris' dream-images then the party sequence doubles this, singularly presenting Chris and Rheya's meeting from the former's point-of-view. Chris enters the party (shot #24) and the camera follows him as he moves through the crowd. Adopting his point-of-view, the camera takes in a scene of the seated Rheya before it tilts up to bring Gibarian, holding his infant son, into view. As Chris moves to join his friend (shots #24–25), diegetic sound from the party gradually replaces the Martinez score, and as Chris and Gibarian converse, another eye-line match cuts to a shot of Rheya. She smiles at Chris, gets up from her seat, and moves towards the bar. Significantly, as Rheya is being surveyed (shot #26), Gibarian says: "[Solaris] seems to be reacting . . . almost like it knows it's being observed." Chris excuses himself and heads towards Rheya, the camera (once again adopting a position on his shoulder) pulling focus to come to rest on a medium close-up of Rheya (shot #28) whereupon she utters her first (embodied) line: "Don't blow it." Again, the sequence returns to a view of Chris sleeping on the Prometheus (shot #29), the sound of the party continuing as they exchange three lines: "You start." "I did," replies Rheya. "Really?" asks Chris. Shot #30 returns to the party, and then shot #31 shows Chris in the same elevator (as shot #22), but this time descending with Rheya. In a voice-over Rheya says "Try poetry," and Chris quotes a single line from Dylan Thomas: "And death shall have no dominion."[35] If the coincidence of dream-images and the restricted point-of-view of recollection-images has, to this point, been complex, then the relationship becomes even more ambiguous in the next passage.

As Chris and Rheya stand in the elevator joining hands, the Martinez music returns and gradually displaces the diegetic sounds of the party. Shot #32 returns to Chris "sleeping" in his cabin, but he now opens his eyes, further confusing—in this waking sleep—the distinction between memory and dream, cognition and imagination, past and present. A reverse-shot (#33) reveals only a shadowy point-of-view. Shot #34 again shows Chris (eyes wide). A door opens and Chris enters his apartment with Rheya. Another shot of Chris in his cabin (#36) motivates a second shadowy point-of-view shot (#37), but this time the indistinct shape materializes in the form of an extreme close-up of Rheya's face. There follows a seventeen-shot sequence (shots #38–54) depicting Chris and Rheya's lovemaking, but the previous shot (#37) serves to quite literally collapse narrative space and blur the distinction between past and present. At the end of the lovemaking, the camera returns to a close-up shot of Chris sleeping (#55) eyes now again closed, and then a medium shot (#56) of the same. With shot #57—a medium close-up of the sleeping Chris—ambient sound again replaces the musical score. Rheya's hand entering the frame to reach over Chris' shoulder brings the "first sleep" to an end. Chris' visitor—a fully realized being born of his deepest memories and desires— has materialized.

The appearance of Rheya—a "copy" or "facsimile," as Gordon later describes her, of Chris' long dead wife—not only recalls the "remarriage" scenarios of Soderbergh's earlier features, but also announces *Solaris* as a self-reflexive remake, one that directly addresses the issue of originals and (remake) copies. Furthermore, as Dillon points out, Rheya's presence and uncertain status—she is a reflection of Chris' own conscience (his feelings of domestic betrayal and guilt)—raises "the same philosophical questions about identity and consciousness" that pertain to the replicants (the synthetic humans) of Ridley Scott's *Blade Runner* (1982).[36] Like the replicant Rachel, *Solaris's* Rheya is a perfect simulation, a "copy" that pushes to the limit the distinction between reality and reproduction, such that "the unreal is no longer that of dream or of fantasy . . . [but] is that of a *hallucinatory resemblance of the real with itself.*"[37] Rheya looks and sounds human, has feelings and emotions, but like Rachel, whose memory is similarly tied to a photograph, what Rheya lacks is a past history (a temporal continuity) and real memories. In another instance of the slippage between experience and recollection that characterizes both film versions, Rheya quizzically tells Chris: "I'm not the person I remember. I do remember things but I don't remember being there. I don't remember experiencing those things." And later, as Rheya begins to understand her situation and something of her relationship to the planet Solaris, she continues: "Don't you see [Chris], I came from your memory of her." These observations are anticipated in Gibarian's comment to Chris at the party (a reprise of words uttered by cyberneticist Snaut in Tarkovsky's film): "We don't want other worlds. We want mirrors." And later, as Gordon strives to convince Chris that he needs to let go of the illusion—the subjective perception—that is Rheya, she tells him: "She's a mirror that reflects part of your mind. You provide the formula." Like the dream of cinema, the dream of *Solaris* and *Vertigo* before it is ultimately a dream of illusion, one that gives way to nothingness.[38]

Chris' incredulity at Rheya's (initial) appearance—"How are you here?" he asks—leads him to reject the visitor, sending her off into space in a small pod. But following Chris' "second sleep," an episode that recalls (in a series of extended flashbacks) Chris and Rheya's courtship and marriage, Chris accepts the Rheya he once again finds at his side. Gradually the circumstances of the disintegration of the couple's marriage and of Rheya's suicide, for which Chris blames himself— he found her dead, clutching Thomas's "And Death Shall Have No Dominion"— are revealed. As Dillon points out, whereas Tarkovsky keeps the detail of Kris and Hari's life together vague, Soderbergh's frequent flashbacks not only visualize the past but render it entirely subjective and, as a result, unreliable, and even contradictory.[39] Chris nevertheless sees in Rheya's return an opportunity for him to make amends—"this is my chance to undo that mistake" he says—but Gordon, who has grave concerns as to Solaris's motivation, constructs a device that has the potential to destabilize and destroy the visitors, including the second Rheya. Around this point, the dead Gibarian comes to Chris in his "sleep"—it is unclear whether this is a visitor or a vision—reminding him that Rheya is part of Solaris and that his ambition to take her back to Earth is doomed to fail. The second Rheya—having already attempted suicide by drinking liquid nitrogen, and increasingly uncertain of whether she is "really a human being"—implores Chris to let Gordon use the annihilation device on her. Chris refuses and seals the both of them in his quarters. Again, Chris sleeps. In another direct (albeit, oblique) quotation from Tarkovsky—the startling scene in which a panicked Hari claws her way through a metal door—the camera pans from Chris, sweat drenched, eyes wide shut, to a tangle of torn metal and blood. Next, in a further reference to Tarkovsky, Chris "dreams" three medium close-up images of Rheya—on the train, in a red-walled room, in the rainy street—before turning to a series of recollections (perhaps premonitions) of Rheya's suicide. Chris awakens to find a video recording—a second "suicide note"—from Rheya: "Chris, don't blame Gordon," she says. "It's not her fault. I begged her to do it [to use the annihilation device]. It's better this way. I found the suicide note. I went through your things. The page torn from the book of poems. And I realized that I'm not her. I'm not Rheya. I know you loved me, though." She then continues, gesturing towards the film's resolution: "I wish we could just live inside that feeling forever. Maybe there's a place where we can, but I know it's not on Earth and it's not on this ship. That's all I can say right now."

With the Prometheus now falling towards the surface of Solaris, Gordon reactivates the ship's computer navigation system and prepares a shuttle for return to Earth. In one of the most substantial departures from the Tarkovsky (and Lem) version, Chris and Gordon discover Snow's body stowed in the ceiling space. Confronting Snow's (identical) visitor, Chris and Gordon are told that Solaris has responded to the use of the annihilation device and is pulling the space station towards it. Gordon and Chris make ready the Athena shuttle for departure, but just as Chris is about to enter he hesitates. At this point (around ten minutes before the end of the film) a close-up of Chris looking into the shuttle dissolves to a repetition of the opening shot: rain falling on a window pane. There follow four shots (#2–5)—Chris: seated on his bed, walking through a crowd, commuting on a train, approaching an apartment building—each one a variation of the opening shots of the film. Accompanying these shots—at once recollections and projections: memories of the past-present to be used in the future-present—is Chris' subdued, somnambulistic voice-over: "Earth. Even the word sounded strange to me now. Unfamiliar" (shot #2). "How long had I been gone? How long had I been back? Did it matter?" (shot #3). "I tried to find the rhythm of the world where I used to live. I followed the current. I was silent and attentive. I made a conscious effort to smile. Nod. Stand" (shot #4). "And perform the millions of gestures that constitute

life on Earth. I studied these gestures until they became reflexes again. But I was
haunted by the idea that I remembered her wrong. Somehow I was wrong about
everything" (shot #5). The repetition of shots continues with a sequence of seven
shots (#6–12) of Chris slicing vegetables in his kitchen. Once again he cuts his
finger, but this time, as he runs it under water, the wound disappears. Chris responds with mild surprise. He turns to look at the refrigerator door—blank in the
opening sequence ("[there are] no pictures on the fridge" Rheya has earlier re-
called)—to now find, in another reprise of Tarkovsky, a photograph of Rheya
planted on its surface.

The sequence of (near) repeated shots ends with a dissolve back to Chris on
the Prometheus. He does not join Gordon on the shuttle, but runs instead back
through the space station, calling Rheya's name, eventually to be overcome by an
intense roar as the satellite plummets towards the surface of Solaris. Chris awakens to find the boy—Gibarian's son, Michael (Rheya was seen with him before
her second suicide)—at his side, their hands touching in imitation of Michelan-
gelo's *Creation of David* (and/or Steven Spielberg's *E. T.: The Extra-Terrestrial*,
1982). This scene dissolves to the earlier point-of-view shot of Rheya's picture on
the fridge door (shot #1). A reverse-shot shows Chris looking (#2), and then
Rheya's voice—"Chris . . . Chris," she says—initiates a series of shots/reverse-
shots of the couple (#3–9). "Am I alive, or dead?" asks a bewildered Chris. And
Rheya replies: "We don't have to think like that anymore. We're together now.
Everything we've done is forgiven. *Everything.*" The next four shots (#10–13)
have the couple embrace and kiss, before a lap dissolve leads to the last shots of
the film: three ever closer views (shots #14–16) of Solaris. By this point, it is unclear whether Chris' (present) experience is generated by his own (past) mem-
ory/desire or by disturbances and failures of memory: "I was haunted by the idea
that I remembered her [Rheya] wrong," Chris has earlier said. More than this, if
Soderbergh's revisitation of *Solaris* has been characterized by a failure to connect—by the inability of two people to understand one's experience of the other—
then the film's movement is ultimately towards some kind of *inter-subjective*
experience. The final sequence works to effect, then, a kind of universal breakdown, or what Gilles Deleuze calls an "un-founding," one that resolves all contradiction so that there is no more past or present, object or subject, body or sprit,
reality or dream, but rather the indisceriniblity of a mutual-image.[40]

Michael Wilmington describes Soderbergh's *Solaris* as "a poem of lost, per-
ilously recaptured love as moving and haunting as Hitchcock's *Vertigo*," and Amy
Taubin says that the *Solaris* remake has "more than a touch of *Vertigo's L'amour
fou* as déjà vu."[41] The latter description, in particular, draws attention to the way
paramnesia—disturbances of the memory, or the experience of déjà vu—might
aptly describe the mutual-image of *Solaris's* conclusion, where, as Deleuze describes it, "there is a recollection of the [past] present, contemporaneous with the
[present] present itself [so that] actual existence . . . whilst it is unrolled in time,
duplicates itself along with a virtual existence, a mirror-image."[42] The "eternal

sunshine" of *Solaris's* precariously happy ending is one which understands that "the only subjectivity is time, [a] non-chronological time grasped in its foundation."[43] This would seem consistent not only with Soderbergh's career interest in interiorized states and fractured temporalities, but also with an approach to cinematic remaking that seeks to understand a revision—such as *Solaris*—not as something secondary to some logically prior original, but rather as a disturbance to the usual hierarchization of original and copy. As in Eric Cazdyn's account of "transformative adaptation," every reorganization—every remaking—not only transforms the original but also its anterior adaptations: "each adaptation organizes the elements of the original literary [or film] text in a certain way in order to wrap it up with meaning," yet the transformative adaptation "implies that the original is not only what it is, but also that it exceeds itself."[44] That is, just as the original *Solaris* is reflected in Tarkovsky's own *Mirror* (1975), and other deeply personal works (his "universe of memory"), Soderbergh's film remakes not only *Solaris* and/as *Vertigo* but an entire authorial vision and cinema of romantic yearning.[45]

# Notes

1. Steven Dillon, *The Solaris Effect: Art and Artifice in Contemporary American Film* (Austin: University of Texas Press, 2006), 3.

2. Dillon, *The Solaris Effect*, 8.

3. Stanislaw Lem, *Solaris* (London: Faber, 1971).

4. For a concise account of Tarkovsky's *Solaris* see Vida Johnson and Graham Petrie, "Ethical Exploration," *Sight and Sound* 13, no. 2 (February 2003): 17–18. See also *Solaris* DVD, directed by Andrei Tarkovsky, Criterion, 2002.

5. Dillon, *The Solaris Effect*, 8.

6. Dillon, *The Solaris Effect*, 2.

7. Dillon, *The Solaris Effect*, 17.

8. Amy Taubin, "Back to the Future," *Filmmaker* 10, no. 4 (Summer 2002): 78.

9. For an extended discussion of authorship and remaking see Constantine Verevis, *Film Remakes* (Edinburgh: Edinburgh University Press, 2006), 58–78.

10. Jonathan Romney, "Future Soul," *Sight and Sound* 13, no. 2 (February 2003): 14.

11. Vida T. Johnson and Graham Petrie, *The Films of Andrei Tarkovsky: A Visual Fugue* (Bloomington: Indiana University Press, 1994), 98–110.

12. Johnson and Petrie, *The Films of Andrei Tarkovsky*, 100.

13. Michael Wilmington says that, like *Vertigo*, *Solaris* "is a film about romantic illusions and second chances, a lyrical tale of love and death." Review of *Solaris* (2002), *The Chicago Tribune*, <http://www.chicagotribune.com> (30 January 2005).

14. Quotations transcribed from *Solaris* Region 4 DVD, Paramount, 2003. Similar comments can be found on the *Solaris* official Web site, <http://www.solaristhemovie.com> (30 January 2005).

15. Todd McCarthy, "Clooney's Star Shines in Soderbergh *Solaris*," *Variety*, 25 November 25–1 December 2002, 22.

16. Romney, "Future Soul," 14.

17. Andrew O'Hehir, Rev. of *Solaris*, *Salon*, <http://www.salon.com> (30 January 2005). O'Hehir says *Solaris* and *Ocean's Eleven* "are adjacent chapters in the same larger work, driven by the same iMac ice blues and brilliant crimsons." Romney makes a similar point: "I can't see much connection here with any other Soderbergh film so much as with *Ocean's Eleven* . . . partly because the [earlier] film's most striking feature—a certain shade of blue . . . makes a welcome reappearance here." "Future Soul," 17.

18. Philip Strick, Rev. of *Solaris*, *Sight and Sound* 13, no. 3 (March 2003): 54–55.

19. Dillon, *The Solaris Effect*, 31.

20. Taubin, "Back to the Future," 81.

21. Quoted in Taubin, "Back to the Future," 83, emphasis added.

22. Anthony Kaufman, "Introduction," in *Steven Soderbergh: Interviews*, ed. Anthony Kaufman (Jackson: University Press of Mississippi, 2002), x. See also Dave Kehr, "The Hours and Times: The (Film) World According to Steven Soderbergh," *Film Comment* 35, no. 5 (September–October 1999): 41.

23. Kaufman, "Introduction," x.

24. Quoted in Anne Thompson, "Steven Soderbergh," *Premiere* 14, no. 4 (December 2000): 60.

25. Kaufman, "Introduction," xiv.

26. Adrian Martin, "Soderbergh's Planet Casts Psychic Spell," *Age*, 27 February 2003, 5.

27. Kehr, "The Hours and Times," 41.

28. Quoted in Sheila Johnston, "The Flashback Kid," *Sight and Sound* 9, no. 11 (November 1999): 12.

29. Kehr, "The Hours and Times," 41.

30. Mark Le Fanu, *The Cinema of Andrei Tarkovsky* (London: British Film Institute, 1987), 54.

31. Quoted in John Gianvito, ed. *Andrei Tarkovsky Interviews* (Jackson: University Press of Mississippi, 2006), 167.

32. Dillon, *The Solaris Effect*, 39.

33. Dillon, *The Solaris Effect*, 40.

34. Amy Taubin, "Steven Soderbergh Follows Andrei Tarkovsky into Space for a Walk with Love and Death," *Film Comment* 38, no. 6 (November–December 2002): 22.

35. Even though there is no poetry in Tarkovsky's version, Dillon describes its use as "the most Tarkovskian element in Soderbergh's remake" for the fact that Tarkovsky's father was a poet and Tarkovsky—who spoke at length about cinematic poetry—included poems in the latter two films of his "central triptych": *Solaris*, *Mirror* (1975), and *Stalker* (1979). See *The Solaris Effect*, 40.

36. Dillon, *The Solaris Effect*, 10. During Gibarian's visit, Chris says "you're not Gibarian . . . [you're] a puppet." Gibarian replies: "And you're not? Maybe you're my puppet. But like all puppets you think you're actually human. It's the puppet's dream, being human." Here we can see not only the connection Dillon makes to *A. I.* but also to *Blade Runner*, in particular the segment in which the replicant Pris masquerades as a puppet in Sebastian's workshop.

37. Jean Baudrillard, *Simulations* (New York: Semiotext(e), 1983), 142. For a discussion of Baudrillard's theory of simulacra and simulation with reference to *Blade Runner* see Giuliana Bruno, "Ramble City: Postmodernism and *Blade Runner*," *October* no. 41 (Summer 1987): 61–74.

38. Dave Kehr makes a similar point in relation to *Solaris* prototype, *Vertigo*. See

"Hitch's Riddle," *Film Comment* 20, no. 3 (May–June 1984): 16.

39. Dillon, *The Solaris Effect*, 42.

40. Gilles Deleuze, *The Logic of Sense* (London: Athlone, 1990), 263. The terms recollection-image, dream-image, and mutual-image are taken from Gilles Deleuze, *Cinema 2: The Time-Image* (Minneapolis: University of Minnesota Press, 1989), 44–97.

41. Wilmington, Rev. of *Solaris* (2002). Taubin, "Steven Soderbergh Follows Andrei Tarkovsky into Space for a Walk with Love and Death," 22.

42. Deleuze, *Cinema 2*, 79.

43. Deleuze, *Cinema 2*, 82. Soderbergh seems to understand this when he says *Solaris* is about "being present, all the time." See Taubin, "Back to the Future," 83.

44. Eric Cazdyn, *The Flash of Capital: Film and Geopolitics in Japan* (Durham, N.C.: Duke University Press, 2002), 117.

45. See Gianvito, *Andrei Tarkovsky Interviews*, 167.

*Chapter 10*

# Ape Redux: *King Kong* and the Kiwis

## Stan Jones

It was so terrific back in 1933. It's no less terrific now.
—Peter Jackson[1]

*King Kong* is exactly what it was meant to be: a highly entertaining, shrewdly conceived
work of pure cinema.[2]

Peter Jackson's remake of the 1933 film *King Kong* (Merian C. Cooper and Edward Schoedsack) proves that, in the political economy of popular global filmmaking, nothing succeeds like success. However, examining how an eventual
triumph comes about reveals an ironical history. The nod for Jackson's version
came in 2003, but that was only some years after the continuing success of the
monster genre had produced remakes like *Mighty Joe Young* (Ron Underwood,
1998) and *Godzilla* (Roland Emmerich, 1998) at Disney and Tri-star respectively.
In 1997 Jackson and his collaborators had already taken a *King Kong* into pre-pro-
duction, but the prospect of competition on such a large scale motivated Universal Pictures to cancel the project. In retrospect, this development in the motif's
history appears doubly ironic, as the original *King Kong* had arguably established
the monster genre in popular filmmaking. Less ironically, and much closer to home
for Jackson, his first movie for Hollywood had already flopped. The horror/thriller,
comedy *The Frighteners* (1996) did not produce the sort of returns in the States that
Universal was looking for when it commissioned the then-untried New Zealand director to make a Hollywood movie. However, out of this frustration came an ultimately ironic development. As Richard Taylor of Weta Workshop puts it: "It's

arguable that *The Lord of the Rings* would never have been made if we had made *King Kong*."[3] One of the trilogy's prime movers sees the success of *LOTR* as deriving from the initial failure to remake *King Kong*. By the time Jackson and associates were gathering Oscars by the armful in 2004, he was already confirmed as a bankable auteur director on a global scale. So, in 1998 Jackson invoked the *LOTR* project to keep his career and his *King Kong* production team together, sold it successfully in Los Angeles, and then created a global triumph of a film in New Zealand. That success then won him the right to the resources needed to make probably the most expensive single Hollywood film in cinema history, with much of the *LOTR* team in New Zealand—again.[4]

The 207 million dollars his re-remake eventually cost also allowed Jackson, as endless interviews, articles, and commentaries confirm, to pursue a strand of his biography further.[5] Ray Bradbury describes the impact of the original film on fans: ". . . a mob of boys went quietly mad across the world, then fled into the light to become adventurers, explorers, zoo-keepers, film-makers."[6] In his generation, Peter Jackson's reaction to the film shares this existential intensity and resulted in a *King Kong* which corresponds closely to David Wills' definition of the remake:

> What distinguishes the remake is not the fact of its being a repetition, rather the fact of its being a precise institutional form of the structure of repetition . . . the citationality or iterability that exists in and for every film.[7]

As a child, Jackson had set out to remake the original film by devising his own models and set, but he gave the project away when the stop-motion filming proved too arduous; by 2003 he could command all the experience, reputation, and capacity he needed to create cinema in whatever form he chose.

## The Blockbuster, Irony, and Allegory

The scale of the original *King Kong*, in all senses from its aesthetic to its cult status, means that filmmakers responding to it through a remake *qua* remake have to produce that most institutional form of film—the blockbuster. A version in any smaller format would invite inevitable comparisons with the original, and thus compromise the remake's own integrity as a film. Ironically, Jackson's particular version began on the small scale of New Zealand television. One Friday night in 1970, the nine-year-old saw the original, courtesy of the State broadcaster, the only channel then permitted. His reaction and his ensuing ambition to remake the film are particularly acute examples of the effect of US product penetrating New Zealand media. Accounts of the production history suggest that the creation of his blockbuster was partially motivated by an attitude belonging more to independent and art house creativity than to Hollywood production. What this means for the political economy of contemporary Hollywood, and for that of filmmaking in New

Zealand, is a topic needing a considerable study in its own right.

Jackson's version of this icon of American cinema may be an attempt to counteract the irony of his remake's production history, and indeed to counteract any sense of irony today attached to the original. The ape is so firmly embedded in cultural history worldwide that any remake, whether blockbuster, copy, satire, persiflage, travesty, or whatever, can reckon with a ready but knowing audience practically anywhere it is released.[8] If the *Kong* myth is to be recycled, it has to be what Constantine Verevis calls a *true remake*, which may cite the original but goes beyond homage and does not compete with it.[9] Such a remake seeks instead to maintain the relevance of its model by updating it according to the prevailing industry standards from technological to textual. Emphasis, therefore, has to shift from simple content to narrative process, to the plot. Phillipa Boyens, who worked on the script for this *Kong* with Jackson and Fran Walsh, confirms that they intended such a shift: "This is a retelling," Boyens says, "I think stories are meant to be retold, and that's what we have done."[10] Her remark is not surprising from a scriptwriter, and it challenges the designation *remake* itself by implying that their version of *Kong* possesses unique value, a proposition to which this study will return. Their script does not, however, produce a version anywhere near as radical as the 1976 remake (*King Kong*, John Guillermin, De Laurentis/Paramount). This version kept the scale of the original blockbuster and its essential narrative content but was retold in such a manner that it deconstructed the myth, revising the original plot so drastically as to appear like some sort of perverse homage via the agency of camp persiflage.

The 2005 version manages to follow the look and the content of the original closely while revising the plot significantly. It then appears to redirect the cultural history of the *King Kong* phenomenon, by, in effect, trying to redeem it from universalizing interpretations, from the encrustations of meaning attached to it. The fate of the original film has, in fact, been to furnish more or less precise allegories for largely negative phenomena such as racism, colonialism, economic or sexual exploitation, and so on. Yet it does not do this because its style or narrative is cryptic and invites interpretation. Its fantasy has much rather proved particularly accessible and hence popular with a huge global audience over a long period. To investigate this apparently contradictory effect, this study will proceed from Cynthia Erb's reflection on the nature of allegorical meaning attached to the Kong myth: "Allegory carries a certain arbitrariness or contingency of meaning that invites the contemplative activity of the critic or poet."[11] Drawing on Walter Benjamin's concept of the "Trauerspiel" in German drama, she reads Jackson's remake as centered on a metaphor for melancholia and attaches that to the wider social-historical implications of its cityscape post-9/11.

Directly opposed to Erb's approach is the German critic Georg Seesslen's evaluation of the film as connoisseur's kitsch:

Und Weil Jacksons "King Kong" ein paar tatsächlich poetische Momente enthält,

Disneyanismus ohne den Kitsch-Overkill, zum Beispiel in den fast taoistischen
Augenblick der Ruhe, da Kong, die weisse Frau zu seinen Füssen, von seinem
Bergthron aus weit über das Meer hinausblickt, oder in der Szene, in der sich,
kurz vor dem dramatischen Ende, King Kong und seine Geliebte wie Kinder auf
dem zugefrorenen See im Park vergnügen, der vom Glanz der weihnachtlich
geschmückten Bäume erleuchtet ist. Kitsch muss man können, und Peter Jackson
kann Kitsch. [And because Jackson's "King Kong" contains a few genuinely poetic moments, Disneyfication without the kitsch-overkill, for example in the almost taoistic moment of peace, as Kong, the white woman at his feet, looks out
far over the sea from his mountain throne, or in the scene where, shortly before
the dramatic end, King Kong and his beloved play like children on the frozen
lake in the park, which is illuminated by the brilliance of the Christmas decora-
tions on the trees. You have to be able to do kitsch, and Peter Jackson can do
kitsch].[12]

The potential of the King Kong myth for kitsch had already asserted itself in the
1976 remake. Here, showing Kong's journey to America meant depicting the ape
at the bottom of a holding tank on a ship. One sequence invokes an anthropomor-
phism so exaggerated as to establish a yardstick for the ultimate *mise en abîme* of
the Kong motif. A scarf from Dwan (Jessica Lange)—this remake's version of Ann
Darrow—flutters into the ape's hand, quite by chance, and drives him into a rage.
She breaks off a tryst with her lover and consoles the ape from on high by assuring him he is going to the US to be a star. When she subsequently falls into his tank,
Kong catches her but lets her climb back out again. With this sequence, Kong's
characterization undergoes a radical overhaul: the wild beast suddenly becomes
the noble savage, as the film ostensibly allows us an insight into his complex psyche. It presents him recognizing how the object of his desire belongs with those
holding him captive. Beneath the pelt is, then, a soul noble enough to attain the
tragic moral greatness of self-denying love, possibly motivated by recognizing her
good faith in her assurance of celebrity. The final shot is underscored by melodramatic strings as it cranes down to the calmed beast peacefully sleeping after
doing the right thing. This abrupt suggestion of an advanced moral consciousness
in Kong obliterates any vestige of the ape's significance as a tragic figure, and the
monster is left merely laughable.

The seeds of this development were already embedded in the illusionism of the
1933 original version, which was powered by Willis O'Brien's special effects.
Does that mean that the first *King Kong* was, and still remains, ultimately a piece
of kitsch cinema? Not so: in the original these effects were at the service of a classical Hollywood narrative that developed well-tried trajectories of heroism in order
to contain the potentially disorientating consequences of its visual fantasy and
hence reassure its audience as it offered them the opportunities for the fear and
wonder for which they had, after all, paid. Considered as a blockbuster in the context of its times, the original film avoids the propensity of the Kong motif for generating kitsch. Any remake of it, has, however, to face the same questions. So does
Jackson's remake, in its times, offer its audiences nothing more than indulgence in

nostalgia for the style of a lost age of cinematic innocence, coupled with the knowing pleasure in the spectacle of technologically sophisticated cinematic kitsch, a kind of post-modern irony that indulges in nihilism? Does Jackson in the last analysis construct an opportunity for audiences simultaneously to shudder at and sympathize with a freak of nature—the Beast? And does this mean that any critique of meaning or ideology in Jackson's film is deluded? To find out means analyzing the remake's potential for allegory operating through "arbitrariness and contingency of meaning" to try to establish what sort of value, if any, can be allotted to Jackson's remake.

## Reception and Retelling

Pragmatic forms of editing have been carried out on the film from the very beginning. Cooper himself edited out the "spider pit" scene, where giant insects devour crewmembers, because the horror of its imagery distracted test audiences and because it slowed down the narrative pace. Additionally, scenes of Kong disrobing Ann Darrow and biting and trampling humans have also been censored in various territories, in some cases for almost forty years.[13] Beyond such pragmatic reactions, the history of *King Kong's* reception is complex. Because it depicts filmmaking itself, critics even debate the original film's genre. Is it fantasy/horror, or even sci-fi? From a sociohistorical viewpoint, its racist, colonialist, and misogynistic ideology is undeniable, and it may also include a capitalist and even an imperialist subtext, particularly in regard to the historical situation of the economic Depression of the early 1930s. A psychoanalytical approach compares it to a dream, links it to myths, such as that of Cupid and Psyche, variously reads allegories of sexuality into it, and raises the controversial topic of miscegenation through the depiction of human/animal relations, which can also extend to universalizing interpretations of a dialectic between nature and civilization.

I do not intend to recapitulate the critical, historical, or cultural reception of the film, although I shall examine what influence locating production in New Zealand may have had. The film's cultural history and its potential range of meanings are already well covered by Orville Goldner and George E. Turner, by Rolf Giesen, Cynthia Erb, Karen Haber, Paul A. Woods, Joshua David Bellin, Ray Morton, Ted Gott and Kathryn Weir, and Daniela Gehrmann, and in innumerable articles in academic and specialist cinema journals, fanzines, and the popular press, on fan Web sites, and, of course, in the ancillary material accompanying the DVD editions of the cinematic release.[14] The reception of the remake by fans is worth a study of its own. However, this study concentrates on the form of the remake itself and will reference the extended version (including the swamp scene cut from the theatrical release) available on DVD.[15]

The remake of *King Kong* illustrates much of what Robert Stam calls "transformations":

These transformations are conducted within the limits of a specific historical situation, and the remake performs these transformations along multiple axes, absorbing and altering the genres and intertexts available through the grids of
ambient discourses and ideologies, and as mediated by a series of filters: studio
style, ideological fashion, political constraints, auteurist predilections, charismatic
stars, economic advantage or disadvantage and evolving technology.[16]

"Transformations" in the remake double its length over the original and slow down
its narrative pace decisively. It displays a range of alterations and additions to characters and scenes. Of the original figures, Carl Denham (Jack Black) becomes
younger and shiftier as a result of his 2005 backstory, where he tries to get more
money out of his producers. Ann Darrow (Naomi Watts) resembles Fay Wray
closely but also has much more backstory. She is identified in the vaudeville establishing sequence within the context of a constellation of supporting roles, which
are then rapidly dropped. The figure of Jack Driscoll (Adrien Brody) shifts his role
radically, being transformed into an intellectual, a playwright seeking recognition
in the theater and only supplying scripts to Denham for the money. Englehorn mu-
tates from an avuncular, vaguely English-sounding captain in late middle age to a
much younger German, a sardonic and dubious collector of wild animals, and very
effective in crises. The minor but essential New York fruit vendor (Tiriel Mora) appears on cue, and the ship's crew has its Chinese cook, now called Choy (Lobo
Chan), who is furnished with a gruesome fate all his own. As ensembles there are
sundry crewmen, three film producers, Skull Islanders, New Yorkers (on the streets
and in two theaters), police and army who also support the plot and the leads as
necessary (in many cases as incidental casualties). And in a profoundly ritualistic
homage to the original film, Jackson himself and a group of other filmmakers follow the original cameo roles of Cooper and Schoedsack in crewing the planes that
kill off Kong.

    Of the figures added, Hayes (Evan Parke) is the most significant because he
takes over the Driscoll function as first mate but comes with his own backstory, as
a heroic black Marine from the First World War with his own fate in a heroic death.
It is incidental to the plot but significant in terms of reflecting a cultural shift. A further addition brings in Jimmy (Jamie Bell), a stowaway turned crewman, who
functions as Hayes' protégé/son and has the most melodramatic role. Denham himself now has three assistants: PA, Preston (Colin Hanks), a sound recordist, Mike
(Craig Hall), and a cameraman, Herb (John Sumner), only one of whom survives
the trip. He also brings along an actor, Bruce Baxter (Kyle Chandler), whose comic
cowardice and vanity parodies the original Bruce Cabot role of Driscoll the tough
guy. Among the crew, there is a figure dropped from the original but now rein-
stated and given significant screen time, although his function is completely unnecessary to the plot: Lumpy the cook (Andy Serkis). The role provides gratuitous
comedy, including the figure's grotesque death amid a nest of suspiciously phal-
lic monster slugs, a scene which reflects Jackson's earlier splatter-horror oeuvre.
Lumpy only deviates from his role at one point to go into melodrama where he ex-

travagantly grieves over Choy in a scene irrelevant to the plot but, as with the figure of Hayes, signaling a shift in the film's cultural significance. In technical terms, however, Serkis has one of the most important functions in the entire cast, reprising his role as a motion-capture figure (Gollum from *LOTR*), this time in a specially designed ape suit. Serkis also provided facial expressions and voiced sound effects, all of which were then combined through CGI to create Kong himself.

The filmmakers kept the original's three-act structure, but they expanded the entire diegesis with additional scenes, and these inevitably reinforce the film's potential for allegory right from its first shots. Elaborate images of the New York zoo and of shantytowns in Central Park introduce a montage, crosscutting between the vaudeville acts and images of the Depression, of families being evicted, protest marches, and prohibition. Backstage shots of Ann's interaction with fellow artists establish her credentials for becoming the heroine, her ambition for higher things, and her generous, optimistic spirit. The succession of scenes establishing how she becomes involved with Denham—from him first seeing her to her stepping onto the gangplank—sets the seal on the film's function as allegory. The encounter is elaborately prepared for by adding the scenes of Ann and the theatrical agent and of her walking away from the burlesque job. Denham's character is prepared equally well, as he flees his producers in the cab, where his dialogue with Preston telegraphs the details of his deceptive project to the audience. By the time Ann comes on board, Denham has been established as a version of the lovable rogue character, and her personal qualities have defined her as the heroine even before she is hired to play that role. The film-in-the film allegory comes strongly to the fore as Denham sees her projected, as it were, by her reflection from behind him in the glass of the display cabinets at the burlesque theater. Yet she removes her image by acting according to her moral principles and walking away from the job despite her need. Immediately afterwards, the allegorical potential of their meeting intensifies when the remake follows the original to have him using his wits to rescue her with his money (when she appears to succumb to temptation in the form of an apple, no less). So Ann is saved by the lovable rogue, from prosecution and then from hunger, as he takes her to the cafe. Jackson then rounds off the significance of the encounter by first upping the narrative pace through the added scene of Denham hustling everyone on the dock prior to departure, only to insert a pause through the close-up shot of her foot hesitating over the first step onto the gangplank. For her character in the plot, this marks the point of no return, but it also melodramatically emphasizes the implications of the heroine, in all senses, now being committed to the rogue.

In order to establish the new Driscoll character in relation to Denham, some funny business is added, and this leads to the running gag of the scriptwriter caged in the ship's hold. The extended voyage slows down the narrative pace and allows the audience time to understand the cast of characters before their discovery of Skull Island. And in the 2005 version, the ship itself has to be saved before Ann's abduction becomes apparent, and they all have to set out to save her. The 'making of' material depicts the actual ship Jackson bought for the film, the modeling of it at Weta Workshops, and their extensive CGI treatment of it almost being wrecked. Presumably the plot could not drop all that investment.

The island itself as mise-en-scène is much more elaborate than that of the original. It suggests the prehistory of a great civilization long since gone into decay. The remake adds one major scene to the content of the second act on Skull Island: the insects in the ravine, with which the survivors battle after Kong has shaken them off the log.[17] Ann's encounter with dinosaurs receives much additional screen time, including aerial choreography of the fight suspended in the vines.

The third act back in New York shows Driscoll and Ann at separate theaters while Denham is presenting the monster, scenes clearly added to retard the moment of his escape by manipulating the film audience's point of view. The musical number played out before the shackled beast, what Jackson in his DVD commentary calls the "Vegas version of Kong," has the same function and prepares for a major addition to the third act when Kong is presented with a false Ann as part of the musical number and then breaks his chains.[18] Altering the motivation for his rage from the exploding flashes of the newspaper cameramen in the original film to the trick Denham plays on him shifts the motivation of his character and its ultimate meaning. It also leads up to the most significant addition in the third act, if not in the entire film: Ann coming to meet him in front of Macy's department store in Manhattan. The ape does not ransack hotel bedrooms in her pursuit but is instead distracted by the car chase staged by Driscoll, which the writer only just survives when she intervenes. With her back safely in paw, Kong refrains from any further mayhem, like wrecking the overhead railway, and instead carries Ann off to skate on the ice in Central Park. This leads to the scene of Ann Darrow once more on top of the Empire State building and screaming, but now she is screaming at the approaching humans in their planes, screaming at them to go away.

## The Logic of the Plot and Genre Identity

The 2005 remake may display such "transformations" in retelling, but it still remains a fantasy film driven by an absurd plot. After all, how can you stand up atop the Empire State Building? With the iconic gate in the wall on Skull Island, for instance, Jackson's film remains true to the illogical nature of the original: why build it big enough to let the monsters through, anyway? Does it suggest that there may have been a time when the civilization that built the protecting wall dominated the creatures with which it shared the island? The gate icon could well initiate a prequel. Logic aside, the gate is vital to the quintessential spectacle of the ape smashing through to the human side, a scene that anticipates his eruption from the New York theater. The logic of the 2005 plot does at least avoid a gap that exists in the original by giving us a scene of Driscoll and Ann escaping down the river after parachuting from Kong's mountain lair by holding onto a very nasty bat-monster.

With that, the film introduces a CGI monster worthy of any horror film to bridge the original's almost comic lapse when, after the couple fall into the sea, the 1933 Driscoll subsequently explains their escape with the throwaway line about them coming down the river! However, the remake retains the fantastical cut from Denham triumphant at Skull Island to the neon sign announcing his "Eighth Wonder of the World" in New York. In his DVD commentary, Jackson confirms that they here kept faith with the original, but goes on to emphasize the fantasy of the stage show still further by speculating on the "real question" as to how Denham got Kong into the New York theater unobserved.[19]

The original's fantasy already has an "unusually mobile" genre identity.[20] It shares much with the jungle film genre of its times and in its brand of monster has clear elements of straight horror, above all where the beast bursts from the theater onto the streets of the iconic twentieth-century city. In the remake, the horror genre predominates in Jackson's treatment of the Skull Islanders, which far exceeds the native/white man encounter scenes of the original. Grotesque costuming and make-up reminiscent of orcs from *LOTR* combine with the shock effect of Mike's death and the sudden violence of the ritual sacrifice. The manufactured uncertainty of handheld camera style merges with slow motion, disorienting the audience and suggesting that some strange point of view has subverted their normal perception of the events on screen—until the white man's technology reasserts itself in the form of Englehorn's pistol. When Ann and Driscoll then come back through the huge gate, slow motion returns with them, but here it is firmly tied to her viewpoint as a sort of technique to convey her recognition of Denham's ruthlessness. Horror as outright excess of spectacle appears with the prehistoric beasts, as in Driscoll's underwater escape from the jaws in the swamp, Ann's extended session of dodging the same on land, and above all in the monstrous insects in the inescapable ravine. As sources of horror, they can outdo the dinosaurs because they are scaled up from creatures plausibly existing in everyday reality.

Yet, as in Jackson's earlier work, horror effects readily combine with comedy, as when the rampaging Kong, the incarnation of the Beast erupting into civilization, suddenly loses control of his faculties, and hence of his role, as he begins slithering about Times Square. Other comic scenes precede this one. On Skull Island, the bat monster/parachute suddenly switches role in mid-attack from that of yet another horrific predator to that of a convenient dupe allowing an incredible escape from a hopeless situation. Denham machine-guns the raft into halves in a comedy of misplaced heroism: he heroically steps up to save the party but actually endangers them still further by his ineptitude. The cowardly Bruce becomes comic as the character who has to find out what the audience already knows when he realizes he is being eyed by a dinosaur as he tries to hide from the stampede. The character Lumpy sports a permanent grimace, yet switches from a sardonic leer to the look of a simpleton with his comment that Kong's paw print is that of the abominable snowman. His death is both comic and horrific and marks the grotesque extreme of spectacular excess, just as the insect scene almost parodies itself as horror.

The musical genre surfaces in the final "Vegas" number and with Ann in a chorus line show elsewhere. Parallel to her, Driscoll appears in the audience watching his comedy in a New York theater; he is still trying to make his name as a playwright. By having both characters shun Denham, the 2005 scriptwriters produce a twist on the original plot to generate something that plot certainly never offered—melodrama. Driscoll subsequently rushes out of his own play, mistakenly thinking he will find his beloved with Denham and the ape, and Ann (dressed only in an evening gown despite the New York cold) returns to console the beast at a crossroads rendered infinitely deep by CGI. Earlier, Lumpy grieved over the dead Choy in full close-up, and Jimmy took over Hayes' cap from his mentor, still noble in death. Such melodrama offers the film audience the pleasures of sentimentality and even melancholy, but it also combines, not unexpectedly, with scenes of cruelty. Kong on the seashore no longer collapses before a knot of small figures at the bottom of the frame. He is harpooned by Englehorn and is finally brought down by Denham smashing a bottle of chloroform over his skull, like a pub fighter. The cruelty of Kong's death is undeniable—did no one have a few bottles of chloroform handy in the theater? Why not just wait to see if he'll come down, now that Ann is on his side?—and combines with the CGI-generated moment of leave taking and death before shifting into the outright spectacle of his fall into the depths.

On cue, Driscoll appears, the love story between the humans is reasserted and order restored so that the fantasy can be over. With that, the remake answers a French critic's question concerning the 1933 ending:

> Another possible ending would have removed the major uncertainty overshadowing the second appearance of the bestial creature, a mystery still unsolved: what expression would King Kong have assumed if, in those last shots, Ann had loved him?[21]

In 2005, the original love story is turned upside down, when Ann rescues Driscoll in New York by going with Kong. Jackson's plot started out with the comedy of her mistaking Driscoll's identity and then confirmed the relationship with their shipboard declaration of love. But then the leap in editing with the famous cut from the capture of Kong to his display in the New York theater also leaps in this remake over the fates of the Venture's crew and the fact that Ann and Driscoll have gone their separate ways. Despite his heroics in rescuing her from Kong's lair, distracting the beast in New York and fighting his way through to the top of the skyscraper, Driscoll appears second best to Kong in her affections.

By leaving the heroine's true affections ambiguous, Jackson's remake complicates the love story and reprises the flexible genre identities already generated by the original film. Yet their furthest extension appears in his film's self-reflexive references to cinema itself. Denham's early reference to Fay Wray working at RKO provides an early joke for the knowing audience. The film goes on to create its icon (and symbol for the cinematic apparatus) for self-reflexivity in Denham's camera, in one scene passed up to him by his cameraman literally from the jaws of a (CGI) dinosaur![22] In the film's syntax, the scenes of Denham on the run from the producers after his unsuccessful pitch, and then of their grotesque *bonhomie* for the cameras on his triumphant opening night, similarly reinforce this self-reflexivity by satirizing their venality. One level removed are intertextual references to Jackson's own Kong memorabilia, which are used in the decor of the Venture's saloon. There are also gas bombs nestled among the ship's stock of chloroform and references to Jackson's own oeuvre, when a notice in the hold warns of the "Sumatran Rat Monkey," which was the vector of the zombie virus in his *Braindead* (Wingnut Films, 1992). Rewarding a true fan's insight is the styling of Jack Black, wig, pipe and all, as Orson Welles in Harry Lime mode. Welles himself wanted to do his own jungle film by adapting Conrad's *Heart of Darkness,* and Jackson privileges the novel in a scene where the black character Hayes explains to the white character, his protégé Jimmy, that that story's situation is not theirs (that is, in their film?). At this level, the blockbuster/fantasy/remake is catering to an audience of art house cinephiles—and it is coming close to kitsch in telegraphing a self-conscious awareness of its capacity to generate meaning.

The original plot has Denham wanting to find Skull Island because he knows about the creature Kong, whereas the remake's character does not know what might be there. Jackson generates the mystery in order to exploit it melodramatically in the scene where Denham and Driscoll puzzle over the map's strange inscription and then lose it overboard so that it floats in foreground close-up as the Venture enters the fogbank. The original Denham reforms a rescue party and rapidly abandons the camera for the rifle, whereas Jackson's character is all for leaving once the ship is freed. When he goes on the rescue, he keeps on filming. He then becomes obsessed with capturing Kong, regardless of the cost to anyone else, when he finds his images ruined in his wrecked equipment at the bottom of the ravine. Add to this the scarred Preston exchanging somber looks with him on opening night in New York, and the obsessive filmmaker/showman has gone from being a possibly deluded, lovable rogue to possibly a villain. The 2005 remake far exceeds the original in inviting judgement of Denham—and hence invites an allegorical interpretation from its viewers. In the terms of the 1933 original, Denham's showman ego was justified, along with the cost in lives of his project, because he was dealing with a brute beast. By 2005, Kong's relationship with Ann has become that much more complex and ambiguous, and the scriptwriters have introduced so many extra individual fates, that the remake invites judgment of the showman's ego by leaving open the question as to the cost of the sort of spectacle Denham wishes to stage and then the cost of the final spectacle of the dead beast, over which he speaks Kong's obituary: "It wasn't the airplanes, it was beauty killed the beast." His pronouncement now plays like a piece of self-exculpation by the guilty party, as he resorts to an allegorical statement.

## The Extended Context

The extended context of the remaking becomes significant, because it demonstrates how the film tries to keep all options open for the film's reception. From the production and postproduction diaries posted on the Internet concurrent with the production, through the commentary by Jackson and Boyens, to the mockumentary on the natural history of Skull Island, the audience for this film is invited to wonder at the—heroic?—efforts of a huge team of filmmakers, at the cost of their undertaking, at their sheer creative talent, yet also at their reverence for their model. What the film means no longer depends on its reception on screen. Instead it operates by inviting viewers to identify with the filmmakers and their art. The most extreme example of this invitation occurs at the very end of the postproduction diaries where Jackson has himself filmed on the completely empty car park at his studio in Wellington. The point of view shifts back a step so that the filming of Jackson's final comments is itself recorded, implying that the perspective could indeed go back to the viewpoint of each individual viewer. By contrasting this scene with the filmmaking activity previously on view, there is thus provided a position for the viewer as active participant, and, in fact, as one somehow able to be present at the location in New Zealand.

The New Zealand production context is of minor importance to the 'making of' reports, particularly when compared to its importance in the text of *LOTR* and for accounts of that project's production. Jackson comments on the decision to render Skull Island virtually:

> When we were starting *Kong*, I think everybody was assuming that New Zealand was a great location. We've got sort of rain forests here, but at the end of the day, when you go into these forests, they just look like Hawaii or anything else you've seen a million times on film. We had some wonderful conceptual art done—beautiful renderings—with these huge, over-scale, twisted, deformed trees and rock bridges and endless chasms that plummet down. It's like a jungle from hell—the most twisted, tortured terrain you can imagine. And I just knew looking at the pictures that we were never going to find a location like that. So we decided, very early on, that if we were really going to make Skull Island look like the conceptual art, that creating it artificially was the only way to do it.[23]

A certain cultural camouflage is at work here, and it is the corollary to the creation of 1933 New York exclusively in the studio because filming the city today is so difficult. Historical research into 1930s New York architecture was fed into a "building bot" software program, which rendered a cityscape graded in detail depending on the requirements of a particular shot. Demonstrations of this program at work in 'making of' accounts display the technology, showing scenes of the city rising up in a sort of reverse disaster movie.[24]

References to the local New Zealand context do appear in the film, with Driscoll fighting off giant CGI versions of what is already called a Giant Weta, the world's heaviest insect. Beyond this arcane reference, however, the 'making of' material does not refer to New Zealand in any detail, although one location here may have influenced the scale set for Kong, namely the Civic theater in Auckland.[25] It doubles for the New York theater and is itself an "atmospheric theater," a concept imported from the US and realized here in 1929.[26] It may be that the dimensions of the Civic helped to decide the scale set for Kong or that the interior of the Civic and the people in it have been manipulated digitally. In any case, this theater is today arguably only available for a film location, or anything else, because Aucklanders saved it from property developers in the late 1980s. The spectacle of Kong wrecking it is, then, particularly ironic for anyone familiar with the location.

## The Global Reception of *Kong*

Jackson's project in remaking *King Kong* deals with the inevitable encumbrance of allegory by turning to deliberate archaism using the most advanced cinematic technology currently available. To demonstrate this analytically, I proceed from what Emmanuel Burdeau sees in such archaism as both bad—"le mauvais archaïsme de la representation" ("the bad archaism of representation")—and good—"le bon archaïsme de la nouvelle nature numérique" ("the good archaism of the new numerical nature").[27] The bad part is that it encourages simple realism. The good part is that it transforms appearances into filmic reality. A scene illustrating very simply the transition from representational realism to filmic reality comes where the Venture leaves New York harbor. The spectacular night skyline behind the ship has been enhanced by shifting the Empire State Building south from its real location. Jackson has clearly understood the way that the effects created by O'Brien for the original *King Kong* are today signifiers of illusion rather than being illusory themselves. He has then sought to counteract this effect, in the good sense of cinematic archaism, by restoring the capacity for illusion to his remake with massive applications of virtual imagery. In that way, he is trying to recreate what he imagined to be the "terrific" impact of the original in 1933.

Thematically, this has meant radically revising the ape's tragedy, as he finds his affection now reciprocated, and making Ann's role as victim more tragic. Her character shifts from the sacrifice through asserting herself by stabbing Kong in the bone yard scene and then telling him off when he goes too far in the vaudeville act they stage in his mountain lair. Despite her role in his capture, she secures his trust, but in the end all she can do is to witness his slaughter. In 2005 Kong himself is not simply laughable, as is his 1976 incarnation, yet he is no longer simply a source of horror as the monster. He remains ferocious in New York, but also comic. In this respect, the ape's fate shifts the figure further towards a human identity (he responds to Ann's prompting on seeing the sunset as "beautiful").[28] As noted by a range of critics, in the remake the plot and the iconography of the characters sidestep the original disrobing scene, replacing it with Ann's vaudeville. Similarly, racial and colonialist implications from 1933 are countered by the extreme horror spectacle of the villagers. In 1933, Denham called them out to resist Kong's onslaught; in 2005 they disappear from the scene. Their significance shifts, then, from that of "natives" whose savagery contrasts with the civilized whites to that of a further fantastical index of the island's dangerous reality. Jackson's film avoids any realism in their depiction and thus downplays any implications of racism. Indeed, where the remake does depict "natives," it satirizes the crass racism inherent in Denham's musical staged before the captive Kong. We, the audience, are shown this performance from Driscoll's viewpoint, and this helps us to understand it. The roles of Hayes, Jimmy, Lumpy, and Choy also deflect any suspicion of racism and even begin to reconstruct the gender identities of a set of tough guys by hinting at hidden emotional bonds. Where the remake's plot is weak is where it follows the original too closely and simply forgets about the secondary characters from the ship in the third act, after spending so much time developing them in the first two acts. In this respect, a sequel to the remake could well trace Jimmy's further doings, particularly as a character whose understanding of the Kong story is determined by his understanding of Conrad's *Heart of Darkness*.

In a wider cinematic perspective, this remake of *King Kong* calls to mind Sean Cubitt's comments on neobaroque style:

> Films like *the Matrix, Desperado, Strange Days* and *Pi* share with others like *Twelve Monkeys* an allegorical structure of this kind, symptomatized in the hyper-detailing that, in a curious inversion of Bazinian realism, dematerializes the image in its excess of signifiers and functions as an allegorical fugue on themes of hyperreality, illusion and the Code. At this juncture, narrative conclusions become almost impossible because of the allegorical burdens they have to bear.[29]

The remake does not refer its audience to any other reality than that of the original's illusionism. After all, the 1933 *King Kong* would never have established its iconic status simply by means of its conventional studio sets or its linear narrative structure. It works through O'Brien's efforts and his special effects to overcome any suggestion of a layered, constructed framing of its fantasy. Its kind of allegory lies in the very spectacle of a diegesis which demonstrates the complete control of all creative resources. This is what Peter Jackson's version extends seventy years later, not only in its production but also in the accompanying array of merchandizing, Web sites, DVD commentary, and so on. The extent of such control is most apparent in the accounts of the extensive use of digital previsualization of shots before going to conventional 35mm shooting (in this sense also, Jackson's *King Kong* was remade twice). With such techniques, it embellishes its retelling of the original, both in its screen version and in the accounts of its making, to offer its audience the pleasure of a dual role of viewers investing in the fantasy and of connoisseurs of the machinery of illusion. However, as it reiterates the style, narrative, and thematics of the original, its own allegorical potential becomes contradictory. Can love still conquer all? But whose love for whom? Exploitation of the natural world may be condemned, but in a celebratory recreation of a great city. And finally, the dubious showman-filmmaker speaks the last word and then just walks away.

Given that a huge range of potential meaning is already implanted in global audiences before they even see this remake, *King Kong* impresses by trying to shift the tense, in the linguistic sense, of its reception. It goes from the future perfect (knowing before the event what will have happened and what it will have meant) to the present, but a cinematic present of over seventy years ago. In this way, this remake opposes the contemporary sense of allegory, as Ismail Xavier interprets it:

> Seen from our present experience, allegories make evident their vocation to express the central role played by time and culture in individual lives. For Paul de Man (1969), they form a kind of "rhetoric of temporality," when the impulse to memorize and identify with a previous moment (of history, of a personal life) ends up communicating the crisis and separation from the irretrievable past.[30]

Jackson and his collaborators seek to overcome any such crisis and loss by restoring the memory of the original film. Their remake renders homage to the original by seeking to emulate the status granted it by dint of being so consistently remembered: they are, in fact, seeking nothing less than timelessness. To this end, they try to come out the other side of allegory, even at the risk of becoming caught up in the self-awareness of kitsch. Using all the armory of twenty-first century cinematic illusion, they went back to Skull Island on the quest to bring back and display a fantastical beast—pure cinematic pleasure. As an entertainment, their beast will survive as part of the cultural history of *King Kong*. Yet the final irony associated with the 2005 *King Kong* lies in the fact that it cannot escape its fate of carrying a wide range of meaning, not the least of which is illustrating the state of cinema in the early twenty-first century.

# Notes

The author thanks the Libraries of the Hochschule für Film und Fernsehen (Potsdam, Germany) and of the Deutsche Kinemathek (Berlin, Germany); Dr. Rolf Giesen (Deutsche Kinemathek, Berlin, Germany); Professor Sean Cubitt (School of Culture and Communication, University of Melbourne); and particularly to Professor Cynthia Erb (Wayne State University).

1. *King Kong*, Deluxe Extended Edition DVD No. 824 5948.18 (Universal Pictures Germany GmbH, 2005), Disc 1.

2. Orville Goldner and George E. Turner, *The Making of King Kong: The Story behind a Film Classic* (New York: A. S. Barnes and Co., 1975), 9.

3. *King Kong*, Disc 3.

4. As the success of the 1933 *King Kong* saved RKO from collapse, and indirectly per-

mitted the eventual making of *Citizen Kane,* so *LOTR* restored the fortunes of New Line—
a further historical irony attached to Jackson's involvement with Hollywood. From a very
different historical perspective comes Fay Wray's wry comment on *King Kong*'s success:
"If we'd had a percentage deal we wouldn't be such nice people. We'd be rich." Goldner
and Turner, *The Making of King Kong,* 195.

    5. Jackson made an ape suit in 1986 and startled motorists by emerging in it from the
bush near his home. A newspaper photograph of the event subsequently got him his first
piece of special effects work. Brian Sibley, *Peter Jackson: A Filmmaker's Journey* (London:
HarperCollins, 2006), 102–105. Dr. Rolf Giesen of the Deutsche Kinamathek in Berlin confirmed that Mr. Jackson bought the Kinamethek's collection of *King Kong* memorabilia
during preproduction. Interview with Stan Jones, 15 November 2007.

    6. Quoted in Cynthia Erb, *Tracking King Kong: A Hollywood Icon in World Culture*
(Detroit: Wayne State University Press, 1998), 155.

    7. David Wills, "The French Remark: *Breathless* and Cinematic Citationality," in *Play
It Again, Sam: Retakes on Remakes,* ed. Andrew Horton and Stuart Y. McDougal (Berkeley: University of California Press, 1998), 148.

    8. There are numerous links to film history: *King Kong* was apparently among film-
buff Adolf Hitler's favorite viewing. Kong fought his own progeny, so to speak, in *Kingu
Konu tai Gojira/King Kong Versus Godzilla* (Isohirô Honda, Beck/RKO/Toho/Universal,
1962). Stanley Kubrick famously satirized the name as his Major T. J. "King" Kong rides
the H bomb to the world's end in *Dr. Strangelove or: How I Learned to Stop Worrying and
Love the Bomb* (Stanley Kubrick, Columbia Pictures, 1964). In 1976, *Queen Kong* (Frank
Agrama, cine Art Produzione/Dexter Films, 1976) produced a parody/travesty on gender
role reversals. Universal Studios in Los Angeles offers menace from a mechanical Kong
head as one of the thrills on its studio tour. In New York, a King Kong puppet was hung from
the Empire State Building in 1983 to celebrate the film's fiftieth anniversary. From a personal perspective: in 1950s Yorkshire, England, my late uncle, Ted Atkinson, was known
among our family as "our Kong," a nickname not implying any monstrous characteristics
but simply his physical strength. Berlin boasts the "Kingkongklub," <http://www.king-
kong-klub.de/> (12 February 2008).

    9. Constantine Verevis, *Film Remakes* (Edinburgh: Edinburgh University Press, 2006),
13.

    10. Jeff Goldsmith, *"King Kong," Creative Screenwriting* 64 (November–December
2005): 33.

    11. Cynthia Erb, *"King Kong's* Melancholy (a Reading of Peter Jackson's *King Kong),"*
in Cynthia Erb, *Tracking King Kong: A Hollywood Icon in World Culture* (Detroit: Wayne
State University Press, forthcoming).

    12. Georg Seesslen, "Alter Affe, Kein Angst," *Neues Deutschland,* 13 December 2005.
Translation by Stan Jones.

    13. Ray Morton, *King Kong: The History of a Movie Icon from Fay Wray to Peter
Jackson* (New York: Applause Theatre and Cinema Books, 2005), 83–84.

    14. Joshua David Bellin, *Framing Monsters: Fantasy Film and Social Alienation* (Car-
bondale: Southern Illinois University Press, 2005); Cynthia Erb, *Tracking King Kong;*
Daniela Gehrmann, *Von Katzenfrauen, Affenmännern Und Werwölfen: Das Tier Im Men-
schen* (Marburg, Germany: Tectum, 2006); Rolf Giesen, *Alles Über King Kong* (Ismaning,
Germany: Taurus Video, 1993); Rolf Giesen, "Von Skull Island Bis Neuseeland," *film-di-
enst* 58, no. 25 (2005): 8–10; Goldner and Turner, *The Making of King Kong;* Ted Gott and
Kathryn Wier, ed., *Kiss of the Beast: From Paris Salon to King Kong* (Brisbane, Australia:

Queensland Art Gallery Publishing, 2006); Karen Haber, ed., *Kong Unbound. The Cultural Impact, Pop Mythos and Scientific Plausibility of a Cinematic Legend* (London: Simon and Schuster, 2005); Morton, *King Kong*; Paul A. Woods, ed., *King Kong Cometh* (London: Plexus, 2005).

15. Peter Jackson, *King Kong* Deluxe, Universal Studios, 2005.

16. Robert Stam, "Beyond Fidelity: The Dialogics of Adaptation," in *Film Adaptation*, ed. James Naremore (London: Athlone, 2000), 68.

17. See <http://www.numberonestars.com/kingkong/production_notes/king_kong_notes_13.htm> (11 January 2008).

18. Peter Jackson, *King Kong* Deluxe, Universal Studios, 2005, Disc 1.

19. Peter Jackson, *King Kong* Deluxe, Universal Studios, 2005, Disc 2.

20. Cynthia Erb, *Tracking King Kong*, 126.

21. Claude Ollier, "A King in New York," in *Focus on the Horror Film*, ed. Roy Huss and T. J. Ross (Englewood Cliffs, N.J.: Prentice Hall, 1972), 120.

22. See note 8.

23. As an exercise in cinematic archaeology, Jackson and his crew allowed themselves a pure remake of this scene, which was famously lost after Cooper cut it. Concurrent with the big picture, they reconstructed the original scene from existing evidence and shot it using stop-motion for the monster insects and themselves for the crewmen devoured. See "Recreating the Eighth Wonder: The Making of *King Kong*" (Michael Pellerin) on Peter Jackson, *King Kong Special*, Universal Studios, 2006, Disc 2. The same documentary shows a similar exercise where the armature of Willis O'Brien's original Kong puppet is brought to the set in New Zealand and reverently handed among the crew before it is copied at Weta Workshops, dressed with fur, and used to reconstruct O'Brien's techniques of background and glass painting as setting for stop-motion effects. The sheer power of Weta's digital technology for creating the same cinematic fantasy is then emphasized in contrast. Shots of the New York set were also added using the period camera that served as model for the (rubber) prop Denham lugs around Skull Island.

24. *King Kong*, Disc 3.

25. An element is missing from the remake—smoking. According to Jackson, the filmmakers simply could not include it because New Zealand law forbids smoking in any workplace. *King Kong*, Disc 2. He speculates on a possible exemption for filmmaking, which suggests the remake may also have dropped the motif out of political correctness. Although Jackson's *King Kong* was made in New Zealand, it is no more a "New Zealand film" than is *LOTR*.

26. See <http://www.historic.org.nz/Register/ListingDetail.asp?RID=100> (15 February 2008).

27. Emmanuel Burdeau, "Les Sens Du Poil," *Cahiers du cinéma* 608 (2006): 32–33. Translations by Stan Jones.

28. For the extreme of the anthropomorphic ape figure, see Franz Kafka's satire on human self-awareness, "Ein Bericht für eine Akademie/A Report to an Academy," <http://www.mala.bc.ca/~johnstoi/kafka/reportforacademy.htm> (18 February 2008). By contrast with the persona here narrating his own story, albeit in print and not visually, the 1976 monster on the oil tanker impresses truly as what he really was—an actor in an ape suit.

29. Sean Cubitt, *The Cinema Effect* (Cambridge, Mass.: MIT Press, 2004), 234.

30. Ismail Xavier, "Historical Allegory," in *A Companion to Film Theory*, ed. Toby Miller and Robert Stam (Malden, Mass.: Blackwell, 1999), 349.

*Chapter 11*

# Distinct Identities of *Star Trek*
# Fan Film Remakes

Daryl G. Frazetti

Fan films are not-for-profit creations of individuals who do not work in the television or film industry. These individuals are usually amateur filmmakers who have made recreating their favorite science fiction television series and films into a serious hobby. Fans of the *Star Trek* franchise have found creative ways to keep the ideals of *Trek* alive while also giving each fan production their own interpretation. Fans create story lines that are set in the familiar world of *Star Trek* and recreate their favorite characters, develop new ones, or combine the old and familiar with the new. These filmmakers also pay for the costs involved and handle all aspects of production themselves. Their productions vary in both length and quality, ranging from short clips or trailers to full-length feature productions. With no *Trek* on the air since 2005 when *Enterprise* was cancelled, and despite the amount of time and funding that is required for these strictly amateur productions, fan films have revitalized the franchise and have given it sustenance.

Putting together the final product takes time, funds, and hours of commitment by volunteers who serve as writers, set designers, film crews, directors, and producers. Finding locations or altering a location to look like a set can also be challenging. Fan filmmakers have become quite creative in how they utilize their environments and resources. The digital technologies and computer programs available today assist in overcoming funding constraints and help to enhance the overall quality of production. Fan filmmakers face many challenges to produce quality work with little funding. These efforts have attracted the attention of many

199

ex-*Star Trek* professionals, such as former makeup supervisor Kevin Haney and famed writer Dorothy Fontana, in addition to many actors such as Walter Koenig, George Takei, Grace Lee Whiney, and Denise Crosby. This has further enhanced the quality of productions while sparing budgets since all of these professionals donate their time to this worthy cause. All of this has also greatly expanded the fan base. Fan films have certainly grown exponentially over the past three decades in many ways and continue to evolve today, with a positive future ahead.[1]

Fan film growth has been due primarily to improved technologies and the Internet. Such works were once only known through bootleg sales at science fiction conventions. Now there are conventions and Web sites dedicated solely to these works. Conventions such as Fanzilla, chat rooms like those found at trekunited.com, and Internet sites like Fanfilms.com, fanboytheatre.com, and iFilm.com, along with videos offered on YouTube.com, like *Star Trek: Hidden Frontier*, have allowed fan films to grow and evolve, creating their own niche not only in the world of *Star Trek*, but in science fiction in general.

These productions have allowed fans to create more in-depth *Trek* characters and plots. In many instances this has allowed productions to address social issues beyond those addressed by *Trek*, such as exploring the gay community. Fan films do this by recapturing the original ideals of *Trek* and merging them with original story and character ideas. This results in the production of films with more serious ambition. There is also a lighter side to some fan films. There are those who wish to capture and explore the humor of *Trek* through an array of parodies. These works have indeed revitalized the spirit of the original *Star Trek* series from the 1960s. For example, the online series *Hidden Frontier* not only addresses the gay community, but also tackles many other political, religious, and racial issues, as has *Star Trek: New Voyages* (which was renamed *Star Trek: Phase II*), which set out to recreate the original series and complete the Enterprise's initial five-year mission. It too tackles social issues in the fashion of the original series. *New Voyages* is also in the process of adapting a controversial *Next Generation* script focused on homosexuality and an AIDS-like disease. This script was passed over by the producers of *Next Generation* due to the level of controversy involved. On the other hand, numerous parodies made purely for fun also exist. *Stone Trek* merges the *Flintstones* and the original *Star Trek* series, while shows like *Beavis and Butthead* merged their characters with the *Next Generation*. Regardless of whether or not fans produce ambition films or parodies, one thing is clear: *Star Trek* fan films are unquestionably labors of love.

Fan remakes of the world of *Star Trek* have continued developing distinct identities through the ways in which individual filmmakers choose to combine known characters with the ideals of *Star Trek*, their personal interpretations of what *Trek* means to them, and new characters they may choose to develop. These productions have also thus far remained free to access. Despite the fact that fan productions are unauthorized and subject to legalities, a status quo of sorts exists now between the fan filmmakers and Paramount (the owners of the *Star Trek* franchise), as the number of fan films continues to increase.[2] This essay examines some of the history behind the rise of *Star Trek* fan films, the variety of remakes, the challenges they face, and some of the public outlets for promoting works. Along the way, it will become clear how these films and their creators have worked to develop distinct identities, creating a subculture with a fan following all its own with a bright and expanding future ahead.

## The Rise of Fan Films

Ever since the early days of the professional television and film industries, there have been television shows and films that have sparked the creative minds of a select few in fandom. Many who work in these industries today tell stories of how they have been influenced by their favorite show or film when they were growing up and how this may have prompted them to start putting together their own homemade plays or short films. From the old 8 mm cameras to the high-tech digital video available today, fans have found creative ways to document their stories and to play the parts of their favorite characters. After all, who has not pretended to be Captain Kirk, blasting the aliens and saving the day for the Federation? Fan filmmakers have access to increasingly more sophisticated technologies and have developed into serious filmmakers in the amateur realm. Though still a hobby, fan filmmaking has become both competitive and expensive.

Fan films, whether using the simplest technologies of 8 mm film or today's high-tech video options, have always been costly. The costs of film, developing, editing and splicing, along with early attempts at special effects like slow motion or double exposure, required a fair amount of funds. But through hard effort and patience, fan films were born. Fan films have always faced financial and technological challenges. But non-professionals have managed to produce works ranging from short, simple parodies created for play to full-length feature episodes or films of great seriousness.[3]

One of the first subjects ever treated by fan movies was the original *Star Trek* series. Some of the first story lines were lifted from fanzines (fan publications in which fan writers could create continuing stories involving their favorite characters or create whole new ones based on the canon of *Star Trek*). At the same time that fan clubs began sprouting up in the 1970s, fanzines were also making their debut. Some fanzines were a part of club newsletters. Simultaneously, early fan films were making their mark at fan club gatherings and the early fan conventions. *Paragon's Paragon* was created by John Cosentino in the late 1970s and is considered to be the first *Star Trek* fan film. The film was shot in Super 8, and Cosentino developed his own aerial optical printer in order to create special effects such as beaming. Other vintage *Trek* fan films include *Yorktown II*, which also starred original series actor George Takei, and the parody *Turkish Trek*. The most well-known fan of the early fan film era is Art Binninger. His goal was to create stop-motion (frame-by-frame animation) parodies. Binninger began making films in 1974, but his goal was cut short following a cease-and-desist letter from Paramount.[4]

Despite their rising popularity, fan films were highly criticized and written off as something obsessed fans did who had nothing else to do with their lives. *Star Trek* fans, or nerds and geeks in general, began to gain a reputation as people who did nothing else with their lives and never left home to go out on their own. It wasn't until the *Star Wars* fan films debuted in the late 1970s and early 1980s that the image of the fan film began to change. *Star Wars* fan productions gave legitimacy to all fan works. Ernie Fosselius was inspired to create a parody titled *Hardware Wars* and found a slot for it on a cable station looking to fill a programming void. *Hardware Wars*, along with a variety of other short films, was bought and distributed by the cable industry, earning it international fame. Fosselius went on to produce a variety of other parodies and eventually landed work in the film industry as a serious filmmaker. As costs have dropped and access to the digital world has become easier for amateur filmmakers, the fan film industry has grown at a phenomenal rate. The advent of the Internet, along with the beginning of the fan film convention Fanzilla Con, gave fan films their biggest boost of all, and many films and even audio drama reproductions have gained status and a fan following of their own. *Star Trek* fan films have grown to the point that they have managed to keep the franchise alive through tough times over the past decade.

*Star Trek* has always been a favorite of fan filmmakers, due in part to its message of acceptance and its focus on the various social, political, and environmental problems faced in today's world. At the same time, it has also been a source of humor, supplying good material for an array of parodies, such as *Stone Trek* and *Star Trak: The Next Hesitation*. *Star Wreck: In the Pirkinning* is most likely one of the best examples of the strength that these films have. It is a remake, made in Finland, based on the animated version of *Star Trek* and *Babylon 5*. *Star Wreck* is considered innovative because it took over seven years to produce, is the first full-length feature film science fiction parody, and features some of the best special effects among fan films. It has also led to a spin-off role-playing game. *Star Wreck* stands as a testament to the longevity of *Star Trek* fan films. Its Web site reports over four million downloads to date. In addition to these fan films, audio dramas formatted in the style of 1950s radio dramas have also had a strong hold on fan remakes of *Star Trek* stories and have contributed to the remake industry. Regardless of the type of remake one is dealing with, the quality of work varies greatly, and both legal and financial issues continue to impact fan films.

The quality of the overall production of fan films tends to vary a great deal due to financial support, equipment quality, and the abilities of those acting, directing, and editing. Some films look as though they were indeed filmed in a backyard, while others look as good as, if not better than, Hollywood productions. Along with an increase in the quality comes a rise in interest by the professional studios that actually own the rights to the original franchises. It can be difficult to cater to the fans making these films and to keep a protective eye on copyright. There are those who have become accepting and supportive of fans. George Lucas, for example, though it took years for him to decide to do so, supports fan films. Others like Warner Bros. have been publicly and highly adverse. Paramount has remained cautious in recent years with respect to *Star Trek* fan films, watching to be sure that their own profits are not adversely affected.[5]

Despite all the legal mazes, fans supporting fan films have been outspoken on the subject of the studios cracking down. Legalities will always remain a part of the amateur filmmaking process, but fans will continue producing these pieces regardless of the occasional calls by studios to halt production. The Internet and fan film conventions such as Fanzilla Con have created a large fan base—one that will continue to grow stronger with time and fans will continue also to impose demands on these amateur filmmakers while continuing to offer support. Fans want to make films that continue to allow them to create their own characters and stories based on new interpretations of the messages in *Star Trek*, or to try to create new messages based on the *Trek* canon, while simultaneously keeping their favorite characters alive.

## The Ideals of *Trek*

So just what is it that makes *Star Trek* so special? The basic ideals of *Star Trek* are key to its popularity. These include a world where everyone is respected and every individual has a place in its future. This is the basis for the IDIC (Infinite Diversity in Infinite Combinations) philosophy created by Gene Roddenberry. People in the world of *Star Trek* are long over petty differences and are able to come together to focus on larger scale social, political, economic, and environmental problems. The characters in this future world seek out new challenges beyond their worlds. By encountering new species and new planets, there is a continuing challenge to how these people of the new Earth define themselves. The biggest question *Star Trek* addresses is: What does it mean to be human? Another question addressed is: What is the role of human beings in the greater context of the universe? These basic questions have been addressed throughout the many incarnations of *Star Trek*. *Star Trek*'s message is that the final frontier is not the exploration of space, but the exploration of the human condition. This had a tremendous impact when the original series aired in the 1960s during turbulent times in the United States. The Vietnam War, Civil Rights struggles, and the Cold War left many hoping that a future still existed for the human species. Roddenberry offered his vision of a future where all would be accepted and achieve equality and where all humans would learn to work together amongst themselves and finally with other species around the universe in peace and for the greater good.

Though none of the series that followed the original captured Roddenberry's vision in quite the same way, each went on to reflect the times during which it was produced. *Star Trek* has offered one of the few hopeful visions of the future in all of science fiction. Socially aware fans have always been attracted to what *Star Trek* has to say, and they are aware of the character development that tends to represent the common struggles of humans in contemporary times. Characters throughout *Star Trek* have faced numerous personal struggles revolving around individual identity, family, and religion. Also, women and minorities have always been portrayed as equals regardless of when the particular *Trek* series was produced.[6] All of this has great appeal to the fan base and has been the reason for the success of fan films. Fan films have reinterpreted the characters and the messages in *Trek* and have recreated them in order to address important cultural issues. Most notably, these include technological progress, social progress, environmentalism, and the concept of 'boldly going.'

## Technological Progress in *Trek*

Gene Roddenberry's vision of the world of *Star Trek* began with the premise that humans would continue to evolve morally and would also coevolve with their technologies. This in turn would lead to social evolution and the utopian future that fans have been so drawn to. Roddenberry was working from a technologically optimistic view that saw resources as limitless and where advancing technologies could solve any social, economic, or environmental problem. Since *Star Trek* has frowned upon dependencies of any kind, personal or technological, Roddenberry's goal was to show humans controlling their technologies and maintaining their individuality. He believed in the power of technology to solve problems, but did not want to see it consume humanity. It is evident that he succeeded at blending the two.[7] In each of its incarnations, stories have dealt with the promotion of self-sufficiency and independence through a balance of science and reason. *Star Trek* has fueled interest in the pursuit of technological advances. It has done so by combining the promotion of individuality and open-mindedness with optimism and idealism. Roddenberry has been accused of wrongly promoting technology as inherently good, but when used without sacrificing the individual or the society of the future, perhaps it is good, so long as it is balanced with social change and utilized to promote positive consequences for individuals. In fact, to highlight this point, the Borg could be said to represent the dangers of abusing technologies and inaugurating the one thing Roddenberry had been so vehemently against throughout his life: the elimination of the individual and of the diversity that individuals can bring to the whole. According to Roddenberry, the idea of a common mold must be destroyed, and diversity must be embraced if humans are to go out and survive in the future as a species. *Star Trek* does indeed promote the idea that technology can be the way to a better world, but only if and when humans learn to open their minds, become willing to accept change, alter their understandings of the realities around them, embrace the differences each individual in the whole has to offer, and strive towards basic humanistic moral and ethical standards. A number of fan films have focused on explicit technological issues, including *Star Trek: U.S.S. Hathaway's* "Genesis" episode that addresses questions related to the Genesis device as the terraforming tool it was designed to be and the dangerous weapon some perceive it to be, and the first animated *Trek* fan film, "Borg War," which reintroduces the Borg. In this fan film, the Borg and their process of assimilation and technology can be seen as an emphasis on technology overtaking the individual. Whenever the crews of *Trek* have taken on the Borg and have been victorious, it can be interpreted as technology being in harmony with the individual and individuality being maintained. Fan films will continue this critical focus on the values associated with technology.

## Social Progress: Infinite Diversity in Infinite Combinations

Roddenberry created a social phenomenon with his choice of the original series cast. They were chosen in order to do something no other science fiction creation had done before: depict a world in which all humans live and work together as equals. For example, Uhura's African heritage and Chekov's Russian background were never intended to affirm "racial" ties but to affirm the potential for different types of humans to exist in harmony. Roddenberry's futuristic world was designed to be one in which all forms of sentient life could come together for the common goal of a better existence for all. *Star Trek* paints a vision of the future in which social issues such as hunger and racism no longer exist. Humans are depicted in a positive light in which all are able to work together to advance beyond their individual histories. Roddenberry's original 1960s creation was driven by the radical social reformation of the times. The end result was the most optimistic and diverse vision of a future to come out of any science fiction production to date.

*Star Trek* has also not only changed with the times but perhaps has had a hand in shaping them. The original series did depict diversity among the main characters, but women still were considered to have a lower status. Starfleet did not allow them to captain ships, for instance. By the time *Next Generation*, *Deep Space Nine*, and *Voyager* appear on the scene, women and other minorities are given greater responsibilities, including the opportunity to become starship captains, as depicted in the characters Katherine Janeway (*Voyager*) and Benjamin Cisco (*Deep Space Nine*). These characters reflect the changing times and perhaps coevolve with them. *Star Trek* has taken great pride in holding itself up as an example for the rest of the world. It has been preaching about diversity and acceptance for the last four decades and has dealt with an array of social issues such as women's equality, drug abuse, slavery, mental illness, parental rights, racism, nuclear disarmament, biological warfare, cloning, homosexuality, terrorism, overpopulation, religious freedoms, environmentalism, and many others. *Star Trek* and its fan base have prided themselves on their blueprint for how to deal with such issues in contemporary times in order to create a better future. It has formed the basis for a real community: a community that hopes to someday create a world where there is no prejudice concerning ethnicity, sexual orientation, gender, or physical abilities; a world where crime, hunger, and pollution have been eliminated; a perfect world of acceptance and equality. Fans seek what contemporary society cannot offer them. This is also quite evident in the types of fan productions being created. Social issues abound in fan films. *Star Trek: Andromeda's* "Communications" has dealt with ethnic struggles, *Hidden Frontier* is best known for its regular gay characters but also has covered issues of war and genocide, and *Tales of the Seventh Fleet* deals with a secretive religion of the Efrosians which is incorporated into their service in Starfleet. In these films, on-screen roles for women and minorities are abundant, as are their roles behind the scenes in many fan productions. *Star Trek: Phase II* has gone forth to produce the rejected *Next Generation* script focused on homosexuality and an AIDS-like virus in the episode "Blood and Fire." One example that cannot be ignored, *Star Trek: Of Gods and Men*, addresses contemporary concerns over freedom and security.

## Environmentalism

Roddenberry's future world is for the most part environmentally neutral due to the technological developments which have allowed many problems of the past to be resolved. Humans have also found ways to ensure safe conditions for other forms of life, to better control or adapt to climate changes, eliminate fossil fuels, and solve overpopulation problems on other worlds. Kirk took on overpopulation in "Mark Of Gideon" as well as an invading species in "The Trouble With Tribbles." The tribbles served as an example of the disruption of the natural predation cycle. In a *Next Generation* episode, "A Force of Nature," Picard wrestles with the discovery that warp drive engines may be detrimental to a particular planet and surrounding space. In "Final Mission" he must deal with the discovery of abandoned radioactive waste. *Star Trek* has always tried to incorporate contemporary issues. One thing it has never veered from is addressing the hard fact that humans themselves are often responsible for problems. One example that stands out to most is the original cast film *Star Trek IV: The Voyage Home* in which Kirk and crew must restore humpback whales to Earth's oceans after discovering the damage caused in the past after humans hunted them into extinction. Another fine example comes from "Home Soil," a *Next Generation* episode that deals with finding a way to share a planet when it is discovered that humans have been inadvertently destroying small crystal beings that live in the sand. *Star Trek* has taken on an array of environmental issues in its forty years of television and film production, and in doing so has continued to reflect the times, offer alternative solutions, and force people to stop and think about their actions and their impact on the planet. These types of story lines are also being picked up on by fan films, particularly *Star Trek: The*

*Continuing Mission*, an audio fan production, and *Star Trek: U.S.S. Hathaway's* "Genesis."[8] Fans producing these works are also on a unified environmental mission of sorts. Despite numerous media reports over the years, fan filmmakers are succeeding in their attempts to get *Star Trek* fandom itself off the endangered species list.

## Boldly Going

One of the most well-known monologues ever delivered consists of the opening words to the original series: "Space, the final frontier. These are the voyages of the starship Enterprise. Its five-year mission: to explore strange new worlds, to seek out new life and new civilizations, to boldly go where no man has gone before." But what is the history of these words? As a response to the Soviet Sputnik satellite program, a 1958 White House document provided the inspiration for Roddenberry. Here is an excerpt from the document titled "Introduction to Outer Space": "The compelling urge of man to explore and to discover, the thrust of curiosity that leads men *to try to go where no one has gone before.*"[9] The five-year mission aspect was a standard time frame written into Starfleet as the average time of a starship's time away from Earth. These two pieces of information combined for the now iconic *Star Trek* monologue, which has changed only slightly with the airing of *Next Generation* and its delivery by Leonard Nimoy in *Star Trek II: Wrath of Khan*, and in 2008 for the *Star Trek XI* trailer. Over time, it has become more gender neutral, or more politically correct. The term *man* was changed in the 1980s to *one*.

Roddenberry had read the original 1958 document, as well as many others relevant to the space program, in his preparations for the show. Dwight D. Eisenhower's science advisory committee originally drafted the 1958 document. James Killian, scientific and intelligence advisor, is credited with the actual creation of the final document. Since it was not written as a technical document, it was also released as a public brochure following Eisenhower's review. Its overall purpose was to help better explain the space program and its goals of peaceful exploration and the sharing of knowledge among all nations for the benefit of all mankind. These are the same goals of Starfleet and the United Federation of Planets. During a chaotic time in history, both this aspect of the space program and *Star Trek* seemed to merge to bring about a true air of a hopeful future for all. This is the sort of original ambiance that fans have returned to in their filmmaking.

## Perspectives: Fans and Scholars

*Star Trek* is perhaps the most analyzed science fiction franchise of all time. For as long as there has been *Trek*, there have been those who are curious about its messages and their meanings. The original fans see the show as groundbreaking in its liberal values. They praise it for its multiracial cast and for boldly challenging the network and airing the first interracial kiss in television history. They continue to be faithful through their multitude of expressions in fandom and refer to *Trek* as a blueprint for life.[10] In contrast, many who have studied it from a scholarly perspective tend not always to share the same views. Some have claimed the original series was both racist and sexist and reinforced many stereotypes. There have also been claims that the many writers held deep political biases. The more recent critiques focusing on issues of imperialism, though, may suffer from the inability to view the original series, the one most often criticized, in its original context. Also, what once seemed bold for television in the 1960s seems rather commonplace today. To be fair though, there does appear to be some merit to these critiques.

White European-American males primarily ran the Enterprise, and the same was true of guests in command roles. Women were still not allowed to hold positions of true authority and were dressed in miniskirts. During the original run of the series, Roddenberry expressed in an interview that there were indeed limitations as to how far he was allowed to go by the network: "Today in TV you can't write about Vietnam, politics, labor management, the rocket race, or the drug problem realistically."[11] Roddenberry also went on to state how even though science fiction was one of the greatest vehicles for contemporary issues, and even though he could mask many political messages in his stories with metaphor, the networks still insisted on certain standards in order to get and keep the original series on the air.[12]

Nicholas Evan Sarantakes has argued that Roddenberry "wanted the United States to play a constructive role on the world scene" and claims that "they used the television show to critique U.S. foreign policy."[13] Sarantakes has also been one of the few researchers to have actually studied original source materials from the show. It has also been argued that the Prime Directive is meant more to preserve and perpetuate the culture of the Federation rather than to preserve the cultures of others. Arthur Itwaru is among those who have made such arguments. In his book, *Negative Ecstasy: The Star Trek Seductions and Other Mass Deceptions*, Itwaru claims that technocapitalism has deceived viewers into believing that a partnership between two of the world's most socially destructive forces could eliminate all problems of society. His argument is that the merger of capitalism with technology is especially destructive in *Star Trek* as it has reached out into space to create intergalactic patrols, borders, and wars. Itwaru continues by discussing how the Federation and Starfleet perceive of themselves as free, democratic, and acting to maintain peace, yet they do nothing but implement and enforce Federation values. Starfleet's true mission, he says, is to maintain the status quo. Since Starfleet uses military control to uphold peace, he argues that peace now has no meaning. Only a state of repressive tolerance exists. The Federation, according to Itwaru, is engaged in nothing different than the early expansionist European missions of conquest. In Itwaru's view, the audience is so enthralled by this techno-military approach that they fail to recognize its futuristic dangers. He states that the popularity of *Trek* has been due to the "colonization of consciousness . . . There is a strong relationship between—*to boldly go where no one has gone before*—and to boldly imperialize where no one has imperialized before."[14]

There are obviously clashing views about how fans and those who study them perceive the work and intentions of Roddenberry. Despite some scholarly perceptions, fans still cling to the values of the futuristic utopian vision and have not only continued to live by them, but have gone on to keep them alive through fan films. From the fan perspective, *Star Trek's* vision is a model for how humans should interact and treat one another regularly in order to secure a future for humanity. Values such as individual growth, discipline, self-worth, mutual respect, hard work, honesty, and integrity are all values fans claim they have learned more about through their dedication to *Trek*. They claim that it has made them look beyond barriers and look at how changes that they see in the shows can be incorporated into their daily lives to make them better people—better as individuals and better contributors to their societies. This open-mindedness is key to their personal success and to the hopes they have for the future. Many feel that if *Trek* had not been a part of their lives then they would not be the individuals they are today. *Trek* is credited for enhancing optimism, encouraging idealism and innovation, and fostering appreciation of the differences in our world and the potential for human existence. One thing that *Star Trek* fan culture has always had is the motivation to participate in the franchise and to shape it. There is also a general feeling that through participation in fandom and "practicing" *Trek* in one's daily life, one is able also to give something back. To some extent, there has been a coevolution of the franchise and fan culture.[15] Fan filmmaking is very individualized but also reflects common values. Fan filmmaking makes use of individual interpretations of *Trek* in order to maintain the original views of Roddenberry, incorporate personal perceptions, reflect today's social and political issues, reinforce the unity of fandom to ensure it has a place in the continued evolution of the franchise, and to also give something back to *Trek*.

## The "Wikimediacation" of *Trek*: The Role of Video and the Internet

The efforts and focus of fan films, and their availability to satisfy the still-strong thirst for *Trek* among fans, have all led to an increased growth in their popularity. Due to this growth, studios have sometimes discovered that fan films are more of a benefit than a cost in the effort to boost interest in the franchise. In *Trek's* case, this was a boost most assuredly needed over the past five to ten years. Fans have always played a large role in the success of *Star Trek*, and fan films based on it are also reliant upon fan support. To gain this support, they need all the exposure they can get. Fan films have been on display at conventions since the late 1970s. However, with the advent of the Internet, fan sites, fan sites with podcasting, and now fan sites with free download content, fan filmmaking has been on the rise. This availability on the Internet has led to a leap in exposure on higher levels. Fan films have begun to attract a great deal of media attention to the point where there are now fan film conventions, chats, Web sites, and fan film journals that have sprung up in recent years devoted solely to fan filmmaking.

In his book *Convergence Culture: Where Old and New Media Collide,* Henry Jenkins, while emphasizing the role of fans in both developing and supporting fan films, rightly notes, "we might think of fan fiction communities as the literary equivalent of the Wikipedia: around any given media property, writers are constructing a range of different interpretations that get expressed through stories."[16] Through fan films, fans have the ability to add to the *Star Trek* lore via what has been described by Jenkins as *wikimedia.* Wikimedia is a form of media that is open to all and is always changing due to new content being added or by changes made to existing content. It is not governed by any formal institution, therefore, it is an ideal outlet for fan expression. Fan films can be promoted through wikimedia. Increased exposure due to advances in technology has opened the door for the growth of the fan film industry. In addition to advances in broadband and wireless technologies, advances in filming technologies and the easier access created by decreases in costs and availability have also increased the visibility and therefore the growth of fan films and fan film fandom. This growth in exposure, availability, and greater fan involvement has kept *Trek* fan films in the forefront of the fan film industry and has also helped to keep interest in the franchise strong.

The fan fiction movement that eventually gave rise to the fan film movement can be traced as far back as 1869 when fans of Lewis Carroll's work offered revisions, parodies, and even alternate endings to his work.[17] Beginning in 1884 with the invention of the mimeograph machine, technology grew, allowing for the mass production of fan works and a trend towards more access to technology at more reasonable costs. That trend continues today. Ever since there have been films to inspire fans, there have been fan films. These works have a history that can be divided into two main categories: pre-Internet and post-Internet.[18]

In the pre-Internet era, fan fiction got its first fanzine dedicated to the expression of fan stories. The magazine was called *The Comet* and debuted in 1930. Things continued to evolve when the first copy machines were made available to the masses in 1959. Shortly thereafter in 1967, the first *Trek*-related fanzine, *Spokanalia,* was published. In 1972 *Grup* became the first adult-oriented *Star Trek* fanzine. Also in 1972, the first *Star Trek* fan convention was held and fan fiction was off and running on a level never before seen. In 1973 there was an even bigger boost with FTP, which allowed fans to archive fiction works. FTP, or file transfer protocol, made it possible to share information quicker by allowing transfers from computer to computer via the Internet or a network. The 1980s saw an explosion in the growth and expansion of fan fiction, including the precursor to instant messaging, IRC (innovation relay center), technology. From this point on, fan fiction expanded exponentially along with the expansion of the Internet and the online community.[19] As with literary fan fiction, fan films have also evolved, primarily due to advances in technological resources, but also due to the growth of science fiction conventions and the consequent exposure that fan films have been given there. Like other forms of filmic remaking, fan films illustrate the fact that technological progress and filmic reinterpretation go hand-in-hand.

Some of those old films shot in 8 mm, like *Star Trek '76*, a film that came in second place at the *Star Trek* Bicentennial Convention, were films that paved the way for the industry that exists today. In the early days of fan films, fans were creating stories on film using, to quote Spock, "stone knives and bear skins" (*City on the Edge of Forever*). As well, fan films were by no means inexpensive. The old Super 8 or regular 8 mm film was expensive to purchase and just as expensive to have developed. Then there was the need to be able to edit the film and splice it. Stop motion and double exposure were about the only effects available with such equipment. Fans persevered, though. Fan club meetings and conventions began showcasing works, and interest spread. Budding filmmakers were inspired and the fan following grew. The media and masses, though, had not yet become all that interested until one *Star Wars* fan was able to fill a slot on local cable for a programming gap and launched the mass interest in fan films. As previously mentioned, *Hardware Wars*, by Ernie Fosselius, gained international attention when it was purchased in a short film package for HBO. Fosselius also went on to work in the professional realm. It was just about this time—the late 1970s—that the fan film industry began to change dramatically, both in terms of fame and technology.

The video age had arrived, and as cameras and other equipment began to drop in cost, fans had more access to a means with which to create better works, faster and easier than ever before. Home computers were also becoming more affordable, and once their cost was within reach of fans, the quality of special effects and editing improved. A fan film industry was off and running in the late 1990s, and so was its strong fan following. *Star Trek* has continued to be a highly inspirational subject matter as evidenced by the numerous individual films. *New Voyages*, *Hidden Frontier*, and *Starship Exeter* are testaments to the continued interest in keeping the dreams and ideology of Gene Roddenberry's creation alive. As the Internet has grown, so has the fan film industry. Also, since it is illegal to profit from these works, downloads on the Internet remain free, adding to the boom in fan interest and the increased democratic potential for fan remaking. This continued interest has given rise to the numerous outlets for fan-made creations that exist today, and the industry continues to grow at astounding rates. The number of outlets devoted to fan films, and to *Star Trek* fan films in particular, are far too numerous to be covered in as brief an essay as this. However, one thing is certain: *Star Trek* fan films are here to stay and have taken on identities of their own as they have continued to evolve along with technologies, filmmaker creativity, and even with the franchise itself to create wondrous futures for fans, for the world of *Star Trek*, and for the fan film industry of which these works are a part.

## Categories of Fan Films: Ambition Films and Parodies

Fan films are indeed here to stay. In the process of evolving, fan films have separated into thematic categories. Some feel that there are three: special effects focus, parodies, and ambition films that focus on ideology. However, when looking at these works, fan films that do emphasize special effects do so in order to enhance the believability of characters and story lines. So in reality, there are most likely two theme categories: parodies and ambition films. When comparing episodes of *New Voyages, Hidden Frontier,* or *Starship Farragut* to *Hick Trek, Star Wreck,* or *Star Trek: The Pepsi Generation,* one can see a direct correlation between the quality of effects and the role of the effects in the stories. In the more serious films that focus on the ideals of *Trek,* the effects enhance overall believability in both characters and story, as is the case with *New Voyages.* In science fiction, the viewer is required to accept a premise that may not be believed in the real world. Ambition films face this challenge in that they need to find ways to create believability. Stories created around the *Star Trek* universe rely on the quality of acting and special effects in order to enhance believability and to remain consistent within the universe of *Trek.* Therefore, ambition films make great efforts with the limited budgets and equipment they have in order to create effects that do not appear fake. In addition, actions and emotions must also be believable. So, actors need to be able to interact in ways that are also believable. This is where character development becomes important. The character needs to be either as real as the *Star Trek* character he or she is based on or as well developed in his or her own right to be believable. Parodies, however, are quite different. They are based on some part of the original work in order both to entertain and perhaps make a statement about the original work. They also oftentimes exaggerate in order to be effective and humorous.

One such production that utilizes effects exceptionally well is *New Voyages.* This fan production focuses on continuing the original five-year mission of the original series and is dedicated to the development of characters and story lines which fit with the original ideology of Gene Roddenberry. It can also boast some of the best work in special effects seen among fan remakes today, particularly its latest episode, "To Serve All My Days," which made its Internet debut on November 23, 2006. The special effects in this episode are as good as, if not better than, most of the professional shows and films that are currently produced. Though the special effects in fan films vary a great deal due to costs or availability of technology, there are some, like *New Voyages,* that aim for a professional level and make effects a primary goal of the work in order to enhance the believability of characters and story lines. The effects are made a part of the overall production as if they were characters themselves. *New Voyages* has found a way to blend effects and story well, giving this production an identity and quality like no other out there. Others that have done a fine job with a strong focus on effects include *Star Trek: U.S.S. Hathaway*, *Star Trek: Of Gods and Men*, *Starship Exeter*, and *Star Trek: Intrepid*. All of these productions fall under the category of ambition films, and though some are based on the original 1960s series—as *New Voyages* is, or on *Star Trek: The Next Generation*, as *Star Trek: Intrepid* and *Hidden Frontier* are—there is one commonality: they all tackle serious social issues.

The second thematic category, parodies, exhibits a very different side of fan films. Just as there is variety in the ambition films, parodies also display a wide range of variation. The main goal of a parody is to poke fun at the stories or characters of the original professional production, and *Star Trek* has much to offer in the way of material to parody. Some, just as with ambition films, recreate favorite characters and stories, while others create new characters and stories. Ranging from such productions as *Stone Trek* to *Star Wreck*, parodies of the franchise poke fun both at *Trek* and at fandom itself. A classic parody, *Hick Trek*, is based on the film *Star Trek II: The Wrath of Khan*. It is a redneck version of *Trek* where the ship, led by Captain Jerk, is made from a Skoal container, cigarette pack, and Budweiser can. Jerk, Mr. Schlock, and "Horns" McBoy all work towards the goal of stopping the spacecat Fluffy. *Hick Trek* made the convention rounds for several years during the 1980s and 1990s and then was finally released on DVD in 1999. Another of the better-known parodies is *Stone Trek*, which is based on *The Flintstones*. This online animation of the crew of the USS Magnetize keeps count of the number of redshirts that get killed off, mission after mission. This is based on a peculiarity of the original series where it was well known that if anyone was going to die, it was going to be the guy in the red shirt. Finally, one of the best known of the parodies, *Star Wreck*, is also one of the best in quality. This production was originally created in 1992 and was finally released on the Internet in 2005. Coming out of Finland and formally known as *Star Wreck: In the Pirkinning*, it started out as a film with simplistic animated effects but then moved on to become much more sophisticated. In its latest incarnations, live actors were added. The characters in this remake are a mix from the original series and *Next Generation*, including Captain James B. Pirk (Kirk), Mr. Fukov (Chekov), Mr. Dwarf (Worf), and Mr. Info (Data). *Star Wreck* is unique in blending not only different generations of *Trek* characters, but as mentioned earlier, offering a crossover between *Star Trek: The Original Series*, *Star Trek: The Next Generation*, and *Babylon 5*. The story line is based on Pirk's frustration over life in contemporary society and how he sets out to build a new world where he is the dictator with control of a fleet of ships. Universal Pictures in Scandinavia decided officially to release this film. *Star Wreck* has also enjoyed popularity on various international television stations.[20]

What is especially interesting about *Star Wreck* is the way in which it parodies the original series. It has a dark sense of humor which depicts the Federation as an imperial power. In *Deep Space and Sacred Time: Star Trek in the American Mythos*, authors Jon Wagner and Jan Lundeen argue that there is a dictatorial aspect to the Federation in *Star Trek*. They suggest that *Star Trek* not only acts as a mirror of American culture in general, but more specifically the Federation reflects America's imperialist character by policing the universe and imposing the values of the Federation while justifying the violation of the Prime Directive (non-interference directive). This is perhaps more prominent in the original series, but Wagner and Lundeen also argue that the more equivocal approach seen in *The Next Generation* is in response to political shifts during the 1980s when there were no immediate enemies to threaten the imperial position of the United States and when there was a decreasing tolerance globally for its imperialistic position. Similar shifts can be seen in each subsequent series, which follow the political tides of the United States. According to Roddenberry, *Star Trek* was meant to mirror American culture and to show alternative ways to resolve conflicts. However some, like Wagner and Lundeen, and the producers of *Star Wreck*, argue that there may be an underlying imperial agenda within the Federation to spread twentieth-century Euro-American values. *Star Wreck* focuses on just this idea. The "Kirk" character from the original series and the Federation he represents are depicted in *Star Wreck* as imperialistic, a very different take on what most see in *Trek*. *Star Wreck* focuses on this from the perspective of a parody. Its parody of the opening "Kirk" monologue from the original series goes like this: "These are the voyages of the starship, Enterprise. Its five-year mission, to seek out and destroy new civilizations, to bring capitalism to an otherwise peaceful galaxy, to boldly spread the swinger lifestyle to where no man has gone before." It could be that this remake relies on parody in order to provoke serious thought.

Finally, the ever-popular YouTube *Red Shirt Blues* fan production, which also aired on the Sci-Fi Channel in 2001, is a parody that focuses on those poor souls doomed as soon as they put on their red shirts. Inspired by the original series in which the guys in red were usually the guys that were doomed to be dead, *Red Shirt Blues* has gained quite a following of its own. It focuses on what these guys really discuss when the Captain is not looking. It's a purely fun parody that has fans begging for an entire series.[22]

If there is one thing that *Star Trek* fans have, it is a sense of humor about themselves and the world of *Trek*, and parodies have served fandom well. They exist for the pure joy of bringing a smile to the face of the fans by making jokes about their favorite characters and story lines. Both parodies and ambition films are designed to pay homage to the world of *Star Trek* and all it has created with its idealistic vision of the future. Fan films do take much from the original product; however, as seen here, they also take on their own identities through the messages and goals they try to create.

## Expression in Production

From where do fan films spring? Clearly, they develop out of a common interest in the enjoyment of science fiction from the global community of fans and a strong belief in all that *Star Trek* stands for. It is obvious that fans are still quite interested in *Star Trek* based on the number of fan-run and professional conventions around the world, the popularity of reruns for each series, the amount of merchandise that is still in demand, the stir about the newest film, and the success of a variety of academic courses that feature *Star Trek*. After the final series, *Enterprise*, went off the air in 2005, talk about the decline and death of the franchise was rampant in the media. But fans still take advantage of any opportunity to be involved in *Star Trek* and keep it alive. Fandom is far from dead; it is alive and well in fan films, and the number of productions is growing. There are individuals in fandom who still see something new and exciting in the Roddenberry ideals, and there are individuals out there in fandom who crave a vehicle for these ideals. Some fan films, in fact, seek to restore the ideals that some fans feel have been lost by the franchise in the last several years. Once Rick Berman, and then UPN (United Paramount Network), took control of *Star Trek* following the death of Gene Roddenberry in 1991, many fans felt that the quality of the show began to decline. Fans have been outspoken about some of the story lines that have introduced more religious overtones than ever before. They also speculate that the network was out to boost ratings through the depiction of sex and with the introduction of sexy characters like Seven of Nine in *Voyager*, or with T'Pol, the main Vulcan character in *Enterprise*. It has been felt by many fans that the network began to target teenage boys and was losing the original values of Roddenberry. Stories that took on tough social and political issues became sparse. This loss of quality and shift in ideology, in the view of some in fandom, is a big motivation for the fan film movement.

Fan films are also free and accessible and have become a good gauge by which to understand just what it is that *Star Trek* fans really want to watch. Historically, a core of fans around the globe has always supported *Star Trek*, and what they don't get, they will find a way to create. That has become a goal of fan films: to recreate the wonder and the fun for themselves and to share that with others. *Star Trek* fandom is a global community and the fans have become networked consumers, proactive about their interest and the desire to see the ideals of *Star Trek* remain alive.

Fans not only watch the shows; they have used all that is *Trek* as a basis to create more *Trek* in order to keep it alive and in some instances to maintain and promote it as a way of life. This way of life has ranged from creating fanzines and fan literature to a variety of musical expressions, fan art, conventions, and even businesses and careers based on *Star Trek* influences. Fan films are merely another expression of this influence in the daily lives of fans. Fan films also could be thought of as a natural progression from fan literature to filmic productions that can be seen around the world and which are shared more readily via the Internet. To create these works, fans have done what they do best: band together, network, and share ideas and resources within a community that holds a unique cultural identity of its own. Now, on a global scale, *Star Trek* fans are becoming more active and

creative and are even perhaps more connected than ever before. Through the vehicle of fan film remakes, there is a way to keep their hopes and dreams alive, allowing for great freedom of expression. Not only are they using the world of *Star
Trek* as a foundation, but they are also creating new ideas that are going beyond the
original.

Going beyond the original is the goal of some fan remakes. These amateur
filmmakers feel that it is time to address issues that none of the *Star Trek* series ever
addressed. Topics such as alternative lifestyles have become popular. For example,
for a number of years the gay and lesbian community was upset that there has
never been an openly gay character featured in this new, open, accepting, and diverse future. Enter *Hidden Frontier*. Rob Caves began this Internet series in 2000,
and it is just completing a successful seven-year run. This fan series tackled issues that the folks at Paramount had been avoiding for far too long, particularly if
*Star Trek* was intended to be a mirror of contemporary society. Caves felt that the
time for an openly gay character had come long ago, and since Paramount was not
addressing it, this fan series would. This series gave fandom the first male-to-male
kiss in either *Star Trek* or *Star Trek* fan film history. *Hidden Frontier* also takes on
an array of social issues, from characters struggling with depression and posttrau-
matic stress disorder to terrorism.[23]

*New Voyages*, released in 2004, is perhaps the best known of the fan films. Set
in the twenty-third century, it recreates and modernizes the original crew and has
set out to complete the original five-year mission. It was developed by James Caw-
ley, an Elvis impersonator by trade (which is how he finances his productions). It
tackles social issues in the tradition of the original series. However, it has also
gone beyond that with its fourth episode, "Blood and Fire." This was a script that
had been under consideration at one point by the producers of *Star Trek: The Next
Generation*, but it was turned down due to the controversial nature of the story. Its
story line deals with homosexuality and an AIDS-like disease. The willingness of
*New Voyages* to recreate the original ideals of *Trek* and to take on the tough issues,
but also to maintain its high quality of overall production, has attracted the attention of professionals who have actually worked for the franchise.[24]

Many fan film remakes are taking lessons from the likes of *Hidden Frontier*
and *New Voyages* and are aiming for similar quality in their own productions. Other
fan films of note include *Starship Exeter*, which attempts to recreate the original
feel of the 1960s rather than modernize it as *New Voyages* attempts to do; *Andromeda*, set in the twenty-fourth century, is now a successful online series having made the leap from audio drama; *Intrepid*, another well-known fan film,
focuses on the internal strife within Starfleet and the Federation and seeks to restore the original founding principles and ignite the urge to explore once again
within both; finally, *U.S.S. Hathaway*, set in the time of the original, 2285, also
aims to revitalize the ideals of the original series and tackle social issues relevant
to today's world. Though there are numerous other parody and ambition fan films
out there in the *Star Trek* fandom community, only a select few have been high-

lighted here. As all of these filmmakers interpret the world of *Star Trek*, they create new stories and new ways to express the basic ideals that are *Trek*.

## Fan Films: The Final Frontier

It is quite apparent throughout science fiction fandom that there has been a surge of interest in fan films, especially by *Star Trek* fans. These productions have become one of the most interesting and exciting outlets for fans who want more, new *Star Trek* and who desire to see the founding principles of *Trek* renewed, revitalized, and carried on. Fans love to participate since it offers them a chance to create the world of which they once only dreamed of being a part. They may now contribute to a future they hope will come to be. Though many fans who decide to start up their own productions have hopes of being noticed by Hollywood, they are more often concerned with the projects themselves and how well they can recreate the stuff that *Trek* is made of. These filmmakers are a part of what has become primarily an online culture. Professionals now look to this group for hints of trends in their industry's future. As technology and social issues and trends change, so do *Star Trek* fan films. In a sense, fan films, much like *Star Trek* itself, have become part of American mythology. They have become modern folk tales. As Patricia Zimmerman puts it, noting a long tradition in fan fiction of paying homage to directors such as Alfred Hitchcock, "This is part of a long tradition of American cultural practice, about always being in dialogue with mass culture."[25] For as long as there have been films, there have been fans interested in recreating them in their own way, and through hard efforts, patience, and some networking and creativity, fan films have created their own identities and have created their own niche: a subculture within fandom with a fan following of their own. *Star Trek* fan films have led the way, despite often being overshadowed by the *Star Wars* fan movement.

*Star Trek* fans are continuing a long tradition of fan fiction that dates back to the late 1800s and which has evolved from the early days of fan literary fiction magazines (fanzines) to fan films on 8 mm media and continues to grow in an era now dominated by the digital age. In the past ten years alone, the growth in both the quantity and quality of these films has been phenomenal. Filmmaker ambitions are at an all-time high with so many creative venues available for exposure of their work. Fan interest has also kept ambitions high. Despite the financial burdens and the endless hours of unpaid work, fan films have become the true final frontier in fandom. Fans are able to create and market their own interpretations of the Roddenberry ideology, giving their work not only a tie to the *Trek* universe, but also a unique identity all its own. This blend of the *Trek* world and filmmaker individualism, boosted by conventions, the Internet, digital technology access, the attention of the mass media, and a dedicated fan base, has allowed fan films and fan film interest to grow exponentially over the last thirty years, creating a unique subculture with a strong future ahead.

# Notes

1. For more on this future, see, Danny Hakim, "Fans Are Flying the Enterprise in Final Frontier for *Star Trek*," *New York Times,* 18 June 2006. Daniel M. Kimmel, "Enterprising Fans Captain *Trek* Spinoffs: Sci-Fi Fans Are Left to Their Own Devices," *Variety*, 31 July 2005. Curt Holman, "Where No Fan Film Has Gone Before: Fan Films Strike Back," *New York Press* (2007), <http://www.newyorkpress.com/20/6/filmissue/feature.cfm> (1 August 2007). Danny Hakim, "*Star Trek* Fans Deprived of Show, Recreate the Franchise on Digital Video," *New York Times*, 18 June 2006, <http://video.on.nytimes.com/index.jsp?fr_story=a10700b6577259834671d9a137db8f153a87cf6c> (29 June 2007).

2. For more on the legalities of these films, see, Jennifer Granick, "Cyber Rights Now: 'Scotty, Beam Down the Lawyers,'" *Wired*, 9 October 1997, <http://www.wired.com/politics/law/news/1997/10/7564> (27 June 2007). M. E. Russell, "The Fan Films Strike Back," *The Weekly Standard*, 14 May 2004, <http://www.weekly-standard.com/Utilities/printer_preview.asp?idArticle=4083&R=EF1CA30> (2 July 2007). Susan Clerc, "Who Owns Our Culture?: The Battle Over the Internet, Copyright, Media Fandom, and Everyday Uses of the Cultural Commons" (PhD diss, Bowling Green State University, 2002).

3. The range of such remakes is addressed in a number of sources, including, Deborah Netburn, "They Just Keep On Trekking: The *Star Trek* Franchise Lives on Through Fan Films," *Los Angeles Times*, 7 July 2007, <http://www.latimes.com/entertainment/news/la-et-trek7jul07,0,5370738.story?coll=la-home-center> (20 July 2007). Russell, "The Fan Films Strike Back." Tim Bajarin, "Knight Rider Story on *Star Wars* Revelations," Technology Pundits, 17 April 2005, <http://www.technologypundits.com/index.php?article_id=89> (28 June 2007).

4. John Cosentino, "Paragon's Paragon," *Cinemagic Magazine* 6 (Spring 1976). David Friedman, "Interview: Art Binninger, The Ed Wood of 1970s Stop-Motion Animated *Star Trek* Parodies," Ironic Sans, 22 October 2007, <http://www.ironicsans.com/2007/10/interview_art_binninger_the_ed.html> (28 October 2007).

5. Anthony Pascale, "Of Gods and Men Delayed Until April," *Trek Movie.com*, <http://trekmovie.com/2007/01/06/of-gods-and-men-delayed-until-april> (2 July 2007).

6. To read more on the gendered and multicultural issues of *Trek*, see David Alexander, "Interview with Gene Roddenberry," *The Humanist* March/April (1991): 5–34. Kimmel, "Enterprising Fans Captain *Trek* Spinoffs." Thomas Richards, *The Meaning of Star Trek* (New York: Doubleday, 1997), 149–185.

7. Robert Costanza, "Visions, Values, Valuation, and the Need for an Ecological Economics," *Bioscience* 51, no. 6 (June 2001): 459–468.

8. "*Star Trek*: *The Continuing Mission*," <http://www.continuingmission.com> (31 January 2008).

9. United States Government Publishing Office, "Introduction to Outer Space" (1958), <http://www.fas.org/spp/guide/usa/intro1958.html> (5 February 2008).

10. Ken Gelder and Sarah Thornton, ed., *The Subcultures Reader* (Oxford: Routledge, 1992), 46–59, 73–80. Jeff Greenwald, *Future Perfect: How Star Trek Conquered Planet Earth* (New York: Penguin, 1999).

11. Quoted in Nicholas Evans Sarantakes, "Cold War Pop Culture and the Image of US Foreign Policy: The Perspective of the Original *Star Trek* Series," *Journal of Cold War Studies* 7, no. 4 (2005): 79.

12. Alexander, "Interview with Gene Roddenberry."

13. Sarantakes, "Cold War Pop Culture and the Image of US Foreign Policy," 1.

14. Arnold Itwaru, *Negative Ecstasy: The Star Trek Seduction and Other Mass Deceptions* (Toronto: Other Eye, 2000). Quoted from <http://opencopy.org/articles/the-star-trek-seductions> (11 February 2008).

15. Henry Jenkins, *Textual Poachers: Television Fans and Participatory Culture* (New York: Routledge, 1992). William Shatner and Chris Kreski, *Get A Life* (New York: Atria, 1999).

16. Henry Jenkins, *Convergence Culture: Where Old and New Media Collide* (New York: New York University Press, 2005), 255.

17. Will Brooker, "'It is Love': The Lewis Carroll Society as a Fan Community," *American Behavioral Scientist* 48 (2005): 859–80.

18. Lisa A. Lewis, "Something More than Love: Fan Stories on Film," in *The Adoring Audience Fan Culture and Popular Media*, ed. Lisa A. Lewis (London: Routledge, 1992), 135–162.

19. This expansion is detailed in numerous sources, including Joan Marie Verba, *Boldly Writing: A Trekker Fan and Zine History, 1967–1987,* 2nd ed. (Minnetonka, Minn.: FTL, 1996), 1–76. Sheenagh Pugh, *The Democratic Genre: Fan Fiction in a Literary Context* (Jefferson, N.C.: McFarland, 2006), 1–80, 101–260. Patricia R. Zimmermann, *Reel Families: A Social History of Amateur Film* (Bloomington: Indiana University Press, 1995), 12–56.

20. *Star Wreck: In the Pirkinning*, <www.starwreck.com> (20 July 2007). *Hick Trek*, <www.hicktrek.com> (20 July 2007). *Stone Trek*, <www.stonetrek.com> (20 July 2007).

21. Jon Wagner and Jan Lundeen, *Deep Space and Sacred Time: Star Trek in the American Mythos* (New York: Praeger, 1998).

22. *Red Shirt Blues*, <www.redshirtblues.com> (20 July 2007).

23. *Star Trek: Hidden Frontier*, <www.hiddenfrontier.com> (21 July 2007).

24. *Star Trek: New Voyages*, <www.newvoyages.com>, <http://www.startreknewvoyages.com/news_archive.html> (26 June 2007). Michelle Green, "New Voyages Moves Ahead with 'Blood and Fire,'" *Trek Today*, 6 September 2007, <http://www.trektoday.com/news/060907_01.shtml> (27 September2007).

25. Patricia Zimmermann, quoted in John Borland, "Homegrown *Star Wars* with Big Screen Magic Intact." *Cnet News*, 25 April 2005, <http://news.cnet.co.uk/software/0,39029694,39187299-2,00.htm> (12 February 2008). See also Patricia Zimmerman, "The Amateur, the Avant-Garde, and Ideologies of Art," *Journal of Film and Video* 38 (Summer–Fall 1986): 62–85.

*Chapter 12*

# Horror Video Game Remakes and the Question of Medium: Remaking *Doom*, *Silent Hill*, and *Resident Evil*

Scott A. Lukas

The hybrid or the meeting of two media is a moment of truth and revelation from which a new form is born. . . . The moment of the meeting of media is a moment of freedom and release from the ordinary trance and numbness imposed by them on our senses. —Marshall McLuhan.[1]

The meeting of the video game and the motion picture is a perilous one. Like the horrors of modernity, the nightmarish landscapes and improbable realities projected in both video games and motion pictures suggest an interesting hybridity. More and more, there are growing affinities between video games and films, but at the same time, critics and everyday people often seem unwilling to accept such a union. Like the rampaging villagers in films such as *Frankenstein*, audiences are quick to judge a union of the video game and the film as illegitimate. As Marshall McLuhan writes, the meeting of two media forms institutes new and emergent forms and, in the process, inspires critical insights about media that we may take for granted. As well, such meeting problematizes the processes of remaking common, now, across all media. This chapter explores the somewhat unholy meeting of two media forms that have come dangerously close to one another and how this meeting is played out in the films and the commentary surrounding *Doom* (2005), *Silent Hill* (2006), and *Resident Evil* (2002).

Video games and movies are often seen as having separate origins, in part because exemplar forms of each—such as *Pong* and *The Godfather*—seem worlds apart. Film has been around much longer than video games and it also shares a much higher status as a form of high culture. Similarly, video games are associated with a youth demographic that is often written off as uncreative, impressionable, and playful. Interestingly, events of the past show more affinities between these media than differences. Consider, for example, the outrage in the United Kingdom and the United States that erupted concerning purported claims about copycat killings related to *A Clockwork Orange* and *Natural Born Killers*, and also consider the claims that violent video games like *Doom* led to the Columbine massacre. As well, in terms of fan identification with media, films like *Star Wars* and *Star Trek* create loyalties deeper than many religions, as do video games like *World of Warcraft*, *Grand Theft Auto*, and *Halo*. At technical levels films have begun to draw on video games, especially as action movie directors strive to increase the frenetic pace of their films, and video games rely on films, especially as more video games are developing extensive characterizations, story lines, and ambient universes.[2] In a world of increasing intermedia, the effects of video games on films and vice versa are becoming more common and more profound.[3]

In the contemporary world, forms of adaptation, remaking, and translation abound. Etymologically, the prefix *re* refers to "back to the original place," "again" or "anew," "restoration to a previous state or condition," and the "undoing of some previous action."[4] In remaking then—whether a film, video game, text, or theme park ride—there is an inherent subversion of the original. This subversion may be enhanced when one medium crosses into the territory of the other medium. As Constantine Verevis suggests, what generally distinguishes the remake from the adaptation is "the medium of the original artefact."[5] The remake works within the same semiotic register, such as film, while the adaptation moves from one register to another, such as literature to film. However, I wish to expand the consideration of the remake as it applies to video games. Whereas the move of literature to film may be maintained as one of adaptation—since literature is generally the process of inscribing words on a page—the move of video games to film and films to video game increasingly reflect remaking rather than adaptation. This is mainly due to the fact that the lines distinguishing film and video games are becoming less distinct; there is a slippage at play between the film and the video game—that is simultaneously technical, cinematic, literary, and interpretative—that I will explore. I will attempt to show that, contrary to some popular opinions, films based on video games are, in fact, not adaptations, but remakes, and that through the process of remaking a video game into a film, a notable cultural tension between media and about remaking is brought to the surface. Analyzing the affinities between these two media provides the critic with valuable insights about both the process of film remaking in general and the specific circumstances that have led to the controversy over the role of video games in remaking.

In addressing the multiple transformative movements between the worlds of video games and film, I will consider both the remaking of films as video games and, primarily, the remaking of video games as films. I have chosen three popular video games for the analysis—*Doom*, *Silent Hill*, and *Resident Evil*—because they are popular video games that each launched multiple game sequels and numerous product tie-ins and franchising; because like classic films, each is considered a classic videogame; because they are radically different types of games in terms of interface (one is a first-person shooter, the others are third person), narrative (one is focused on visceral combat, the others on cinematic-like suspense and ambiance); because they each emphasize elements of horror, especially through their use of demons and zombies as villains; and because each of the games were remade into popular film versions.[6] In addition to expanding the idea of remaking as a process of inter- (not just intra-) media, I hope to offer insights on the value of video games as influences on film and culture in general.

## A Precedent for the Remake

In a review of the video game–film remake *House of the Dead* (2003), a critic suggests that there is a simple truth that can be applied to the film by Uwe Boll: "Video games aren't movies."[7] This critic's view of Boll's film, unfortunately, states a widely held perception about the affinity of games and films; namely, that the two are worlds apart. This view, which is often held by fans on the Internet as well as film critics, assumes that video games and films are two different media and that no attempt at intertexuality, or certainly remaking, should be imagined. Part of this assumption is rooted in the lack of high culture status that is attributable to video games, while another part is tied to the general lack of understanding of intermedia that is present in the contemporary world. Since the early 1990s, many video games have been remade into films, and the reaction is often complete dismissal. Roger Ebert, responding to a fan discussion of video games, called them "inherently inferior to film and literature," and added that "To my knowledge, no one in or out of the field has ever been able to cite a game worthy of comparison with the great dramatists, poets, filmmakers, novelists and composers . . . for most gamers, video games represent a loss of those precious hours we have available to make ourselves more cultured, civilized and empathetic."[8] Ebert's high culture bias demonstrates that moving from a form that is easily belittled, like video games, to one that is commonly revered, like film, will not be an easy transition.

The relationship between video games and films has always been an uneasy one. Many movies have used video games as a central plot of the film, including *Tron* (1982), *The Last Starfighter* (1984), *Cloak & Dagger* (1984), *Arcade* (1993), *eXistenZ* (1999), and *Avalon* (2001), so there is a precedent for the exploration of the affinities between these two differing media worlds. As well, some films, like *eXistenZ*, *Videodrome* (1983), and *Brainstorm* (1983), play with the idea of media and its tension of translation. In terms of remaking video games, numerous ones have been translated into television shows. Not surprisingly, many have been animated features or cartoons such as *Adventures of Sonic the Hedgehog*, which was based on the popular video game series created by Sega. Like the many feature films that would follow, the cartoon uses the basic characters from the game, including Sonic the Hedgehog and his nemesis Dr. Ivo Robotnik, but later fills in the details, including plot and characterization. A general trend in the remaking of video games as television shows and feature films is the need to adapt the narrative. As will be illustrated with *Doom*, video games have sometimes reflected low plot development and characterization, in part because they are driven by action, not story. When video games are remade into cartoons, there is a market phenomenon involved. Because children are often socialized with video games—in fact, in contemporary society their aptitude for play may actually begin with the electronic play of video games, not traditional forms of it like outside play or board games—there is a tendency for media to be produced around these powerful gaming franchises. What is interesting to note in the remaking of video games as cartoons is the idea that there is more affinity between the two media; part of this is due to the fact that the cartoon, unlike film, is considered to be lower on the cultural scale.[9]

While cartoons, due to their association with low culture, may not be overtly criticized for their relationships with video games and remaking, films do not share the same immunity. The film *Super Mario Bros.* (1993) was the first major attempt to transform a video game into a feature film. Unlike the light-hearted game that was popular with children and teenagers, the feature film opted for a futuristic, dystopian mood. The game world in which many young people had participated was transformed into a *Blade Runner*-like future with parallel universes, dinosaurs, and multiple fantastical species. As well, the plot was surprisingly complex unlike the video game with its minimal story line. Many fans were upset with the adaptation—citing fidelity issues like altering the story line of the game too much, and taking too much liberty with characters, including the alteration of a mushroom person into a human character in the film. Early on the tensions are thus established in the video game–movie remake; notably, the question of how to adapt the video game in terms of its narrative.[10]

The film *Double Dragon* (1994)—directed by Paul W. S. Anderson, who would later direct two of the *Resident Evil* films—was one of many adaptations of the classic fighting arcade video game. The Taito video game was released in 1987, adapted into comic book form in 1991, and later into an animated series for television in 1993. Though not successful as a film remake, *Double Dragon* showed the promise of remaking as a cross-media, synergistic phenomenon. Another popular martial arts fighting game, *Street Fighter*, was produced as a film in 1994, and it included a notable cast with actors Jean-Claude Van Damme and Raul Julia. The film expanded on the video game's somewhat simplistic plot and added elements of comedy and deeper characterization, and like *Mortal Kombat*, the film included an exterior conflict, outside of the fighting itself. Later, video games were released that were based on the *Street Fighter* game; among other things, they included digitized scenes of the actors from the feature film, and, thus, they pointed to the interesting intertextuality that develops in the world of film and video game remakes. The understanding of this phenomenon cannot be told as a linear, A–B movement of either the film to the video game or vice versa, but rather, in the style of a Gadamerian hermeneutics—the interaction of referents from the game and movie properties operates in a circular, non-linear, if not rhizomatic sense.

The adaptation of the popular fighting arcade game *Mortal Kombat* into a movie in 1995 was somewhat less challenging than the earlier efforts, in part due to the format of the video game. The narrative of the game centers on one fact— the mythical tournaments known as Mortal Kombat. This central plot element is one that is suited for both the video game and the feature film. In the case of action video games, fighting is a main purpose, and in action films, fighting is also a major hallmark of the genre. Thus, there is less anxiety in the production of a *Mortal Kombat* remake because the central element of the video game—the fight— is preserved in the film version. As well, stylistic elements like the battle tournaments in the film replicate the approach of the fights in the video game, notably the techno music, pacing, editing, and the use of scenery that resembles the static scenery of the video game.

By the late 1990s, in part due to the expanding role of media companies in people's lives, film remakes of video games had been established as a significant genre. While many of the earliest video game–film remakes had martial arts fighting themes, a shift was prompted due to the increasing popularity of horror and slasher genres in film and the expansion of new genres in video games, which was itself due greatly to the increasing processor speeds and storage capacity of new gaming systems. *Lara Croft: Tomb Raider* (2001) was a popular remake of the video game that emphasized the exploits of a female game heroine, much in the style of *Indiana Jones* with quests, epic battles, and multiple locations. Like Mario, Pac-Man, and Donkey Kong before her, Lara Croft became an iconic character, and this helped establish branding that would be necessary in all of the spin-off games, films, and other adaptations. Unlike the earlier characters, which are somewhat flat in their characterization, Croft is given an extensive biography that, though later retooled, provides a sense of depth that would be necessary for the character requirements of film. Later video games, including *Resident Evil* and *Halo*, would develop characterizations of multiple characters to help move the narrative of the game. In the case of *Lara Croft* remade as a film, the biographical details of Croft are used to similarly create plot. As Lara Croft becomes an iconic gendered figure, models and fans such as Karima Adebibe gain notoriety by recreating Lara Croft for purposes of advertising and public appearances at video game conventions.[11] By 2000 video game–film remakes were beginning to focus on the horror genre. There have been numerous horror films that have found translations as video games, including *A Nightmare on Elm Street*, *The Evil Dead*, *Halloween*, *Hellraiser*, and *The Thing*, so there is a precedent in exploring the worlds of horror that are, in some cases, created conterminously in both video games and movies.

## Recasting *Doom*: Adding More to Less

*Doom*, released in 1993 by id Software, is one of the most popular video games of all time. Like many video games to follow it, *Doom* inspired numerous copies, official sequels, and spin-off media. *Doom* is a FPS or first-person shooter, meaning that the player sees the action on the screen as he or she would in real life. *Doom* is associated with two video gaming pioneers, John Carmack and John Romero. They created the first real first-person shooter called *Wolfenstein 3D*. What is significant in *Doom*, as a quasi-adaptation of previous horror and science fiction films, is Carmack and Romero's use of key figures, symbols, and situations from previous horror, science fiction, and fantasy media. Both designers were heavily influenced by the interactive role-playing of *Dungeons & Dragons*, and both were fans of J. R. R. Tolkien's fantasy worlds and the various worlds of *Star Trek*. The sense of interactivity and fantasy from these varied worlds was combined with references to their favorite horror and science fiction films, including *Evil Dead*, *The Thing*, and *Aliens*.[12]

In fact, one of the reasons behind the increasing prevalence of video game–film remakes is due to the increasing overlap of media worlds. While critics and fans are sometimes unwilling to accept the practice of cross-citation, for those in the cultural avant-garde, such forms of cross-referencing are possible, if not desirable. Carmack and Romero used such horror and science fiction citations as they went about making the fantasy world of *Doom*. Unlike a feature film, *Doom* lacks clear plot. The only information given to the gamer in the game's instruction manual and in short messages within the game is that the player is a marine, deported to Mars, and forced to work for the Union Aerospace Corporation (UAC). The UAC is working on secret experiments involving teleportation between Mars' two moons when something goes awry. The result is the opening of gateways that teleport in demons and other creatures. Soon the creatures take over and kill humans and turn others into zombies. The player, who is unnamed but referred to by fans as Doomguy, is the last one left alive to combat the invaders. Like many science fiction and fantasy films, the theme of an evil corporation's experiments ending in abomination is the starting point for the game. Unlike later games, like the *Resident Evil* series, there is little emphasis on a central narrative or characterization; in fact, the most memorable characters are the various demons and other creatures that pop up on the numerous levels, and this fact creates less identification between the player and the avatar. In some ways, this fact of the game—which allowed players to focus on the pure carnal act of violence in shooting hordes of creatures—made it such a hit with fans.[13]

*Doom* was eventually adapted in multiple media. Two sequels of the game were produced and, most significantly, in the third installment there was a lessening of the number of monsters in any given space and a refocus on a more cinematic experience, with high-quality graphics, textures, mood lighting, sound, and more artificial intelligence and personality behind the tormenting monsters. The game lessens its identity as a video game and heightens its cinematic feeling. *Doom 3* signaled that video games were now approaching cinema in their ability to deliver complex scenery and special effects. The *Doom* franchise was even used by the US Marines to help train combat teams—a fact that would later inspire other video games in military applications, especially *America's Army*.[14] The video game was later adapted in novels like *Knee-Deep in the Dead* and *Hell on Earth*, and with these textual efforts there is a greater development of the plot and characters. The marine is named Taggart and other characters, unknown in the original game, are also named and developed. The novels that adapt *Doom*, similar to the film remake of it, struggle with the tension of adapting a video game that is inherently shallow in plot and characterization. The games' creatures and mechanics are also altered—while in the game there are clear references to demons that travel from hell, these creatures become aberrations of genetic engineering. One of the controversies of the original game was the 'Satanic' tone criticized by some religious organizations. As well, the novels dealt with the demise of zombies by means of the traditional headshot that is key in many zombie films, while in the video game rapid shots to all parts of the zombies' bodies did the trick.

In the movie *Doom*, the plot centers around an Ark that was discovered by archaeologists in the Nevada desert.[15] Similar to situations in the video game, the Ark represents a portal to another world and a team of marines uses it to teleport from Earth to Mars. The corporation from the video game, the UAC, is retained and is described as a corporation that "does make the odd, tiny mistake." A key point of the film is that the various monsters that inhabit the Mars research facility have been created through genetic engineering. Like the novels based on *Doom*, the film takes the plot of the corporation meddling in nature and producing horrible monstrosities that wreck havoc on humans and their world. Throughout the 1990s, the theme of the evil corporation using science that produces negative outcomes becomes a mainstay of both video game worlds and filmic ones—what develops is an intertextuality of science and the corporation that, like the role of the zombie, influences the worlds of video gaming and film simultaneously.

When asked about the movie version of *Doom*, *Doom* gamers often responded negatively to the movie's treatment of plot elements. Many gamers compared *Doom* to other movie remakes of video games, including *Mortal Kombat* and *Resident Evil*.[16] Predictably, some criticisms of the gamers focused on the inability of a movie to provide an interactive experience, but like the fidelity argument relative to film–film remakes, this one focuses on an essentialized notion of the medium. According to one of the most positive reviews of the film, the film was an effective remake of the video game because it focused on "things that make the game so popular: the first-person perspective, the buckets of gore, and the gnarly weapons."[17] The same reviewer, commenting on critics who cite problems with the plot development of the film, offers that "*Doom* is made to resemble and glorify a video game. . . . [and does] not include weaving a delicate tale of human interaction or composing a story that makes a lot of sense."[18] Endemic to the review is the idea that the film attempts to mimic key elements from the video game and it is thus a faithful remake. According to the film's special effects supervisor, "We tried real hard to make it [the film] look like the environment in the game."[19] One of the most famous scenes of the film is the final few minutes of the film in which the character played by Karl Urban moves through the film's corridors in a manner reminiscent of the FPS action of the video game world.

Similar to *House of the Dead*, the DVD of *Doom* includes an opening screen with the iconic *Doom* logo from the game and a selection screen that resembles menus from the games. One of the included DVD features is "Doom Nation," a discussion of actors, including Dwayne Johnson (The Rock), and their memories of playing the video game. Additionally John Carmack and other id Software designers are interviewed about their inspirations behind the game. Like many film–film remakes, the DVD package of *Doom* creates a dialogic relationship with the game; it suggests, in many ways, that homage is due to *Doom*, but often fails to state the explicit relationships between the video game and the film. On the Internet, where fan interpretations of both the *Doom* film and video game abound, commentary about the nature of the film remake focuses on characters, the weapons from the game (which make a major appearance in the film, especially the BFG or "Big Fucking Gun"), and the technical issues of the film, such as editing. While there is no consensus on the 'accuracy' of the remade film, the interpretations give insight into the tensions involved in intermedia remakes. In the case of *Doom*, there is the tension involving the intermedia aspect, which results in some fans and critics exclaiming that the media are too different to share any affinity. There is a secondary tension of adaptation that, unlike the tension of adapting novel–film in which more information is condensed to less, involves an increase in the information from less plot and characterization to more. There is the final tension of the brand and marketing of *Doom*. As many video game–film and film–video game remakes establish, audiences from one medium do not necessarily overlap with those of another. In the case of *Doom*, like in the case of film–film remakes, a problem of cross-marketing develops. While *Doom* is unfairly criticized by critics who lament the impossibility of transforming video games into film, it offers a powerful look at the possibility and challenge of intermedia remakes.

## A Tension of Interface

In the complex world of video game and film remakes, there is often a tension of interface at play. In the 1983 game *Dragon's Lair* by Cinematronics, a new hybrid emerges—that of the cartoon/video game. The game, unlike others at the arcades at the time, operated with a laserdisc system.[20] The player had to manipulate the gaming controls in precise timing, which then affected the outcome of subsequent scenes. The revolutionary appeal of *Dragon's Lair* was the idea that a player was not simply controlling a pixilated character on the screen, but actually motivating the outcome of a story. Like the popular book series for children that was released in the late 1970s, *Choose Your Own Adventure*, *Dragon's Lair* played with the idea of outcome—something which film has been unable to achieve. Whereas in film, suspense can lead to a viewer being involved in trying to predict the outcome of the next scene, the scene has been predetermined; in *Dragon's Lair*, at least in theory, the player could manipulate the story in order to achieve the desired effect. Of course, the flow of the narrative of *Dragon's Lair* was predetermined, and thus a tension develops at the interactive level of the medium. More recent games, including the Nietzchean game *Fahrenheit*, utilize the concept of *Dragon's Lair* with updated technology and graphics. This same tension is present in video games like *Resident Evil*, but in the case of these modern versions, there is an even greater development of plot and characterization, and due to processor speed and storage capabilities, the game provides more possible decisions as compared to *Dragon's Lair*. In various *Resident Evil* games, different characters can be played and manipulated, which results in different outcomes of the game and different cut scenes. For some gamers the tension of interface—which results in differential amounts of agency in the medium—relates to their lack of enthusiasm for the filmic remakes of video games. In a game like *Doom*, individuals spend countless hours fighting demons, spiders, and other horrible creatures all at a fast if not frenzied pace. In the film version of *Doom*, which involved pacing, there is a lessened emphasis on such a frenetic approach.

There is a noticeable difference in the viewer/player interfacing with films as compared to video games. In video games the emphasis is often on frenzied pace, depending on the game, or on specific tasks that must be completed—such as killing all of your opponents in a death match. In *Doom* there are legendary competitions known as speedruns in which players try to complete the game as fast as possible. In film, even in a fast-paced action film like *Terminator* or *Die Hard*, the emphasis is on the viewer moving through the story, which may take one to two hours to complete. This difference in the speed of the interfacing thus creates tension when a video game is made into a film. Much has been written on the last few minutes of *Doom* the film, particularly a segment that replicates the frenetic action of the FPS game in a similar first-person perspective. For some this moment in the film was too much like a video game: in the discomfort that is created when one medium strays too far into becoming like another, individuals often react with outrage. As Hutcheon says, the "film *Resident Evil* will be experienced differently by those who have played the video game of the same name, from which the movie was adapted, than by those who have not."[21] This fact creates problems for the remake; whether it is a movement from film to game or game to film, the producers of the new medium will have to deal with the interface tensions endemic to media and their translation. Creators of video game–film remakes, of course, cannot predict which demographic will come to theaters and rent DVDs of their movies, but they can create movie versions that attempt to play to multiple audiences as well as employ effective marketing strategies.

In both film and video games, there are multiple ways in which perspective is a form of experimentation. Since Eisenstein's famous use of montage in film, it has been possible to radically alter the viewer's perspective as he or she views a film. In video games a similar alteration of perspective is achieved, albeit with a different outcome. In the video game *Doom*, new graphic technology allowed for rooms that were not simply squares, and primitive lighting effects allowed for a further atmospheric contrast. *Resident Evil* offered radically new approaches to camera angle and perspective. In this third-person game, there are numerous occasions in which the edit is used to move the avatar from one scene to the next and in which the second scene involves a shift in visual perspective. This shift creates noticeable moments of tension in the game and achieves a cinematic effect; the difference is that unlike in cinema, the individual playing the game can react to the tension and, using skills, attempt to alter the outcome of the scene. The cybernetic relationship between the game and the player is a key truth of interfacing that is not shared by cinema. When video games become films, this cybernetics is lost, and many gamers thus complain not about the plot but about the inability to interact with the film. Likewise, a filmgoer might complain about a video game adaptation of a classic film like *The Godfather* because the mode of reception has shifted from a passive to a middle voice.[22]

## *Silent Hill*: The Promise of Atmosphere

The game *Silent Hill*, released by Konami in 1997, is, like *Resident Evil*, considered to be one of the iconic games of the survival horror video game genre. Survival horror involves the concept of the player being caught in the middle of a horror film.[23] The player must move through the environment that resembles a 3–D horror film, solve puzzles, and use their wits and weapons to defeat zombies, monsters, and other obstacles, including limited ammunition for their weapons and scarce supplies. Like the complications of a horror film, in survival horror the player must negotiate an unknown fantasy landscape. Though *Resident Evil* popularized the genre, it can be traced back to the early Atari game of 1992, *Alone in the Dark* which itself drew on the macabre mythos of writer H. P. Lovecraft. In 2005, *Alone in the Dark* was remade as a film by Uwe Boll. The Japanese game *Clock Tower*, which will also likely be made into a film, similarly emphasizes the suspenseful elements characteristic of horror films, including the J-Horror genre like *Ringu*, *Ju-on*, *Tomie*, and others, many of which are based on manga animated features. It is clear that survival horror, as a video game genre, is influenced by conventions of cinema. Once computer technology evolves, as it did with the making of *Resident Evil*, the conventions of horror films—including pacing, lighting, editing, and camera angles—become technologically realizable in video games.

One of the main ways in which survival horror games distinguish themselves from FPS games like *Doom* is the emphasis on a story-driven experience. Both *Silent Hill* and *Resident Evil* use an evolving story and characters to move the gaming experience along, and both eschew the first-person approach of *Doom* for a third-person one that promotes a different connection between the player and the environment—the visceral is abated for the literary. For players to successfully complete the game, they must use textual and aural clues to make appropriate decisions. The remake of *Silent Hill* the video game into the movie offers interesting insights into the specific affinities between survival horror and horror film. In "Path of Darkness: Making *Silent Hill*," a documentary from the *Silent Hill* DVD, director Christophe Gans describes the inspiration that led him to the movie. He was playing a long session of the video game and realized that it "was one of the few games that actually could become a movie."[24] One of his producers doubted his sincerity and asked him if a game could be frightening, to which Gans replied that the video game was "one of the most absolute fears I have experienced in my whole life." Gans goes on to describe the translation of the game to the film as a process of trying to relive the experience that he had playing the game and of "preserv[ing] the atmosphere of the game."[25] During the filming of *Silent Hill*, the production team went back and forth between the video game and their production efforts, and they emphasized repeating specific elements from the game, including lighting and camera movements. One of the effective horror elements in the video game is the avatar's movement through very dark interior spaces and foggy streetscapes. Though the two media of these versions of *Silent Hill* are arguably different, and thus more typical of adaptations, the close relationship that the production team established in trying to recreate circumstances from the video game—especially the ability to look at one form in order to influence the other—suggests principles of remaking that are typical of films being remade as films. In fact, in some film–film remakes only a loose understanding of the original film may be the case, and thus many video game–film remakes reflect a more nuanced understanding of the previous and inspirational medium.

As *Resident Evil* will illustrate, video games often lend themselves to filmic remakes because built into the games are interweaving memes of familiarity—the classic zombie and all of the associations with it (such as the head shot), the use of suspenseful music to signify something foreboding, and mood lighting and atmospheric effects that create visceral sensation in the player. In many ways, *Resident Evil* is more conventional and thus, as the game is remade into a film, the convention is carried. For *Silent Hill*, both the gaming experience and the filmic one are somewhat more surreal. In a review of both games from a psychoanalytical perspective, Santos and White argue that *Silent Hill* "like an avant-garde artist, undermines the genre conventions established by *Resident Evil*."[26] The plot of *Silent Hill* is less modernist than that of *Resident Evil* (or *Doom*). Instead of an evil corporation conducting mad experiments, the protagonist is thrown into a fictional New England town named for the game. In it a man (changed to a woman in the film) seeks to relocate his lost daughter in the surrealist, haunted community. Moving through the town, the protagonist encounters eerie landscapes, fog-laden streets, and surreal creatures that bespeak of the town's horrific past. Demons, sewn-together limbed creatures that resemble artist Hans Bellmer's dolls, monster nurses, flaming children, demon dogs, and other monstrosities create a symbolic order that is counter even to the dystopian realties of zombie worlds.

Within survival horror video games like *Silent Hill*, there is a "dynamic experience that oscillates between doing and not doing."[27] Often, film can be classified as a passive experience in terms of the viewing—save performative films like *Rocky Horror*—though the reception of the film in the viewer's mind and the interpretative processes associated with film can be quite active. Reading a novel can be an active experience in that the reader is able to control the pace of the read, go back over pages, or even flip forward, but the story itself has a passive dimension in terms of the outcome. Video games occupy a space of the middle—neither completely active nor passive—and can be classified as a form of the middle voice. Instead of acting on a thing (active voice), or being acted upon by a thing (passive voice), middle voice operates through the thing acting and being acted upon, simultaneously, as in the German "*ich rasiere mich*" (not "I am shaving," but "I am shaving myself.") In video game worlds the middle voice exists in the connection between the player and the avatar or character being deployed in the gaming environment. The form is even more noticeable in *Silent Hill*, as compared to *Doom* and *Resident Evil*, for there is a moral ambiguity present—in many ways, the demons and monsters of *Silent Hill* can be read as psychological and dream projections of the characters, while in *Doom* and *Resident Evil*, there is a clear moral authority of the protagonists who attempt to defeat the monstrosities that are results of the misguided experiments of powerful corporations. The middle voice makes the medium of video games a difficult fit with other discursive forms of media, and this discursive form means that forms of adapting and remaking—such as translating *Doom* into a novel or into a film—are not simple accomplishments.

The difficult reception of *Silent Hill* may reflect the film's play on the margins of the video game. In a conversation with an audience member following the screening of the film, critic Roger Ebert offered, "I guess this was like a video game that you like had to play in order to like understand the movie."[28] Interestingly, in remakes like *Silent Hill*, and numerous others, when film critics and fans dislike the film they refer to it as a video game.[29] Perhaps in some ways Gans' remake was too consistent with the original video game. There are scene-for-scene shots in *Silent Hill* that were translated from the video game into the film (including the eerie opening sequence of fog and "snowflakes" in the town), not unlike the efforts in Gus Van Sant's *Psycho* (1998). But whereas Van Sant's efforts were deemed as marring the original film by Hitchcock, the reaction in this case goes back to the dismissal of the entire medium from which *Silent Hill* emerged—video games. In cinematic ways, the video game *Silent Hill* may have surpassed cinema itself. The film's adoption of atmospheric tone and ambiance in lieu of under-standable plot, though, suggests that the film acts more as a video game. At the same time noticeably sparse and simple dialogue in the video—such as this line from early in the game: "This is not a Dream. What's happening to this place?"—suggests that *Silent Hill* as a video game is not yet entirely cinematic. What is clear is that the remake of *Silent Hill* suggests that the world of cinema may have powerful and profound influences on horror video games.

## *Resident Evil*: Towards a Zombie Intertextuality

In the original George A. Romero script of *Resident Evil*, the remake of the popular video game series, a character, reacting to an invasion of zombies, utters the line, "Christ, this is like . . . *Night of the Living Dead*!"[30] Romero's version of the video game, which was never used, referenced the deep and complex intertextuality of the zombie. While the zombie has its cultural origins in religions of Haiti and West Africa, it has become a popular culture archetype.[31] The zombie becomes a cultural figure through multiple interpretations, cultural transformations, and political modifications. Like the general process of remaking that governs the multiple permutations of the filmic remake, the zombie, as a figure, is one that reflects "a practice of cultural intertextuality."[32] The zombie never appears in the same way, but its remaking as a figure is conditioned by the previous versions that have been imagined.

In a playful sense, *Shaun of the Dead* (2004) emphasizes the way in which adaptation and citation reference objects across all forms of media. In the film, the soundtrack includes references to a song by the band Zombie Nation, while the store where protagonist Shaun works has the name Foree, which refers to the actor from *Dawn of the Dead*, Ken Foree. Of course, the title of the film also pays homage to Romero's *Dawn of the Dead*. *Shaun of the Dead* also parodies the British zombie film *28 Days Later* with a reference to the "rage virus" near the end of the film. *Shaun of the Dead* provides an interesting reflection on intertextuality in the age of multiple media. Like the proverbial cereal box within a cereal box, the video gaming, musical, filmic, and textual references of the zombie all combine at a meta-zombie level. Throughout the film, video games are referenced (including *Halo*) by couch potato characters obsessed with them, while television serves an interesting commentary in that the characters rely on it for advice on dealing with the zombie outbreak. *Shaun of the Dead* is not a remake in the traditional sense, but it is an intertextual film that draws on the many previous zombie films and cultural forms. It was very well received by critics, and this is perhaps due to its playful approach to the corpus of zombie films and media. Whereas direct game-to-film zombie adaptations struggle with the cross-genre effect, this particular zombie film uses any tension between media and between zombies of different origins as a source of inspiration.

Interestingly, *Shaun of the Dead* was inspired by a bit from the British situation comedy show *Spaced*. In one episode an individual playing *Resident Evil 2* fantasizes that he is really fighting zombies and this becomes the inspiration for the feature film. Unlike *Shaun of the Dead*, the film *Resident Evil* was attacked by critics as being banal, uninspired, and "look[ing] like its better predecessors."[33] In citing their concerns about the film, critics referenced the intertextual dimension that is prominent in the film. In choosing *Resident Evil* as a remake, the film's producers knowingly enter into the textual world of the remake. It is a world that, even more so than the video game worlds of *Doom* and *Silent Hill*, is conditioned by multiple permutations of the zombie archetype. Zombies suggest a complex intertexuality that spans multiple media: "the circulation of signs, products and representations in the resonate space linking film and videogaming is a rich and multi-layered phenomenon."[34] Like the inspirations behind the monsters in the video game *Doom*, *Resident Evil* builds a world of monsters, primarily the zombie, through a complex citation of previous zombies, from both video game and filmic worlds. Thus, the zombie itself, as it emerges in the many media versions of *Resident Evil*, helps illustrate how remaking is a complex process that spans multiple media and multiple stories.

*Resident Evil*, the video game, is associated with helping create the popular survival horror genre. As *Silent Hill* emphasized, survival horror is a genre that "remakes" the previous conventions of horror, suspense, and action that were once only familiar in film. This new video game genre remakes the entire genre of horror in a new interactive format. In the video game, the experience of the player is heightened by the ways in which cinematic horror conventions are brought to life. Cinematic cut scenes, like in a traditional film, both advance the narrative and impact suspense. Players can see that something menacing is about to befall them. Eerie mood music and atmospheric lighting add to the sense of horror as players move through the mansion. One of the most suspenseful elements is an effect of technological limitations. As players move from one room to the next, a short pause occurs as an image of a door appears on the screen. The image actually allows the game console's processor to catch up on the next scene, but the effect is to create more suspense—exactly what will be waiting behind the door? In some cases, there is nothing, which like in a film, adds to the overall narrative of suspense and waiting. In others there is an additional cut scene showing a monster, while in others the live action camera angle shifts—creating disorientation in the player—and a group of zombies surprise the player. Sound also plays a major role in the game, from creaking doors to echoing footsteps that could signal the approach of zombies or other creatures. The game also includes the ability to save the player's progress on a typewriter, which recalls the convention of the novel in which the reader can leave the story and return to it later.

In translating the video game into a movie, director Paul W. S. Anderson stated that the game "has a real brooding suspenseful atmosphere that translates well into movies."[35] Anderson recognizes the cinematic aspects of the game, as did Capcom's head of production, Yoshiki Okamoto, who said that "We have been told that the game contains movie elements, and we hoped that the game would become a movie as soon as possible."[36] Like many directors, Anderson, himself a part of the new video game generation, became inspired by a video game and then was asked to write the script and direct the movie. Interestingly, George A. Romero, as already noted, produced a script that was eventually rejected and he also directed a short television commercial for the *Resident Evil 2* video game. Perhaps Romero's version would have stuck more closely to the zombie archetype that he established in his *Night of the Living Dead* (1968), but for Anderson, he wanted to specifically avoid references to the zombies of 1970s and 1980s film.[37] As well, Anderson explored an *Alice in Wonderland* motif in the film—including the protagonist named Alice and symbolic references like the Red Queen, a white rabbit, and a mirrored door—which has no relation to either Romero's work or the *Resident Evil* video game. This major difference in how the video game is remade as a film illustrates that though multiple interpretations of the zombie pervade popular imagination, certain ones are more popular with fans than others.

In the film version, the action begins with an ominous statement about the Umbrella Corporation—it is the leading supplier of computers, medical technology, and healthcare, and its products are found in nine out of ten homes in the United States. Unknown to most, however, its profits are the result of military technology, genetic engineering, and viral weaponry. The first scene shows an Umbrella worker, clothed in a protective suit, working on a laboratory experiment. A vial is dropped and an unseen menace moves through the laboratory's underground ventilation system. The experimental T-Virus, when released, creates aberrations in the people and dogs that are a part of the "Hive" laboratory. Interestingly, the creatures, though they are clearly zombies, are never referred to as such in the film, and instead are called "things." Perhaps equally significant to the intertextuality of the zombie is the fear of the multinational corporation, specifically the one that is involved in military and genetic experimentation. According to director Paul W. S. Anderson, the rich world of the video game—which includes genetic testing, viral research, underground labs, and an evil multinational corporation—was perfectly suited for the movie remake.[38] It is a plot that is suited to be remade, reworked, and revitalized. In video games, including *Doom*, *Resident Evil*, and *Half-Life*, there is a pronounced emphasis on corporate and/or military experimentation gone wrong, and the theme is also picked up in numerous film remakes, such as *The Manchurian Candidate*. Like the zombie, the evil corporation serves as a foundation for the remake, in part due to the prevalence of the idea in people's minds. Just as the zombie is an archetypal image in people's minds, so too is the evil corporation; and it is this latter archetype that serves as a foundation for the remake.

While *Resident Evil* preserves many elements of the video game, including the prominent role of Umbrella in unleashing a genetic-based terror on the world, it fails to follow the game's characterization and setting. As well, in stylistic terms, fans of the original video game cited the corny lines and bad delivery of dialogue as a positive, campy element of the gaming experience. After defeating a plant monster in the game, one character says, "Looks like we got to the root of the problem," while in a scene in which character Jill is nearly crushed, another character offers, "That was too close. You were almost a Jill sandwich!" Comedy of this sort is completely absent in the remake, and suggests a situation that changes the tone of the original game (not unlike the alteration of tone that occurs in the remake of the film *Stepford Wives* in 2004). In terms of technical issues, members of the film's cast, including Michelle Rodríguez (who also played a voice role in the video game *Halo 2*), suggest that the film operates with principles that made the survival horror video game popular, including the suspense involved in moving in narrow corridors and being attacked by zombies.[39] But, unlike the game, this suspense is never really achieved in the film. The archetypal suspense and unknowing of the video game is lessened, in part due to the limitations of cinema, the setting is never claustrophobic enough, and zombie attacks do not surprise as they do in the video game. The debate here is whether this is a result of the choices that the producers, director, and designers make or whether this is a result of the change in medium that occurs as the production moves away from the video game.

 *Resident Evil* has proven to be a popular movie franchise, with sequels including *Resident Evil: Apocalypse* (2004) and *Resident Evil: Extinction* (2007). The second version of the film develops more of the plot elements from the many *Resident Evil* video games than the first film. The third film follows conventions of other contemporary horror and fantasy film remaking and draws on a number of other references that exist outside of the zombie intertext. Most notable is a referencing of the ragtag caravan in the post-apocalypse (*Mad Max*) and a reworked version of a classic archetype with zombie birds (*The Birds*). The popularity of the *Resident Evil* franchise has offered yet another intermedia effect, this time in theme parks. In 2008, Fuji-Q Highland theme park of Japan opened up a *Resident Evil: The Experience* haunted house, complete with characters from the films and video games. There is no doubt that video game enthusiasts and film fans will continue to debate the meanings of video game remakes like those associated with the *Resident Evil* series. The following tables suggest that video game–film remakes still suffer from negative perceptions in the minds of both critics and fans.

## Table 3.1. Remake Reception (Video Game Movies)[40]

| Film | Year | Rating A (%) | Rating B (/10) |
|------|------|--------------|----------------|
| *Street Fighter* | 1994 | 27 | 3.0 |
| *Double Dragon* | 1994 | 0 | 3.2 |
| *Super Mario Bros.* | 1993 | 6 | 3.6 |
| *Mortal Kombat* | 1995 | 20 | 5.1 |
| *Mortal Kombat-Ann.* | 1997 | 4 | 2.9 |
| *BloodRayne* | 2005 | 4 | 2.5 |

| Film | Year | Rating A (%) | Rating B (/10) |
| --- | --- | --- | --- |
| *Alone in the Dark* | 2005 | 1 | 2.2 |
| *Doom* | 2005 | 20 | 5.2 |
| *Lara Croft: Tomb Raider* | 2001 | 20 | 5.2 |
| *Lara Croft Tomb Raider: The Cradle of Life* | 2003 | 23 | 5.2 |
| *Resident Evil* | 2002 | 33 | 6.2 |
| *Resident Evil: Apocalypse* | 2004 | 20 | 5.7 |
| *Resident Evil: Extinction* | 2007 | 22 | 6.3 |
| *Final Fantasy* | 2001 | 44 | 6.4 |
| *House of the Dead* | 2003 | 4 | 2.0 |
| *Silent Hill* | 2006 | 28 | 6.5 |
| *Wing Commander* | 1999 | 9 | 3.5 |
| *Alone in the Dark* | 2005 | 1 | 2.2 |
| *In the Name of the King* | 2007 | 2 | 4.2 |

**Table 3.2. Remake Reception (Traditional Horror Movies)**

| Film | Year | Rating A (%) | Rating B (/10) |
| --- | --- | --- | --- |
| *The Thing* | 1982 | 76 | 8.1 |
| *The Evil Dead* | 1981 | 100 | 7.5 |
| *Evil Dead 2: Dead by Dawn* | 1987 | 100 | 7.8 |
| *Blade Runner* | 1982 | 92 | 8.3 |
| *Night of the Living Dead* | 1968 | 100 | 7.9 |
| *Night of the Living Dead* | 1990 | 69 | 6.4 |
| *Dawn of the Dead* | 1978 | 97 | 7.9 |
| *Dawn of the Dead* | 2004 | 78 | 7.4 |
| *Day of the Dead* | 1985 | 80 | 6.8 |
| *Land of the Dead* | 2005 | 74 | 6.6 |
| *The Shining* | 1980 | 85 | 8.4 |
| *The Cabinet of Dr. Caligari* | 1919 | 100 | 8.2 |
| *Metropolis* | 1927 | 99 | 8.4 |
| *The Exorcist* | 1973 | 86 | 8.0 |
| *Shaun of the Dead* | 2004 | 90 | 8.0 |
| *Psycho* | 1960 | 98 | 8.6 |
| *Psycho* | 1998 | 36 | 4.7 |
| *Halloween* | 1978 | 90 | 7.9 |
| *Halloween* | 2007 | 27 | 6.0 |

# The Meeting of Intermedia

In the DVD release of the teen horror film *Final Destination 3*, a unique feature allows the viewer to alter the course of the story. In certain scenes from the movie, a heads or tails symbol appears and the viewer can choose how the scene will develop, ultimately allowing the viewer to save the life of a character in the movie.[41] Full-length interactive movies, including *Tender Loving Care* (1999), combine multiple story lines that can be acted upon by the viewer. With this new technology, similar to the *Choose Your Own Adventure* book series, the movie becomes a video game, albeit with a primitive sense of control. While the viewer cannot move freely within scenes, he or she can alter the text in an episodic way. Similarly, in games like *The Getaway*, sixty minutes of live-action footage are featured, and so there is a convergence in the opposite direction, with video games featuring full-length movie sequences.[42] For both commercial and artistic reasons, more major directors see a close connection between video games and films. Peter Jackson and Steven Spielberg have both been involved in video games related to their movies.[43] Another common occurrence is the hiring of film directors to rework the story lines or develop camera angles, editing, and even characterization in video games.[44] The trend, from an industry perspective, is a closer marriage of video games and film, and thus the remaking of each, in both directions, will also increase.[45] As well, the dissolution of genre and medium benchmarks will continue.

From a fan perspective, there is a similar force of remaking. Games like *Doom* helped establish the popularity of the WAD, short for "Where's All the Data?" A WAD allows a player to customize a game engine like *Doom* and then create a new scenic universe that maintains the game play and action of the original engine. WADs, like machinima that would follow them, provide for an insurgent form of remaking that has since been neglected in analyses of remakes. The insurgent remake is created not by a media company or film studio but by an everyday individual. Using WADs, fans have remade films and television shows like *The Simpsons*, *Batman*, *South Park*, *Star Wars*, *The X-Files*, *Aliens*, *Predator*, and many others. In some cases the WADs incorporated key iconic images from the films into the *Doom* engine (such as a backdrop), in others they involved sampling audio from the movies or television shows and using them in the game, and in others actual characters or sprites, such as the creatures from *Aliens*, are incorporated as enemies which the player battles. Though the weapons may remain the same, the landscapes and the enemies that are engaged are altered by the player's use of the insurgent WAD. One of the most famous total conversions of the *Doom* engine was *Aliens TC*, released in 1994 and based on the popular film *Aliens*.[46] In the case of machinima, players use the video game engines of games like *Doom*, *Quake*, and others to produce their own films, complete with dialogue, actors, and action sequences. Early games like *Stunt Island* (Disney Interactive, 1992) and later ones like *The Movies* (Lionhead Studios, 2005) allow for complex forms of homemade movies, further expanding the affinity of motion pictures and video games. Even George Lucas used the *Unreal* video game engine for storyboarding purposes on some of the *Star Wars* films.[47]

Contrary to shallow critics and fans who cite adaptation anxiety, video games and film share many affinities, and their relationships will continue to evolve. Along with theme park rides that maintain connections with both, film and video games will reflect more of a coevolution than has been previously understood. The noirish video game *Max Payne*, with its bullet-time feature, draws on the cinematic sequences of *The Matrix*, which themselves have been produced with heavy CGI and "virtual cinematography," suggesting a further link back to the world of video games. The popular series *The Sims* draws inspiration from television, including soap opera formats.[48] Video games now incorporate dramatic cut scenes that approximate cinema, while film uses CGI-generated characters that are the equivalent of video game monsters and characters. Some films, like *Run Lola Run* and *Memento*, experiment with time and sequence, mimicking a video game's structure in which a player can go back over and replay scenes.[49]

Whether clearly a remake in the true sense of the term, the video game transformed as film problematizes the category of the remake and also complicates the genre and territorial distinctions of video games and cinema. The remake is not simply about the technical issues of media, nor is it about simplistic notions of originals and copies, and it is not limited to movement within one medium. As the remaking of video games into movies illustrates, the process is much more complex, less linear, and more palimpsestous than has been imagined. As the film continues to impact the video game and as the video game does the same to the film, the genre distinctions will begin to break down and, along with other emergent experiential media (such as theme park rides), the new forms of intermedia will produce new and interesting ways of reimagining the stories of horror, science fiction, and fantasy.

# Notes

The author wishes to thank Dr. Talmadge Wright (Loyola University of Chicago) for some early suggestions about references used in the research.

1. Marshall McLuhan, *Understanding Media: The Extensions of Man* (Cambridge, Mass.: MIT Press, 1994), 55.

2. As some have suggested, "games remediate aspects of cinema (including certain forms of plotting or point-of-view structures), while cinema, in return, remediates aspects of games (especially in the use of digital graphics in special effects)." Geoff King and Tanya Krzywinska, "Introduction: Cinema/Videogames/Interfaces," in *ScreenPlay: Cinema/Videogames/Interfaces*, ed. Geoff King and Tanya Krzywinska (London: Wallflower, 2002), 1.

3. Intermedia is associated with the ideas of performance artist Dick Higgins who envisioned the combination of presumably disparate media, like poetry, painting, and performance.

4. *Oxford English Dictionary*, <http://dictionary.oed.com/> (10 October 2007).

5. Constantine Verevis, *Film Remakes* (New York: Palgrave Macmillan, 2006), 82.

6. Incidentally, I also chose them because they are two of the most memorable video games that I have played. I recall spending hours and hours trying to advance through the increasingly difficult levels of *Doom*, and many more working through puzzles and battling cunning zombies and other creatures in *Resident Evil*.

7. Mark Palermo, Review of *House of the Dead*, *The Coast* (Halifax, Nova Scotia), 15 October 2003.

8. Roger Ebert, "Answer Man," 27 November 2005, <http://rogerebert.suntimes.com/apps/pbcs.dll/section?category=ANSWERMAN&date=2 0051127> (10 October 2007). Specific to the remaking of films based on video games, a similar negative tone is often the case. See Peter Hartlaub, "Hey, Grandma—Video Games Based on Movies Usually Stink," *San Francisco Chronicle*, 8 May 2007, <http://sfgate.com/cgi-bin/article.cgi?file=/c/a/2007/05/08/DDGVNPJR0K28.DTL> (10 October 2007).

9. In general, I agree, following Linda Hutcheon, that in understanding the concept, a notion of remaking that is horizontal, not vertical, is desirable. Linda Hutcheon, *A Theory of Adaptation* (New York: Routledge, 2006), xiii.

10. In some cases, these tensions are reflected at absurd levels. In Roger Ebert's review of the film *Doom* (2005), he begins by stating the film is not enough like a video game—using the word inspired in quotes—and ends by criticizing a closing sequence of the movie "that abandons all attempts at character and dialogue and uncannily resembles a video game." Roger Ebert, Review of *Doom*, <http://rogerebert.suntimes.com/apps/pbcs.dll/article?AID=/20051020/REVIEWS/51012003/1023> (12 October 2007).

11. For more on the issues of identity and Lara Croft see Diane Carr, "Playing with Lara," in *ScreenPlay: Cinema/Videogames/Interfaces*, ed. Geoff King and Tanya Krzywinska (London: Wallflower, 2002), 171–180.

12. David Kushner, *Masters of Doom* (New York: Random House, 2003), 19, 25, 31, 91, 128.

13. My recollection of first playing the game was that I was compelled to make it to the next level and anticipate the next slew of creatures to be challenged.

14. For more on *Marine Doom* see, By Rob Riddell, "*Doom* Goes to War," *Wired* 5, no. 4, <http://www.wired.com/wired/archive/5.04/ff_doom_pr.html> (10 June 2008).

15. Like many video games that are remade as films, careful attention is paid to the kinship between the two media. In the closing credits of *Doom*, the prominent text is seen: "Based on the video game by id Software."

16. Jose Amntonio Vargas, "*Doom* Takes a Shot at the Gamers," *Washington Post*, 21 October 2006, C01.

17. Chris Carle, "*Doom* Review: The Best Videogame-to-Film Adaptation Yet," <http://movies.ign.com/articles/658/658956p1.html> (1 November 2007).

18. Carle, "*Doom* Review."

19. Neil Davidson, "*Doom* Hits the Big Screen," *Times Colonist,* 24 October 2005, D2.

20. See The *Dragon's Lair* Project for examples, <http://www.dragons-lair-project.com/games/>.

21. Hutcheon, *A Theory of Adaptation*, 8.

22. In one account of *The Godfather* video game, it is written that the director of the *Godfather* film, Francis Ford Coppola, was very upset with the way in which the game was remade from the films. *Reuters*, "Bruckheimer Q&A: Fueling Video Games," *Reuters*, 18 May 2007, <http://entertainment.tv.yahoo.com/entnews/va/20070518/117950358400.html> (1 November 2007).

23. For an excellent discussion of the origins of the survival horror genre see, Chris Pruett, "The Prehistory of Survival Horror," <http://www.dreamdawn.com/sh/features/prehistoryofhorror.php> (1 November 2007).

See also, Brett Todd, "A Modern History of Horror Games Part 1," GameSpot, <http://uk.gamespot.com/gamespot/features/pc/history_horror_pt1/index.html> (1 November 2007).

24. "Path of Darkness: Making *Silent Hill*." DVD documentary for *Silent Hill*.

25. "Path of Darkness." Another member of the team described the video game as the "Bible" that they followed in making the film version of *Silent Hill*. In fact, in an interview, director Gans explains that Konami granted rights to the game in part due to the director's explanation of his love for the game. See "Exclusive: Director Christophe Gans," Comingsoon.net, <http://www.comingsoon.net/news/movienews.php?id=14165> (1 November 2007).

26. Marc C. Santos and Sarah White, "Saving Ourselves: Psychoanalytic Investigation of *Resident Evil* and *Silent Hill*," Game Career Guide, 30 January 2007, <http://www.game-careerguide.com/features/334/features/334/saving_ourselves_psychoanalytic_.php> (1 November 2007).

27. Tanya Krzywinska, "Hands-On Horror," in *ScreenPlay: Cinema/Videogames/Interfaces*, ed. Geoff King and Tanya Krzywinska (London: Wallflower, 2002), 207.

28. Roger Ebert, Review of *Silent Hill*, <http://rogerebert.suntimes.com/apps/pbcs.dll/article?AID=/20060420/REVIEWS/60421001/1023> (1 November 2007).

29. Nathan Lee, Review of *Silent Hill*, *New York Times*, 22 April 2006.

30. George A. Romero's original script for *Resident Evil* may be viewed at <http://www.dailyscript.com/scripts/resident_evil_romero.html> (1 November 2007).

31. For more on the popular culture history of the zombie, see Max Brooks, *The Zombie Survival Guide* (New York: Three Rivers Press, 2003).

32. Pedro Javier Pardo García, "Beyond Adaptation: Frankenstein's Postmodern Progeny," in *Books in Motion: Adaptation, Intertextuality, Authorship*, ed. Mireia Aragay (Amsterdam: Rodopi, 2005), 240.

33. Mike Clark, Review of *Resident Evil*, *USA Today*, 14 March 2002, <http://www.usatoday.com/life/movies/2002/2002-03-15-resident-evil.htm> (1 November 2007).

34. Derek A. Burill, "'Oh, Grow Up 007': The Performance of Bond and Boyhood in Film and Videogames," in *ScreenPlay: Cinema/Videogames/Interfaces*, ed. Geoff King and Tanya Krzywinska (London: Wallflower, 2002), 181.

35. "The Making of *Resident Evil*." DVD documentary included with *Resident Evil*.

36. "The Making of *Resident Evil*."

37. "The Making of *Resident Evil*." Interview with the director.

38. "The Making of *Resident Evil*."

39. "The Making of *Resident Evil*."

40. Rating A is based on Rotten Tomatoes movie critic reviews, which includes most major worldwide newspapers and publications, <http://www.rottentomatoes.com/> (1 November 2007). Rating B is based on Internet Movie Database fan film voting, which on the movies listed in this chart included between 2,700 and 112,000 voters, <http://www.imdb.com> (1 November 2007). While these sources do give a sense of critic and fan interest in films, they do not suggest a scientific ability to compare these originals to their remakes.

41. CBS News, "Pick A Flick, Choose Your Own Ending," CBS News, 1 August 2006, <http://www.cbsnews.com/stories/2006/08/01/earlyshow/main1853874.shtml> (1 November 2007).

42. Brad King, "Games: The Movies You Play," *Wired*, 25 May 2002.

43. Laura M. Holson, "*King Kong* Blurs Line Between Films and Games," *New York Times*, 24 October 2005.

44. Laura M. Holson, "Out of Hollywood, Rising Fascination with Video Games," *New York Times*, 10 April 2004.

45. There is even a trend in which classic video games, like *Centipede*, are remade. In such cases, like with classic movies that ship with film remakes, there is an inclusion of the classic arcade game along with the remade version. Richard Rouse, "Everything Old Is New Again: Remarking Computer Games," *Computer Graphics* 33, no. 2.

46. See Doomworld's "The Top 100 WADs of All Time," <http://www.doomworld.com/10years/bestwads/> (1 November 2007). For more on WADs and issues connecting video games and everyday violence, see Scott A. Lukas, "Behind the Barrel: Reading the Video Game Gun," in *Joystick Soldiers: The Military/War Video Games Reader*, ed. Nina Huntemann and Matt Payne (New York: Routledge, 2009, forthcoming).

47. Leander Kahney, "Games Invade Hollywood's Turf," *Wired*, 9 July 2003.

48. King and Krzywinska, "Introduction," 7.

49. Margit Grieb, "Run Lara Run," in *ScreenPlay: Cinema/Videogames/Interfaces*, ed. Geoff King and Tanya Krzywinska (London: Wallflower, 2002), 165.

*Chapter 13*

# Film Remake or Film Adaptation? New Media Hollywood and the Digitizing of Gothic Monsters in *Van Helsing*

Costas Constandinides

Count Dracula, an undead host, and Frankenstein's monster, a precursor to the cyborg, ensured that the notorious lines "I bid you welcome" (*Dracula*, Tod Browning, 1931) and "It's alive" (*Frankenstein*, James Whale, 1931) will be repeated as long as filmmakers continue to aspire toward the cinematic perfection of these monstrous bodies through the use of new technology and stylization. For instance, the cinematic medium itself seems to amplify Dracula's supernatural qualities as shape-shifter and undead by transforming his filmic body in accordance with the current cinematic technology. Equally, Frankenstein's monster and its narrative have been read as the progenitors of the cyborg, being compared to Arnold Schwarzenegger's Terminator role in the film of the same title, as well as to narratives that depict the invention of artificial intelligence as the original sin of the twenty-first century.[1] These transformations do not only apply to the above characters, but to other cinematic monsters as well, such as King Kong, Godzilla, and the Alien among others. However, a main disparity here is that these latter monsters were invented for the cinema, rather than by literary authors.

Although the origins of Dracula and Frankenstein are literary, their continuous journeys through the diverse landscape of cinema have detached them from their creators' written portraits. The Count's image has been adapted and regenerated by celebrated film directors such as F. W. Murnau, Tod Browning, Francis

Ford Coppola, and Werner Herzog. Similarly, Frankenstein's monster has been re-animated by James Whale and Kenneth Branagh. The bodies of Dracula and Frankenstein's monster in each of these films have been reinterpreted as images that bear no traditional relationship to the original texts. These interpretations, nonetheless, have not been perceived as inferior to the source texts and they have been studied as independent texts. Consequently, these films have acquired a kind of detachment from their literary sources, which establishes them as distinctive moments in cinematic history. *Van Helsing* (2004) seems to be an extreme example of this detachment.

Robert Stam in his seminal essay "Beyond Fidelity: The Dialogics of Adaptation" attempts to marginalize the issue of fidelity in film adaptation studies by undermining the concept of the author and authorial meaning.[2] Stam suggests that the filmmaker cannot be faithful to something that itself is not firm, conscious, or clear about its intentions. To reinforce his assumptions and undermine the author's function, Stam refers to the Bakhtinian translinguistic conception that understands the author as a coordinator of preexisting discourses. Therefore, Stam seeks to weaken preconceptions of film adaptation as an inferior and subordinate form of expression by putting forward critical arguments that stem from structuralist and post-structuralist theoretical developments. These arguments are applied to render the film adaptation as an open structure which is similar to the form of the novel as a text. This approach allows the film itself to be studied as a text of visual signs that can generate an excess of readings.

The Gothic literary tradition is a genre that has been formed by oral preexisting discourses about the unspeakable and the macabre. This is reflected on the verbal signs that constitute the conventions of this tradition and will be described in the following section of this chapter. The Gothic novel itself is the forerunner of an intensified generic hybridity that is overtly visible in *Van Helsing*. The Gothic stitches together a preexisting oral tradition along with melodrama, romanticism and the epistolary novel, which essentially moves away from the simple form of the folklore and embraces the literary culture of its time.

Similarly, *Van Helsing* is a film that is not preoccupied with the literary antecedents of the monstrous bodies it depicts, but with the visual culture that these bodies have shaped. *Van Helsing* could also be described then as a carnivalesque remediation because of the semiotic overload, its chaotic torrents of intertextual allusions, and its combination of old and new media with various sorts of popular culture, such as Hollywood, popular novels, animation, comic books, and music: Dracula's Brides' transformation into animated flying freaks is highly reminiscent of Marilyn Manson's androgynous body on the cover photo of his 1998 album *Mechanical Animals*. *Van Helsing* manipulates this culture through the medium of digital cinema as understood by Lev Manovich (2001).[3] This raises certain questions about the coding and reading of these bodies and how they function within convergence culture; a culture that has essentially replaced Boris Karloff and Bela Lugosi with other movie monsters, from Freddie Kruger to *Jurassic Park's* T-Rex.

*Van Helsing* brings together the creatures of Gothic literature, cinema, and the Golden Age of Hollywood horror films into a new, overtly stylized space. How does this space change the way we perceive the representations of these monsters in older media? This essay attempts to explore further the significance of the digital image as expressed in the work of new media theorists such as Lev Manovich, David Bolter and Richard Grusin, Henry Jenkins, and Anna Everett, along with others who celebrate the "shift from the computer as a tool . . . to the computer as a medium of communication, education, and entertainment."[4] At the outset, the challenges that the filmmakers of creature movies face today are not how the audience is going to react to gory scenes, macabre settings, and blasphemy, but how to create the *total* image—an image that aims perhaps to pay homage to, and certainly competes with, the older medium of film. There is a challenge to explore the limits of contemporary cinematic technology, possibly "to fulfill our apparently insatiable desire for immediacy," and offer new thrills to audiences in the form of fast-moving action.[5] The visual images of Frankenstein, the vampire, the werewolf, or Mr. Hyde do not have the libidinal power they once had, but they have the potential to be transformed into superheroes in order to communicate effectively with younger generations. Before I look at *Van Helsing* in detail, given that I will be referring throughout this essay to key texts from the early and late-nineteenth-century Gothic genre, it will be useful to offer a short account of the literary and cinematic development of the Gothic genre.

## From Literary Text to Screen Text

It is commonly acknowledged that the rise of the Gothic novel took place in the late-eighteenth century with Horace Walpole's medieval narrative *The Castle of Otranto* (1764). E. J. Clery notes that "histories of the literature of terror written from the 1920s onwards routinely identified Walpole as the progenitor of a genre," the Gothic novel.[6] The generic term *Gothic novel* was a twentieth-century development within the context of literary studies, the term *Gothic* obviously taken from Walpole's subheading *A Gothic Story* and a handful of related works of fiction that feature the word *Gothic* in their subtitles from the 1790s onwards.[7]

Key works of the late-eighteenth-century novel that were influenced by Walpole's formula were Ann Radcliffe's *The Mysteries of Udolpho* (1794) and Matthew Gregory Lewis' notorious *The Monk* (1797), among others. These works in turn shaped the topographical descriptions of the Gothic that were translated for the language of cinema to form the generic visual trappings of horror cinema. Fred Botting comments that in eighteenth-century Gothic literature "certain stock features provide the principal embodiments and evocations of cultural anxieties. Tortuous, fragmented narratives relating mysterious incidents, horrible images, and life-threatening pursuits."[8] The predominant topography of the early Gothic novel was the castle, which is described by Botting as "decaying, bleak and full of hidden passageways, the castle was linked to other medieval edifices—abbeys, churches and graveyards especially—that, in their generally ruinous states, harkened back to a feudal past associated with barbarity, superstition and fear."[9] The labyrinthine castles and uninviting forests were populated by bandits, demons, monsters, ghostly apparitions, evil feudal lords, and persecuted fair maidens as "suggestive figures of imagined and realistic threats."[10] The popularity of the Gothic novel, its institutionalization, and mainly its potential for iconographic richness lured the film industry to adapt this tradition, which provided opportunities of experimentation with make-up, special effects, film technology, and interpretation; elements that are appealing to mass culture and filmmakers. These are the main reasons that the Gothic tradition is continuously revisited.

In the late-nineteenth century, the Gothic returned with a vengeance after it had become relatively familiar and lost its radical ideological and aesthetic shock value. The infamous works of the Victorian, or fin de siècle, Gothic like Robert Louis Stevenson's *The Strange Case of Dr. Jekyll and Mr. Hyde* (1886) and Bram Stoker's *Dracula* (1897) together with Mary Shelley's *Frankenstein* (1818) gave birth to cult characters that generated an array of standardized images in horror and science fiction cinema, such as the crazy scientist, the vampire hunter, and the abject creature. These have influenced the history of cinema and the development of special effects ever since. Botting states that such works, "in the many film versions of them that have been made, have spanned the history of cinema itself. Early films featured Gothic texts: *Frankenstein, The Edison Kinetogram* (1910) adapted Shelley's novel, while scientists and vampires were the focus of German expressionist films."[11] Undoubtedly, the films that have been most influential to the later horror/terror, film noir, and dystopian science-fiction cinema are the tour de force films produced throughout the silent period by the German studio UFA. The most important of these films, which draw on the themes and narratives of Gothic literature, are Robert Wiene's *The Cabinet of Dr. Caligari* (1919), F. W. Murnau's *Nosferatu* (1922), and Fritz Lang's *Metropolis* (1927), which, as Botting notes, "with their grotesque villains and stylized sets, played on the gloomy artificiality of Gothic scenes of terror."[12] The film this chapter will focus on, *Van Helsing*, draws on these sorts of powerful German influences from the iconography of 1930s Hollywood Gothic. As S. S. Prawer states, "the use of German expressionist techniques in the Gothic films of the 1930s . . . is no matter of coincidence or even indirect influence, for the late 1920s and early 1930s brought a raft of these German directors to America . . . where they exerted an immense influence on Hollywood filmmaking for the next two decades."[13] Tod Browning's *Dracula* (1931) and James Whale's *Frankenstein* (1931) are the two central films of Hollywood Gothic that spawned a number of horror films produced by Universal featuring these two characters. The bulk of these films constitute the golden age of horror. In introducing the characters of the blood-sucking aristocrat and the big robotic monster, these texts brought before us the actors Bela Lugosi as Count Dracula and Boris Karloff as the monster, who since then have become cultural icons. Collectibles, figurines, and DVDs of their legendary cinematic roles are still popular and in demand. Apart from the monstrous Gothic bodies, which I will be referring to in more detail later, German Expressionism and Universal Studios established a consistent iconography and filming techniques marked by sublime artificial landscapes (matte paintings, miniatures, sets) and unconventional cinematography.

The modus operandi of German expressionist films and of their successors involved, according to Prawer, "chiaroscuro lighting effects, distorted backdrops, claustrophobic spaces, extreme camera angles, and shadows disproportionate to the objects that cast them, all techniques which serve to externalize a psychological crisis in the subjects on screen."[14] These cinematic stylistic choices were applied to the Hollywood Gothic film adaptations by émigré filmmakers such as Karl Freund and began to form the generic conventions of the golden age of horror film that later influenced the development of the horror film in general. Misha Kavka, in her essay "Gothic on Screen," offers a short description of the topography and iconography of the film adaptations of Gothic novels by Universal Studios:

> The ruined castle or abandoned house on a hill made hazy by fog; the dark cemetery dotted with crosses and gnarled, bare branches; the heavy-built wooden doors that close without human aid; the high, arched or leaded windows that cast imprisoning shadows; the close-ups of mad, staring eyes (often above a cape drawn across the lower face); the towering, square body of a leaden-footed galvanic creation; even the passing of a black cloud across a full moon; these are the elements by which the historically mutable Gothic has become Gothic film.[15]

These are the conventions that *Van Helsing* revisits and plays with, and I purposefully use the word *play*, as *Van Helsing* is certainly not just a horror film. It is a hybrid of many genres from horror to *James Bond* films and it becomes a playground for the filmmakers to experiment with and for the audience to cognitively interact with by discovering the intertextual connections. The audience is also invited through exhilarating action sequences to enjoy a 'theme park ride' that showcases cult cinematic characters and flamboyant sets that the viewer will be able to relive as an interactive experience through the widely advertised video game of the film. On its narrative level *Van Helsing* is doing what the hugely successful play *The Complete Works of William Shakespeare (Abridged)* (The Reduced Shakespeare Company, 1994) did, but it is using a significant spectrum of Gothic texts instead, mainly filmic references from the golden age of horror. After the gradual demise of this era, 1960s and 1970s Britain saw the return of Gothic texts such as *Frankenstein, Dracula*, and *Jekyll and Hyde* in various versions, which as Botting writes were "inflected by concerns with the social and sexual liberations of the period."[16] Produced by Hammer Film Productions, these films, as Heidi Kaye remarks "offer a highly colored, highly sexualized image of the traditional Gothic texts, tending towards the flamboyance of Grand Guignol instead of suspense."[17]

At this point I would like to focus on the monstrous bodies featured in *Van Helsing*, mainly Dracula and Frankenstein's monster, and briefly note how they have been read and how they evolved as characters. This will be useful as the perception of the monstrous body in popular culture, especially in the culture of digital cinema, may carry unique connotations. For instance, Judith Halberstam argues that the monstrous body "makes flesh itself Gothic and . . . maps out a new geography of terror."[18] According to the latter "within the nineteenth-century Gothic, authors mixed and matched a wide variety of signifiers of difference to fabricate the deviant body—Dracula, Jekyll/Hyde, and even Frankenstein's monster before them are lumpen bodies, bodies pieced together out of the fabric of race, class, gender, and sexuality."[19] Monstrous bodies have dramatized fears caused by racial and sexual prejudices, as well as class-consciousness awakening, which threatened Englishness and its values. In the beginning was Dr. Frankenstein's monster:

> Frankenstein's monster has attained mythic status within both the popular imagination and the critical project of literary history. Exhaustive studies of Frankenstein have read the monster's symbolic value in terms of sex, gender, and class. The monster, in various readings then . . . is class struggle, the product of industrialisation, a representation of the proletariat; the monster is all social struggle, a specific symbol of the French Revolution, the power of the masses unleashed; the monster is technology, the danger of science without conscience, the autonomous machine.[20]

Does Frankenstein's monster in *Van Helsing* suggest these issues, urging the viewer to think critically about our contemporary condition? Certainly not in the same way the novel does; because obviously the film does not intend primarily to address the critical viewer. But on the other hand Frankenstein's monster in *Van Helsing* announces its first appearance as a digitally composited body; that is, a blend of live-action and computer-generated elements. Does this choice bring new interpretations of what this body represents and how is this related to the context of the film?

The other legendary monster of Gothic fiction is, of course, Dracula. Halberstam argues that in the context of Stoker's novel "Dracula is otherness itself; a distilled version of all others produced by and within fictional texts, sexual science and psychopathology. He is monster and man, feminine and powerful, parasitical and wealthy . . . he lives forever but can be killed. Dracula is indeed not simply a monster but a technology of monstrosity."[21] Interestingly, Halberstam uses the word *technology* in both descriptions, and in the case of *Van Helsing*, both monstrous bodies in specific scenes are indeed the bodies of technology, of digital morphing and assembling. What they both desire to denote rather than connote along with the other monsters of the film is an aesthetic superiority in the manner they are constructed, in the manner they morph, in the manner they perform their powers. They have become characters out of a graphic novel, a cluster of superheroes and super villains that inhabit a space filled with signs of a hyperconscious confused temporality.

## Intertextuality in Van Helsing

The story of *Van Helsing* largely departs from literary Gothic texts, which it was inspired by, and in fact its originating texts have been lost in the course of numerous film, television, and comic book adaptations. It is even doubtful that these treatments refer back to a single text as their source of inspiration. *Van Helsing* is obviously based on films like *House of Frankenstein* (Erle C. Kenton, 1944), and *House of Dracula* (Erle C. Kenton, 1945), which feature all the movie monsters of Universal horror just as *Van Helsing* does.

*Van Helsing* recounts the adventures of an undercover agent (Hugh Jackman), whose mission is to destroy evil. He is a member of the Knights of the Holy Order, a secret religious institution that fights the "unspeakable." This version of the character is not the traditional middle-aged father figure of preceding versions, but an amalgam of action film heroes. His costume and unruly appearance call to mind Indiana Jones and Wild West outlaws; a wanted poster of him emphasizes his image as a western hooded outcast, the anti-hero. Gabriel Van Helsing has no memory, thus no identity, but the film hints that he might be the fallen Archangel Gabriel. Van Helsing's mission is to eliminate Dracula (Richard Roxburgh) and his werewolves before the Count destroys the world. With the help of the Transylvanian Princess Anna Valerious (Kate Beckinsale), his assistant Carl (David Wenham), and Frankenstein's monster (Shuler Hensley), Van Helsing prevents Count Dracula's evil plot.

Prior to the film's opening sequence, the Universal logo turns in black and white and then bursts into flames. The burning globe beautifully cuts to a lit torch, one of the many held by an angry mob. The use of black and white is a tribute to the classic Universal horror movies and the opening sequence draws inspiration mainly from Whale's *Frankenstein* (1931). The film furthermore alludes to Frankenstein's castle/laboratory, the animation sequence, the windmill sequence, and other Gothic trappings from the classic films. It even integrates some of the methodologies utilized in expressionist films, like the use of canted camera work and the play of shadows. This is an indication that *Van Helsing's* main points of reference are the monster movies of the thirties and forties, which may be regarded as source works, since they have gained a historical significance and scholarly attention over the years. However, it is not possible to appropriate the film's use of quotations to a single source as *Van Helsing* draws from a number of popular images and media forms, past and modern.

In the "Mr. Hyde" sequence, where Van Helsing is introduced to the audience for the first time, the location is Paris, specifically Notre Dame; obviously Notre Dame, the Hyde monster and his apelike movements allude to the tradition of the filmic representation of Quasimodo in *The Hunchback of Notre Dame* by Victor Hugo (1831), in films such as *The Hunchback of Notre Dame* (Wallace Worsley, 1933), and even in Disney's animated feature (Gary Trousdale and Kirk Wise, 1996). Noticeably, the Hulk-like Hyde is pure CGI, an option that enables the filmmakers to play with his proportions, his grotesqueness, his power, and most importantly his acrobatic movements in order to produce an exhilarating action sequence. The animation used to depict Mr. Hyde provides the audience with a sense of a comic book, which helps to establish the Van Helsing character as a superhero. This effect is enhanced through the low-angle long shot of his dark silhouette standing on the edge of the roof of Notre Dame with a faint moon and black clouds as a background. Furthermore, the digitally animated Hyde monster functions in juxtaposition to the black and white beginning of the film, highlighting the abilities of contemporary film technology, and demonstrating that the process of remediation is partly to be perceived as a constructive/creative antagonism between the two media. Thus, the abominable transformations and actions of the monsters in early horror films that were impossible to depict are no longer seen through the dark silhouettes of Expressionism.

When Van Helsing eliminates Hyde, he returns to his base, which is a secret underground location in the Vatican. The superhero motif as well as the *James Bond* motif is very strong in this sequence as Van Helsing receives instructions for his next mission. Van Helsing moves around a vast lab filled with priests and monks from various religions, who invent gadgets and weapons for the destruction of supernatural evil. After Van Helsing is informed by the head Catholic priest and father figure of the Holy Order about his mission, he joins Friar Carl, who is a nineteenth-century version of *James Bond's* Q, a clumsy inventor who supplies him with weaponry and gadgetry in order to face the enemies. However, inconsistencies raise a number of ideological concerns regarding the meaning of this sequence. The Holy Order certainly works as a kind of nineteenth-century NATO coalition, although in a religious version. Christianity employs under its authority the rest of the world's religions. To an audience outside the US this must seem absurd.

The use of an Oriental person as a guinea pig, unconsciously or consciously, reflects the sociopolitical context of the production, wherein the Orient is being labeled and treated in Western countries as a source of terrorism. The allusion to Bond films reinforces even more the stereotype of the Western white male preventing foreign invaders or terrorists with peculiar accents from destroying the world. The costumes of Dracula's three brides do not appear to be innocent either. The brides are dressed like Oriental belly dancers, or harem girls, and this codes them as exotic, unruly, and uncivilized. Accordingly, Kraidy states that "Hollywood's ideological manufacturing of the Orient is one of the most enduring sites of Otherness in American popular culture."[22] Moreover, the Eastern inhabitants of the barbaric land of Transylvania are depicted as uncultured, grotesque, dumb, and dirty. In other words, Transylvania sets up the dangerous world of the Other. In her reading of Disney's *Aladdin* (1992) as a postmodern text, Kraidy writes that the film, beneath its harmless surface, is "a myriad of semiotic constellations [that] engage a plethora of signs in a powerful field of signification where constructions of race, class, and gender are imbricated in monolithic formulae and reductive conventions converging in the power dyad of a glamorized Self and a postulated Other."[23] Thus *Van Helsing*, interestingly yet unnecessarily, places these familiar Gothic narratives in a space where a "carnival of intertextuality . . . and American foreign policy, disseminate a quasi-infinity of signifiers."[24] The above are examples of the Western postulations on otherness and the Orient that are prevalent throughout history and popular culture. They present a reductive and stereotyped image of the East. In "Crisis [in Orientalism]" Edward Said illustrates how Orientalism, that is, the discourse of the West about the East, constructs stereotypes that articulate an imperialistic discourse and superiority over the Orient that still exist twenty-nine years after his study. Said affirms that the "the scope of Orientalism exactly matched the scope of empire, and it was this absolute unanimity between the two that provoked the only crisis in the history of Western thought about the dealings with the Orient. And this crisis continues now."[25]

Another recent stereotype that the film employs is the empowered female heroine, referring back to the comic book tradition and films such as *The Matrix*. Anna (Beckinsale), unlike typical Gothic heroines, is emancipated and wears tights instead of a long dress. She rules the community and knows how to defend herself, yet she is beautiful and alluring, hence she is closer to what Bukatman describes as "the spectacle of the female body" and the complete "fetishism of breasts, thighs, and hair" of superheroines in comic books.[26] These stylizations do imitate images of recent science fiction cinema, which were borrowed from comic books, but they also enter into a dialogue with the earlier cinematic representations of the main female lead or character, which were usually standardized as damsels in distress or persecuted maidens in the specific genre of horror cinema. This transformation is of course interesting to study, however the main focus of this essay remains the transformation of the monsters and the character of Van Helsing as digital and superhero bodies.

Digital media provide choices that allow flexibility, excess, and larger-than-life cinema, basics that certainly render the Gothic monsters and otherworldly settings as the best selection to play with and adapt. Should we consider the implementation of animated digital cinema a curse then? Digital animation is overtly used in specific categories of films that demand extravagant representations and which could not be seen as a threat to the essence and existence of indexical cinema and most of all to fantasy literature. In fantasy films, this may actually be more of a blessing than a curse. *Van Helsing* unleashes the creatures from more mundane representations and lets them roam in playful narratives. These creatures do not threaten us directly anymore as creatures of the unknown. They are overtly known and visible, unlike the shadowy and eerie representations of early Gothic cinema. They are visible because digital cinema desires to exhibit the perfection/detail of the computer generated monstrous body and the action elements of the film. In "Games, the New Lively Art" Henry Jenkins argues:

American popular culture is responding to Asian influences with the rise in violence in mass market entertainment a property of heightened competition between Japan, India, Hong Kong, and Hollywood for access to international markets. Action elements surface, not only in games but also in film, television, and comics, because such elements are more readily translated across linguistic and national boundaries.[27]

This film then can be seen as a symptom of this competition as these creatures can succeed in the mainstream only if their stylization fits the demands of the market and can blur the aesthetics of digital blockbuster cinema and video games. In the representations of early Hollywood Gothic, the bodies of the creatures usually wore dark attire so as to blend with the chiaroscuro lighting effects and create a sinister expressive mood. Boris Karloff (1931) wore dark clothes as Frankenstein's monster, whereas in *Van Helsing* the viewer can see the stitched upper body of the monster where at parts the skin is removed and the artificial mechanics of the monster's inner functions are visible. *Van Helsing* then does not merely adapt the narrative of a specific Gothic text, but it presells familiar characters, creatures, and their attributes as portrayed in Gothic novels and older horror films. They are transported into the visual experience, that is the digital image, and transformed into a revived character type—the superhero.

## *Van Helsing* and the New Intertextual Commodity

In the remaining sections I argue that *Van Helsing* is an example of an adaptation rather than a remake due to its transference of content from the medium of indexical cinema to digital cinema. The film also involves the "intensification and elaboration of the intertextual matrix" as the "industrial response to the heightened value of both interactivity and play for audiences."[28] This intensification is characterized by David Marshall as the "New Intertextual Commodity." Essentially, this is the culture/media industries' strategy to capture audience interest in a product through its association with other cultural forms. The product does not remain only within the boundaries of traditional media forms, such as film genres or novels, but becomes part of a wider network of related media products that are designed by the industry to maintain a "process of cultural knowledge that flows back and forth between the audience and the individual text as the audience member injects" these products into the main text. These products range from magazines to video games.[29] Marshall locates the beginning of this strategy in the music industry, where popular music was distributed and promoted through different formats, from cassettes to concerts, and, by the 1980s, through videoclips. Moreover, Marshall draws a parallel between John Hartley's (1999) description of television, which persistently tells its viewer how to enjoy and watch the medium, and children's culture, which connects toys to other products or media forms to "provide a wide range of interactions and play."[30] Today, culture/media industries move beyond children's culture and television and are "providing elaborate patterns of play across media forms" to capture the attention of a wider range of interactive audiences.[31] In this regard, the *Van Helsing* production team has released or re-released a range of products: a theme park attraction, twelve-inch action figurines, hand-painted busts of the original movie monsters *Van Helsing* was based on, a video game, the animated prequel, and three DVD collections of Universal's monster movies apart from the DVD editions of the main text.

The "Mr. Hyde" sequence from *Van Helsing* employs a strategy of incompleteness that contemporary media industries utilize as part of the intertextual commodity regime. The story of Hyde within the film marks the completion of a narrative developed in the animated short film *Van Helsing: The London Assignment* (Sharon Bridgeman, 2004), which depicts Hyde's atrocious actions. Jekyll transforms into Hyde to steal the essence of beautiful women by murdering them. He then uses this essence in a formula that keeps a person young. This short film functions as the beginning of the main film's narrative, but is presented in cartoon animation. That is one of the main reasons why Mr. Hyde and parts of *Van Helsing* in general retain a cartoonish look; it creates visual continuity with the animated prequel. This strategy imitates the collaborative texts of *The Matrix* franchise, specifically the *Animatrix* DVD (2003), which provides short animated backstories to *The Matrix* narrative and, of course, indirectly indicates the visual influences of the film by Japanese anime. In the case of *Van Helsing* the incompleteness of the main narrative involves another adaptation process. The animated characters of the short film are transferred to digital cinema. The digital image, then, not only has to imitate the cinematographic process in order to merge effectively with live action, but it also has to retain elements of cartoon animation to suggest a continuous visual style from one text to another. The main narrative of the film begins in a way that does not explain the Mr. Hyde case, thus it provokes the viewer's curiosity to see the prequel. *Van Helsing* promotes within its main narrative and its official Web site the incompleteness of the text. In other words, the main narrative is a commercially controlled text that is consciously created with gaps to be filled by other products/texts and not only by the cultural knowledge of the viewer.

Indeed, the official Web site for *Van Helsing* contains information regarding the origin of each monster.[32] But the audience that possesses this cultural knowledge belongs to another uncontrollable intertextual network that exists beyond *Van Helsing*'s event-effect. This consists of novels, scholarly books, television documentaries, online reviews, fan-based Web sites, and other popular sources. *Van Helsing*'s commercial intertextuality then is an example of a film that according to Marshall heralds a "confluence of cultural forms" rather than a single cultural form.[33] *Van Helsing* is an adaptation on two levels: firstly, it announces the transition of Gothic monsters from a filmic iconography to a computer-generated image. Secondly, its intertextual commodity purposely partakes in the strategy of incompleteness and the promise of interactivity, thus differentiating it from the traditional understanding of film adaptation. The audience of *Van Helsing* is not "defined by narrative relationships of pleasure and mastery of the text, but a form of interactivity with cultural forms."[34] The next section of this essay explains how the aesthetics of digital cinema—as exploited and used in new media Hollywood— contribute to the establishment of the new intertextual commodity and to the change of relationships between audiences and already known images.

## *Van Helsing* and New Media Hollywood

*Van Helsing* belongs to a group of post-millennium films that reanimate famous screen monsters and bring them together in a stitched narrative. Other examples are *Underworld* (Len Wiseman, 2003), *Alien vs Predator* (Paul W. S. Anderson, 2004), and *Freddy vs. Jason* (Ronny Yu, 2003). Undeniably, this trend toward creating a visual monster orgy is evocative of the early Hollywood horror films of the 1930s and 1940s and particularly Universal's marketing strategies of repeating and re- producing the horror formula. Those films expressed "audiences' dreams, fears, and social concerns, and thus inevitably reflected social mores, conflicts, and ide- ologies."[35]

The challenges that contemporary monster movies are presented with are quite different than those faced by the society, film technology, and film industry of the 1930s and 1940s. A new breed of Hollywood directors can be seen as the "league of extraordinary" directors who make films that include intertextual, dark, exces- sive settings and bodies, which tend to undergo digital morphing. If we consider the *auteur* as a director who has a particular style in composing his/her mise-en- scène and who uses similar patterns/themes throughout his/her work, certainly these directors know how to bring together pixels, traditional special effects, crea- tures, and stylish live-action photography like no one else in the industry; thus they are able to compose an effective multi-layered and expressive mise-en-scène. However, they are not *auteurs* in the way French auteurists define the word since they work within the constraints of Hollywood action spectacle cinema and adopt the language system of new media. Yet, they have made a name in the industry for mastering the digitally composited fantasy cinema. Directors such as Alex Proyas (*The Crow*, 1994; *Dark City*, 1998; *I, Robot*, 2004), Guillermo Del Toro (*Mimic*, 1997; *Blade II*, 2002; *Hellboy*, 2004; *Pan's Labyrinth*, 2006), Stephen Norrington (*Blade*, 1998; *The League of Extraordinary Gentlemen*, 2004), and Stephen Som- mers (*The Mummy*, 1999; *The Mummy Returns*, 2001) are part of this new breed. Simultaneously, the products of these directors belong to a "body of films that downplay authorial originality by foregrounding intertextuality. Such productions present their makers not as originary artists but as transmitters of cultural knowl- edge."[36]

As discussed in the previous section, it is impossible to see the above direc- tors as the sole transmitters of this knowledge within the industrial system of Hol- lywood. Hollywood does not give much freedom to directors to choose their own projects; in fact, the director is frequently chosen to undertake a project as a salable commodity himself/herself. Hence, the production of Hollywood blockbusters decentralizes the possibility of an individual author given that many people, processes, and presold texts are employed. Geoff King, in his study *New Hollywood Cinema: An Introduction*, argues that the absence of an individual author in Hollywood products lines up with Roland Barthes' declaration of the death of the author:

> This description might be quite fitting for many of the products of New Hollywood, with its multiple re-writes of scripts and a development process designed to fabricate projects that draw on and rework earlier films and seek to include various elements to appeal to different audience groups. More generally, the point is to emphasize the extent to which all texts draw on multitudes of pre-established meanings and devices that are not all determined, controlled or limited by the creation of any individual author.[37]

With the convergence of digital media the director is not always in control of the moving images or frames of the film since computerized images are generated with tools that do not require traditional skills in special effects making or set building. This poses a number of questions regarding the authorship of Hollywood blockbuster cinema and contemporary experimental digital cinema.

What has been generally acknowledged in new media and hypertext theory remains an issue in traditional film adaptation studies. Yet, it is questionable whether the writers of literary masterpieces should be seen today as sacred authors of texts with a single meaning, related to a specific context, since their texts have become hypertexts. Indeed, it is possible to read all great Anglophone literature online, hyperlinked, and free. In "Homer to Home Page: Designing Digital Books," William J. Mitchell describes how the reader can interact with the hypertext of *Odyssey*: "I can click on hot-linked words to discover where they show up in other ancient Greek texts. And . . . I could go back to the original Greek at any point and click on words to find dictionary entries, run morphological analyses, and even analyze frequencies of occurrence in different contexts . . . The digital text has new pleasures."[38] This remediation of the older medium of print culture to the computer screen dismantles traditional views of how to approach and, most importantly, respond to a classic text. It is also indicative of the possible meetings of other media in representing a classic text online, such as photography, painting, digital film, and the potentials of interaction between medium and reader/viewer. The original text itself becomes a hybrid and this process raises a number of theoretical considerations regarding the traditional values of the 'original.' Therefore, the concept of adaptation today expands rapidly as the result of numerous remediations that an artifact can undergo. The concept *film adaptation* as used in film studies must be replaced by one that does not suggest restrictions in terms of the media involved in such an interplay of familiar and commodified content.

Today's political paranoia dictates that monsters, viewed as the Other in cultural theories, might be living next door. The anxieties that the horror films of the past dealt with—such as the Cold War anxieties located in the fear of communist invasion—are different anxieties from those of today. Reality hardcore video or snuff films of beheadings have been introduced by terrorist organizations. This directly horrifies and threatens the recipient culture; a condition that triggered a shift in horror movies to films like *Saw* (James Wan, 2004)—and its sequels—and *Hostel* (Eli Roth, 2005). Beheadings of hostages by Iraqi guerilla groups, similar to the *Faces of Death* series of films in the 1970s and 1980s, may have brought forth a genre that triggers our morbid curiosity to the extreme. Who is interested in fictional vampires and werewolves when horror and the sinister Other are threatening the Western subject's immediate public/private space? It seems that filmmakers and film companies are still interested in representing monsters of the past, but in new ways. This interest derives from the early cinematic and aesthetic failure to represent fantastic environments and monstrous creatures convincingly. It is now possible to simulate these worlds credibly via the possibilities of computer animation programs. *Van Helsing* enters a new arena of heightened market competition that blurs the distinctions between video games and cinema through maximum movement, gory fight and battle sequences, limitless weaponry, and creation of exaggerated dystopias. Jenkins observes that today "action film directors combine circus acrobatics and special effects with rapid-fire editing and stylized sound effects to amp up the intensity of a fight sequence. Similarly, game designers use movement, camera angle, sound effects, and other devices to exaggerate the impact of punches or to expand the flight of a skateboarder."[39] The crossover borrowing of style is obvious in blockbuster cinema as the video game versions of films try to imitate the expressive mood and style of the movie, and the movie itself promotes the experience of the video game through hyperbolic action sequences like the one between Van Helsing and Mr. Hyde. Of course, such amplifications of movement and style are only possible via digital compositing and by giving a new visual identity to these characters. Like typical superheroes with their alluring undisclosed pasts, secret powers, superhero costumes, cool stunts, secret hideouts, and Professor-X-like father figures who help them control their powers, they become images for consumption. Ironically, Gothic monsters are becoming the very thing they inspired. With the characters of *Batman* (DC comics), *Hulk* (Marvel comics), *Blade* (Marvel comics), *The Crow* (James O'Barr), and *Wolverine* (Marvel comics), the connection is apparent.

Anna Everett, in her essay "Digitextuality and Click Theory," offers a possible interpretation of the success of digital films like *The Matrix* (Wachowski Brothers, 1999) suggesting that these films have the ability to "challenge the digital literacy and scopic competencies of contemporary media audiences more concerned with questions of technological magic than with believable representations of reality as markers of success."[40] Accordingly, Lev Manovich, in his online article "Image After '*The Matrix*,'" refers to the competitive nature of film companies as regards film technology, stating that "in order to sell movie tickets, DVDs, and all other merchandise, each new special effects film tries to top the previous one in terms of showing something that nobody has seen before. In *The Matrix* it was bullet time; in *The Matrix: Reloaded* it was a scene where dozens of identical clones fight Neo."[41] In his work *Spectacular Narratives: Hollywood in the Age of Blockbuster*, Geoff King introduces his study with the following paragraph:

> From epic landscape to sumptuous interior; from visions of space, aliens and future cityscapes to explosive action and adventure: expansive vistas spread out across the width of the big screen, their presence magnified by the aural impact of multichannel sound. Everything is larger than life; not real but hyperreal, leading us into the imaginary worlds of the cinema but also leaving us to sit back and wonder at its creations. That is the intention, at least.[42]

King justifies this Hollywoodish highlighting of spectacle as a means to compete with the medium of television. Everett relates the spectacular results of the developments of the digital media to André Bazin's views in his essay "The Myth of the Total Cinema" and his statement that "cinema has not been invented yet!"[43] She proposes that "digital media's new technological advances bring us closer to a realization of Bazin's ideas in the myth of total cinema—in short, finally the cinema *has* been invented! Its invention is achieved through magical digital tools."[44] Quite similarly, Lev Manovich in *The Language of New Media* argues that cinema is not any more the art of the index as the "logic of the filmmaking process is being redefined" by the computer.[45] Prior to the latter concluding remark, he poses an interesting question relatively ignored in contemporary film studies since the question could be applied to the study of cinema as well:

> But what happens to cinema's indexical identity if it is now possible to generate photorealistic scenes entirely in a computer using 3–D computer animation; to modify individual frames or whole scenes with the help of a digital paint program; to cut, bend, stretch and stitch digitized film images into something which has perfect photographic credibility, although it was never actually filmed?[46]

Manovich suggests that "the manual construction of images in digital cinema represents a return to nineteenth-century pre-cinematic practices, when images were hand-painted and hand-animated . . . Consequently, cinema can no longer be clearly distinguished from animation. It is no longer an indexical media technology but, rather, a sub-genre of painting."[47] Manovich's argument that artificiality becomes a central key and live action becomes raw material in the production of contemporary Hollywood cinema, and that this mode recalls early pre-cinematic viewings, is quite interesting. However, there are certain differences between digital painting software systems and hand-painting, and between digital compositing and optical printing as the computer mainly executes these latter functions. In their notable study *Remediation: Understanding New Media*, Bolter and Grusin point out that "digital graphic images are the work of humans, whose agency, however is often deferred so far from the act of drawing that it seems to disappear."[48]

Digital compositing, according to Manovich, "runs against Eisenstein's aesthetics with its focus on time. Digital compositing makes the dimensions of space (3–D fake space being created by a composite and 2½–D space of all the layers being composited) and frame (separate images moving in 2–D within the frame) as important as time."[49] In other words he argues that in contemporary American mainstream cinema, editing privileges space as the layers of images are spatially ordered within the image. In *Van Helsing* the "Mr. Hyde" sequence contains many clear examples of this spatialization of editing. In this film, seamless spatialization of layers is the aim. For instance, when the fight between Van Helsing and Mr. Hyde continues on the rooftop of a simulated Notre Dame and the latter grabs Van Helsing by the collar of his coat and drags him to the edge, a virtual camera movement rapidly pulls out towards the ground of the building, keeping both bodies in the shot while descending. During this descent the body of Van Helsing obviously becomes animated, as the final image of the shot is a low-angle shot of the digitally composited building. While it is not possible to provide in detail the elements or databases used to create this shot, it is obvious that its composite consists of a 3–D virtual space, a 2–D space of the live-action footage, a layer of 2–D movement, and a layer of Mr. Hyde's 3–D movements. Sophisticated digital compositing enables the continuity of space and the merging of a digital and a live-action character in one shot without a cut. This same shot would have been done in more than two cuts in the language of pre-digital cinema or even early digital cinema.

I shall quote Manovich's definition of digital cinema and comment further on these observations:

> digital film = live-action material + painting + image processing +
> compositing + 2–D computer animation + 3–D computer animation.[50]
>
> *We can finally answer the question "what is digital cinema?" Digital cinema is a particular case of animation which uses live-action footage as one of its many elements.*
>
> *Born from animation, cinema pushed animation to its periphery, only in the end to become one particular case of animation.*[51]

In his definition Manovich names animation as the most significant constituent of digital cinema. However, his definition might be problematic, since it is questionable whether the "painterly" actually supersedes live-action photography in contemporary Hollywood cinema in general. The main problem here is that he does not give a satisfactory number of examples to illustrate this definition. Certainly, I would say that this definition is mostly relevant to blockbuster fantasy/science fiction films rather than Hollywood cinema per se. However, Manovich's radical statements help us to understand why the digitally animated, processed, and edited image is an important component of today's cinema and why it transforms the Hollywood blockbuster into a different medium from the older medium of film. Consequently, this brings us closer to seeing that the images of monsters and Gothic trappings in *Van Helsing* are in fact post-celluloid adaptations of earlier filmic representations and that they communicate a cultural logic that pertains to the new intertextual commodity.

Indeed, the images and characters in *Van Helsing* are sometimes completely animated, as in the case of Mr. Hyde. This choice has been analyzed as a strategy to create aesthetic unity between the collaborative products of the film, such as the prequel and the video game. Another visual style that the film remediates is that of comic books, which are also appealing to fandom. The characters are amalgams of cult images and superheroes. They have extraordinary weapons and powers and we do not see them changing their attire at all—a fact that may also suggest that the one costume they wear serves as an iconic marker, like the costume of the superhero.

Arguably, the style *Van Helsing* adopts is close to the written descriptions of Gothic texts, which were all about imagination, excess, the sublime, illusion, uncanny locations, narrative chaos, intertextuality, blurring of boundaries, and bad weather conditions. Furthermore, the epistolary form of Gothic novels such as Mary Shelley's *Frankenstein* (1818), Bram Stoker's *Dracula* (1897), and Robert Louis Stevenson's *The Strange Case of Dr. Jekyll and Mr. Hyde* (1886) foreground the absence of an omniscient third-person narrator, or even of a consistent first-person narrator; thus the accounts of the characters within the novels have a level of uncertainty, which provides an openness and playfulness to the reception and adaptation of the novels. It might be argued that the absence of the narrator invites the viewer and potential user of the collaborative texts to become an author by interacting with the images and completing the backstory of each character. These observations urge us to ask whether fidelity issues—questions regarding authorial intentions and faithfulness to the narrative—are relevant to the process of adapting or remaking popular Gothic stories that were themselves obviously inspired from preexisting folk legends and earlier literary products. It is not productive to engage in a sterile, comparative elemental study of omissions and additions. It is rather preferable to examine how the film as an example of post-celluloid adaptations inhibits such considerations via its modes of production and consumption.

Thus far, I have suggested that *Van Helsing* adapts Gothic monsters into the new medium of digital cinema. Therefore the filmmakers do not repeat or imitate their predecessors; they simply attempt to compete with them by engaging the viewer (particularly the one who has seen a considerable number of horror classics) in a playful iconographic comparison rather than narrative/content comparison. What concerns this essay is adaptation in the present, yet it can be seen as a response to earlier adaptation studies that tend to bind the subject in Arnoldian ideas and Kantian aesthetics, inevitably, returning to the issue of fidelity/superiority. I am also responding to formalist studies that point out the already obvious differences between the two media, providing *how to* guidelines. Finally, I am responding to studies that overlook new media theory. There are film adaptation studies that stress the need to assimilate current approaches to texts and raise significant issues for further research. Deborah Cartmell's and Imelda Whelehan's *Adaptations: From Text to Screen, Screen to Text*, for instance, explores a range of texts including non-canonical literature, and offers examples of analyses devoid of fidelity issues. In her introduction to the second part of the book, Cartmell suggests that "the search for an original or for a single author is no longer relevant in a postmodern world where a belief in a single meaning is seen to be a fruitless quest."[52] The multiplicity of texts inherent in adaptations is the main concern of the book and not fidelity. Cartmell also emphasizes the fact that the contributions in the specific edited volume show the need for a broader understanding of the concept of film adaptation. Similarly, Robert Stam's essay "Beyond Fidelity: The Dialogics of Adaptation" in James Naremore's *Film Adaptation*, provides a range of radical arguments and in fact advocates the impossibility of fidelity:

> The shift from a single-track, uniquely verbal medium such as the novel, which has "only words to play with," to a multitrack medium such as film, which can play not only with words (written and spoken), but also with theatrical performance, music, sound effects, and moving photographic images, explains the unlikelihood—and I would suggest even the undesirability—of literal fidelity.[53]

Stam indeed moves beyond the traditional reception of the concept of fidelity to suggest that the end product of a film adaptation should be more faithful to the essence of the film medium than to the source text. Like the editors of *Adaptations: From Text to Screen, Screen to Text*, Stam foregrounds conscious/unconscious intertextuality within film adaptation as an active process that enables an infinite set of readings, arguing that the literary text itself is an "an open structure . . . to be reworked by a boundless context."[54] Hence, an adaptation such as *Van Helsing* is "made of and from the accumulation of information that, through memory and quotations, presents a rereading and rewriting of things so that the act of communication tends to supersede the content of the communication."[55] Degli-Esposti uses the latter account in her introduction to *Postmodernism in the Cinema* to describe the prominent processes engaged in postmodern cinema. Present-day filmmakers are exposed to all kinds of accessible cult texts and thus communicate a more cognizant and overt intertextuality in order to take the spectator to "another level of seeing. He/she is not only seeing differently, but is aware of seeing himself/herself see."[56]

The term *intertextuality* has also undergone evolution due to the impact of digital media and convergence media. The neologism *digitextuality* is introduced in Anna Everett's essay "Digitextuality and Click Theory." Everett argues that "new digital media technologies make meaning not only by building a new text through absorption and transformation of other texts, but also by embedding the entirety of other texts (analog and digital) seamlessly within the new."[57] Thus, apart from the traditional study of non-computerized technical choices within a movie, the film/film adaptation critic should start engaging with the meaningful negotiations of the digitextual image and should be equipped with the skills to identify and interpret the diverse texts of convergence cinema.

The 'original' work might have already lost its historical significance, or worthiness, through processes of uninhibited unraveling and journeys across old media and new media, but the constant refashioning of borrowed images and contents in another medium unconsciously redefines our cultural and historical moment through ideological, social, and feminist considerations, which, ultimately, emerge through the interplay between the historical context of the text and that of its adaptation. *Digital cinema adaptation* could in fact form a term that is legitimated by this repetition of images. It is useful to develop such a term not only in order to study texts that share the same narrative, but also because it reflects the convergence culture of today that media industries have learned to manipulate through different media channels. A language is needed to describe the images that originated in traditional media but are being adapted in new media. Correspondingly, Stam argues that "the greater the lapse in time [of an adaptation of a classic text], the less reverence toward the source text and the more likely the interpretation through the values of the present."[58] The controlled incompleteness of the main text, then, is an important part of the digital cinema adaptation process as it amplifies this need to interact with the main narrative object and its space. Intertextual and digitextual practices in Hollywood blockbusters are not solely about *seeing yourself see* as Cristina Degli-Esposti suggests. *Van Helsing*, to a certain extent, involves a process of *seeing yourself consume* as the viewer today becomes aware of his/her participation in the whirl of the intertextual commodity of these products.

# Notes

1. Sean French, *The Terminator* (London: BFI, 1996).
2. Robert Stam, "Beyond Fidelity: The Dialogics of Adaptation," in *Film Adaptation*, ed. James Naremore (London: Athlone Press, 2000), 54–78.
3. Lev Manovich, *The Language of New Media* (Cambridge, Mass.: MIT Press, 2001).
4. Henry Jenkins, "The Work of Theory in the Age of Digital Transformation," in *A Companion to Film Theory*, ed. Toby Miller and Robert Stam (Oxford: Blackwell, 1999), 236.
5. David Bolter and Richard Grusin, *Remediation: Understanding New Media* (London: MIT Press, 2000), 5.
6. E. J. Clery, "The Genesis of 'Gothic' Fiction," in *The Cambridge Companion to Gothic Fiction*, ed. Jerrold E. Hogle (Cambridge: Cambridge University Press, 2002), 21.
7. Clery, "The Genesis of 'Gothic' Fiction," 21–22.
8. Fred Botting, *The Gothic* (London: Routledge, 1996), 2.
9. Botting, *The Gothic*, 2–3.
10. Botting, *The Gothic*, 2.
11. Botting, *The Gothic*, 165–66.

12. Botting, *The Gothic*, 166.

13. S. S. Prawer, *Caligari's Children: The Film as Tale of Terror* (Oxford: Oxford University Press, 1980), 214.

14. Prawer, *Caligari's Children*, 214.

15. Misha Kavka, "The Gothic on Screen," in *The Cambridge Companion to Gothic Fiction*, ed. Jerrold E. Hogle (Cambridge: Cambridge University Press, 2002), 210.

16. Botting, *The Gothic*, 167.

17. Heidi Kaye, "Gothic Film," in *A Companion to the Gothic*, ed. David Punter (Oxford: Blackwell, 2000), 186.

18. Judith Halberstam, *Skin Shows: Gothic Horror and the Technology of Monsters* (Durham N.C.: Duke University Press, 1995), 28.

19. Halberstam, *Skin Shows*, 3.

20. Halberstam, *Skin Shows*, 29.

21. Halberstam, *Skin Shows*, 88.

22. Marwan M. Kraidy, "Intertextual Maneuvers around the Subaltern: *Aladdin* as a Postmodern Text," in *Postmodernism in the Cinema*, ed. Cristina Degli-Esposti (New York: Berghahn Books, 1998), 46.

23. Kraidy, "Intertextual Maneuvers around the Subaltern," 45.

24. Kraidy, "Intertextual Maneuvers around the Subaltern," 54.

25. Edward W. Said, "Crisis [in Orientalism]," in *Modern Criticism and Theory*, ed. David Lodge and Nigel Wood (New York: Pearson Education, 2000), 281.

26. Scott Bukatman, *Matters of Gravity: Special Effects and Supermen in the 20th Century* (Durham, N.C.: Duke University Press, 2003), 65.

27. Henry Jenkins, "Games, the New Lively Art," <http://web.mit.edu/cms/People/henry3/GamesNewLively.html> (9 December 2007).

28. David P. Marshall, "The New Intertextual Commodity," in *The New Media Book*, ed. Dan Harries (London: BFI, 2002), 69.

29. Marshall, "The New Intertextual Commodity," 70.

30. Marshall, "The New Intertextual Commodity," 72.

31. Marshall, "The New Intertextual Commodity," 73.

32. *Van Helsing* Official Web site, <http://www.vanhelsingmovie.com/> (9 December 2007).

33. Marshall, "The New Intertextual Commodity," 74.

34. Marshall, "The New Intertextual Commodity," 80.

35. Douglas Kellner, "Culture Industries," in *A Companion to Film Theory*, ed. Toby Miller and Robert Stam (Oxford: Blackwell, 1999), 207.

36. Virginia Wright Wexman, *Film and Authorship* (New Brunswick, N.J.: Rutgers University Press, 2003), 13. One of these directors, Guillermo del Toro, has announced his interest in producing new *Hellboy* films that will feature battles against the classic Universal monsters, including Frankenstein, Dracula, and the Wolf Man. Scott Collura, "Exclusive: Hellboy vs. the Universal Monsters? Del Toro Hopes to Revive the Classic Characters," IGN.com, 16 October 2006, <http://movies.ign.com/articles/739/739203p1.html> (6 June 2008).

37. Geoff King, *New Hollywood Cinema: An Introduction* (London: I. B.Tauris, 2002), 110.

38. William J. Mitchell, "Homer to Home Page: Designing Digital Books," in *Rethinking Media Change: The Aesthetics of Transition*, ed. David Thorburn and Henry Jenkins (Cambridge, Mass.: MIT, 2004), 204.

39. Jenkins, "Games, the New Lively Art." See also, *ScreenPlay:Cinema/Videogames/Interfaces*, ed. Geoff King and Tanya Krzywinska (London: Wallflower, 2002).

40. Anna Everett, "Digitextuality and Click Theory: Theses on Convergence Media in the Digital Age," in *New Media: Theories and Practices of Digitextuality,* ed. Anna Everett and John T. Caldwell (New York: Routledge, 2003), 9.

41. Lev Manovich, "Image After *The Matrix*," <http://manovich.net/> (13 August 2007).

42. Geoff King, *Spectacular Narratives: Hollywood in the Age of the Blockbuster* (London: I. B. Tauris, 2000), 1.

43. Everett, "Digitextuality and Click Theory," 22.

44. Everett, "Digitextuality and Click Theory," 22.

45. Manovich, *The Language of New Media*, 300.

46. Manovich, *The Language of New Media*, 295.

47. Manovich, *The Language of New Media*, 295.

48. Bolter and Grusin, *Remediation*, 27.

49. Manovich, *The Language of New Media*, 157.

50. Manovich, *The Language of New Media*, 301.

51. Manovich, *The Language of New Media*, 302.

52. Deborah Cartmell, "Introduction," in *Adaptations: From Text to Screen, Screen to Text*, ed. Deborah Cartmell and Imelda Whelehan (London: Routledge, 1999), 28.

53. Stam, "Beyond Fidelity," 56.

54. Stam, "Beyond Fidelity," 57.

55. Cristina Degli-Esposti, "Postmodernism(s)," in *Postmodernism in the Cinema*, ed. Cristina Degli-Esposti (New York: Berghahn, 1998), 5.

56. Degli-Esposti, "Postmodernism(s)," 5.

57. Everett, "Digitextuality and Click Theory," 7.

58. Stam, "Beyond Fidelity," 57.

# Selected Bibliography

## Compiled by Scott A. Lukas

Allen, Graham. *Intertextuality*. New York: Routledge, 2000.

Andrew, Dudley. "Adaptation." Pp. 28–37 in *Film Adaptation*, edited by James Naremore. Piscataway, N.J.: Rutgers University Press, 2000.

———. "*Breathless*: Old as New." Pp. 3–20 in *Breathless: Jean-Luc Godard, Director*, edited by Dudley Andrew. New Brunswick, N.J.: Rutgers University Press, 1987.

———. "Notes on the Continuity Script." Pp. 147–152 in *Breathless: Jean-Luc Godard, Director*, edited by Dudley Andrew. New Brunswick, N.J.: Rutgers University Press, 1987.

———. "The Well-Worn Muse: Adaptation in Film History and Theory." Pp. 9–17 in *Narrative Strategies: Original Essays in Film and Prose Fiction*, edited by Syndy M. Conger and Janice R. Welsch. Macomb, Ill.: Western Illinois University, 1980.

Aragay, Mireia. "Introduction, Reflection to Refraction: Adaptation Studies Then and Now." Pp. 11–34 in *Books in Motion: Adaptation, Intertextuality, Authorship*, edited by Mireia Aragay. Amsterdam: Rodopi, 2005.

Aragay, Mireia and Gemma López. "Inf(l)ecting *Pride and Prejudice*: Dialogism, Intertextuality, and Adaptation." Pp. 201–219 in *Books in Motion: Adaptation, Intertextuality, Authorship*, edited by Mireia Aragay. Amsterdam: Rodopi, 2005.

Argent, Daniel. "Evolution: The Development of *The Planet of the Apes* (2001)." *Creative Screenwriting* 8, no. 4 (July/August 2001): 44–46.

Arthur, Paul. "The Written Scene: Writers as Figures of Cinematic Redemption." Pp. 331–342 in *Literature and Film: A Guide to the Theory and Practice of Film Adaptation*, edited by Robert Stam and Alessandra Raengo. Malden, Mass.: Blackwell, 2004.

Ascheid, Antje. "Speaking Tongues: Voice Dubbing in the Cinema as Cultural Vehicle." *Velvet Light Trap* 40 (Autumn 1997): 32–41.

Atkinson, Michael. "Son of Apes." *Film Comment* 31, no. 5 (September/October): 62–66.

Aufderheide, Patricia. "Made in Hong Kong: Translation and Transmutation." Pp. 191–199 in *Play It Again, Sam: Retakes on Remakes*, edited by Andrew Horton and Stuart Y. McDougal. Berkeley: University of California Press, 1998.

Aycock, Wendell and Michael Schoenecke, eds., *Film and Literature: A Comparative Ap-*

*proach to Adaptation* (Studies in Comparative Literature: No. 1). Lubbock: Texas Tech University Press, 1989.

Ball, Sarah McKay. "The Uncanny in Japanese and American Horror Film: Hideo Nakata's *Ringu* and Gore Verbinski's *Ring*." MA Thesis. North Carolina State University, 2006.

Bazin, André. "Adaptation, or the Cinema as Digest." Pp. 19–27 in *Film Adaptation*, edited by James Naremore. Piscataway, N.J.: Rutgers University Press, 2000.

———. "Remade in USA." *Cahiers du cinema* 2, no. 1 (April 1952): 54–59.

BBC. "*Hazzard* Star Blasts Film Remake." *BBC News*, 14 July 2005. <http://news.bbc.co.uk/2/hi/entertainment/4681693.stm> (3 August 2006).

———."*Get Carter* Is 'Worst Film Remake.'" *BBC News*, 31 October, 2004. <http://news.bbc.co.uk/2/hi/entertainment/3969245.stm> (3 August 2006).

Beja, Maurice. *Film and Literature*. New York: Longman, 1979.

Beresford, Matthew. *From Demons to Dracula: The Creation of the Modern Vampire Myth*. London: Reaktion, 2008.

Biguenet, John. "Double Takes: The Role of Allusion in Cinema." Pp. 131–143 in *Play It Again, Sam: Retakes on Remakes*, edited by Andrew Horton and Stuart Y. McDougal. Berkeley: University of California Press, 1998.

Bloom, Harold. *The Anxiety of Influence*. New York: Oxford University Press, 1973.

Bluestone, George. *Novels into Film*. Berkeley: University of California Press, 1961.

Bond, Jeff. "Latent Image: *King Kong*." *Cinefantastique* 36, no. 1 (Feb/Mar 2004): 72.

Boon, Alexander. "In Defense of John Carpenter's *The Thing*." *Creative Screenwriting* 6, no. 1 (Jan/Feb 1999): 44, 66–73.

Boyum, Joy Gould, ed. *Double Exposure: Fiction into Film*. New York: Universe Books, 1985.

Brashinsky, Michael. "The Spring, Defiled: Ingmar Bergman's *Virgin Spring* and Wes Craven's *Last House on the Left*." Pp. 162–171 in *Play It Again, Sam: Retakes on Remakes*, edited by Andrew Horton and Stuart Y. McDougal. Berkeley: University of California Press, 1998.

Braudy, Leo. "Afterword: Rethinking Remakes." Pp. 327–334 in *Play It Again, Sam: Retakes on Remakes*, edited by Andrew Horton and Stuart Y. McDougal. Berkeley: University of California Press, 1998.

Brooker, Will. "*Batman*: One Life, Many Faces." Pp. 185–198 in *Adaptations: From Text to Screen, Screen to Text*, edited by Deborah Cartmell and Imelda Whelehan. London: Routledge, 1999.

Buddrus, Petra. "US Remakes Nordic Films: Tapping the Norse Code." *Screen International*, 10 April 1998.

Canby, Vincent. "Movies Lost in Translation." *New York Times*, 12 February 1989.

Carr, Jay. "Whither Film Noir? Hollywood's Latest Remakes Are Little More than Limp Retreads." *Boston Globe*, 3 April 1988.

Carroll, Noël. *The Philosophy of Horror*. New York: Routledge, 1990.

———."The Future of Allusion: Hollywood in the Seventies (and Beyond)." *October* 20 (Spring, 1982): 51–81.

Cartmell, Deborah and Imedla Whelehan. "Harry Potter and the Fidelity Debate." Pp. 37–49 in *Books in Motion: Adaptation, Intertextuality, Authorship*, edited by Mireia Aragay. Amsterdam: Rodopi, 2005.

Cattrysse, Patrick. "Film (Adaptation) as Translation: Some Methodological Proposals." *Target* 4, no. 1 (1992): 53–70.

Champoux, Joseph E. "Film Remakes as a Comparative View of Time." *Educational Media*

*International* 36, no. 3 (September 1999): 210–217.

———. "Comparative Analyses of Live-Action and Animated Film Remake Scenes: Finding Alternative Film-Based Teaching Resources." *Educational Media International* 42, no. 1 (March 2005): 49–69.

Charity, Tom. "Open Ear Open Eye." *Sight and Sound* 14, no. 3 (March 2004): 26–28.

Chatman, Seymour. *Coming to Terms: The Rhetoric of Narrative in Fiction and Film.* Ithaca, N.Y.: Cornell University Press, 1990.

Clements, Marcelle. "L'Amour Fou: Cinemascoping." *Premiere* 6, no. 12 (August 1993): 53.

Cohen, Alain J. "*12 Monkeys, Vertigo* and *La Jetée*: Postmodern Mythologies and Cult Films." *New Review of Film and Television* 1, no. 1 (November 2003): 49–164

Cohen, Roger. "Aux Armes! France Rallies to Battle Sly and T. Rex." *New York Times*, 2 January 1994.

Connor, J. D. "The Persistence of Fidelity: Adaptation Theory Today." *M/C Journal* 10, no. 2 (2007). <http://journal.media-culture.org.au/0705/15-connor.php> (10 January 2008).

Cooper, Michael. "*Poseidon* Takes Risk with Action-Adventure Remake: Director Wolfgang Petersen Says He Did Not Worry about Re-Making the Classic." *Daily Trojan*, 17 May 2006. <http://media.www.dailytrojan.com/media/storage/paper679/news/2006/05/17/Lifestyle/poseidon.Takes.Risk.With.ActionAdventure.Remake-1997491.shtml> (10 June 2006).

Coyle, William, ed. *Aspects of Fantasy: Selected Essays from the Second International Conference on the Fantastic in Literature and Film.* Westport, Conn.: Greenwood, 1986.

Curtis, Barry. *Dark Places: The Haunted House in Film.* London: Reaktion, 2008.

Cutchins, Dennis. "Adaptations in the Classroom: Using Film to 'Read' *The Great Gatsby*." *Literature Film Quarterly* 31, no. 4 (2003): 295–303.

D'Angelo, Mike. "The Most Brutal Film Ever Made. Made Again." *Esquire* 149, no. 4: 40–42.

Decker, James M. "Literary Text, Cinematic 'Edition': Adaptation, Textual Authority, and the Filming of *Tropic of Cancer*." *College Literature* 34, no. 3 (Summer 2007): 140–160.

Delamater, Jerome. "'Once More from the Top': Musicals the Second Time Around." Pp. 80–94 in *Play It Again, Sam: Retakes on Remakes*, edited by Andrew Horton and Stuart Y. McDougal. Berkeley: University of California Press, 1998.

Delaney, Sean and Potamitis, Nicholas. *16+ Study Guide: Remakes.* London: BFI National Library, 2004. <http://www.bfi.org.uk/filmtvinfo/publications/16+/remakes.html> (10 August 2006).

Deleyto, Celestino. "Me, Me, Me: Film Narrators and the Crisis of Identity." Pp. 243–262 in *Books in Motion: Adaptation, Intertextuality, Authorship*, edited by Mireia Aragay. Amsterdam: Rodopi, 2005.

Desmond, John and Peter Hawkes. *Adaptation: Studying Film and Literature.* New York: McGraw-Hill, 2005.

Desowitz, Bill. "New Apes, New Planet, Old Story: Simians Still Rule." *New York Times*, 13 May 2001, 2A3.

Diehl, Karen. "Once Upon an Adaptation: Traces of the Authorial on Film." Pp. 89–106 in *Books in Motion: Adaptation, Intertextuality, Authorship*, edited by Mireia Aragay. Amsterdam: Rodopi, 2005.

Dika, Vera. *Recycled Culture in Contemporary Art and Film: The Uses of Nostalgia.* Cambridge: Cambridge University Press, 2003.

Dobson, Julia. "Transatlantic Crossings: Ideology and the Remake." Pp. 183–194 in *100 Years of European Cinema*, edited by Diana Holmes and Alison Smith. Manchester: Manchester University Press, 2001.

Doherty, Thomas. "The Remake: A Review." *Cinefantastique* 19, no. 1/2 (January 1989): 98–99.

Dovey, Lindiwe. "Politicising Adaptation: Re-historicising South African Literature through *Fools*." Pp. 163–179 in *Books in Motion: Adaptation, Intertextuality, Authorship*, edited by Mireia Aragay. Amsterdam: Rodopi, 2005.

Druxman, Michael B. *One Good Film Deserves Another*. London: A. S. Barnes, 1977.

———. *Make It Again, Sam: A Survey of Movie Remakes*. Cranbury, N.J.: A. S. Barnes, 1975.

Durham, Carolyn A. *Double Takes: Culture and Gender in French Films and Their American Remakes*. Hanover, N.H.: University Press of New England, 1998.

———. "Three Takes on Motherhood, Masculinity, and Marriage: Serreau's Trois *Hommes et un coffin*, Nimoy's Remake, and Ardolino's Sequel." Pp. 243–272 in *Dead Ringers: The Remake in Theory and Practice*, edited by Jennifer Forrest and Leonard R. Koos. Albany: State University of New York Press, 2002.

———. "Taking the Baby out of the Basket and/or Robbing the Cradle: 'Remaking' Gender and Culture in Franco-American Film." *The French Review* 65, no. 5 (April 1992): 774–784.

Eaton, Michael. "Condemned to Repeats." *Sight and Sound* 1, no. 8 (December 1991): 4.

Eberwein, Robert. "Remakes and Cultural Studies." Pp. 15–33 in *Play It Again, Sam: Retakes on Remakes*, edited by Andrew Horton and Stuart Y. McDougal. Berkeley: University of California Press, 1998.

*Economist*. "Film Makers' Flip-Flops. (Remakes of Films by the Original Director)." *Economist*, 17 July 1993.

Edwards, David. "Film: Remake Special: On The Make; 10 Worst Remakes." *The Mirror* (London), 19 August 2005.

Ellis, John. "The Literary Adaptation: An Introduction." *Screen* 23, no. 1 (1982): 3–5.

Fadiman, William. "But Compared to the Original." *Films and Filming* 11, no. 5 (1965): 21–23.

Fern, Ong Sor. "Hollywood's Asian Affair; *The Departed's* Oscar Triumph Will Lead to More Hollywood Interest in Asian Films—But Not on Asian Terms." *The Straits Times* (Singapore), 4 March 2007.

Fischer, Lucy. "Modernity and Postmodernity: *High Heels* and *Imitation of Life*." Pp. 200–216 in *Play It Again, Sam: Retakes on Remakes*, edited by Andrew Horton and Stuart Y. McDougal. Berkeley: University of California Press, 1998.

Forrest, Jennifer. "The 'Personal' Touch: The Original, the Remake, and the Dupe in Early Cinema." Pp. 89–126 in *Dead Ringers: The Remake in Theory and Practice*, edited by Jennifer Forrest and Leonard R. Koos. Albany: State University of New York Press, 2002.

———. "Sadie Thompson Redux: Postwar Reintegration of the Wartime Wayward Woman." Pp. 169–202 in *Dead Ringers: The Remake in Theory and Practice*, edited by Jennifer Forrest and Leonard R. Koos. Albany: State University of New York Press, 2002.

———. "Remaking *Le Voile bleu*: An Interview with Normal Corwin, Screenwriter for *The Blue Veil*." Pp. 309–336 in *Dead Ringers: The Remake in Theory and Practice*, edited by Jennifer Forrest and Leonard R. Koos. Albany: State University of New York Press, 2002.

Forrest, Jennifer and Leonard R. Koos. "Reviewing Remakes: An Introduction," Pp. 1–36 in *Dead Ringers: The Remake in Theory and Practice,* edited by Jennifer Forrest and Leonard R. Koos. Albany: State University of New York Press, 2002.

Frater, Patrick. "Remakes in English Abound." *Screen International,* 11 April 2003, 3.

———. "What Makes a Good Remake?" *Screen International,* 6 June 2003, 9.

———. "Remade in Their Own Image." *Screen International,* 6 June 2003, 12.

———. "Remaking the Remake." *Screen International,* 30 May 2003, 9–10.

Frater, Patrick and Jeremy Kay. "Diary of a Remake." *Screen International,* 6 June 2003, 10.

Free, Erin and Peter Galvin. "The Big Remake: Out of Time, Out of Place, Out of Ideas." *Independent Filmmaker* 36 (August 2001): 36–41.

Friedberg, Anne. *Window Shopping: Cinema and the Postmodern.* Berkeley: University of California Press, 1994.

Friend, Tad. "Remake Man: Roy Lee Brings Asia to Hollywood, and Finds Some Enemies Along the Way." *New Yorker,* 2 June 2003.

———. "Copy Cats." *New Yorker,* 14 September 1998, 51–57.

Gabbard, Ken. "The Ethnic Oedipus: *The Jazz Singer* and Its Remakes." Pp. 95–114 in *Play It Again, Sam: Retakes on Remakes,* edited by Andrew Horton and Stuart Y. McDougal. Berkeley: University of California Press, 1998.

*Galatta.* "Film Remakes." *Galatta* (India), 21 April 2007. <http://tamil.galatta.com/articles/Film-Remakes.asp> (12 October 2006).

Gant, Dan. "Double Take." *Heat,* 2 April 1999, 38–39.

García, Pedro Javier Pardo. "Beyond Adaptation: Frankenstein's Postmodern Progeny." Pp. 223–242 in *Books in Motion: Adaptation, Intertextuality, Authorship,* edited by Mireia Aragay. Amsterdam: Rodopi, 2005.

Georgakas, Dan. "Robin Hood: From Roosevelt to Reagan." Pp. 70–79 in *Play It Again, Sam: Retakes on Remakes,* edited by Andrew Horton and Stuart Y. McDougal. Berkeley: University of California Press, 1998.

Giddings, Robert, Keith Selby, and Chris Wensley. *Screening the Novel: The Theory and Practice of Literary Dramatization.* New York: Palgrave Macmillan, 1990.

Giddings, Robert and Erica Sheen, eds. *From Page to Screen: Adaptations of the Classic Novel.* Manchester: Manchester University Press, 2000.

Gilbey, Ryan. "Film & Music: Film: I Think We've Seen this One: This Is the Summer of Remakes and Sequels—46 of Them at Last Count. Why Don't the Studios Think up Some New Ideas?" *The Guardian,* 15 June 2007.

Goldberg, Lee. *Television Series Revivals: Sequels or Remakes of Cancelled Shows.* Jefferson, N.C.: McFarland, 1993.

Goodwin, James. *Akira Kurosawa and Intertextual Cinema.* Baltimore, Md.: Johns Hopkins University Press, 1994.

Greenberg, Harvey R. "Raiders of the Lost Text: Remaking as Contested Homage in *Always*." Pp. 115–130 in *Play It Again, Sam: Retakes on Remakes,* edited by Andrew Horton and Stuart Y. McDougal. Berkeley: University of California Press, 1998.

Grindstaff, Laura. "Pretty Woman with a Gun: *La Femme Nikita* and the Textual Politics of the Remake." Pp. 273–308 in *Dead Ringers: The Remake in Theory and Practice,* edited by Jennifer Forrest and Leonard R. Koos. Albany: State University of New York Press, 2002.

———. "A Pygmalion Tale Retold: Remaking *La Femme Nikita*." *Camera Obscura* 16, no. 2 (2001): 133–175.

Grossvogel, David I. *Didn't You Used to Be Depardieu?: Film as Cultural Marker in France and Hollywood*. New York: Peter Lang, 2002.

Guerrero, Edward. "AIDS as Monster in Science Fiction and Horror Cinema." *Journal of Popular Film and Television* 18, no. 3 (Autumn 1990): 86–93.

Hancock, David. *Movie Sequels*. London: Screen Digest, 2004.

Hantke, Steffen. "Academic Film Criticism, the Rhetoric of Crisis, and the Current State of American Horror Cinema: Thoughts on Canonicity and Academic Anxiety." *College Literature*, 22 September 2007.

———. "Japanese Horror Under Western Eyes: Social Class and Global Culture in Miike Takashi's *Audition*." Pp. 54–65 in *Japanese Horror Cinema*, edited by Jay McRoy. Edinburgh: Edinburgh University Press, 2005.

Hark, Ina Rae. "The Wrath of the Original Cast: Translating Embodied Television Characters to Other Media." Pp. 172–184 in *Adaptations: From Text to Screen, Screen to Text*, edited by Deborah Cartmell and Imelda Whelehan. London: Routledge, 1999.

Harney, Michael. "Economy and Aesthetics in American Remakes of French Films." Pp. 63–87 in *Dead Ringers: The Remake in Theory and Practice,* edited by Jennifer Forrest and Leonard R. Koos. Albany: State University of New York Press, 2002.

Harris, Martin. "You Can't Kill the Boogeyman: *Halloween III* and the Modern Horror Franchise." *Journal of Popular Film and Television* 32, no. 3 (Autumn 2004): 98–109

Harrison, Stephanie. *Adaptations: From Short Story to Big Screen: 35 Great Stories That Have Inspired Great Films*. New York: Three Rivers, 2005.

Harvey, Jessamy. "Death and the Adorable Orphan: *Marcelino pan y vino* (1954; 1991; 2000)." *Journal of Romance Studies* 4, no. 1 (Spring 2004): 63–77.

Harvey, Stephen. "Can't Stop the Remakes." *Film Comment* (September–October 1980): 50–53.

Hawkings, Joan. *Cutting Edge: Art-Horror and the Horrific Avant-Garde*. Minneapolis: University of Minnesota Press, 2000.

Herbert, Daniel. "Sky's the Limit: Transnationality and Identity in *Abre los Ojos* and *Vanilla Sky*." *Film Quarterly* 60, no. 1 (Fall 2006): 28–38.

Higashi, Sumiko. "Invasion of the Bodysnatchers: The Pods Then and Now." *Jump Cut* 24/25 (March 1981): 3–4.

Hoberman, J. "They're Back: Do Androids Dream of Electric Sequels?" *Village Voice*, 30 June 2003. <http://www.villagevoice.com/issues/0327/hoberman.php> (10 October 2005).

———. "Paranoia and the Pods." *Sight and Sound* 4, no. 5 (May 1994): 28–31.

Hollinger, Karen. "The Monster as Woman: Two Generations of Cat People." *Film Criticism* 13, no. 2 (Winter 1989): 36–46.

Holmlund, Chris. "Feminist Makeovers: The Celluloid Surgery of Valie Export and Su Friedrich." Pp. 217–237 in *Play It Again, Sam: Retakes on Remakes*, edited by Andrew Horton and Stuart Y. McDougal. Berkeley: University of California Press, 1998.

Holmlund, Christine. "New Cold War Sequels and Remakes: *Down and Out in Beverly Hills* (Paul Mazursky, 1985), *Rocky IV* (Sylvester Stallone, 1985), *Aliens* (James Cameron, 1986)." *Jump Cut* 35 (April 1990): 85–96.

Holston, Kim R. and Tom Winchester. *Science Fiction, Fantasy and Horror Film Sequels, Series and Remakes: An Illustrated Filmography, with Plot Synopses and Critical Commentary*. Jefferson, N.C.: McFarland, 1997.

Horn, John. "Film Remakes That Have Soared, Sunk." *Los Angeles Times*, 13 October 2007.
———. "Just Because It Worked Once . . . Doesn't Mean It Will Work Again, But Holly-wood Keeps Remaking Old Movies." *Los Angeles Times*, 9 October 2007.
Horton, Andrew. "Cinematic Makeovers and Cultural Border Crossings: Kusturica's *Time of the Gypsies* and Coppola's *Godfather* and *Godfather II*." Pp. 172–190 in *Play It Again, Sam: Retakes on Remakes*, edited by Andrew Horton and Stuart Y. McDougal. Berkeley: University of California Press, 1998.
Horton, Andrew and Stuart Y. McDougal. "Introduction." Pp. 1–11 in *Play It Again, Sam: Retakes on Remakes*, edited by Andrew Horton and Stuart Y. McDougal. Berkeley: University of California Press, 1998.
Hutcheon, Linda. *A Theory of Adaptation.* New York: Routledge, 2006.
Ito, Robert. "Remake? Fans of Gory Film Up in Arms." *The International Herald Tribune*, 12 June 2006.
Jess-Cooke, Carolyn and Constantine Verevis, eds. *Second Takes: Critical Approaches to the Film Sequel.* Albany: State University of New York Press, 2009 (forthcoming).
Katovich, Michael A. and Patrick T. Kinkade. "The Stories Told in Science Fiction and Social Science: Reading *The Thing* and Other Remakes from Two Eras." *Sociological Quarterly* 34, no. 4 (November 1993): 619–638.
Kermode, Mark. "What a Carve Up." *Sight and Sound* 13, no. 12 (December 2003): 12–16.
King, Geoff. *New Hollywood Cinema: An Introduction.* London: I. B. Tauris, 2002.
Kirkham, Pat and Sarah Warren. "Four *Little Women*: Three Films and a Novel." Pp. 81–97 in *Adaptations: From Text to Screen, Screen to Text*, edited by Deborah Cartmell and Imelda Whelehan. London: Routledge, 1999.
Kline, Karen E. "*The Accidental Tourist* on Page and on Screen: Interrogating Normative Theories about Film Adaptation." *Literature Film Quarterly* 24, no. 1 (1996): 70–84.
Kline, T. Jefferson. *Screening the Text: Intertextuality in New Wave French Cinema.* Baltimore, Md.: Johns Hopkins University Press, 2002.
Knee, Adam. "The Metamorphosis of *The Fly*." *Wide Angle* 14, no. 1 (January 1992): 20–34.
Kolker, Robert P. "Algebraic Figures: Recalculating the Hitchcock Formula." Pp. 34–51 in *Play It Again, Sam: Retakes on Remakes*, edited by Andrew Horton and Stuart Y. McDougal. Berkeley: University of California Press, 1998.
Konigsberg, Ira. "How Many Draculas Does It Take to Change a Lightbulb?" Pp. 250–275 in *Play It Again, Sam: Retakes on Remakes*, edited by Andrew Horton and Stuart Y. McDougal. Berkeley: University of California Press, 1998.
Koos, Leonard R. "Hiring Practices: Simenon/Duvivier/Leconte." Pp. 203–223 in *Dead Ringers: The Remake in Theory and Practice*, edited by Jennifer Forrest and Leonard R. Koos. Albany: State University of New York Press, 2002.
Kranz, David L. and Nancy C. Mellerski, eds. *In/Fidelity: Essays on Film Adaptation.* Newcastle upon Tyne, U.K.: Cambridge Scholars Publishing, 2008.
Kratina, Al. "In Praise of Horror Remakes that Are Not Horrible." *The Gazette* (Montreal), 1 September 2007.
Kuzyk, Raya and John Sellers. "Adaptation Infinitum." *Publishers Weekly* 254, no. 34 (2007).
Landa, José Ángel Garcia. "Adaptation, Appropriation, Retroaction: Symbolic Interaction with *Henry V*." Pp. 181–199 in *Books in Motion: Adaptation, Intertextuality, Authorship*, edited by Mireia Aragay. Amsterdam: Rodopi, 2005.
Landy, Marcia. "Malombra: Can a Person Have Two or More Earthly Lives?" *Journal of*

*Romance Studies* 4, no. 1 (Spring 2004): 29–46.

Leadbetter, Russell and James Watt. "Coming Soon . . . Yet Another Remake at Your Local Cinema; Which Movie Would You Like to See Reprised and Who Could Star in It?" *Evening Times* (Glasgow), 4 September 2006.

Lee, Nathan. "The Return of the Return of the Repressed! Risen from the Grave and Brought Back to Bloody Life: Horror Remakes from *Psycho* to *Funny Games*." *Film Comment* 44, no. 2 (March/April 2008): 24–28.

Lehman, Peter. "'Tonight Your Director is John Ford': The Strange Journey of *Stagecoach* from Screen to Radio." Pp. 295–309 in *Play It Again, Sam: Retakes on Remakes*, edited by Andrew Horton and Stuart Y. McDougal. Berkeley: University of California Press, 1998.

Leitch, Thomas. *Film Adaptation and Its Discontents: From Gone with the Wind to The Passion of the Christ*. Baltimore, Md.: Johns Hopkins University Press, 2007.

———. "The Adapter as Auteur: Hitchcock, Kubrick, Disney." Pp. 107–124 in *Books in Motion: Adaptation, Intertextuality, Authorship*, edited by Mireia Aragay. Amsterdam: Rodopi, 2005.

———. "Twelve Fallacies in Contemporary Adaptation Theory." *Criticism* 45, no. 2 (Spring 2003): 149–171.

———. "Hitchcock without Hitchcock." *Literature/Film Quarterly* 31, no. 4 (2003): 248–259.

———. "Twice-Told Tales: Disavowal the Rhetoric of the Remake." Pp. 37–62 in *Dead Ringers: The Remake in Theory and Practice,* edited by Jennifer Forrest and Leonard R. Koos. Albany: State University of New York Press, 2002.

———. "101 Ways to Tell Hitchcock's *Psycho* from Gus Van Sant's." *Literature/Film Quarterly* 28, no. 4 (2000): 269–273.

———. "Twice-Told Tales: The Rhetoric of the Remake." *Literature-Film Quarterly* 18, no. 3 (1990): 138–149.

Lhermitte, Corinne "A Jakobsonian Approach to Film Adaptations of Hugo's *Les Misérables*." *Nebula* 2, no. 1 (March 2005).

Limbacher, James L. *Haven't I Seen You Somewhere Before?: Remakes, Sequels, and Series in Motion Pictures and Television, 1896–1978*. Ann Arbor, Mich.: Pierian, 1979.

Lofficier, Randy. "Remake? American Style: American Writers Discuss the Writing and Crediting Process for Remakes of Foreign Films." <http://www.lofficier.com/wgaarticle.htm> (October 10 2006).

Lupack, Barbara T. *Take Two: Adapting the Contemporary American Novel to Film*. Bowling Green, Ohio: Bowling Green University Popular Press, 1994.

Lütticken, Sven. "Planet of the Remakes." *New Left Review* 25 (January–February 2004). <http://newleftreview.org/?view=2491> (6 August 2007).

Lyons, Charles. "Remake *The Wicker Man*? Now That's Scary." *New York Times*, 6 August 2006.

———. "Remakes Remodel Foreign Pix; Execs Look Abroad for Fresh Ideas in Ready-Made Packages." *Variety*, 21 October 2002.

Macnab, Geoffrey. "Movie Remakes are Nothing New, but the Current Crop Contains Some Bizarre Choices." *The Independent*, 27 July 2007.

Magistrale, Tony. *Abject Terrors: Surveying the Modern and Postmodern Horror Film*. New York: Peter Lang, 2005.

Maio, Kathi. "Summer of the Scavengers and Cannibals." *Fantasy & Science Fiction* 88, no. 1 (January 1995).

Mancini, Marc. "French Film Remakes." *Contemporary French Civilization* 13 (Winter/Spring 1989): 32–46.

Mars-Jones, Adam "Film: The Real Thing . . . Only More So if There's One Thing We Know About Film It's That Remakes Are Naff. Nonsense. Remakes Are Film in Its Pomp" *The Independent*, 7 January 1999.

Martin, Sara. "What Does Heathcliff Look Like?: Performance in Peter Kosminsky's Version of Emily Brontë's *Wuthering Heights*." Pp. 51–67 in *Books in Motion: Adaptation, Intertextuality, Authorship*, edited by Mireia Aragay. Amsterdam: Rodopi, 2005.

Mask, Mia. "*Beloved*: The Adaptation of an American Slave Narrative." Pp. 272–294 in *Literature and Film: A Guide to the Theory and Practice of Film Adaptation*, edited by Robert Stam and Alessandra Raengo. Malden, Mass.: Blackwell, 2004.

Maxford, Howard. "Things Ain't What They Used to Be." *Starburst* 277 (September 2001): 76–81.

Mazdon, Lucy. "Introduction: Special Issue: Film Remakes." *Journal of Romance Studies* 4, no. 1 (Spring 2004): 1–11.

———. *Encore Hollywood: Remaking French Cinema*. London: British Film Institute, 2000.

———. "Translating Stereotypes in the Cinematic Remake." Pp. 171–182 in *On Translating French Literature and Film II*, edited by Myriam Salama-Carr. Amsterdam: Rodopi, 2000.

———. "Remaking Paternity: *Mon Père ce héros* and *My Father the Hero*." Pp. 223–233 in *French Cinema of the 1990s: Continuity and Difference*, edited by Phil Powrie. Oxford: Oxford University Press, 1999.

———. "Rewriting and Remakes: Questions of Originality and Authenticity." Pp. 47–63 in *On Translating French Literature and Film*, edited by Geoffrey T. Harris. Amsterdam: Rodopi, 1996.

McCarthy, Margaret. "Adaptation and Autobiographical Auteurism: A Look at Filmmaker/Writer Doris Dörrie." Pp. 125–142 in *Books in Motion: Adaptation, Intertextuality, Authorship*, edited by Mireia Aragay. Amsterdam: Rodopi, 2005.

McCarthy, Todd. "Remake of Japan Horror Pic Sounds a Tinny *Ring*." *Variety*, 7–13 October 2002, 21.

McDonald, Neil. "When Is a Remake a Masterpiece?" *Quadrant*, 1 December 2006.

McDougal, Stuart Y. "The Director Who Knew Too Much: Hitchcock Remakes Himself." Pp. 52–69 in *Play It Again, Sam: Retakes on Remakes*, edited by Andrew Horton and Stuart Y. McDougal. Berkeley: University of California Press, 1998.

———. *Made into Movies: From Literature to Film*. New York: Holt, Rinehart, and Winston, 1985.

McFarlane, Brian. *Novel to Film: An Introduction to the Theory of Adaptation*. New York: Oxford University Press, 1996.

McIntyre, Gina. "Sinister Urge: Sharpening the Saw." *Cinefantastique* 35, no. 5 (October/November 2002): 24–25, 73–74.

McNary, Dave. "Remakes Need a Makeover: H'wood Steps up Its Updates, But Idea Is Far from Surefire." *Variety*, 21 July 2003.

McRoy, Jay. "Case Study: Cinematic Hybridity in Shimizu Takashi's *Ju-on: the Grudge*." Pp. 175–184 in *Japanese Horror Cinema*, edited by Jay McRoy. Edinburgh: Edinburgh University Press, 2005.

Mendik, Xavier and Graham Harper, eds. *Unruly Pleasures: The Cult Film and Its Critics*. Surrey, U.K.: Fab Press, 2000.

Mermelstein, David. "The Remake as a Risky Take on a Classic." *New York Times*, 5 April
    1998.
Michaels, Lloyd. "*Nosferatu*, or the Phantom of the Cinema." Pp. 238–249 in *Play It Again,
    Sam: Retakes on Remakes*, edited by Andrew Horton and Stuart Y. McDougal. Berke-
    ley: University of California Press, 1998.
Milberg, Doris. *Repeat Performances: A Guide to Hollywood Movie Remakes*. New York:
    Broadway Press, 1990.
Minns, Ada. "People: UK: Franchise Fever Sweeps UK." *Screen International*, 14 May
    2004.
Mogilevich, Mariana. "Charlie's Pussycats." *Film Quarterly* 55, no. 3 (Spring 2002): 38–
    44.
Morgan, Janice. "From Clochards to Cappuccinos: Renoir's *Boudu* is Down and Out in
    Beverly Hills." *Cinema Journal* 29, no. 2 (Winter 1990): 23–35.
Morrison, James. *Passport to Hollywood: Hollywood Films, European Directors*. Albany:
    State University of New York Press, 1998.
Mouren, Yannick. "Remake Made in France." *Positif* 460 (June 1999): 90–94.
Mueller, Matt. "You Won't Feel a Thing." *Empire* 49 (July 1993): 68–72.
Nacache, Jacqueline. "Comment penser les remakes américains?" *Positif* 460 (June 1999):
    76–80.
Naremore, James. "Remaking *Psycho*." Pp. 387–296 in *Framing Hitchcock: Selected Es-
    says from the Hitchcock Annual,* edited by Sidney Gottlieb and Christopher Brook-
    house. Detroit: Wayne State University Press, 2002.
———. "Introduction: Film and the Reign of Adaptation." Pp. 1–18 in *Film Adaptation*, ed-
    ited by James Naremore. Piscataway, N.J.: Rutgers University Press, 2000.
———. "Authorship and the Cultural Politics of Film Criticism." *Film Quarterly* 44, no. 1
    (1990): 14–22.
Newman, Kim. "Made in Heaven, Remade in Hell." *Empire* 49 (July 1993): 100–101.
Nowell-Smith, Geoffrey and Joseph Sullivan. "Variations on a Theme: *Yojimbo, A Fistful
    of Dollars* and the 'Servant of Two Masters.'" *Journal of Romance Studies* 4, no. 1
    (Spring 2004): 79–90.
Nowlan, Robert A. and Gwendoline Wright Nowlan. *Cinema Sequels and Remakes, 1903–
    1987*. Jefferson, N.C.: McFarland and Company, 1989.
O'Regan, Tom. "Negotiating Cultural Transfers." Pp. 213–31 in *Australian National Cin-
    ema*. London: Routledge, 1996.
Orr, Christopher. "The Discourse on Adaptation." *Wide Angle* 6, no. 2 (1984): 72–76.
Orr, Mary. *Intertextuality: Debates and Contexts*. Cambridge: Polity Press, 2003.
O'Toole, Lesley. "Video Nasty." *Empire* 165 (March 2003): 92–95.
Paget, Derek. "Speaking Out: The Transformations of *Trainspotting*." Pp. 128–140 in *Adap-
    tations: From Text to Screen, Screen to Text*, edited by Deborah Cartmell and Imelda
    Whelehan. London: Routledge, 1999.
Paige, Linda Rohrer. "The Transformation of Woman: The 'Curse' of the Cat Woman." *Lit-
    erature/Film Quarterly* 24, no. 4 (1997): 291–299.
Pall, Ellen. "Are Some Remakes Much, Much More Than Meets the Eye?" *New York Times*,
    11 March 1990.
Paquet, Darcy, Liz Shackleton, and Mark Schilling. "Asian Remakes." *Screen International*
    26 (September 2003): 15–17.
Patterson, John. "The Guide: Film: If Only . . . People Had to Remake Their Own Movies
    before Touching Anyone Else's." *The Guardian*, 29 September 2007.

Perkins, Claire. "Remaking and the Film Trilogy: Whit Stillman's Authorial Triptych." *Velvet Light Trap* 61 (Spring 2008).

Phillips, Kendall R. *Projected Fears: Horror Films and American Culture*. Westport, Conn: Greenwood, 2005.

Picart, Caroline Joan. *Remaking the Frankenstein Myth on Film: Between Laughter and Horror*. Albany: State University of New York Press, 2003.

Pratt, Steve. "Remake Mistakes." *The Northern Echo*, 26 May 2007.

Prince, Stephen. "Dread, Taboo and *The Thing*: Toward a Social Theory of the Horror Film." *Wide Angle* 10, no. 3 (1988): 19–29.

Quaresima, Leonardo. "Loving Texts Two at a Time: The Film Remake." *CiNéMAS* 12, no. 3 (2002): 73–84.

Rafferty, Terrence. "Screams in Asia Echo in Hollywood." *New York Times*, 27 January 2008.

Randall, Laura. "Which Film Remake Is Next? Eddie Brandt Knows." *Christian Science Monitor*, 12 December 2003.

Ray, Robert. "The Field of Literature and Film." Pp. 38–53 in *Film Adaptation*, edited by James Naremore. Piscataway, N.J.: Rutgers University Press, 2000.

Rosenbaum, Jonathan. "Two Forms of Adaptation: *Housekeeping* and *Naked Lunch*." Pp. 206–220 in *Film Adaptation*, edited by James Naremore. Piscataway, N.J.: Rutgers University Press, 2000.

Roth, Marty. "Twice Two: *The Fly* and *Invasion of the Body Snatchers*." *Discourse* 22, no. 1 (Winter 2000): 103–116.

Roush, Matt. "The Roush Review: Leave our TV Classics Alone!" *TV Guide*, 24 July 1999, 8–9.

Royoux, Jean-Christophe. "Remaking Cinema." Pp. 21–27 in *Cinéma Cinéma: Contemporary Art and the Cinematic Experience*, edited by Marente Bloemheuvel and Jaap Guldemond. Rotterdam: Stedelijk Van Abbemuseum, Eindhoven, and Nai, 1999.

Russell, Jaime. "Close-up: Double Down." *Sight and Sound* 13, no. 10 (October 2003): 78.

Sanders, Julie. *Adaptation and Appropriation*. New York: Routledge, 2005.

Santas, Constantine. "The Remake of *Psycho* (Gus Van Sant, 1998): Creativity or Cinematic Blasphemy?" *Sense of Cinema*, Issue 10 (2000). <http://www.sensesofcinema.com/contents/00/10/psycho.html> (18 August 2007).

Schatz, Thomas. *Hollywood Genres: Formulas, Filmmaking, and the Studio System*. Philadelphia: Temple University Press, 1981.

Schneider, Steven Jay. "Repackaging Rage: *The Vanishing* and *Nightwatch*." *Kinema* 17 (Spring 2002): 47–66.

———. "Thrice-told Tales: *The Haunting* from Novel to Film . . . to Film." *Journal of Popular Film and Television* 30, no. 3 (Autumn 2002): 166–176.

———. "A Tale of Two *Psychos*." *Senses of Cinema*, no. 10 (2000). <http://www.sensesofcinema.com/contents/00/10/psychos.html> (18 August 2007).

Schwartz, Ronald. *Noir, Now and Then: Film Noir Originals and Remakes (1944–1999)*. Westport, Conn.: Greenwood Press, 2001.

Seger, Linda. *The Art of Adaptation: Turning Fact and Fiction into Film*. New York: Owl Books, 1992.

Seguin, Denis. "Repeat Contenders: World Film Proves Ripe for Remake." *Screen International*, 3 May 2002.

Serceau, Michel and Daniel Protopopoff, eds. *Le Remake et l'adaption. CinémAction* 53 (1989).

Shelton, Robert. "Genre and Closure in the Seven Versions of *Invasion of the Body Snatchers*: Finney ('54, '55, '78), Siegel ('56, '56), Kaufman ('78), and Ferrara ('93)." *West Virginia University Philological Papers*, 22 September 2002.

Sibilla, Mark. "Movie Remakes Not Popular among Some Students." *Kansas State Collegian*, 13 October 2005. <http://collegian.ksu.edu/collegian/article.php?a=7400> (18 August 2007).

Siegel, Tatiana and Marc Graser. "U's 'Birds' Redo Takes Flight." *Daily Variety* 297, no. 15: 1–11.

Silverman, Stephen M. "Hollywood Cloning: Sequels, Prequels, Remakes, and Spin-Offs." *American Film* 3, no. 9 (July–August 1978): 24–27, 29.

Simon, Ronald. "The Eternal Rerun: Oldies But Goodies." *Television Quarterly* 22, no. 1 (1986): 51–58.

Simonet, Thomas. "Conglomerates and Content: Remakes, Sequels, and Series in the New Hollywood." Pp. 154–162 in *Current Research in Film: Audiences, Economics, and Law*, Vol. 3, edited by Bruce A. Austin. Norwood, N.J.: Ablex, 1987.

Sinyard, Neil. *Filming Literature: The Art of Screen Adaptation*. New York: St. Martin's Press, 1986.

Skvirsky, Salomé Aguilera. "The Price of Heaven: Remaking Politics in *All that Heaven Allows*, *All: Fear Eats the Soul*, and *Far from Heaven*." *Cinema Journal* 47, no. 3 (Spring 2008): 90–121.

Smith, Iain Robert. "'Beam Me up, Omer': Transnational Media Flow and the Cultural Politics of the Turkish *Star Trek* Remake." *Velvet Light Trap* 61 (Spring 2008).

Smith, Paul Julian. "High Anxiety: *Abre los ojos/Vanilla Sky*." *Journal of Romance Studies* 4, no. 1 (Spring 2004): 91–102.

Snow, Kevin C. "Slash Rehash: Horror Film Remakes, Myths and Meanings." MA Thesis. Pennsylvania State University, Harrisburg, 2004.

Somigli, Luca. "The Superhero with a Thousand Faces: Visual Narratives on Film and Paper." Pp. 279–294 in *Play It Again, Sam: Retakes on Remakes*, edited by Andrew Horton and Stuart Y. McDougal. Berkeley: University of California Press, 1998.

Staiger, Janet. *Perverse Spectators: The Practices of Film Reception*. New York: New York University Press, 2000.

Stam, Robert. "Introduction: The Theory and Practice of Adaptation." Pp. 1–52 in *Literature and Film: A Guide to the Theory and Practice of Adaptation*, edited by Robert Stam and Alessandra Raengo. Malden, Mass.: Blackwell, 2004.

———. *Literature Through Film: Realism, Magic, and the Art of Adaptation*. Boston: Wiley-Blackwell, 2004.

———. "Beyond Fidelity: The Dialogics of Adaptation." Pp. 54–76 in *Film Adaptation*, edited by James Naremore. Piscataway, N.J.: Rutgers University Press, 2000.

Stanley, T. L. "Seen that Movie Before? Hollywood Likes It that Way." *Advertising Age* 76, no. 30 (2005): 10.

Style, John. "Dirk Bogarde's Sidney Carton: More Faithful to the Character than Dickens Himself?" Pp. 69–86 in *Books in Motion: Adaptation, Intertextuality, Authorship*, edited by Mireia Aragay. Amsterdam: Rodopi, 2005.

Sutton, Paul. "Remaking the Remake: *Irma Vep* (Assayas, 1996)." Pp. 69–80 in *French Cinema in the 1990s: Continuity and Difference*, edited by Phil Powrie. Oxford: Oxford University Press, 1999.

Thompson, Kirsten. "*Cape Fear* and Trembling: Familial Dread." Pp. 126–147 in *Literature and Film: A Guide to the Theory and Practice of Film Adaptation*, edited by

Robert Stam and Alessandra Raengo. Malden, Mass.: Blackwell, 2004.

———. "Fantasy, Franchises, and Frodo Baggins." *Velvet Light Trap* 52 (Autumn 2003): 45–63.

Tropp, Martin. "Re-creating the Monster: *Frankenstein* and Film." Pp. 23–77 in *Nineteenth-Century Women at the Movies: Adapting Classic Women's Fiction to Film*, edited by Barbara Tepa Lupack. Bowling Green, Ohio: Bowling Green University Popular Press, 1999.

Tulloch, Lee. "Flipping Out over Angels Remake." *The Age*, 17 May 2000.

Tyler, Bruce M. "Racial Imagery in *King Kong*." *Black Film Review* 3, no. 1 (Winter 1986/1987): 20–21.

Ughes, David. *Tales from Development Hell: Hollywood Film-making the Hard Way*. London: Titan Books, 2003.

Varela, Manuel Barbeito. "John Huston's vs. James Joyce's *The Dead*." Pp. 145–161 in *Books in Motion: Adaptation, Intertextuality, Authorship*, edited by Mireia Aragay. Amsterdam: Rodopi, 2005.

Venuti, Lawrence. "Adaptation, Translation, Critique." *Journal of Visual Culture* 6, no. 1 (2007): 25–43.

Verevis, Constantine. *Film Remakes*. Edinburgh: Edinburgh University Press, 2006.

———. "For Ever Hitchcock: *Psycho* and Its Remakes." Pp. 15–29 in *After Hitchcock: Imitation/Influence/Intertextuality*, edited by David Boyd and R. Barton Palmer. Austin: University of Texas Press, 2006.

———. "Remaking Film." *Film Studies* 4 (Summer 2004): 87–103.

———. "Through the Past Darkly: Noir Remakes of the 1980s." Pp. 307–322 in *Film Noir Reader 4*, edited by Alain Silver and James Ursini. New York: Limelight, 2004.

———. "Once More On to the Beach." *Metro* 127–128 (Autumn/Winter 2001): 156–161.

———. "Re-viewing Remakes." *Film Criticism* 21, no. 3 (Spring 1997): 1–19.

Verini, Bob. "Room with a Deja Vu." *Daily Variety* 294, no. 6: B4–B5.

Vernon, Kathleen M. "Remaking Spain: Trans/national Mythologies and Cultural Fetishism in *The Devil is a Woman* (Sternberg, 1935) and *Cet obscur objet du désir* (Buñuel, 1977)." *Journal of Romance Studies* 4, no. 1 (Spring 2004): 13–27.

Vidal, Belén. "Playing in a Minor Key: The Literary Past through the Feminist Imagination." Pp. 263–285 in *Books in Motion: Adaptation, Intertextuality, Authorship*, edited by Mireia Aragay. Amsterdam: Rodopi, 2005.

Vincendeau, Ginette. "Hijacked." *Sight and Sound* 3, no. 7 (July 1993): 22–25.

Vognar, Chris. "Critics May Boo, But Horror Film Remakes Are Scaring Up Big Bucks." *Dallas Morning News*, 12 May 2005.

Wang, Yiman. "The Phantom Strikes Back: Triangulating Hollywood, Shanghai and Hong Kong." *Quarterly Review of Film and Video* 21, no. 4 (2004): 317–326.

Warden, K. S. "Adapting Film Across Culture: Four French Farces and Their American Remakes." MA Thesis. University of Maryland, Baltimore County, 1996.

Watt, Mike. "Night of the Living Dead." *Cinefantastique* 34, no. 3/4 (June 2002): 116–119.

Waxman, Sharon. "A Matter of Deja View: French Cry Faux Over U.S. Film Remakes." *Washington Post*, 15 July 1993.

Webster, Andy. "A Haunting Intruder from the Darkroom." *New York Times*, 22 March 2008.

Weis, Elisabeth. "*M\*A\*S\*H* Notes." Pp. 310–326 in *Play It Again, Sam: Retakes on Remakes*, edited by Andrew Horton and Stuart Y. McDougal. Berkeley: University of California Press, 1998.

Wells, Paul. "'Thou Art Translated': Analysing Animated Adaptation." Pp. 199–213 in

*Adaptations: From Text to Screen, Screen to Text,* edited by Deborah Cartmell and Imelda Whelehan. London: Routledge, 1999.

Welsch, Janice R. and Syndy M. Conger, eds. *Narrative Strategies: Original Essays in Film and Prose Fiction.* Macomb: Western Illinois University Press, 1980.

Welsch, Tricia. "Sound Strategies: Lang's Rearticulation of Renoir." Pp. 127–149 in *Dead Ringers: The Remake in Theory and Practice,* edited by Jennifer Forrest and Leonard R. Koos. Albany: State University of New York Press, 2002.

Whelehan, Imelda. "Adaptations: The Contemporary Dilemmas." Pp. 3–19 in *Adaptations: From Text to Screen, Screen to Text,* edited by Deborah Cartmell and Imelda Whelehan. London: Routledge, 1999.

Whipp, Glenn. "Bloody Hell Horror Film Remakes Ride a Rising Tide of Gore." *Los Angeles Daily News,* 10 March 2006.

White, Dave. "I Spit on Your Horror Movie Remakes, Sequels: A Horror Fan Laments the Current State of One of His Favorite Genres." MSNBC.com, 25 October 2005. <http://www.msnbc.msn.com/id/9805698/> (12 October 2007).

Wicks, Ulrich. "Studying Film as Integrated Text." *Rhetoric Review* 2, no. 1 (September 1983): 51–62.

Wildermuth, Mark E. "Electronic Media and the Feminine in the National Security Regime: *The Manchurian Candidate* before and after 9/11." *Journal of Popular Film & Television* 35, no. 3 (Fall 2007): 121–126.

Williams, Alan. "The Raven and the Nanny: The Remake as Crosscultural Encounter." Pp. 151–168 in *Dead Ringers: The Remake in Theory and Practice,* edited by Jennifer Forrest and Leonard R. Koos. Albany: State University of New York Press, 2002.

Williams, Michael. "*Plein soleil* and *The Talented Mr. Ripley*: Sun, Stars and Highsmith's Queer Periphery." *Journal of Romance Studies* 4, no. 1 (Spring 2004): 47–62.

Williams, Michael and Christian Monk. "Remake Stakes Are Up: Hollywood Hastens Pursuit of French Pic Properties." *Daily Variety,* 19 April 1993.

Wills, David. "The French Remark: *Breathless* and Cinematic Citationality." Pp. 147–161 in *Play It Again, Sam: Retakes on Remakes,* edited by Andrew Horton and Stuart Y. McDougal. Berkeley: University of California Press, 1998.

Woolnough, Damien. "Disturbing the Classics." *The Advertiser* (Australia), 7 April 2007.

Yockey, Matt. "Somewhere in Time: Utopia and the Return of Superman." *Velvet Light Trap* 61 (Spring 2008).

Young, John. "The Best French Films You'll Never See." *New York Times,* 30 October 1994.

Zagt, Ab. "All Change Again." *Screen International,* 6 June 2003, 11.

Zanger, Anat. *Film Remakes as Ritual and Disguise: From Carmen to Ripley.* Amsterdam: Amsterdam University Press, 2007.

Zurbrugg, Nicholas. "Will Hollywood Never Learn?: David Cronenberg's *Naked Lunch.*" Pp. 98–112 in *Adaptations: From Text to Screen, Screen to Text,* edited by Deborah Cartmell and Imelda Whelehan. London: Routledge, 1999.

# Index

critic, 14, 38, 190, 227, 228, 233, 236, 238,
    261
critical geography, 145
Crosby, Denise, 200
cross-citation, 226
Crow, The (1994), 254
Crow, The (comic book), 256
crowd, 26, 28, 93, 96, 98, 102, 103, 104
Cubitt, Sean, 194
cultural imperialism, 16, 108, 111, 113,
    123. See also imperialism
cultural production, 147, 158
cultural specificity, 116, 119, 122, 144
culture, 8, 16, 17, 29, 85, 89, 90, 110, 147,
    148, 157, 214, 252, 253; high, 222,
    223; low, 224
Cupid, 185
Cure (1997), 155
cybernetics, 230
cycle, 15, 117
cynicism, 48

Daiei Motion Pictures, 134, 136
Dallas, Texas, 38
Danse Macabre, 64
Darfur, 15, 40, 47
Dark City (1998), 254
Dark Water (2002), 122
"Darkness," 61
Da-sein, 94
Dawn of the Dead (1978), 63, 72–75, 81,
    237
Dawn of the Dead (2004), 63, 75–77, 233,
    237
Day of the Dead (1985), 81, 237
Day of the Dead 2: Contagium (2005), 62
DC Comics, 256
De Laurentis, 183
De Man, Paul, 195
Dead Rising, 81
death, 25
death match, 229
Deep Space and Sacred Time: Star Trek in
    the American Mythos, 213
Degli-Esposti, Cristina, 260, 261
dehumanization, 15, 46–47, 59
déjà vu, 176
Dekalog (1989), 156

Del Toro, Guillermo, 254, 262n36
Deleuze, Gilles, 176
democracy, 104, 208
demography, 11, 222, 230
demon, 223, 226, 229
Dendle, Peter, 64
Denmark, 147, 153
Departed, The (2006), 144, 153
Depression, 185, 187
desegregation, 29
Desperado (1995), 194
destiny, 90
dialogue, 12, 14, 15, 236
Die Hard (1988), 229
diegesis, 152, 194
digital, 193, 199, 217, 251, 254, 255, 256,
    257, 258, 259, 261
digital cinema adaptation, 261
digitextuality, 259, 260
"Digitextuality and Click Theory," 256,
    260
Dillard, R. H. W., 64
Dillon, Steven, 167, 168, 169, 171, 174
dinosaur, 189, 224
director, 14, 80, 116, 118, 169, 167–77,
    181–95, 202, 238, 254
disaster, natural, 31
disease, 40, 48, 50, 62, 80
dismemberment, 66
Disney, 181, 249, 250
Disney Interactive, 238
Disneyfication, 184
Divine Emperor, 133
DNA (deoxyribonucleic acid), 26, 57, 58
domestic violence, 155, 158
Donkey Kong, 225
Doom (2005), 10, 221, 226–28, 229, 237
Doom (video game), 222, 223, 224, 226–
    28, 230, 231, 232, 234, 235, 238
Doom 3, 227
Doomguy, 226
"Doom Nation," 228
double, the, 49
Double Dragon (1994), 224, 236
double exposure, 211
Dower, John, 132, 133
Doyle, Chris, 117
Dr. Strangelove or: How I Learned to Stop

# Contributors

**Shane Borrowman** is an assistant professor of English at the University of Nevada, Reno, where he teaches courses in rhetorical history and theory, advanced memoir, and freelance writing. His first book, *Trauma and the Teaching of Writing*, was published in 2005, and his first-year composition textbook *Promise of America* appeared in 2006. Currently he is editing a second FYC textbook, a collection of essays on the perils of writing program administration for untenured faculty, and a collection on technologies that affected writing instruction prior to the advent of the personal computer. Aside from zombie movies, his most recent research passion focuses upon the reintroduction of Aristotle into medieval Europe by Islamic scholars such as Ibn Rushd. His twins, John and Samantha, are impressed by none of this.

**Costas Constandinides** is a lecturer in the communications department at the University of Nicosia, Cyprus. He teaches film studies, television production courses, and media. He is the co-founder of the first bi-communal experimental theater group in Cyprus, the Rooftop Theatre Group. He has co-produced three performances and he is currently involved as a multimedia practitioner in a UNDP (United Nations Development Programme)-sponsored project entitled "Voicing and Staging the Experience."

**Daryl G. Frazetti** graduated from the University of Massachusetts at Boston in 2002, studying both biology and anthropology, and later completed graduate work at Northern Illinois University in anthropology, graduating in 2004. He has taught anthropology at Lake Tahoe College where he has offered courses including "The Anthropology of *Star Trek*," "Xenolinguistics," and "Anthropology of *Lord of the Rings*." He been attending fan conventions since 1989, and at them, has entered his *Star Trek* cats in numerous costume contests.

Along with his cats, Frazetti has appeared in the *Trekkies I* and *Trekkies II* documentaries, and is mentioned in William Shatner's book *Get a Life*. He has also participated in many *Star Trek* fandom-related fundraising and community service events and is an avid Tribble collector.

**Daniel Herbert** is currently a visiting lecturer in screen arts and cultures at the University of Michigan. He is a Ph.D. candidate in critical studies at the University of Southern California, working on contemporary transnational film remakes. His essays appear in *Film Quarterly* and *Millennium Film Journal*.

**Ils Huygens** worked for two years as a researcher in the theory department of the Jan Van Eyck Academy in Maastricht. There she developed her current research on body, affect, and emotion in film studies, which culminated in the organization of a two-day symposium, "Thinking Through Affect." She has published articles in magazines and in book collections on affect and emotion in cinema and on David Lynch and Deleuze. Currently she is in the process of coediting a collection of papers based on the affect symposium, together with Barbara M. Kennedy. Aside from her academic research, she is editor in chief of the Belgian online short film magazine Kortfilm.be and is one of the organizers of the Brussels film festival Offscreen Film Fest.

**Stan Jones** was born in Yorkshire and has lived in New Zealand for almost thirty years. He is senior lecturer in screen and media at the University of Waikato. In 1987 he co-founded the first film studies program in New Zealand. It has since developed into "Screen and Media." He has written on German Expressionism, modern German literature, Wim Wenders, Marcel Ophüls, and New Zealand film on the German market. His writing has appeared in *European Identity in Cinema*; *Twin Peaks*; *European Cinema: Inside Out*; *Writing Europe's Pasts*; *Lord of the Rings: Popular Culture in a Global Context*; *Schirmer Encyclopaedia of Film*; and *New Zealand Filmmakers*. His current research interest is in cross-cultural appropriation in the context of national/global identity in cinema.

**Scott A. Lukas** received his Ph.D. in cultural anthropology from Rice University. He has taught anthropology and sociology at Lake Tahoe College and at Valparaiso University. In 2005 he was the recipient of the McGraw-Hill Award for Excellence in Undergraduate Teaching of Anthropology by the American Anthropological Association. He is the author of the volume *The Themed Space: Locating Culture, Nation, and Self* (Lexington Books, 2007), as well as *Theme Park* (Reaktion Books, 2008), *Recent Developments in Criminological Theory* (coeditor with Stuart Henry, Ashgate, 2009), and *Strategies in Teaching Anthropology* (coeditor with Pat Rice and David McCurdy, Prentice-Hall, 2010).

**John Marmysz** teaches philosophy at the College of Marin in Kentfield, California. His philosophical interests center on the problem of nihilism and its cultural manifestations. He is the author of *Laughing at Nothing: Humor as a Response to Nihilism* (SUNY Press, 2003) and *The Path of Philosophy: Truth, Wonder and Distress* (Cengage/Wadsworth, forthcoming).

**Zília Papp** is assistant professor of art history and media studies of the School of Global and Interdisciplinary Studies at Hosei University, Tokyo, and she is currently submitting her Ph.D. dissertation at the University of New South Wales in Sydney, Australia, receiving advisory supervision from Professor John Clark, director of Australian Centre for Asian Art and Archeology, University of Sydney. She currently lectures on contemporary art and media of the Asia-Pacific region and animation studies as well as contributes articles to the *Japan Times* daily newspaper published in Japan.

**Myoungsook Park** was born in Seoul, Korea, and attended Seoul National University, receiving a B.A. in art history and English literature. She has master's degrees in art history from the University of California at Santa Barbara and in film studies from the University of Iowa. Through her work she hopes to expose rhetoric commonly employed by Hollywood to support its continued dominance of global cinema. She currently lives in New York City.

**Juneko J. Robinson** is an Arthur A. Schomburg Fellow in Philosophy at the University at Buffalo with interests in continental philosophy, existentialism, and aesthetics. Like many horror fans, she has an inquisitive mind and the heart of a small girl. She keeps it in a jar on her desk.

**Constantine Verevis** is senior lecturer in film and television studies at Monash University, Melbourne. He is the author of *Film Remakes* (Edinburgh University Press, 2006) and coeditor (with Carolyn Jess-Cooke) of *Second Takes: Critical Approaches to the Sequel* (SUNY Press, forthcoming).